To our parents

Clement Nat Stockard
Anita Stockard McMilan

and

Herbert Neal Massey
Leola Paullin Massey

6, content

SEX AND GENDER IN SOCIETY

SECOND EDITION

Jean Stockard
Miriam M. Johnson
University of Oregon

PRENTICE HALL, Englewood Cliffs, New Jersey 07632

L[illegible]s Cataloging-in-Publication Data

Stockard, Jean.
Sex and gender in society / Jean Stockard, Miriam M. Johnson. -- 2nd ed.
p. cm.
Rev. ed. of: Sex roles. 1980.
Includes bibliographical references and indexes.
ISBN 0-13-807496-8
1. Sex role. 2. Social role. 3. Socialization. 4. Sex differences (Psychology) 5. Sexism. I. Johnson, Miriam M. II. Stockard, Jean. Sex roles. III. Title.
HQ1075.S74 1991
305.3--dc20

91-22129
CIP

Editorial/production supervision
and interior design: Kari Callaghan
Acquisitions editor: Nancy Roberts
Cover design: Carol Ceraldi
Prepress buyer: Debbie Kesar
Manufacturing buyer: Mary Ann Gloriande

Previously published under the title:
Sex Roles: Sex Inequality and Sex Role Development.

A Simon & Schuster Company
Englewood Cliffs, New Jersey 07632

Printed in the United States of America
10 9 8 7 6 5 4 3 2 1

ISBN 0-13-807496-8

Prentice-Hall International (UK) Limited, *London*
Prentice-Hall of Australia Pty. Limited, *Sydney*
Prentice-Hall Canada Inc., *Toronto*
Prentice-Hall Hispanoamericana, S.A., *Mexico*
Prentice-Hall of India Private Limited, *New Delhi*
Prentice-Hall of Japan, Inc., *Tokyo*
Simon & Schuster Asia Pte. Ltd., *Singapore*
Editora Prentice-Hall do Brasil, ltda., *Rio de Janeiro*

Contents

Preface

The first edition of this book appeared in 1980, entitled *Sex Roles: Sex Inequality and Sex Role Development*. Changes in terminology commonly used in the field have led us to use a different title for this edition, *Sex and Gender in Society*. As we describe in Chapter 1, many scholars now prefer to talk about gender inequality and development rather than sex inequality and development, to emphasize the social, rather than biological, basis of most distinctions between males and females.

In 1980 a great deal of scholarly work on gender inequality and gender development had already appeared in various disciplines, from sociology to economics, anthropology, biology, psychology, psychoanalysis, and social history. We tried to produce a work based on broad scholarship that did justice to these different disciplinary perspectives and the different insights and visions of individual theorists and researchers, but that also synthesized and transcended this work to some extent. We especially wanted to achieve an integration between work that focused on the development of gender identity and gender differences in personalities and work that focused on gender inequalities in social roles and institutional structures.

Since 1980 the scholarly literature on gender has mushroomed, as, not coincidentally, more and more women have entered academe. These new studies on gender are not only numerous, they are high quality. Almost every issue of the leading sociological journals has at least one article that bears on areas discussed in this book. This edition of *Sex and Gender in Society* incorporates this new work. We maintain an emphasis on broad scholarship and attention to basic research findings in the wide variety of fields that produce work related to gender. The general outline used in the first edition has been retained, but every part of the book has been altered and updated with the most current theoretical and empirical writings.

The most recent wave of the feminist movement began over a quarter of a century ago, and many changes in the status and relationships of men and women, as well as norms regarding gender, have occurred within all western, industrialized societies. Laws guarantee women treatment equal to men. Women are much more likely to be in the paid labor force, both women and men have access to higher education, divorce is more common, fewer women marry, and more women have children outside of marriage. In contrast to earlier decades, both women and men overwhelmingly approve of women working outside the home and of men helping to care for their children. Our society, and other advanced industrial societies, may have entered a postfeminist era, in which many of the ideologies of the latest feminist movement have been accepted by the general populace, and a large number of the aims of the movement have been incorporated into law and practice.

Yet gender inequality has not disappeared. Women, especially in the United States, earn far less than men, even when they have similar training and skills. Job segregation remains very strong, with women holding different jobs from men and receiving different types of educational training. Married women still do far more than their share of housework and have less influence on family decisions than their husbands do, even when they work outside the home. Although the lower incidence of marriage has resulted in more women living independently of men, this has also resulted in vast increases in the number of women and children living in poverty. Often single mothers not only face financial strains, but also carry enormous stress from the many family duties they must assume by themselves. These problems are usually even more intense for women in ethnic and racial minorities.

Many scholars now believe that the laws that guarantee women treatment equal to men are not sufficient to end gender inequality. Institutional structures that promote gender inequality and male dominance appear to be very deep seated. Moreover, they are promoted and maintained by the day-to-day decisions of individual men and women. To understand the basis of gender inequality it is important, then, to explore these institutional structures, both in our society and in other societies, and also to examine the reasons people choose to maintain these discriminatory practices. We must understand not just how gender inequality appears in our social institutions, but also how individuals conceive of themselves as men and women, how these conceptions develop, and how these self-views help maintain and promote gender inequality. The two parts of this book address these issues.

In the first part we show how inequality is built into our social institutions and into the whole system of cultural symbols through which we interpret experiences. We not only describe how gender inequality pervades our cultural symbol systems, but we also try to give a picture of how most women are constrained in their everyday lives not to challenge this system. On the institutional level, we explore the wealth of evidence on how gender stratification operates in the polity and economy of our society, with men dominating the positions with greatest power and authority. We critically examine the theories of economists regarding women and job discrimination, as well as sociological theories concerning the impact of women's family roles on their status in the labor force. We also examine changes in the family over the years and how the family and educational institutions help reinforce gender inequalities in the economy. We then broaden our scope and examine women's status in social institutions in other countries and, finally, across human history. We describe how anthropologists explain some of the variations and similarities in women's status and roles in societies with various kinds of kinship structures and at different stages of technological development.

Having established the foregoing institutional framework, we turn in the second part of the book to a consideration of gender development. In our canvass of theories and findings in this area, we describe biological differences between the sex groups, but argue that they cannot directly account for social role differences and certainly cannot account for socially defined gender inequality. After discussing on their own terms theories from academic psychology and psychoanalysis about the acquisition of gender typing, and their implications for understanding gender differences and male dominance, we turn to a more sociological, role-oriented analysis. Among other things, we suggest that institutionalized patterns that make women primarily responsible for early child care affect both male and female motivation and personality structure, and help reproduce male bonding and male dominance. We argue that gender-differentiated personalities and men's psychological motives to dominate are ultimately reproduced by institutional and cultural arrangements that give men access to greater power resources than women.

This linkage of gender development and institutional gender inequality provides clues as to why changes in our laws have not prompted greater gender equality, and how the system of male dominance may be altered. This topic is elaborated on in the last chapter of the book, which describes changes in the economy and the family that will be important in promoting greater gender equality.

We hope that this edition will continue to be used as the text, or one of the texts, in courses dealing with gender at a variety of levels and disciplines, including sociology, psychology, anthropology, political science, and women's studies. The book may also be used as a supplement in other courses focusing on social problems, social issues, the family, and social psychology. We hope that the book will be useful to the general public and especially to those involved professionally and/or personally in issues of gender. It can be a guide to understanding the wealth of material that has been written on gender, and for developing a perspective on how change might come about.

ACKNOWLEDGMENTS

I began serious work on this second edition while spending a sabbatical leave at Duke University in 1988–89. Among the Duke faculty I thank Ken Land for arranging my stay in the Sociology Department, Jean O'Barr for her support and the hospitality of the Women's Studies Program, Elizabeth Bramm-Dunn and the entire staff of Perkins Library for their assistance in obtaining materials, Ida

Harper Simpson and Angela O'Rand for their friendship, Naomi Quinn for her very insightful and helpful advice on the revision, and, especially, Wendy Luttrell for the support and kindness she and her family showed my family and me throughout our stay. Others in the North Carolina "triangle area" also helped make my sabbatical year both fruitful and enjoyable, and I thank Rachel Rosenfeld of the University of North Carolina, Barbara Risman of North Carolina State, and, especially, Peter Bearman of UNC, Ann Fisher, and their family.

I finished the revision at the University of Oregon. Among members of the faculty here, I am most grateful to Beverly Fagot, Pat Gwartney-Gibbs, David Jacobs, and Marilyn Whalen for sharing their extensive knowledge with me, their reading suggestions, and their support and encouragement. Diana Sheridan, Kate Sprauer, Beth Long, and Elizabeth Stiegler of the Center for the Study of Women in Society provided invaluable help in obtaining references; Mary Freer on the staff of the Department of Sociology coped with all the problems of mailing manuscripts; and I thank all of them for their assistance. The Center for the Study of Women in Society also provided some appreciated assistance with copying costs.

Although she did not actively participate in preparing this edition, Miriam Johnson read all of the material and provided invaluable feedback. Miriam has been a most important source of intellectual support and inspiration throughout my career, and I will always be grateful for her presence. Although she probably does not agree with all of the material I chose to include in this volume, her insightful and concise comments on this revision have no doubt made it better than it would have been, and I thank her for her input.

Others who provided feedback on this edition of the book are Clyde W. Franklin, II, of Ohio State University; Linda Haas, Indiana University; Dana V. Hiller, University of Cincinnati; Susan Tiano, University of New Mexico; and Amy S. Wharton, Washington State University. I am very grateful for their comments. Any errors that may remain in the book are, of course, my own responsibility.

Finally, I must thank my family. My husband, Walt Wood, has always done more than his share of work around the home and has been a delightful companion for more than twenty years. Our children, Beth, John, and Tim, were born after the first edition of this book appeared. The second edition would undoubtedly have been completed a number of years earlier without their presence, but life would never have been so enjoyable.

We continue to dedicate the book to our parents. My father and both of Miriam's parents died a number of years ago, but we and many others will never forget them. My mother remains a constant source of inspiration through her energy, her courage, and her zest for life.

Jean Stockard
Eugene, Oregon

PART ONE

GENDER INEQUALITY

chapter 1

Gender Inequality in Cultural Symbolism and Interpersonal Relations

"Is it a boy or a girl?" This is the first question we ask when a baby is born, and the answer will profoundly affect the child's future. From birth on, we feel the need to know a person's sex in order to interact comfortably with her or him. Similarly a person needs to feel that she or he is indeed one sex or the other. Although the decision to classify a child as a girl or a boy is obviously based on the child's physical characteristics, it results from the social distinctions we make between the sex groups and has a major impact on the child's life.

Societies vary in the degree to which they train children differently according to their sex group. Some societies segregate the sexes quite early and begin training for differentiated adult roles right away. In others, as diverse as some nomadic hunting and gathering societies and the modern United States, girls and boys receive fairly similar early training. On the other hand, all human languages make a definite distinction between the sex groups, and all societies use sex categorization as a basis for assigning people to different adult roles. In the United States, men and women tend to enter different occupations and have different activities and opportunities in the economic world. Here too, as everywhere, women are more involved with nurturant and domestic activities than are men.

Furthermore, the social roles assigned to women and men are not simply different, they are also differentially evaluated and differentially rewarded. For instance, in the United States, not only is the labor force sex-segregated, but also among full-time employees, women earn on the average only about two-thirds as much as men. As more women enter the labor force, women's work continues to be defined as both different from and less important than men's. As we shall see in subsequent chapters, it is not women's inferior performance that causes an occupation held predominantly by women to be less rewarded, but rather the fact that it is a woman's occupation. This hierarchical ranking of the sex groups that involves their differential access to both resources and rewards is called *gender stratification* or *sex stratification*.* Obviously there are other group inequities in societies besides sex-based ones, most notably in the United States those based on class and race. Yet, because families include both sex groups, inequities based on sex occur within both class and racial groups.

Gender stratification reflects the actual organization of societies and is reinforced by the shared symbol systems of a culture. These shared symbol systems provide the common understandings that people use in interaction. *Male dominance* refers to the beliefs and cultural meanings that give higher value and prestige to masculinity than to femininity, and that value males over females, men over women. Many anthropologists consider all known societies to be male dominant to some degree.

Male dominance does not mean that individual males in a society consciously conspire to keep women subordinate. Neither does it mean that women are helpless victims who have no way to prevail against men. Indeed, male dominance is hard to see unless one has become sensitized to it. The difficulty arises because male dominance is imbedded in our language and ways of thought. These built-in presuppositions limit the potential of all people and have personal costs for both males and females. In this chapter, we show how male dominance operates at the level of culture and in our everyday interactions.

CULTURAL SYMBOLISM AND MALE DOMINANCE

A cultural level of analysis or way of viewing human action focuses on the shared meanings individuals use in their interactions. Male dominance is passed from one generation to another partly through these shared symbol systems, including language and religions, as well as the mass media. These symbol systems picture and define our world for us and constrain us to interpret the world in masculine terms.

---

*Social scientists have used several other terms besides gender stratification, such as sex or gender discrimination, sex/gender systems, sexism, and patriarchy to describe sex-based inequalities. The term *gender discrimination* tends to focus attention on individuals and their unequal access to opportunities. We prefer the term *gender stratification* because it focuses attention on the systemic or built-in nature of sex inequality. We do, at times, however, use the term *gender discrimination* to refer to individual actions that promote and maintain the system of sex stratification. Although the term *sex/gender systems* uses the word *gender* to remind us that the roles assigned to the sexes are social roles and not biological necessities, it does not imply any inequality in the system. The term *sexism* is derived as a parallel to *racism* and points to a parallel between sexual inequality and racial inequality. There is some truth to this analogy, but it should not be carried too far because the sources of sexism and racism are probably far from identical. Moreover, although the sex groups are joined in families, an important aspect of racism is the prohibition of intermarriage. Although the term *patriarchy* has recently been used by some feminists to refer to all situations which involve male dominance, the term actually comes from anthropology and is used in that field to describe Old-Testament type pastoral societies in which one older man has absolute control over his wives, children, and other dependents.[1] Such societies are, in fact, only a minority of all societies anthropologists have studied, and, as we shall see, societies vary a great deal in the extent to which men control the lives of women and children. The use of the term "patriarchy" to describe all situations of gender stratification glosses over these distinctions.

It is important to remember that culture is ultimately a human product: We humans construct our social world. However, no one individual ever constructs an entire culture single-handedly. Most of our culture was originally made by other people, and some of it is quite old. This is the reason why we often see cultural meanings as if they were facts of nature, like the weather, objective necessities that exert an irresistible control over us, rather than the products of human activity. Thus, humans are both creators and victims of culture. But because culture is a human product, created and re-created in human interaction, it can be changed and controlled by human will.

Language

Language, the means of our thought and of our communication with others, embodies male dominance. What is male in a language is generally basic; what is female is usually subsidiary and/or deprecated. Some languages, such as Japanese, are used differently by male and female speakers. Although the basic form and syntax of the language do not change, males and females use different prefixes and suffixes, and at times the two "languages" sound quite different. When this happens, however, the language that the males use is always seen as the language of the society; the female version is called "women's language." Other languages such as those in the Romance and Germanic families use gender-differentiated pronouns for both the singular and plural forms, but again the male form is basic. In French, while *elles* refers to a group of females and *ils* to men, only *ils* may be used to describe a group of mixed sex. In English, this same practice appears in the use of the generic *he*. To refer in a general sense to a single person, one must use the masculine singular pronouns *he, him,* or *his*. The result can be absurd: "No person may require another person to perform, participate in, or undergo an abortion against his will."[2] In other instances, the term *man* is used to refer to all human beings. We have many phrases with this meaning, including "good will to men," "man in the street," and even "all men are created equal."

English often describes females in terms of males. Thus, we may speak of a seamstress, a stewardess, an actress, even a tigress and a lioness. With occupations, we usually attach qualifiers, such as in lady doctor or woman lawyer, to signify that the occupant is not a male. Only with traditionally female occupations do we signify that the occupant is a male, such as in male model or househusband, or in the family-related term *widower*.[3] The terms of address Mrs. and Miss indicate a woman's marital status. There are no comparable terms in the language to indicate whether a man is married. Even the attempt in English to use the undifferentiated Ms. for women may have been subverted. Although the originators of the term hoped it would be used to refer to all adult women, it now appears that Ms. is primarily used as a form of address in professional correspondence, especially when the marital status of the woman is unknown.[4]

Finally, language may deprecate and devalue women. Some usages trivialize what women are and do, as in the phrase "wine, women, and song" or the term *girl* to refer to females of all ages. One of our mature students described how she developed new sensitivity when a college choir director regularly called for women's voices with the phrase, "Now, girls," while eliciting male vocalization with, "Now, men." To call a full-grown adult male "boy" is an insult, but until recently it was no insult at all to call a full-grown adult female "girl." Actually, the words *woman* and *female* themselves have several deprecatory meanings. For example, the 1956 edition of Webster's dictionary gives, in addition to neutral meanings, the following meanings for *woman:* "One who is effeminate, cowardly, emotional, or weak, used of a man, as, he seemed to me a very woman." Another meaning given was "to cause to act like a woman, to subdue to weakness like a woman." In 1967, the Random House dictionary eschewed the foregoing list but noted that the word *female,* which used to be interchangeable with *woman,* had now developed a contemptuous implication, as in "a strong-minded female." The 1916 collegiate edition of Webster's dictionary was even more straightforward. It defined male as "denoting an intensity or superiority of the characteristic qualities of anything:—contrasted with female"!

Perhaps the ultimate form of this deprecation involves sexual overtones to words connected with women. One study found close to 1,000 English words and phrases that describe women in sexually derogatory ways, and many fewer such phrases describing men. Although there are over 500 synonyms for prostitute, there are only about 65 for the masculine term of whoremonger. Even terms that were once sexually neutral (such as hussy, which comes from an old English term for housewife; broad, which meant a young woman; and spinster, which once meant someone who ran a spinning wheel) have over the years developed negative meanings with sexual overtones.[5]

These language patterns reflect our male-dominated culture. They may also, however, reinforce and reproduce this culture because language reflects the ways in which we see the world.

Religion

Religions generally do recognize and include both masculine and feminine principles. For instance, Taoism includes both the principles of yin, symbolizing the feminine elements, and yang, symbolizing maleness. Hinduism and other indigenous belief systems throughout Oceania, Asia, Africa, and the Americas contain a theme of two basic masculine and feminine principles. Recently discovered writings of early Christian sects also show a strong feminine element in their conception of God.[6] All of these stress that the masculine and feminine principles are interdependent, both needed for the completion of the deity and the universe.[7]

Even so, the two principles have different functions. The female image is usually linked with fertility, the earth, and nurturance. Figures of full-breasted pregnant women have been found in archeological excavations of preagricultural hunting societies dating from 2000 to 4000 B.C. They suggest the possible centrality in pre-Hebraic and pre-Greek cultures of a feminine deity who symbolized birth and renewal.[8] Although these themes were carried over into later religious traditions, male images became predominant.[9] For instance, in Christianity the image of Jesus, the son of a male God, brings rebirth and everlasting life to the faithful.

Sister Marie Augusta Neal has suggested that in the West, God has usually been symbolized as the father of a family. Men, at times, have been depicted as the servants of God, whereas women in many societies and across classes in the same society have been seen as the servants of men. Although the concept of the Virgin Mary does allow women a spiritual existence that was not allowed in earlier times, her image represents less of the nurturing mother than that of the pure and chaste asexual "lady."[10]

The major functionaries of religious systems are also male. For instance, although there have been a few strong women prophets, the major prophets and figures of Western religions, including Moses, Jesus, and Mohammed, were male. Females are included in biblical stories, but their role is generally minor. They may be maternal and devoted helpmates as Mary Magdalene and Ruth were, or they may be evil or stupid, as were Lot's wife, Jezebel, and, most especially, Eve.

Religions have different official roles for males and females, and males always have the closest ceremonial ties to the deities. In the Catholic church, men are priests and women are nuns. Although nuns teach, nurse, and may hold very responsible administrative positions in hospitals and schools, they cannot celebrate Mass. Only priests may perform the ceremony that links the faithful directly with God.

This is justified by the tenet of apostolic succession, even though scholars can find no historical evidence of this tradition in the early church.[11] In some Protestant groups, only elders and deacons—who are men—may make the congregational decisions. Among conservative and orthodox Jews, only men may be rabbis. Jewish women serve important functions in the home, but in the orthodox and conservative synagogues they are seated apart from the men and are not involved in the official prayers and ceremonies.

Finally, religious rituals reflect and reinforce systems of male dominance. This occurs partly because the major religious functionaries are usually male. Thus, in Christianity, men ordain other men; in most denominations only men serve communion; and men generally perform wedding ceremonies. Sometimes the ceremonies themselves embody the principles of male dominance. For instance, the religious Jewish male regularly repeats a prayer in which he thanks God that he was not born a woman. The initiation rites of males through which young men learn the sacred rules of a society may serve to bond men together and to separate them from and elevate them over women. Even female initiation rites serve to promote male dominance by legitimizing and helping women rationalize men's control over their lives.[12]

Because religion defines the ultimate meaning of the universe for a people, the impact may be deep and often emotional rather than intellectual. When male dominance is embodied within religion, it enters the arena that a society considers sacred. This may make it even less open to question and more resistant to change than other social areas.

The Mass Media

The media have an important impact on people's everyday lives. Americans spend an enormous amount of time with the mass media, especially television. Over 95% of the homes in this country have at least one television set. By the time an average child is 15 years old, she or he has spent more time watching television than going to school. In adulthood, people do not break the habit. An average adult spends 5 hours a day with the mass media, four of these with electronic media such as radio and television and typically another hour with newspapers, magazines, and books.[13] The way men and women are depicted in the media—in television shows, popular magazines, advertisements, music videos, and even children's storybooks and school textbooks—reflects the assumptions of a male-dominant society.

Many studies have demonstrated that women tend to be both underrepresented and misrepresented in television programming, including national news, prime-time entertainment, children's programs, and daytime game and talk shows. When women are depicted, they are more likely to be young than old and tend to be found in romantic or domestic roles.[14] Examination of the interactions within prime-time shows also indicates that men are more likely to dominate women than the reverse, especially in crime shows, and even when women are the star of the show.[15]

Since the start of the television era, the roles women play have changed to reflect actual changes in women's activities. For instance, while Lucy Ricardo, of "I Love Lucy," was a housewife in the 1950s, Mary Richards, of "The Mary Tyler Moore Show," had a career, and Maude was actively involved in community affairs in the 1970s. In the 1980s Murphy Brown and the "Designing Women" debuted as single women with challenging jobs, while Kate and Allie and Roseanne were working mothers. Yet, even if television women in the late 1980s were less often portrayed at home or as married, their shows depicted a male-dominated culture in which attracting and pleasing men were often prime concerns.

The changes in women's roles on prime time have been linked not to feminism, but to financial concerns of network owners and advertisers and the growing diversity of television with the advent of many new cable stations. Market researchers have discovered that women are more likely than men both to watch prime-time network television and to buy products typically advertised at that time such as cosmetics and household goods. As network programming has become slightly more oriented toward female viewers, males have increasingly turned to cable channels, which are much more likely to present women in demeaning and subservient roles on stations such as the Playboy Channel or in shows such as "Full Contact Karate" and "Reform School Girls."[16]

Magazines, like television, are aimed at perceived markets. The highest circulating men's magazines in the United States are *Playboy, Penthouse, Sports Illustrated*, and *Hustler*. Each of these magazines may be seen as emphasizing power, either over women or over other men.[17] In contrast, although high circulation women's magazines, such as *Good Housekeeping, Redbook*, and *Family Circle*, may encourage a woman to pursue a career and an independent life, they also imply that she should be a good wife and mother.[18] This message seems to hold across magazines aimed at different markets. The fiction in magazines such as *Redbook*, developed for the middle class, and those such as *True Story*, aimed at the working class, may differ in theme, literary style, and emphasis. *True Story* tends to publish confessions and romances, whereas *Redbook* examines psychological conflicts of domestic life. Yet they share a basic message that a woman's happiness and fulfillment in life come through a love-dependent relationship with a man.[19]

Advertising may well be the most subtle aspect of the media, embedded within magazines and television and often receiving only peripheral attention. Numerous studies of print media and television indicate that males and females are portrayed in stereotypic roles in advertisements, with women often shown as decorative or sexual objects and dependent on men.[20] The messages in advertisements aimed at women often emphasize the importance of beauty and romance, suggesting that use of the touted product will help women gain men's attention.[21] When a woman is placed in an authoritative role in advertisement, she is usually selling household cleaning, beauty, or hygiene products. The vast majority of voice-overs, the authoritative statement of an advertisement, are done by males,[22] even though research indicates that both male and female audiences perceive that female voices are as effective as male voices.[23]

An analysis of music videos played on Music Television (MTV) and Black Entertainment Television (BET) cable channels also illustrates male dominance. Of all the videos shown on MTV in a typical period, 83% featured white male singers or bands led by white males, whereas only 11% featured white female singers or band leaders, and 1% featured African-American female singers. Similarly, African-American male performers were featured almost three times as often as African-American female performers on the videos shown on BET. Although love and sex predominated as themes of the videos, a significant number depicted stories in which a woman is rescued by a man or tries to gain the attention of a man who ignores her.[24]

Finally, a number of studies have examined children's reading, mathematics, science, and social studies textbooks and found similar results there. Females are less often included as characters and, when they are included, are much less likely to be the main character. The behaviors that characterize the children and adults of each sex group in the stories also differ. Men are often portrayed outdoors, in business, and at school; women are much more often portrayed in the home.[25]

In short, these images of males and females in the mass media as well as in school curricular materials attest to the male-dominant culture. That females are less often portrayed than males has been called a "symbolic annihilation," the removal of women from our cultural imagery.[26] Women are more limited in the roles they hold and may be shown in devalued characterizations and in interactions controlled by men. While these portrayals reflect the male-dominated culture, by their very existence they—like religion and language—may also reinforce and support the existence of male dominance on the cultural level.

INTERPERSONAL RELATIONS AND MALE DOMINANCE

Not only does male dominance pervade our language, religion, and media, it also influences the everyday interactions of males and females. Gender segregation and the devaluation of women appear in everyday life. This involves *social roles,* individuals' actions in social groups based on the expectations of others in the group. When people are expected to play certain roles simply because they are males or females, these roles are called *sex roles* or *gender roles.* They are both different and differentially evaluated. Like culture, our social roles are such an expected part of our lives that we usually do not realize the extent to which our day-to-day activities reflect, re-create, and reinforce both gender differentiation and male dominance.

A Note on Terminology

There has been a good deal of uncertainty and controversy over the use of the terms *sex* and *gender* in the past few years. Males and females are assigned different social roles on the basis of physical differences related to biological sex. Yet many people today prefer *gender* to *sex* because the term *gender* implies a social rather than a biological basis of role assignment and avoids the double meanings associated with physical sexuality and the term *sex.* When discussing physical differences between males and females and their categorizations into these groups, we generally use the terms *sex* and *sex group.* When discussing social arrangements, including expected behaviors, we generally use the terms *gender* and *gender role,* and will, in fact, err on the side of using *gender.*

Some sociologists, especially those associated with the ethnomethodological tradition, avoid the use of the term *roles* altogether and instead use the term *gender* to refer to the social arrangements and activities that differentiate between males and females, including what we have called gender differentiation, male dominance, and gender stratification. They contend that the use of the term *roles* obscures the fact that these differentiations are reproduced in everyday activities.[27] Other scholars have objected to the use of the term *roles* because they believe it ignores the unequal power relationships of men and women.[28]

Although we agree with the view that everyday activities both reflect and reinforce male dominance and gender differentiation, we retain the more traditional use of the term *roles,* primarily because it includes the notion of patterned social expectations and behaviors. We also retain the separate terms of *male dominance* and *gender differentiation* because, as we note throughout this book, they are analytically and empirically distinct. Gender roles are multifaceted, and men and women play many different roles in their lives. The amount of power attaching to each of these roles differs, both within our own culture and cross-culturally. Using the concept of *roles* allows us to examine the areas in which women have relatively more and relatively less power and influence.

Gender Differentiation in Everyday Life

Extensive role segregation appears in day-to-day interactions at home, at work, and in organizations. For instance, in the United States, men more often change the oil in the car and mow the lawn, and women more often dust and clean closets. At work, women much more often use a word processor or copy machine; men more often use a dictaphone. Although both upper-class men and women belong to exclusive clubs, the men may belong to the city clubs or the university clubs, and the women belong to the Junior League or have auxiliary membership in their husbands' groups. Middle- and working-class organizations are also gender segregated. Usually only men belong to the Elks Club, the Moose, the Eagles, the American Legion, and the Junior Chamber of Commerce. Although women are now allowed in most of these groups, only a few actually join, and most participate in organizations that primarily serve women.[29] (These groups have also been segregated by race and religion. Nonwhites and non-Protestants have sometimes formed their own lodges, which are also sex-segregated.)[30]

The intensity of people's feelings about this role segregation is most apparent in organizations threatened by change. For a number of years the Episcopal church had a strong controversy over the ordination of women into the priesthood. Before women were officially ordained, dissident priests who allowed women to give communion were threatened with excommunication. Even after women joined the priesthood, dissent has continued. Some clergy and some parishes have even left the established church for other church bodies or their own fellowship. Similarly, the United States Jaycees once expelled several chapters when they admitted women. Supporters of integrating the group took the case to court, and the Jaycees spent much time and money fighting the possibility of integration.

The Devaluation of Women in Everyday Life

Not only women's activities, but also their very being are devalued in everyday interactions. This is well illustrated by the way men avoid anything feminine. For instance, if nursery-school boys display behavior usually associated with girls, they tend to redefine the activity as masculine. Linda Heuser told about a boy who one day wore white tights and a woman's wig. He vehemently rejected other children's derision of his "girlish" behavior by explaining that his tights were "boy's tights" and his wig covered his balding head! Heuser did not find the parallel behavior of girls avoiding masculine activities.[31] It is far worse for a boy to be called a sissy than for a girl to be called a tomboy. Grown men continue this pattern. The unisex fashion pattern primarily involves women adopting masculine clothes such as pants and T-shirts. Men may wear brighter clothes and jumpsuits and even carry purses, but they never wear skirts or dresses, and the purses they carry are always, as the fashion coordinators say, distinctively masculine.[32]

Even the attribution of womanly traits may be considered an insult. In an informal basketball game we observed, when a boy would miss a basket the other boys would call him "woman"! On another occasion, we heard a younger boy turn to an older boy in the midst of an argument and say, "Shaddup, boy!" in the most deprecating tone he could muster. The older boy, however, immediately gained the upper hand by saying to his younger brother, "You shaddup, girl!" There is no comparable phenomenon among women, for young girls do not insult each other by calling each other "man."[33]

By adulthood most men temper the open comments they make about women as they become more intimately involved with them. Yet signs of men's devaluation still appear, especially in all-male settings. In his classic study, *The American Soldier*, Samuel Stouffer described how training for combat becomes entwined with the soldiers' definitions of themselves as men:

> The fear of failure in the role [of combat soldier], as by showing cowardice in battle, could bring not only fear of social censure, but also more central and strongly established fears related to sex-typing. To fail to measure up as a soldier in courage and endurance was to risk the charge of not being a man. ("Whatsa matter, bud—got lace on your drawers?")[34]

Even in modern times men are urged on to war by threats to their masculinity. Wayne Eisenhart described an "endless litany" from the drill sergeant in the Vietnam War along the lines of "Can't hack it, little girls?"[35] Although women were closer to the front lines in the Persian Gulf War than in any previous conflict involving the United States, formal combat roles were still limited to men.

Men's sexual jokes may also reveal antagonistic attitudes toward women. Jokes about dumb blondes or traveling salesmen and the farmer's daughter are typical ways to convey devaluation of females. The woman in these jokes "is represented as naive or simply stupid, easily outmaneuvered by the male, who gets what he wants without cost."[36]

Although women may not often witness military combat or even hear men's jokes, they do come into contact with men at work. Here men's devaluation of women may be most clearly expressed through sexual harrassment. Numerous studies have documented the unwanted and unsolicited sexual attention male supervisors and co-workers give women workers.[37] Whether it takes the form of sexual comments, pressure for sexual relationships, touching, or actual assault, these actions reflect men's devaluation of women colleagues as well as male dominance.

The Reproduction of Male Dominance in Everyday Interactions

In the final analysis, cultural patterns of gender segregation and devaluation continue to exist because individuals perpetuate them. Gender segregation is usually much more strongly supported by men than by women, and it is men who express jokes and comments that devalue women. Men communicate their expectations of role segregation and devaluation to one another and thus reinforce these views. Obviously some men do not care as deeply as others about maintaining gender segregation. However, because they must actively work against long-established traditions and the often deeply held views of others, their attempts to end gender segregation and devaluation usually meet a good deal of opposition. Women also may reinforce gender segregation, the devaluation of women, and male dominance through their responses to these expectations.

Male power in everyday life In male-dominant societies, men have, as a group, greater power than women. Verbal communications both reflect and reinforce this power differential. Males and females in our society tend to speak in different ways, although the exact nature of these differences may vary from one social context to another.[38] In general, contrary to the popular stereotype, when women and men are in the same group, the men actually dominate the conversation and talk more than the women do. Topics men introduce result in extended conversations much more often than topics women introduce. Women are also much more likely to provide conversational niceties, such as questions showing interest, in order to maintain smooth interaction.[39] Interruptions in conversations are linked to power in interactions, with the more powerful partner more likely to interrupt[40] and to be perceived by others as more successful and driving.[41] Men tend to interrupt women when they are speaking more than women interrupt men. Although both females and males interrupt one another in conversation, one study showed that women allowed men to have twice as much uninterrupted speaking time as men allowed women.[42]

Men's greater power also shows in nonverbal interactions. For instance, high-status people tend to take up more space relative to their bodies than low-status people do, and men take up more space than women do, even when the size of their bodies is taken into account.[43] Even if women adopt men's nonverbal behavior, this may not affect their relative status. In groups composed only of women or of men, people tend to see the person seated at the head of the table as the group leader. One study demonstrated that when women sit at the head of the table in mixed gender groups, both men and women participants tended to see one of the men in the group, regardless of where he was sitting, as the leader.[44] These studies suggest that women and men both recognize that men have greater power and reinforce this in their interpersonal relations. The exact nature of the relationship between nonverbal behavior and male dominance, however, remains to be fully delineated.[45]

Women's responses to expectations of gender differentiation Expectations of gender differentiation often follow the lines of the *instrumental-expressive* distinction. Expressive actions are oriented toward relations within a group. Instrumental actions are oriented toward goals outside a group. Women are usually expected to be able to deal with the emotions and feelings of others, to be supportive and warm teachers, mothers, or nurses. Men are usually expected to be rational and analytical and to gain recognition in occupational and other nonfamilial arenas of achievement and creativity. Actually, however, both men and women must be both instrumental and expressive. It is virtually impossible for any adult to avoid both instrumental and expressive tasks. But how, given expectations of gender segregation as well as the overriding situation of male power and women's recognition of this, do women respond to men's expectations of gender differentiation?

First, women may confine their instrumental tasks to typically female spheres. Here, even though they are instrumentally competent, they do not encroach on males' areas of endeavors and thus cannot threaten men's self-definitions. Housewives and mothers typically engage in many instrumental tasks, yet their work is seen as "women's work" and not at all in men's sphere. Many middle-class women routinely engage in volunteer work in their communities. The sociologist Arlene Daniels has studied the volunteer efforts of upper-middle-class and upper-class women in a large city on the West Coast. She reported that many of these women engaged in high-level executive decisions, managed large charity budgets, and coordinated complex organizations and activities. Yet, perhaps because its ultimate aim was charity, their work was seen as feminine.[46] Most of the women who work outside the home work in predominantly female fields and do not challenge expectations of role segregation, for the job itself—no matter what it is—becomes defined as appropriate for women.

Some women do participate directly in fields that include a substantial number of men. What may these women, who are directly challenging expectations of gender segregation, do? One possible response is for the women to degrade their achievements, especially when compared to male colleagues; another is to redefine their work as actually being more in line with "feminine" roles.

Attempting to degrade one's own achievements seems most common when women directly compete with men in school or in sports, as grades or a game score give concrete evidence of the achievement of both the man and the woman. A number of years ago, Mirra Komarovsky noted a tendency for women students to play down their academic achievements when talking with men friends. One young woman said, "When a girl asks me what marks I got last semester, I answer, 'Not so good—only one A.' When a boy asks the same question, I say very brightly with a note of surprise, 'Imagine, I got an A!'" Similarly, when a woman beats a man in tennis or in any sport at which the man typically excels, a woman may say (if she wants to play with the man again), "Oh, I just got lucky." Although probably few women use this tactic very often and the tendency for women to disparage their achievements may be generally declining, tensions regarding competition between men and women have not disappeared.[47]

The world of work lacks game scores or exam grades to compare. The reaction women may give then to males' expectations of gender segregation is to redefine their activities as appropriately "feminine." The reasons women give for wanting to enter male professions often fit with an expressive orientation more than the ones men give. In our own research, we have found that, regardless of the kind of occupation, young women say much more often than young men that they want to enter a job because they want to work with people or help people. The reasons women give correspond to the expectations of what women should do. Because they have "feminine" reasons for wanting to be a lawyer or a doctor, the young women may defuse male objections to their actions.

Studies of women in male-dominated arenas suggest that women who emphasize some aspect of a feminine role meet with the fewest interpersonal problems on the job. Lynn Zimmer has studied women who work as guards in men's prisons. She found that women guards tend to alter the "macho, competitive role" men guards typically take toward inmates. They adopt a more caring, nurturing, and motherly role and spend much more time listening to inmates' problems and helping them make plans for release. The women guards are best able to meet their job requirement of inmate control by utilizing aspects of traditional female roles in their day-to-day interactions.[48] Similarly, interviews with female professionals suggest that women who "act professional, but not especially formal or aggressive, who try to be gracious as women and not be one of the boys, face the fewest problems in male dominated work situations."[49] Being feminine may take the form of playing the mother who is sympathetic and helpful to others, the sex object or seductress who plays on her sexuality, or the "pet" or kid sister who encourages the men in their work or acts as a mascot.[50]

If women enter male areas but do not redefine their activities as feminine in nature, they may be seen as the "hard-boiled executive" or an "iron maiden."[51] This response directly challenges male expectations of gender-typed behavior by asserting that the woman is indeed competent and is doing what the men are doing. There are two reasons why this response is relatively rare. First, it directly challenges male expectations, and men may react negatively. Second, women who marry and have families, if they are not well to do, still usually carry a heavy load of typically female household chores. Thus, even if they wanted to, only a small minority of married women would be able to limit their behavior totally to the male sphere of activities.

Women's responses to devaluation Just as none of women's reactions to gender segregation directly challenges it, the ways that women deal with males' devaluation of them do not directly contradict these sentiments. Instead, women often use coping mechanisms that maintain their self-esteem without directly challenging the system of male dominance and the associated female devaluation. All people, men and women, have a need to be loved, to feel good about themselves, to see themselves as worthy. Thus, women are motivated to find other ways to interpret men's devaluation than to see it for what it is. Even if women perceive the devaluation, they also know that men have greater power than they do, and they cannot challenge the devaluation directly without jeopardizing their own security.

One possible reponse to devaluation is for women to see it as correct on a general level but to insist that "it doesn't apply to me because I'm not like other women." Thus, women who have made it in a man's world often attribute their success to their being better than and fundamentally different from other women. Isolated professional women may feel, "I made it. Why can't the rest of you?"

Women may also deny that men's devaluation of women is true and may even put men down themselves. We suspect that this devaluation of men occurs almost exclusively in all-female groups. This would, of course, be expected given the views and the power of men. Many of the put-downs occur as small elements in conversations, as simple asides. Women, at least in this culture, apparently do not have the repertoire of jokes or insults that men use to indicate their devaluation of women. Much less do they base their solidarity on their power over men. Yet the bits of conversation are telling. Women often agree with the grandmother who said, "We really are smarter than men; we just can't let them know it!"

Perhaps implicitly believing this statement, women have typically countered male dominance in day-to-day life by manipulation. Studies of interpersonal power document that this indirect manipulation is the most common means women use to assert control over men.[52] Women use their interpersonal skills to manage and control men whom they may think of as "fools" or "babies" that can be skillfully managed. This is reflected in the folk adage: "The best way to get a man to do something is to let him think it is his own idea." A television commercial once showed a mother and daughter preparing sandwiches for the family's lunch. Even though the father and son insisted that they didn't want mustard, the mother and daughter wanted to use a new brand and put it on the sandwiches anyway. Father and son liked it, and the women and their new brand of mustard triumphed.

Finally, women may deny that men devalue them by accepting the role of angel on the pedestal. For these women, the fact that men open doors and hold chairs for women and extend them courtesies indicates the high regard men have for women. These women may encourage men to give them special treatment by being especially appealing. Unfortunately, these special courtesies have more often than not been associated with a view of women as dependent, weak, and incompetent.

Just as all the responses to gender segregation except the relatively rare "iron maiden" response do not directly challenge gender differentiation, none of the responses just described challenges the devaluation of women as a group. These responses do allow individual women to maintain a favorable self-image in a male-dominated culture, but they do not challenge the system itself. Indeed, individual women may get farther by accepting the system, and they may have much to lose by challenging it. In short, as long as a culture *is* male dominant, women are constrained to play the game to survive, and many have done so almost automatically. In so doing, however, the basic rules of the game tend to remain unquestioned and unchanged.

THE FEMINIST RESPONSE TO MALE DOMINANCE

Feminist movements have made people more aware of how our cultural symbolism and day-to-day interactions reinforce male dominance. Although there have probably always been individual women who have resisted male dominance, feminist movements are broad-based social actions that challenge the entire range of social institutions and cultural definitions. They have appeared only in modern times.

Although the term *feminism* was not used until the 20th century,[53] the first movement in the United States calling for greater legal rights, education, and employment opportunities for women occurred before the Civil War. By the late 19th century, the movement attracted many more women, but narrowed its focus to obtaining suffrage and protective legislation for working women. When these goals were attained by the early 20th century, the movement abated and did not appear again in force until the late 1960s. This recent upsurge of the feminist movement returned to the widespread concern about male dominance that characterized the movement of the early 19th century.[54]

In recent years feminism has influenced scholarship as well as social change efforts. Feminist scholars have called for changes in social policy and have also developed extensive theories that try to account for the origins of male dominance and gender inequality. While they do not always agree with one another on either analysis or strategy, they do tend to share a common desire for greater gender equality and less gender differentiation.

Three theoretical traditions are commonly distinguished within contemporary feminist scholarly writings in the social sciences, each focusing on different aspects of the problem of male dominance: liberal feminism, socialist and Marxist feminism, and radical feminism.[55] While there are many permutations and elaborations to each perspective it is possible to briefly describe the views of each group. Liberal feminists focus on philosophical issues of rights and justice and the equal application of these to men and women. Thus they tend to emphasize equal educational opportunities, changes in attitudes, and legislative reform as the most important ways to promote gender equality.[56] In contrast, socialist feminists focus not on individuals, but on how social relations and social institutions preserve and promote male dominance. Marxist feminists, who share many of the views of socialist feminists, specifically focus on how societal arrangements promote not just gender inequality, but also capitalism. Socialist feminists also often examine the relationship of inequalities stemming from social class, race and ethnicity, and gender. Both socialist and Marxist feminists call for radical restructuring of social institutions and social relationships.[57] Radical feminists generally see women's reproductive capacities and sexual relations as basic to their oppression. They sometimes emphasize the superiority of some typically female characteristics and suggest that male dominance can only be eliminated if women build upon their own strength, using the resulting arrangements to replace the male dominant society. This emphasis has also sometimes been labeled cultural feminism.[58]

In the last quarter century liberal feminists have called for changes in our language, in media representations of women, and even in religious practices. These attempts have met with such success that some authors have suggested that we are in a postfeminist era.[59]

For instance, publishers now often require that at least their textbook authors phrase their writings in ways that do not use masculine referents for all people, and individuals appear reluctant to use the generic masculine pronoun in public discourse.[60] Before 1975, women were rarely seen as newscasters on national or local television. Although men are still the majority there, most local stations now have both women and men as news anchors, and women reporters are much more common. In addition, many more network entertainment shows feature women in nontraditional roles. Women in a wide range of religious groups have also called for change, and they have met with some success. Although women have generally been more likely than men to attend church and to express religious beliefs,[61] they have rarely held leadership positions. Women religious leaders are still the exception, and only about half of all denominations in the United States allow the ordination of women. Yet the enrollment of women in religious seminaries has mushroomed in recent years, a number of denominations have altered liturgy to include female imagery of the deity, and feminist theology has called for widespread changes in theological interpretations and religious practices.[62]

Feminists have also encouraged people to challenge male dominance in their day-to-day interactions. For instance, contemporary feminists questioned the existence of male-only organizations and brought costly lawsuits against many of them, forcing them to allow at least some women to join. They also encouraged women to try to replace manipulation with assertiveness in order to gain directly what they want in their daily lives. It is clearly true that less direct maneuvers tend to support male dominance. Attitudes toward women's roles have, in fact, changed markedly. Certainly, both men and women are much more supportive of women's labor-force participation today than they were in the 1960s.[63]

Even though many of the original goals of the liberal branch of the feminist movement have been incorporated within the general culture, male dominance has not disappeared. Just as earlier feminists found that male dominance did not end with the extension of voting rights to women, so today's feminists have found that institutionalization of some of the reforms they advocated in the late 1960s has not stopped male dominance or gender stratification. Male dominance is so deeply embedded within our culture and our patterns of social interaction that the solutions proposed by liberal feminists have not been sufficient to basically alter the situation.

We believe that gender stratification goes beyond cultural symbols and day-to-day interactions and is built into social institutions and the personalities of individuals. Our analysis incorporates in many ways the specific concerns of liberal, socialist, and radical feminists. Like the liberal feminists, we assert that guarantees of equal treatment for men and women are important and necessary for greater gender equality. Like the socialist feminists, however, we believe that these changes are far from sufficient to end male dominance and that it will be necessary to deal directly with the structure of social institutions and how gender inequalities are related to inequalities based on social class and race and ethnicity. Like the radical feminists, we believe that a world without male dominance must incorporate values and orientations that have traditionally been defined as feminine, and that changes need to address institutional patterns that define women's roles as mothers and wives. This requires an analysis that looks at gender inequality and male dominance from a variety of perspectives or levels. In the chapters to follow we first consider in detail how social institutions embody and perpetuate gender stratification and then explore how these institutional arrangements generate individual motives and attitudes that help maintain gender stratification. Gender inequality is a problem that must concern social scientists both as scientists and as individuals who profess to believe in human equality. We believe that our multi-level analysis of gender stratification can help point the way toward change.

SUMMARY

Male dominance pervades both cultural symbols and day-to-day interactions. Males are depicted in different roles from women and are given more value and authority than women in languages, in religions, and in the mass media. In day-to-day interactions, men show their devaluation of women, and the roles of men and women are often sharply differentiated. Although the actions of women often reinforce differentiation and devaluation, contemporary feminists have challenged these patterns of male dominance. Some changes may be observed in both cultural symbols and social interactions, but these changes have not been extensive.

SUGGESTED READINGS

BARON, DENNIS. 1986. *Grammer and Gender*. New Haven, Conn., and London: Yale University Press. An extensive historical and contemporary discussion of gender-linked language forms and usage.

BRIGGS, SHEILA. 1987. "Women and Religion." Pp. 408–441 in Beth B. Hess and Myra Marx Ferree (Eds.). *Analyzing Gender: A Handbook of Social Science Research*. Newbury Park, Calif.: Sage. Shows how feminism has affected the language and practices of contemporary religious movements.

CHAFETZ, JANET SALTZMAN, and ANTHONY GARY DWORKIN. 1986. *Female Revolt: Women's Movements in World and Historical Perspective.* Totowa, N.J.: Rowman & Allanheld. An extensive discussion and analysis of the precipitating conditions of women's movements both cross-culturally and historically.

FERGUSON, MARJORIE. 1983. *Forever Feminine: Women's Magazines and the Cult of Femininity.* London and Exeter, N.H.: Heinemann. Uses Durkheimian theory to analyze women's magazines in the United States and Great Britain.

FERREE, MYRA MARX. 1987. "She Works Hard for a Living: Gender and Class on the Job." Pp. 322–347 in Beth B. Hess and Myra Marx Ferree (Eds.). *Analyzing Gender: A Handbook of Social Science Research.* Newbury Park, Calif.: Sage. Describes how women resist male dominance and devaluation with special attention to women who are not in professional-level jobs.

HALL, JUDITH A. 1984. *Nonverbal Sex Differences: Communication Accuracy and Expressive Style.* Baltimore: Johns Hopkins University Press. A meta-analysis of many studies of gender differences in nonverbal behavior.

JAGGAR, ALISON M. 1983. *Feminist Politics and Human Nature.* Totowa, New Jersey: Rowman and Allanheld. An extensive philosophical discussion of liberal, radical, and socialist feminist theories.

LIPS, HILARY M. 1991. *Women, Men and Power.* Mountain View, California: Mayfield. Explores inequalities of personal, collective and institutional power between women and men.

THORNE, BARRIE, CHERIS KRAMARAE, and NANCY HENLEY. 1983. *Language, Gender and Society.* Rowley, Mass.: Newbury House. Includes several articles analyzing male dominance in language and social interactions and a very extensive annotated bibliography of material in the area.

WEST, CANDACE, and DON H. ZIMMERMAN. 1987. "Doing Gender." *Gender and Society* 1:125–151. Ethnomethodologists distinguish between *sex, sex category,* and *gender* and show how gender is continually produced in social situations.

chapter 2

Gender Inequality in the United States: The Polity and the Economy

Compared to men, women play a minor role in the polity (political organizations and institutions) and the economy of our society. Much of the power men wield results, in fact, from their control of these institutional areas. Although we now have laws that guarantee women's rights, the inequities these laws are designed to counteract remain and are especially striking in the economy. In this chapter, we explore gender differences in political attitudes and participation and describe the important laws that affect gender stratification. We examine past and current trends in gender segregation in the labor force and gender differentials in wages. Finally, we consider the economic theories advanced to account for women's lower wages.

THE POLITY

Although women definitely have views on political issues, participate in political parties, and are represented in political posts on the local level, they rarely hold national office. A number of laws have restricted women's activities in the past, yet the legal principles of the U.S. Constitution and some federal and state laws are designed to end gender stratification and promote equality in our institutions. Much of this legislation has come about through the efforts of feminists, although some now doubt if it will be as effective as they once hoped.

Gender Differences in Political Attitudes

Attitude polls and voting behavior over the past 40 years show some consistent gender differences in political views. Polls throughout the 1960s and 1970s show that women were much less likely than men to support U.S. involvement in the Vietnam War. In the late 1980s only half as many women as men supported giving assistance to guerrilla forces opposing the Sandinista government in Nicaragua, and women were far less likely than men to support the Persian Gulf war in 1991. Similarly, polls from 1937 to the present day show that women are less likely than men to support capital punishment even though women are more aware than men of increases in crime and more fearful of personal attacks. Women are also more supportive than men of what has been called "prosocial aggression," including the jailing of child abusers and drunken drivers. Even though women tend to oppose military aid to other countries more than men do, they are more supportive of nonmilitary aid. In fact, after World War II, women were much more willing than men to return to rationing so that food could be sent to other countries.[1]

In the 1980 and 1984 presidential elections Ronald Reagan received substantially more support from men than from women, especially among whites.[2] Other politicians have sometimes received more support from one sex group or the other. This does not, however, indicate that women form a voting bloc in the sense that African-Americans, Hispanics, or union members traditionally do. Women do not tend to identify politically with one another to the extent these other groups do, and the differences among women are often as great or greater than the differences between men and women.[3]

Political Participation

Even though women rarely appear in the national political scene, both men and women are involved in politics. Women's social activism has reflected all points of the political spectrum. Historically many women were active in the abolition, suffrage, and prohibition movements. In more contemporary times women have advocated issues such as political conservatism,[4] feminism,[5] and both sides of the abortion issue.[6] Activists have ranged from women employed at high levels of the government[7] to working-class and minority women.[8] Despite this activism, gender stratification influences women's participation in the polity. This is especially true in electoral politics.

Women's right to vote was first supported at a women's rights convention in 1848, yet suffrage was not won until 72 years later, when the Nineteenth Amendment to the Constitution was finally ratified in 1920. Although fewer women than men actually voted at first, in recent years the proportions have been almost the same. Because there are more adult women than men in this country, more women than men actually turn out at the polls.

Men and women are quite similarly involved in party activities at the lower levels. Since the 1960s there have been few differences in the proportions of men and women who wear buttons or display bumper stickers in support of candidates, who attend political meetings, or who actively work for the election of a candidate. Men, however, have been more likely to contribute money to a party, probably simply because they have more money and perhaps also because they are more often employed and thus are solicited for contributions. Probably because they have more leisure time and financial resources, professionally employed, white, middle-class women are also more likely to be politically active than African-American and working-class women.[9]

Beginning in the 1920s both national parties included a man and a woman from each state on their national committees. On the local level, both precinct committee women and men are elected for each party. Over the years, more women have gone to the national conventions and, in recent years, have occasionally had highly visible roles such as that of keynote speaker. Women, then, are active in their party, but this activity still reflects gender stratification and male dominance. Women are much more likely to stuff envelopes and answer phones, whereas men make decisions and plan campaign strategy.[10]

Women are also political candidates and hold political offices, but they are much more likely to do so at the local than at the national level. Their chances of being elected may also be greater in urban than in rural areas. For instance, it was estimated in 1985 that 4% of all the mayors and members of municipal and township governing boards were women. Yet by the late 1980s women were mayors of 11 of the 100 largest cities in the United States.[11]

More women are being elected to state legislatures; by the beginning of 1991 they represented 18% of all state representatives and senators.[12] However, probably because the lower houses in each state are larger, they are much more commonly found there, rather than in the state senates. Women legislators tend to be more common in the New England states and, to some extent, in the West than in other areas.[13] Although their representation is associated with low pay, an even more important correlate of women's participation appears to be a lack of competition for legislative seats. The New England states generally have very large bodies, perhaps as an extension of the town meeting practice. Because there are many legislative seats relative to the total population of the state, the competition for the seats is relatively low. In states with such large legislatures in relation to the population, women tend to predominate.[14]

Until 1973 only three women had been elected as state governor, and all of them succeeded their husbands. Only in 1974 were two women elected on their own credentials: Ella Grasso of Connecticut and Dixie Lee Ray of Washington. Since then other women have been elected in their own right, but there have never been more than three women state governors at the same time. By the end of the 1990 elections women governors were found in only three states: Ann Richards in Texas, Betty Roberts in Oregon, and Joan Finney in Kansas. Women are, however, gradually gaining more representation in lower-level state positions. By the end of the fall 1990 elections there were 6 women lieutenant governors, 10 secretaries of state, 3 attorney generals, and 12 state treasurers.[15]

Women are only gradually moving into the U.S. Congress. By the end of the 1990 fall elections, only 29 of the 435 members of the House of Representatives were women, one more than in the previous session. Only two women were senators. Few of these women have served long enough to have sufficient seniority to be on major committees or to hold powerful decision-making posts. Moreover, informal norms of cronyism may lock women out of many informal, behind-the-scenes decision-making meetings.

For a long time many of the women in Congress were widows of former congressmen and senators.[16] That trend has virtually disappeared, and almost all women legislators now earn office on their own merits.[17] Nevertheless, the increase in women's representation has been glacially slow, leading one political commentator to note that equal representation of the sex groups in Congress would not occur until the 24th century if the current pace continues.[18]

More women are running for all political offices,[19] but few of them win. Relatively few people today appear to vote against women simply because of their gender,[20] and women do not seem to be negatively affected by a second primary system[21] or to receive less campaign financing once variables such as incumbency are controlled.[22] Once women enter electoral politics they are less likely than men to aspire to other offices, perhaps because they are often somewhat older,[23] and this may hurt their representation, at least in higher-level offices. But the major reason women continue to be underrepresented in electoral politics is the power that accrues to incumbents in our political system.

Very few women are incumbents, and most who run for political office face incumbents. In fact, women appear more likely than men to be recruited by party leaders to be sacrificial lambs to run against incumbents in contests they have virtually no chance of winning.[24] Women candidates tend to fare better in open contests, where there is no incumbent, and in multicandidate districts, where several candidates are elected at large.[25] African-American women have fared somewhat better than white women in winning elections,[26] primarily because recent increases in African-American voter registration and voting as well as the creation, often by court order, of African-American majority legislative and congressional districts has opened up new political territory and negated the power of incumbency.[27]

Women are notably absent in high-level appointive positions. Until the appointment of Sandra Day O'Connor, no women had served on the Supreme Court. Women are still noticeably rare in lower court positions on both the state and federal levels. Few women have been cabinet members, although presidents typically have at least one woman as a token member. Both women and men serve on the staffs of senators and representatives, but because civil service regulations do not apply to their own appointments, women staff members often earn less than men in similar jobs.[28]

Laws and Gender Stratification

Legislation codifies and reinforces societal norms regarding women's status and roles, but legislation can also help break down barriers to equality.[29] Since the mid-19th century, feminists have pressed for legal changes that they hoped would improve women's lives. Much of the legislation they have advocated has been enacted, but sometimes with unintended results.

For instance, many feminists, labor unions, and social reformers in the late 19th century advocated protective legislation laws to protect women from dangers in occupations such as mining, bartending, and policing. The laws limited the hours women could work, the tasks they could perform, and the situations in which they worked. Although the original intent of some of this legislation may have been to bar women from certain jobs, many of the laws were originally developed to eliminate the tragic sweatshop conditions under which many women labored and to improve the health of women and their children.[30]

Yet a byproduct of these efforts was to exclude women from certain jobs. Some early 20th-century feminists were concerned about this exclusion and opposed special treatment for women. They advocated a policy of equal treatment that would remove all legal distinctions between men and women. Beginning in the 1920s, they proposed an amendment to the Constitution, the Equal Rights Amendment (ERA), which would guarantee this legal equality.[31] The feminists on both sides of this controversy were clearly concerned about women's welfare; they disagreed on the best way to ensure it.

The Equal Rights Amendment to the Constitution was never ratified. Although it was approved by Congress in 1972 and Congress extended the period needed for ratification, only 35 of the required 38 states voted to approve it before the alloted time ended.[32] Nevertheless, state and federal laws, court decisions, and various administrative regulations from the 1960s to the 1980s have accomplished most of the legal goals of those who advocated the ERA.[33]

Many of the changes came from using the courts to challenge laws that restricted women's opportunities. The basis for these challenges comes from the U.S. Constitution and the constitutions of the various states, laws passed by Congress, and various administrative regulations. The Fourteenth Amendment to the Constitution requires that no state shall "deny to any person within its jurisdiction the equal protection of the laws." This provision has been used in several lawsuits as the reason for requiring equal protection or equal treatment for men and women. Such court cases often prove lengthy, costly, and time consuming, and Congress and state legislatures have passed other laws that deal more directly with elements of gender stratification in social institutions. An example is the Equal Pay Act of 1963, which requires that men and women be paid equal wages for the same work.

The most important prohibition against occupational segregation is Title VII of the 1964 Civil Rights Act. This landmark legislation prohibits discrimination on the basis of race, color, national origin, religion, and sex in any term or condition of employment. Although the original intent of the act was to deal with racial discrimination, the inclusion of the criterion of sex, largely through the quiet efforts of women legislators, such as Martha Griffiths, has led to important legal support for women seeking to end occupational discrimination.[34] The act specifically forbids an employer "to limit, segregate, or classify his employees in any way which would deprive or tend to deprive any individual of employment opportunities . . . because of such individual's sex."

Another important legal tool for employment equality is affirmative action, an executive order that requires employers with federal contracts to take affirmative steps to make up for past inequities that minorities and women have faced. Affirmative action plans are now also common in the private sector. Despite the growing conservative makeup of the Supreme Court, a 1987 decision strongly upheld an affirmative action plan that gave preference to female employees for promotions in order to remedy a long-standing gender imbalance.[35]

Other court decisions and legislation have ensured equal treatment for women and men in many areas. For instance, the Supreme Court forced all-male organizations such as the Jaycees to admit women, and it invalidated state laws that gave preference to men as administrators of estates and that established higher legal drinking ages for men than for women. Specific laws passed by Congress and state legislatures have attempted to ensure equal treatment for men and women in areas ranging from pension benefits to custody of children in divorce cases.[36] Title IX of the Educational Amendments of 1972 prohibited gender segregation and discrimination in almost all areas of academic and extracurricular activities at the elementary, secondary, and college levels.

Although legislators and the courts sometimes are reluctant to intrude on the family because it is seen as a sacred and private area, the 1973 Supreme Court decision that legalized abortions provided women greater control over their own bodies. Liberal, no-fault divorce laws, now found in virtually all states, were advocated by feminists to make it easier for women to dissolve unhappy marriages. In addition, female children of divorced parents now can receive child support as long as male children.[37] The laws promoting women's equality in the workforce may also help increase their status in the home. Laws pertaining to marriage and family relationships, however, often vary considerably from state to state because states have jurisdiction over domestic matters.

As the liberal feminists who promoted these changes hoped, many women have benefitted from these legal changes.[38] Women who work full time now earn more relative to men than they did several years ago, and more women are entering professional areas once totally dominated by men. Both boys and girls participate in school classes and extracurricular activities that were once limited to one sex group or the other. The belief that women and men are entitled to equal treatment under the law is accepted by the majority of U.S. citizens, and policy changes that highlight this tenet are usually widely supported.[39]

Yet gender stratification is still very apparent, and the changes in the law have not resulted in the alterations envisioned by their feminist promoters. For instance, occupations are still highly gender segregated, and women workers still earn only a fraction of what men workers earn. College athletic budgets are still highly skewed in favor of men's sports, and there are actually fewer women in high-level administrative positions in intercollegiate athletics now than there were a few years ago.[40] Although divorce is easier to obtain, women are much more likely than their former spouses to have a lower standard of living after the dissolution of their marriages.[41] Over half of all families headed by women live below the federally defined poverty level. The notion of equal treatment has even been used against women, as men have charged that they were discriminated against. For instance, women's rights to abortion have been challenged on the basis that a husband should be able to intervene. Controversies have surrounded the provision of medical insurance for pregnancies and job protection for maternity leaves because only women, and not men, can benefit from these policies.[42]

In 1980 Congress passed the Pregnancy Discrimination Act, which requires that employers treat pregnancy as they would treat other disabilities, thus providing "equal treatment." Since that time some states have passed legislation that provides special protection for pregnant workers, such as a requirement that employers grant unpaid maternity leaves to women who request them. Such laws are meant to counteract discrimination faced by pregnant women. Yet, just as with the protective legislation acts from the early part of this century, these laws might result in women losing employment opportunities as employers either fire women who might request maternity leaves or refuse to hire them in the first place.[43] As Ava Baron put it, "The lesson from earlier legislation is that protection is, at best, a double-edged sword."[44]

Recognizing the limitations of the equal treatment approach to legislative reform, many feminist legal scholars informed by radical and socialist feminist theories have recently called for a different philosophy of jurisprudence. Because the legal standard of equal treatment is based on a male-dominant culture, interpretations of laws that may affect men and women differently, such as those discussed above surrounding pregnancies, tend to reach conclusions that are more favorable to men than to women. These scholars suggest that it may be time for a legal philosophy that is committed to equality between men and women, but that also takes into account both the differences between the sex groups and the reality of a male-dominated culture.[45]

THE ECONOMY

The laws that provide the basis for ending gender stratification have been enacted for well over two decades, yet patterns of gender stratification remain. They are especially apparent in the economy, for here real dollars can be used to measure the extent of gender stratification. In recent years, more women have entered the labor force. Yet women tend to work in different jobs and are paid less than men, despite their educational level or job classification. Minority women face a double burden of race and gender and suffer more disadvantages than white women.

Participation in the Labor Force

Since 1900, the participation of women in this country's paid labor force has risen sharply, mainly because of the increased participation of married women. From 1900 to 1940, the percentage of married women in the labor force more than doubled,[46] and from 1940 to the late 1980s it more than tripled. This increase in the labor-force participation of married women has occurred with women of all ages, but was especially noticeable in recent years among women of child-bearing ages. Whereas widows (many of whom are over 65) have a lower labor-force participation rate than married women do, single and divorced or separated women have a higher employment rate.[47]

This increase in women's labor-force participation has occurred steadily over the past century, without any important reversals, through times of depression, inflation, and various ideological eras. Over this time period, jobs considered appropriate for women became much more available, thus increasing opportunities for women's employment.[48] Working outside the home also became more financially attractive, as women's wages, adjusted for inflation, more than quadrupled from 1890 to 1985.[49] Attitudes toward married women's employment have become more favorable over the years, so that now relatively few people object to even mothers of small children working outside the home. The large changes in attitudes, however, occurred after, not before, sharp increases in women's labor-force participation.[50]

Married nonwhite women have participated more in the labor force than have married white women, mainly because the husbands of nonwhite women make substantially less money than the husbands of white women. Married women of Mexican, Puerto Rican, or Native American origin do not have higher labor-force participation rates than white women. Even though their families are poorer than white families, cultural prohibitions against women working as well as a possible lack of jobs and definitely lower educational levels probably influence their absence from the workplace.[51] In recent years the labor-force participation of African-American women has not increased as much as white women's. Although the underlying dynamics of this convergence have not yet been clearly identified, they may be related to inadequate employment opportunities for African-American women in lower socioeconomic groups.[52]

Although married women have continually increased their labor-force participation, the rates for men have declined. Of the married men aged 45 to 64 who were living with their wives, 93% worked in 1960; in 1988 this figure dropped to 82%.[53] Much of this decline can be attributed to lower participation rates of men over 54 years of age, who more often retire early—both voluntarily, as higher pensions become available and involuntarily, as it is more difficult for older workers to compete in the labor market. Although African-American women still have higher labor-force participation rates than white women, since the 1970s African-American men have had lower rates than white men. These differences are especially noticeable among younger, unmarried men, and probably reflect the extraordinary unemployment of African-American men in this group.[54]

Women with small children were traditionally less likely to be in the labor force than other women. This situation changed dramatically in the 1980s. By 1988 more than half of all married women with children 1 year of age or younger worked outside the home. Of all married women with school-age children almost three-fourths were employed. Mothers who are divorced are even more likely to be in the labor force.[55] Although the smaller number of children young mothers have today and a greater availability of part-time work have contributed slightly to this increase, the most important influence seems to be a greater tendency for all young women to work. Jobs considered appropriate for women are much more plentiful now than they were a number of years ago, and young women and the general public are much more supportive of mothers working outside the home. Yet the most important reason for women's employment, whether the women are married or single, is economic necessity. The incomes of young single men have declined substantially since the 1970s. Although men between 25 and 34 years old in 1973 had a median income of $26,879 (adjusted for inflation to equal 1988 dollars), in 1988 men in this age group had a median income of only $20,782. Thus, married couples in which both spouses are employed have substantially higher family incomes than those in which only the husband works outside the home, and the employment of both spouses is usually necessary to maintain a standard of living similar to that which they could have enjoyed a few years ago.[56]

Gender Segregation of Occupations

Although more and more women have entered the labor force, they do not work at the same jobs as men. A number of studies show that the occupational structure in the United States is intensely segregated by gender and that this pattern of gender segregation has persisted since at least 1900.[57] In every decade, over two times more women than we would expect by chance are in occupations that are disproportionately female, given the number of women participating in the labor force as a whole. This gender segregation is so extreme that if men and women were to be represented in occupations the same way that they are represented in the labor force as a whole, almost two-thirds of all men and women would have to change jobs.[58]

Women are much more likely than men to be found in clerical occupations (such as bookkeeper, secretary, and data-entry clerk) and service occupations (such as waitress, practical nurse, child-care worker, hairdresser, and private household worker). Men are much more likely than women to be in scientific, technical, and professional occupations (such as engineering and medicine); skilled crafts (such as carpentry, plumbing, and mechanics); operatives (such as meat cutters, welders, and truck drivers); and laborers (such as gardeners and freight handlers). The majority of women work in occupations that are at least 80% female and an even greater proportion of men work in occupations that are at least 80% male.[59] Half of all working women are employed in only 19 of the occupations listed by the census. About a third of all college-educated women work as teachers, nurses or social workers.[60]

Although broad occupational categories are useful, they can often underestimate the amount of gender segregation and gender discrimination in the labor force. Within a given occupation listed in the census, such as teaching or sales, the more prestigious and usually higher-paid posts are held by men, the less prestigious and less well rewarded posts by women. For instance, in retail sales, men generally sell cars and large appliances, and women sell clothing and small kitchen goods. Also, salesmen tend to serve male customers, and saleswomen serve female customers.

Gender segregation is most apparent when workers' actual job titles are studied. Bielby and Baron examined over 400 firms for a 20-year time period. Over half of these establishments had *total* job segregation, with no job assigned to both men and women. Only 10% of the more than 60,000 workers had job titles that were assigned to both men and women in their workplace, and closer examination of the relatively integrated firms showed that the men and women rarely worked side by side at the same jobs.[61] For instance, women might work day shifts and men might work night shifts. Similarly, although the census figures show that women predominate overall in the profession of teaching, most men teach in high schools and most women teach in elementary schools. Within the high schools, men usually teach the physical sciences and some of the social sciences, whereas women teach languages and literature. In gender-segregated classes, men generally instruct boys and women teach girls.

Occupational segregation declined somewhat in the 1970s, primarily as a result of more women entering male-dominated fields.[62] It is difficult to predict whether this decline will continue throughout the rest of the century. On the one hand, a good deal of evidence indicates that young women more often prefer and work in male-typed occupations than older women do,[63] and that young women working in male-typed areas are not more likely to quit their jobs than are women working in female-type areas.[64] This could suggest that women will continue to pressure employers to alter occupational and job segregation.

On the other hand, case studies of occupations that experienced a large influx of women in the 1970s also indicate that these changes may have been only temporary, and a precursor to occupational resegregation. For instance, women are much more likely now, than a few years ago, to be bus drivers; but women usually drive school buses, whereas men work for large metropolitan transit systems. Women pharmacists are much more common, but they tend to work in hospitals, whereas men hold managerial positions or work in research or retail pharmacies. Women also appear much more likely to be entering male-dominated areas when technological or organizational changes modify the duties to allow less worker discretion and more routinization.[65] For instance, the field of typesetting and compositing was once a highly paid and unionized craft dominated by men. With the introduction of computerized methods in the 1970s, the representation of women rose from 17% to 56% and wages fell.[66]

Women also experience additional discrimination because of their color. Table 2-1 gives the distribution of African-American and white men and women in the major occupational categories used by the U.S. Census. This table shows discrimination by both race and sex. White women are overrepresented in professional specialty fields, such as teaching and nursing, sales occupations, and administrative support fields, including clerical work. African-American women are overrepresented in low-paying service work, including work in private households. White men are overrepresented in executive, administrative, and technical fields; in precision production, skilled craft, and repair work; and in extractive occupations of farming, forestry, and fishing. African-American men are overrepresented in protective service fields and among all the low-level blue-collar fields including machine and transport operators, assemblers, inspectors, and general laborers. Although the aggregate figures show more African-American women than African-American men in executive, professional specialty, and technical fields, closer inspection of the data indicates that these professional women are concentrated in a few traditionally female professions including teaching, social work, counseling, library science, and nursing. Those who do enter predominately male professions such as law, medicine, or dentistry are much more likely than white women in these fields to be employed in public agencies instead of the private sphere.[67]

Table 2-1 Occupational distributions of the four race-gender groups, 16 years and older, 1988 (percentage)

OCCUPATION	WHITE MEN	BLACK MEN	WHITE WOMEN	BLACK WOMEN
Executive, administrative, and technical	14.6	6.8	11.6	7.5
Professional specialty	12.3	6.5	15.6	11.2
Technicians and related support	3.1	2.2	3.5	3.6
Sales occupations	11.8	5.8	13.6	9.4
Administrative support, including clerical	5.5	9.1	28.2	26.1
Private household workers	a	0.1	1.2	3.1
Protective service	2.5	4.4	0.5	1.2
Service, except private household and protective	6.2	13.7	14.7	23.0
Precision production, craft, and repair	20.0	15.6	2.1	2.3
Machine operators, assemblers, and inspectors	7.2	10.3	5.5	9.1
Transportation and material moving occupations	6.4	11.6	0.8	1.0
Handlers, equipment cleaners, helpers, and laborers	5.8	10.8	1.5	2.1
Farming, forestry, and fishing	4.6	3.2	1.1	0.3
Totals [b]	100.3	100.1	99.9	99.9
Total N (in thousands)	56,432	5,915	45,654	6,051

a. Less than 0.05%.
b. Totals do not equal 100.0 because of rounding.
Source: "Household Data," *Employment and Earnings, 38* (January 1991): 184.

Gender Differences in Wages

Men and women earn vastly different salaries, even when they both work full time. In 1960, year-round, full-time male workers over the age of 14 had median annual earnings of $5,435. For full-time, year-round women workers, the comparable figure was $3,296, which is 61% of the male rate.[68] In 1987, the median earnings of full-time male workers was $28,313, comparable women's median earnings were $18,531—65% of the men's wages.* Over this quarter-century, women's wages relative to men's rose only slightly, whether the absolute or the percentage differences between the sex groups are considered. Because only 35% of all working women, but 70% of all working men, are employed full time and year-round, even these comparisons tend to understate the earnings gap. When all working women and men are compared, women's median earnings in 1987 were only 44% those of men.[69] Although single women tend to earn more than married women, the gap between single and married women's incomes is so small that it is not at all comparable to the income gap between women and men.

People who have less education and are members of minority groups generally earn less than people who have more education and are white. Yet, in each of the education and racial/ethnic categories, women earn much less on the average than men do (see Table 2-2).

Even when men and women work in the same occupational category, women tend to be paid less. Table 2-3 compares the mean earnings of men and women full-time, year-round workers in each of the broad census categories of major occupational groups in 1989. In each of these categories women earn far less than men do, even though both the men and women included are working full time.

No matter how one looks at the picture, women workers earn less than men. This wage gap appears in both traditionally male fields such as science and engineering, and in predominantly female areas such as service jobs. Many of the areas where women work require extensive education and training. Yet within specific fields where this is true, such as library science, nursing, teaching, and clerical work, women workers earn much less than men. Their lower pay does not represent lower qualifications than men have or employment in areas that require less education. Within occupational categories where men and women have quite similar educational levels, the women consistently earn less than the men.[70] Similarly, when women and men work in jobs with similar tasks, women earn less than men.[71] Even though men who work in predominantly female fields do earn more than the women in those fields, they generally do not earn as much

*The gap between men's and women's wages becomes more dramatic if the means, or averages, instead of the medians are compared. (Whereas the median denotes the point that divides a distribution in half, the mean is the average, or balancing point, of the distribution and is thus affected by extreme values in the distribution.) Men are much more likely than women to have extremely high incomes. Thus, men's mean incomes were more than $1,500 greater than their median incomes in 1987, whereas only $315 separated the mean and median for women.

Table 2-2 Median annual earnings of year-round, full-time workers age 25–64 by sex, race, and education, 1989

	EDUCATIONAL LEVEL OF MALES						
	Elementary School	High School 1–3 Years	High School 4 Years	College 1–3 Years	College 4 Years	5 Years	Total
Whites	$17,508	$21,341	$26,512	$31,025	$37,440	$45,650	$30,449
African-American	16,061	16,482	20,301	23,965	29,294	36,108	21,285
Total, all races	17,335	20,663	25,856	30,420	36,827	45,146	29,591

	EDUCATIONAL LEVEL OF FEMALES						
	Elementary School	High School 1–3 Years	High School 4 Years	College 1–3 Years	College 4 Years	5 Years	Total
Whites	$11,836	$13,344	$16,929	$20,998	$26,067	$30,671	$20,017
African-American	11,244	13,154	16,465	19,141	25,139	30,784	18,098
Total, all races	11,782	13,261	16,885	20,745	25,959	30,904	19,812

Source: U.S. Bureau of the Census, unpublished data from the Current Population Survey.

Table 2-3 Median earnings of year-round, full-time civilian workers 15 years old and over with earnings by occupation of longest job and gender, 1989

OCCUPATION OF LONGEST JOB	WOMEN	MEN	WOMEN/MEN (RATIO)
Executive, administrative, and managerial	$24,595	$40,085	.61
Professional specialty	27,939	39,499	.71
Technicians and related support	17,577	27,898	.63
Sales occupations	16,057	29,604	.54
Administrative support, including clerical	17,510	25,132	.70
Private household workers	6,882	[a]	—
Protective service	21,650	28,233	.77
Service, except private household and protective	11,683	15,635	.75
Precision production, craft, and repair	17,457	26,490	.66
Machine operators and tenders	13,618	21,899	.62

Table 2-3 *(Continued)*

OCCUPATION OF LONGEST JOB	*WOMEN*	*MEN*	*WOMEN/MEN (RATIO)*
Material moving occupations	21,420	22,976	.93
Handlers, equipment cleaners, helpers and laborers	14,095	18,061	.78
Farming, forestry and fishing	11,305	13,894	.81
Total, all jobs	18,769	27,331	.69

a. Mean earnings not shown when base is less than 75,000 persons.

Source: U.S. Bureau of the Census, unpublished data from the Current Population Survey, 1989.

as other men in the labor force, presumably because they are employed in "female" jobs.

There is some indication that at least younger women's salaries may be improving relative to men's, probably because they are least likely to work in female-typed fields. In 1988 women between the ages of 25 and 34 who worked full time had median earnings 76% as high as men workers in that age bracket.[72] Historically, the wage gap between men and women has been larger for older workers than for younger workers. Although this pattern is still apparent, the differences appear to be somewhat smaller than in the past and may lessen even more if young women continue to enter male-dominated fields and receive higher earnings.[73]

Women and Poverty

At least since 1948, women's unemployment rates in the United States have tended to exceed men's. Women are also more likely to involuntarily work less than full time and to have ceased looking for employment because they were discouraged in their efforts. Thus, official unemployment rates continually underestimate gender differences. The gender differences in unemployment rates tend to be smaller in recessionary periods, when the number of unemployed workers increases and when areas where men predominately work, such as manufacturing and other blue-collar fields, are more heavily affected. These small gender differences in the official unemployment rates occurred several times during the 1980s, even though women continued to be more heavily represented among discouraged workers and those temporarily employed part time.[74] Because women are more likely than men to be working less than full time, they are also less likely to be eligible for full unemployment benefits.[75]

We live in a highly economically stratified society. According to one expert, "less than 1 percent of the population owns roughly a quarter of all the personal wealth in this country."[76] Moreover, the United States has no official policy of minimizing wage differences between occupational categories, and both working-class women and men face economic disadvantages relative to others in the society. Working-class women, however, are disproportionately at the bottom of the income distribution because, if they are married, their husbands often earn less than other men and their own salaries are usually too small to raise the family's income much. If they have no husband and must support families by themselves, their low wages make it even harder to survive.

Almost one-quarter of all families with children are headed by women, and from 1970 to 1986 the number of female-headed families more than doubled.[77] Families headed by a woman are much more likely than two-parent families or families headed by a single man to have incomes below the poverty level. Over half of all female-headed families with children are officially categorized as poor.[78]

All of these patterns affect minority families more adversely than white families. Although African-American women are more likely than white women to be employed, the median wage of year-round, full-time, African-American women workers was 89% of the median wage of year-round, full-time, white women workers, 81% of the African-American black male median, and only 57% of the median wage of the white male worker in 1987 (see Table 2-2). In 1988, 27% of all employed African-American women were private household workers or working in the service sector outside the home, whereas only 16% of all employed white women were in these categories (see Table 2-1). Because virtually no minimum wage legislation applies to these areas, such a pattern exacerbates the poverty of African-American women.

Both minority men and women face discrimination. Employed men in all minority groups in this country earn less than white men and are much more likely to be unemployed. So although many minority women must work for the family to make enough to live on, their earnings still rarely approach the average family income of white families. In addition, many African-American men do not have the economic stability to help support a family. The very high unemployment rate of African-American men, reaching as high as 39% for those 16 and 17 years of age, undoubtedly contributes to the high rate of single mothers and female-headed families in the black community.[79]

Over half of all African-American families with children were headed by women in 1986, and over half of these women have never married.[80] These families have very low incomes and high poverty rates, are very likely to depend on welfare, and are less likely than other families to receive support from absent fathers. In the late 1980s, whereas 15% of all white children lived in families with incomes below the federally defined poverty level, 45% of all black children and 39% of all Hispanic children lived in poor families.[81]

African-American, Hispanic, and Native American families are more likely to be headed by a woman than are white families. (Asian families more often have both parents present than white families.) African-American, Puerto Rican, Mexican-origin, and Native American female-headed families are almost twice as likely as white female-headed families to have children under the age of 6. All minority families tend to be larger than white families.[82] Together, these variables show the extreme economic problems that minority women face. They earn less, their husbands earn less, they are more likely to be unemployed, their families are larger, and they are generally more likely to have to support a family by themselves than are white women.

Explanations of Gender Stratification in the Economy

Social scientists have long been interested in why men and women are unequally rewarded in the economy, and their explanations have tended to focus on the economic institutions themselves. Most of these models were originally proposed to explain racial inequalities and were later expanded to account also for gender inequalities. Although they may all ultimately be used to explain institutional patterns of gender stratification, most of these models eventually use the more individual concept of discrimination—the idea that employers favor one group (men) over another (women)—as an explanatory variable.[83]

Employees and employers Some economic models, often termed neoclassical, examine how the actions of employees and employers in the labor market relate to larger economic patterns. Some of the theorists focus on the characteristics and choices of employees, what economists call a supply-side explanation. The human capital and compensating differentials models fall into this group. Others focus more on the characteristics of the labor market, a demand-side explanation. The notion of statistical discrimination, the overcrowding hypothesis, and the monopsonistic model fall into this category.[84]

Human capital theories are probably the most popular neoclassical explanation of the women's job situation. Human capital refers to the resources of individual people. Economists who advocate this model assume that individuals and families choose to invest in formal education and on-the-job training. They may choose to remain on a job to gain futher experience or to move to another location to attain greater economic rewards. Decisions regarding effort and time devoted to nonmarket activities such as child care and housework are also considered important, for they can affect the ability of individuals to invest in human capital in ways that would enhance earnings. These theorists suggest that men and women differ in their human capital investments, and that these differences in human capital can account for gender differences in occupations and earnings. Because women expect to have shorter and less continuous work careers than men, they choose occupations that require less extensive human capital investments and thus are paid less.[85]

Variables identified by the human capital model do affect earnings. Studies conducted by economists and by sociologists working within the status attainment tradition demonstrate that workers with greater job experience, higher educational levels, more on-the-job training, and greater geographic mobility earn more than other workers. Yet these variables and others identified by the model can account for only a small portion of the wage gap between the sex groups. Even when various human capital variables are taken into account—when the impact of women's disadvantage in work experience, training, occupational status, and so forth is statistically removed—a large wage gap between men and women remains. Moreover, women appear to benefit less than men from advanced education, working in male-dominated areas, and having continuous work histories. These results appear for both white and minority women.[86] Neither do women appear to diminish the effort they devote to work as a result of their household responsibilities. In fact, women allocate more effort to work than men do.[87]

The theory of *compensating differentials* suggests that women choose jobs that have desirable characteristics other than high pay. According to this theory, jobs that have undesirable working conditions compensate by providing higher pay. Because women prefer not to be in these jobs, they earn less than men.[88] There is, however, little support for this theory. Although men are more likely than women to have jobs that involve physical danger, analyses that consider a broad range of job characteristics, defined by workers themselves as desirable, indicate that women's jobs are actually far inferior to men's. Of 14 nonmonetary characteristics considered in one extensive study, women's jobs were better than men's only in the amount of vacation received and the dirtiness of the job, and the gender disparity in nonmonetary characteristics was greater than the differential in pay.[89]

The model of *statistical discrimination* assumes that employers want to maximize profits and that they hold beliefs about the relative stability and productivity of men and women workers. In making decisions about hiring and promotions, they tend to rely on these beliefs about the *average* characteristics of each sex group, rather than the *individual* abilities of males and females. When these average characteristics do not apply to individual workers, statistical discrimination is said to have occurred.[90] In support of this view, as we noted above, jobs and occupations are highly segregated by gender,[91] and a great deal of evidence suggests that employers make hiring decisions on the basis of their views of the average characteristics of men and women.[92]

Some proponents of the statistical discrimination model have suggested that if the perceived average characteristics of men and women used by employers are correct, then women, as a group, do not experience discrimination.[93] Yet individual women who do not possess these "average" characteristics no doubt experience discrimination. Evidence also suggests that many of the stereotyped beliefs employers hold regarding women's work behavior, such as their likelihood of quitting or their administrative abilities, are far from accurate, and these inaccurate beliefs undoubtedly harm women as a group. Moreover, the feedback effects of statistical discrimination may be especially harmful. For instance, if employers view women as less stable and give them less on-the-job training and job assignments with low turnover costs, these women may have little incentive to remain on the job and thus will be more likely to leave. Even though the employers' initial beliefs about women's job stability were inaccurate, women's behavior may eventually conform to these beliefs because of their treatment on the job.[94]

The *overcrowding hypothesis* involves the notion that women tend to be overcrowded in certain areas of the labor force and that this overcrowding contributes to their lower wages. This theory rests on the traditional economic notions of supply and demand and the relation of wages to these variables. Demand refers to the need of employers or consumers for a given group of workers. Supply refers to how much of that group is available. If the supply of workers is higher than the demand for them, then a buyer's market exists and employers can afford to discriminate. The overcrowding hypothesis says that because women's occupations are overcrowded, the supply of workers exceeds the demand and the workers will receive lower wages. This overcrowding occurs because of discrimination, the desire to keep women in their "place"—only in certain jobs—and the acceptance of cultural stereotypes of women as inefficient and incapable of performing male jobs. This benefits not only employers, but also male workers, who do not have to compete with women in their predominantly male occupations.

Empirical studies give some support to the overcrowding hypothesis. Even when jobs are grouped by the training and skills they require, women in each group consistently earn less than men. Men and women with the same skills and experience are placed in different jobs, and these different jobs have different levels of pay. It must be remembered, however, that overcrowding cannot account for all of the gap in men's and women's unemployment rates and wages. Even in the typically female jobs, males appear to be preferred as employees and have a lower unemployment rate and higher wages than women.[95] In addition, even though typically female jobs have expanded much more rapidly in recent years than typically male jobs have, gender differences in wages have changed very little.

The final neoclassical explanation is a *monopsonistic model*. Monopsony, in this case, refers to a system in which employers (the buyers of labor) are in a position to set the wages they have to pay to get the workers they need. Anyone who has such monopsonistic control pays the lowest wage that still attracts workers. Janice Madden applied this model to gender discrimination. She assumed that males hold the power within the society and that is is to their advantage to discriminate against women; it is a "manifestation of male power."[96] She argued that because women are less able to change jobs than men, a firm has greater monopsony power over them.[97]

Because women have fewer choices within the labor market and cannot respond as men do to wage changes, a firm can get women to work for less. For example, in a one-university town the university holds monopsony power. In the past (and often today) the husband's job opportunities usually determined where a family would settle. In such a town a faculty wife, if she wished to work at the university, would be virtually forced to take whatever opportunities they offered her.[98] Similarly, unions have often excluded women from membership or ignored their specific needs, such as maternity leave or child care. Because males are more likely to unionize than females, they develop their own form of monopsony power. In the wage demands they can place on employers they have advantages over nonunionized workers, many of whom are women. Male wages can also be determined relative to other work, whereas female wages may be compared to work at home, which has been given no explicit monetary value.

The organization of work Instead of focusing on the characteristics and motives of workers and employers, some analyses focus on the nature of jobs, occupations, and employing firms and industries. These include models of labor-market segmentation, internal labor markets and careers, studies of specific occupations, as well as analyses of organizations, often a separate field in sociology.

Various *labor-market and industry segmentation* analyses have been used to explain the marginal position of minorities in the economy. Although a great deal of controversy exists over how best to define and measure these segments, all of the conceptualizations try to distinguish "good" jobs, or a primary labor market, from "bad" jobs, or a secondary labor market. Theorists also distinguish a core sector of highly profitable industries from a peripheral sector of less profitable and more competitive industries that generally pay workers less. The primary labor market is characterized by higher pay, substantial opportunities for advancement, and, especially in the upper tier of this market, greater opportunities for individual initiative. In contrast, the secondary labor market, which is found in both core and periphery industries, has jobs with lower pay, little training, and few advancement opportunities. Advocates of this perspective suggest that women's disproportionate representation in the secondary jobs can account for gender differences in earnings and job benefits.[99]

In support of this view, studies using a variety of different measures of economic sectors usually find that women are more likely than men to be employed in the secondary labor market in both peripheral and core industries and that workers in this labor market earn less than those in the primary market. Yet even within each labor market and industrial sector substantial gender disparities in wages remain, and these occur for both white and minority workers.[100] In addition, the traditional classifications of occupations into different labor markets may not be applicable to both male-dominated and female-dominated occupations. Given the extensive gender segregation of occupations, the definition of a good job may vary significantly between the two sex groups.[101]

The *internal labor market* analysis and the study of *career dynamics* can be used to examine the gender segregation that occurs within occupations and work organizations. Both of these approaches deal with the advancement of employees along career ladders and distinguish between entry-level positions, which employees attain when they first enter a firm or an occupation, and positions that are attained through promotions or upgrading. The filling of this second category of jobs is usually determined by administrative apparatus within firms, an internal labor market, and competition among those already employed by the enterprise or launched into an occupation. An individual's advancement opportunities are usually determined by the worker's original entry-level position. Men and women have different entry positions; these entry-level positions are linked with different career lines, and thus it would be expected that men and women would have different jobs and different wages throughout their careers. Moreover, because men's entry positions are more likely to be in the primary sector, where longer career ladders are found, their career trajectories would be expected to be longer and more financially rewarding.[102]

Studies within specific firms and of workers throughout the labor force document white men's clear advantage over white women and both men and women from minority groups in wages in entry positions, in the probability of promotion, and in later career earnings.[103] Fields that women tend to enter, such as clerical work, are especially likely to have short career ladders with few promotional opportunities.[104] Minority women appear to be even more disadvantaged in promotional opportunities than are white women.[105]

With the advent of equal opportunity programs in the 1970s some organizations developed programs that offer bridges from low-level, short career ladders, such as those employing clerical workers, to more highly rewarded, administrative ones. Studies of these programs indicate that these bridging policies have allowed more women and minorities to enter at least the lower rungs of administrative career paths, even though they still remain very underrepresented in administrative positions.[106]

Sociologists have also studied gender discrimination in specific *occupations*. Although women are becoming more common in traditionally male professional fields, they tend to have different career patterns and experiences from men. Women physicians tend to be overrepresented in the specialties of pediatrics, anesthesiology, psychiatry, physical medicine, and public health and underrepresented in surgical specialties (except obstetrics), cardiovascular medicine, gastroenterology, and general practice. They are rarely found in the top echelons of the medical profession, as heads of prestigious clinics, hospitals, or medical schools, or in high-level medical policy making positions in government or industry. Interviews with women physicians indicate that they have not been encouraged to pursue masculine specialties and that they have had only limited sponsorship from older male physicians while establishing their careers.[107] Similarly, even though many more women are now completing law school and entering practice than just a few years ago, they tend to be concentrated in low-prestige and less well-paid specialties such as domestic relations, where many clients are women, or trusts and estates. When they do appear in court, many women lawyers report derogatory treatment by both judges and fellow lawyers that makes direct reference to their gender.[108]

Many more women are attaining advanced degrees, and their representation in academia is slowly growing, although intense gender segregation persists. Women are much more often found within the humanities, and men are more often employed within the sciences and social sciences. Within the sciences, men are more often in fields such as physics, engineering, and agricultural science; women are more often employed in biology and other life science fields.

Within the social sciences, women are much less likely to be in economics or political science than in psychology or sociology. Even within specific fields there is extensive gender segregation. Women psychologists are overrepresented in developmental and school psychology and underrepresented in industrial, consumer, and psychopharmacology areas. Women anthropologists are somewhat more likely to be cultural anthropologists or linguists and less likely to be physical anthropologists or archaeologists than would be expected by chance. Women academics are much more likely than men to be employed part time and to hold lower academic ranks. They also earn less than men, even when their rank, part-time status, education, and publication record are equal.[109]

Although many professional fields such as medicine, law, and higher education are dominated by men, women do predominate in other professional areas, including nursing, social work, teaching, and library science. In the past few years, more men have entered these areas. Yet when men enter these professions, they often do not hold the same positions women do. Men more often teach in higher grades; male social workers are more often community organizers than group or case workers. These different starting points generally presage different incomes and opportunities for advancement.[110] In these traditionally female fields, the proportion of men has gradually increased over a period of years. Yet men are represented in the higher-status and administrative components more than would be expected by chance, and this tendency has not declined as more men have entered the fields.[111] This is especially true when the administrative component of a profession expands. A demand for administrators apparently enhances the tendency of males to dominate the field.

Although the majority of working women in the United States are in nonprofessional jobs, less research has been devoted to their problems. However, they experience both gender segregation and wage discrimination. Some of the occupational gender segregation for blue-collar workers involves segregation by firm. As the dual labor market analysis would predict, women tend to predominate in fields with low profits, relatively unstable employment opportunities, and, thus, low wages. These fields include such jobs as apparel manufacturing workers, beauticians, waitresses, laundry and dry-cleaning workers, and dressmakers. Yet, as an internal labor market perspective would predict, extensive gender segregation also exists within organizations, and because men and women start at different points in the firm, their advancement opportunities and career patterns differ greatly. For instance, the representation of women among road construction workers increased from 2% in 1976 to 6% in 1986. However, few of these women were actually involved in the higher-paying on-site jobs, such as the operation of heavy equipment, and almost one-third were in clerical posts, a traditionally female position.[112] In general, discrimination may occur in promotion patterns, wage advances, or entry points, but the end result is that women always tend to have lower wages and employment levels than men.[113]

Although much of this discrimination results from decisions of employers, some of it arises from union practices. Women workers in the United States have joined forces to protest unfair labor practices since the early 19th century,[114] but organized labor has never been centrally concerned with the needs of women workers. From their beginning many unions have had exclusionary policies, or when women were allowed to join they did not give women's needs high priority. Women have especially been excluded from apprenticeship programs in the skilled trades. Union leadership has been dominated by men, even in unions that serve mainly women, including the International Ladies' Garment Workers and the Amalgamated Clothing Workers unions.[115]

Union organizers have traditionally been reluctant to devote time and money to organizing women workers, believing that clerical workers and workers in some service areas such as waitressing are hard to organize. Although these workers have not formed unions as often as others, women's representation among union members has grown considerably in recent years. This reflects a decline in male membership, especially in traditionally male, blue-collar, industrial, and manufacturing areas, as well as more women joining unions. Women now represent over a third of all union members, a larger proportion than ever before. Minority women and those who are public employees are more likely to be unionized than are white women or those working in the private sector.[116] Recent studies indicate that women nonunionized workers are no more opposed to unionization than similarly situated men workers, and some observors suggest that adding more women to their membership roles will be an important strategy for union survival in the coming years.[117] Research in both the United States and in other countries shows that women can benefit significantly in pay and benefits from participation in unions, especially in the public sector.[118]

To understand how discrimination occurs in labor markets, sociologists have examined *women's experiences in work organizations.* One of the most influential theoretical views in recent years was developed by Rosabeth Moss Kanter and suggests that women's relative disadvantage in organizational power and opportunity, as well as gender differences in work behaviors and attitudes, stems primarily from women's disadvantaged location in work hierarchies. She suggests that individual women in higher-level positions experience problems to the extent that they work in predominantly male groups and are tokens. According to Kanter, any group in an extreme minority will suffer the problems managerial women do, and once women are less visible as tokens, their problems should disappear.[119] In this sense, the theory may be seen as gender-neutral; it can apply to any group and avoids discussions of gender discrimination.[120] From this theory, one would predict that both men and women, when a numerical minority within an organization, would have more problems, including less support from colleagues and fewer advancement opportunities.

Tests of this model have generally not been supportive. Both workers' gender and their place in an organization's hierarchy may influence their workplace behaviors.[121] Yet there is little evidence that discriminatory actions toward women decline when they become less than a token presence within an organization or that being part of a numerical minority harms men in the same way that it harms women. For instance, two studies have found that negative attitudes toward women workers are actually less pronounced when there are fewer women on the job than when women are more common.[122] Other research has found that both race and gender influence the interactions and relationships of workers in organizations, even when the workers hold similar positions.[123] In addition, although both men and women who work in atypical fields may experience opposition and teasing, the processes and outcome are not at all comparable. The opposition that women tokens face when they enter male-dominated fields tends to be hostile and debilitating; the opposition that men tokens face tends to be more transitory and is overshadowed by the advantage they seem to have in gaining career advancements and promotions. In contrast to what Kanter's theory would predict, the experience of tokens within organizations does not appear to be gender neutral, but instead reflects the male dominance of the wider society.[124]

Capitalism Some contemporary social scientists informed by Marxism use an analysis that focuses on the segmentation of the labor force to show how the segregation of minorities and women into certain occupations and their lower pay benefits capitalists, private owners of businesses, and capitalism as a system. These theorists accept the notion of primary and secondary sectors and the division of the primary sector into subordinate and independent primary jobs. They suggest that although the independent jobs require and encourage creativity and problem solving, subordinate jobs are routinized and require dependability, discipline, and responsiveness to authority.[125] Beyond these divisions, they recognize that the labor market is segmented by race, with minorities more often in the secondary sector and the subordinate part of the primary sector, and by gender as we discussed earlier.

These theorists, then, suggest that this labor-force segmentation benefits the system of capitalism. First, segmentation of the labor force increases capitalists' profits and forestalls challenges to the system as a whole by dividing workers among themselves and undermining unions that promote workers' interests. Because labor-force segmentation usually follows ethnic, race, and gender lines, when one group of workers goes on strike, another group of a different race, ethnicity, or gender may be enticed by the employers to be strikebreakers. For instance, when workers in paper mills on the West Coast, who are mainly men, went on strike in the late 1970s, the salaried and nonunionized clerical workers, who are mainly women, were required to work in the mills if they wanted to keep their jobs. These theorists also suggest that labor market segmentation limits women workers' aspirations for mobility and legitimizes inequalities between individuals. Most important, segmentation of the labor force is profitable. For instance, even though the women who worked in the West Coast paper mills during the strike were paid more than they earned as clerical workers, their wages were still less than those the men workers had before they went on strike. Thus, not only were the mill owners able to continue operations during the strike, they even made greater profits.

It would seem that rational employers would always prefer to hire women, to whom they could pay such low wages, rather than men. Yet many employers continue to hire men and still make profits. The reason may be partly that men workers tend to predominate in monopoly sectors with high profit rates and women workers predominate in less profitable industries such as the service areas and garment industry, which are also more competitive. The capitalists in the latter areas profit from hiring women workers, because they help keep their prices low and competitive. The employers in the monopoly sectors, because they can essentially set the prices they pass on to consumers, also make a profit and can still afford to refuse to hire women.[126]

Comment In the sections above we have reviewed several explanations of gender inequality in the economy. With a neoclassical model, the human capital theorists try to account for women's lower wages through their lower accumulation of education, job experience, and other such variables. Inequities that remain after the impact of these variables has been accounted for are attributed by some theorists with this perspective to discrimination. The theory of compensating differentials suggests that men earn more money than women to compensate for the undesirable characteristics of their jobs, a position that is unsupported by empirical evidence. The model of statistical discrimination suggests that women's lower wages reflect employers' views about the average capabilities of men and women, and individual women experience discrimination when they differ from these average characteristics. The overcrowding hypothesis suggests that because women are crowded into fewer occupations than men are, they can be paid less than their skills and abilities would warrant. The monopsony approach recognizes that discrimination exists and that men have greater power than women in the economy. Because women are crowded into fewer occupations and hence become a less elastic labor supply than men, firms can discriminate more against them. In other words, women have to take what they can get.

Other analyses focus on the discrimination women face within work organizations. They suggest that because women generally start at different points within the labor market, they have different opportunities and experiences than men do and that within work organizations, even when given responsible positions, women face discrimination. Finally, a Marxist orientation accepts many of the findings of the other approaches, but adds the idea that segregation of the labor market benefits capitalism itself.

In explaining gender inequalities in the economy, each of these theories falls back eventually on the idea that employers discriminate by confining women to certain jobs and by not rewarding women for their actual contributions. Although these theories explore how this discrimination occurs, they do not deal with the questions of why occupational gender segregation exists or why males and females are not rewarded equally for their work. In other words, they do not answer the *primary* question of why gender inequalities exist in the first place.

Gender segregation of occupations and discrimination in pay are specific examples of the tendency for males to differentiate their activities from those of women and to devalue women's roles. Men and women tend to have different job titles, even when the nature of their work is quite similar. Women and men workers with similar skills, experience, and responsibility are paid different amounts.

These patterns of discrimination are institutionalized in an economic system. Although to some extent we can understand the perpetuation of occupational gender segregation and gender discrimination in incomes as stemming from the continuance of these traditional patterns, it is important to realize that these patterns are continually reproduced and reinforced by individuals who make decisions about the nature of the workplace. These gatekeepers to the economic world make decisions on job classifications, hiring, firing, and income levels. They may be employers, personnel managers, and even union officials, but they are generally men, or women whose superiors are men.[127]

Undoubtedly, the socialist feminists and Marxist-oriented theorists are correct when they see gender segregation of the occupational force as benefiting capitalism. Yet not just employers, but male workers as well, benefit from gender discrimination against women in the economy. Moreover, countries that have explicitly tried to eliminate profits of capitalists and to minimize the overall discrepancies in income still have occupational gender segregation and gender discrimination in wages (see Chapter 4). Thus, gender inequalities in the economy appear to be rooted in the system of male dominance. To end them, we agree with both the socialist and radical feminists who assert that we must deal with the system of male dominance itself and its perpetuation from one generation to another.[128]

SUMMARY

Although women and men have similar voting behavior and political participation at the local level, men are much more frequently in the upper echelons of decision making. Women's labor-force participation has risen throughout this century in the United States. Yet men and women generally work in very different occupations, and women, even with the same training and skills, earn much less than men. Women, especially those who are the sole providers for their families, are poorer than men in similar circumstances. Indeed, women represent a much higher proportion of those classified as poor than men. Explanations of this gender stratification in the economy may focus on the characteristics and situation of the employees and employers, on the nature of the job and work organization, and how patterns of gender discrimination serve capitalism.

In recent years, laws have been passed that guarantee more equality to men and women; yet the wage gap and gender segregation of the labor force remain high. An underlying assumption behind discrimination in the economy and the polity is that women's primary social roles are in the family and that men's primary social roles are in the economy and occupational world. It is assumed that women should devote their major attention to their roles as wives and mothers and that the major focus of men's attention should be to the world of work outside the home. Thus, women's family roles are often used directly and indirectly as reasons for denying them equal access to public roles, even though the majority of women with children at home are now employed.

SUGGESTED READINGS

BERGMANN, BARBARA R. 1986. *The Economic Emergence of Women.* New York: Basic Books. Examines women's economic position in the labor force and the family; includes many examples of discrimination reported in court cases.

BLAU, FRANCINE D., and MARIANNE A. FERBER. 1986. *The Economics of Women, Men and Work.* Englewood Cliffs, N.J.: Prentice Hall. A textbook written by economists that examines research on women, men, and work in the labor market and the household.

BOOKMAN, ANN, and SANDRA MORGEN (Editors). 1988. *Women and the Politics of Empowerment.* Philadelphia: Temple University Press. Case studies of working-class and minority women's responses to discriminatory treatment in the workplace and community.

CARROLL, SUSAN J. 1985. *Women as Candidates in American Politics.* Bloomington: Indiana University Press. Uses results of national survey of female candidates for nonlocal offices to analyze reasons for women's underrepresentation in political office and the possibility of change.

HOFF-WILSON, JOAN. 1987. "The Unfinished Revolution: Changing Legal Status of U.S. Women." *Signs: Journal of Women in Culture and Society* 13:7–36. Explores changes in the legal status of women from the ratification of the Constitution to the end of the 1980s, with special attention to the divisions between those who advocated "special" and "equal" legal treatment for women in the law.

MARINI, MARGARET MOONEY. 1989. "Sex Differences in Earnings in the United States." *Annual Review of Sociology.* 15:343–380. A sociologist reviews and assesses theories that try to account for the gender gap in wages.

Monthly Labor Review and *Employment and Earnings.* Two monthly government publications that are excellent sources of the most current data on gender differences in wages, unemployment, and occupational sectors of employment.

SIDEL, RUTH. 1986. *Women and Children Last: The Plight of Poor Women in Affluent America.* New York: Viking. Describes the extent of women's poverty in the U.S., its sources, and policies that can change this situation.

TILLY, LOUISE A. and PATRICIA GURIN (Editors), 1990. *Women, Politics, and Change.* New York: Russell Sage Foundation. Includes wide-ranging essays regarding women in political movements and electoral politics.

WILLIAMS, CHRISTINE L. 1989. *Gender Differences at Work: Women and Men in Nontraditional Occupations.* Berkeley: University of California Press. A subtle, qualitative analysis of the experiences men and women face in nontraditional jobs.

Women and Work: An Annual Review. Newbury Park, Calif.: Sage. Volumes issued annually contain articles by scholars from a variety of disciplines, all focusing on women and work.

chapter 3

Gender Stratification in the United States: The Family and Education

Industrialization in this country has involved the separation of the world of the family from the world of paid work. The family has come to be seen as the seat of personal and private life, and work has become a means to sustain it. Although, as we saw in the previous chapter, women have increasingly entered occupations outside the family, men continue to be defined in terms of their outside work in a way that women are not. In the United States a man's primary role is his job or occupation, whereas a woman's primary role is her home and family, even when she works outside the home. The separation of the family from economic production has important consequences for gender inequality because the family serves the economy far more than the economy serves the family.

With industrialization, education designed to prepare people for work and family roles has become a system of formal training removed from both the home and the workplace. In general, people in this society see education as a potential way to equalize opportunity for people from various socioeconomic class levels and for the two sex groups. There is less gender inequality in education than in the occupational world. In addition, our educational system is an area where many strenuous efforts are being made to overcome gender inequality in other institutional areas. We need to assess to what extent equal access to educational facilities for men and women can in fact bring about their equality.

THE FAMILY

In this section we trace the emergence of the family as we know it today and ask how changing views about what families are supposed to do and be have affected the status of women. Certainly not all of the changes involved in industrialization have been detrimental to women. In fact, these changes have provided a new basis for women's equality. We shall also examine the situation of women today from the perspective of the interconnections between family and housework roles and paid work roles. We look at inequality within the family itself and directions of change with special reference to the areas of sexuality, love, and child care.

The Emergence of the Modern Family

In the predominantly rural, preindustrial society of the colonial period, family life and work life were one and the same. Privately owned family farms were the basic enterprises, and other businesses were also usually family owned and operated. In the early period of capitalism, the family unit was the basic affectional unit and also the basic work unit. This early family also was likely to contain nonfamily members, such as servants (usually the children of other householders) and apprentices. The preindustrial family was not only the workplace; it was also "church, reformatory, school and asylum."[1] With increasing industrialization and urbanization, these functions were given over to other agencies, and the family became a more "specialized" structure whose main functions were the early socializing of children and managing tensions, or stabilizing adult personalities. Talcott Parsons called this process of assigning functions to increasingly specific structures "structural differentiation."[2] The cultural ideal that dominated the "modern family" held that although the husband/father provided for the family by his outside work, the wife/mother assumed major responsibility for housework, child care, and making a happy home. Thus, the male role became anchored in the occupational sphere outside the family, and the female role was anchored in the family. Parsons described this whole process as highly functional for industrial society. The privatization of the family, its separateness from nonfamily members, made it easy for a family to pick up and move with the worker/husband wherever occupational opportunity led him. Parsons gave the impression that this arrangement was ideal and implied it would continue indefinitely.

Eli Zaretsky, a contemporary Marxist, analyzed the relationship of the family to the economy in a manner that does not contradict Parsons's analysis, but put the emphasis in a different place. For Zaretsky, the changes Parsons called structural differentiation have had the effect of removing work "from the center of life to become the *means* by which life outside work was maintained."[3] He has seen this "radical disjuncture" between personal life and work as a distinctive feature of developed capitalist societies. For Zaretsky, as the world of paid work becomes increasingly impersonal and alienating, the subjective world of the family becomes increasingly important to the individual. Both Parsons and Zaretsky see the family as very much needed by individuals in contemporary society precisely because it is the place we have come to expect to find personal fulfillment.

Although this more specialized family may be functional for industrial society according to Parsons and for large-scale capitalism according to Zaretsky, its beginnings can be traced back to ideological, structural, and demographic changes that preceded both industrialization and large-scale capitalism. The Protestant idea that children were not just miniature adults or workers, but individuals whose souls (we would now say personalities) needed parental care and guidance, had been emerging for a long time.[4] It is also true that certain demographic changes preceded industrialization by at least several decades. Both mortality and fertility declined before industrialization, suggesting (because the fertility decline occurred among married couples) that the attitude toward children had already changed.[5] A variety of factors besides industrialization, including urbanization, declining fertility, and increased schooling for children, contributed to families devoting more attention to fewer children for longer periods of time.[6]

Whatever the ultimate and proximate causes of the change, historians tell us that from about 1825, ideas and ideals about family life that are familiar to us today were disseminated from the pulpit and in middle-class periodicals.[7] The type of family, then, that Parsons and Zaretsky have described—the family that is the cradle of personal life, the specialized family that is removed from the world of work—emerged as both ideal and partial reality a little over 160 years ago. This family ideal posits love as opposed to financial considerations as the only legitimate basis for marriage, stresses the importance of mother love for children, and sees the home as a domestic unit, a psychological haven apart from the rest of society.

In the Colonial period before industrialization, women too were producers. In addition to housekeeping, women made bread, churned butter, spun yarn, wove cloth, and made soap, candles, and medicines.[8] Women also had important roles in the community that were later to become the jobs of male professionals. For example, the functions performed by midwives were taken over by obstetricians, almost all of whom are male.[9]

Some have argued that because women did play these productive roles, their status was higher in the Colonial period than in the 19th century, when work and family became more separate. Even though women's competence as workers was recognized and valued in the early days of this country's history, it must not be forgotten that married women did not have anything like equal status with their husbands. They were next in command, but they were certainly not the boss of these small enterprises unless the male head died or became seriously incapacitated. In addition, married women's legal and property rights were more limited than men's.[10] Women were not given higher education until well into the 19th century, and women were not allowed to vote until the 20th century.

The new image of the family that began to emerge in the 1800s defined women in a very different way than as workers. The home began to be discussed in highly sentimental terms as a retreat, and it was already clear that meaning and satisfaction in life were to be found at home and not in the workplace.

This ideal of the home as a retreat from the harsh and evil world had the effect of connecting women to domesticity and sentiment in a way unknown in the Colonial period. It further sharpened the perceived differences between the sex groups, and it associated feeling and sensibility with women and intellect and assertion with men.[11] On the other hand, the sentiment and feeling associated with women were also associated with morality, and there were advantages for women in this new image. Even though 19th-century middle-class men were clearly the heads of their households, they were, nevertheless, exhorted by popular moralists to model themselves on the virtues of their wives, who were "purer" beings. The purity and morality assigned to 19th-century women became a vital opening wedge for increasing women's political and educational rights. After all, because the home was seen as the moral bedrock of society, society would be helped by helping the home, which was represented by women. Thus, women's benevolent and temperance activities became, in part, a seedbed for feminist activities.

The first concern of 19th-century feminists was to reform the property laws and upgrade women's power inside the family. This goal was met with the Married Woman's Property Acts of the second quarter of the 19th century, which established a wife's right to act in economic and family matters with the same powers as a husband. Next, feminists sought to gain the vote in local elections by arguing that family morality and interests should be represented in the community. This approach was also used in 1920, when women secured the right to vote in national elections and thereby, at least formally, became the political equals of men. The rhetoric women used to get the national vote was that women's concerns with home and morality would clean up dirty politics. At about the same time that women got the vote, education for women in general began to be justified on the basis of their family role. Thus, women's loss of their productive roles by the separation of family and economy in the 19th century may have actually helped them attain greater legal equality.

The view of the family as a haven of sentiment and morality was far more characteristic of middle-class families in the 19th century than of working-class families. These families, for whom economic survival was relatively precarious, could ill afford the luxury of sentiment. In the first half of the century, families often retained their rural base while supplementing their incomes with the earnings of daughters who went to work in the textile industry. In other cases, whole families operated as a work unit in the manufacture of some item. Even when different family members worked in different places at different jobs, work continued to be a family enterprise in that each member's work was considered to be for the family and was regulated by an overall family survival strategy.[12] On the other hand, most of the working-class women who worked outside of the home were not married. In the 19th century, 95% of women who were married did not work outside the home.[13] By allowing children, rather than wives, to work outside the home, the role of the wife as protector of the domestic sphere was preserved even for those in difficult economic circumstances.[14]

African-American men and women were both forced by the system of slavery to assume active roles in the economy, often working side by side in the fields. Yet, in the years after the Civil War and emancipation, most African-American women either stopped or greatly reduced the time spent working in the fields, even though many continued to work as domestic servants. When they had the freedom to choose their activities, African-Americans followed the strong cultural tradition already institutionalized among their white working- and middle-class contemporaries, and began to strongly differentiate the roles of husbands and wives.[15]

In the middle class, the 19th-century idea of the housewife creating perfect bliss within the home on the basis of intuition later became transformed into a more "scientific" attitude toward home management. The Domestic Science Movement was formally begun by middle-class women at the turn of the century with the Lake Placid Conference on Home Economics. This movement, in essence, sought to professionalize the role of the housewife. As a result of this effort, scientific principles of health, sanitation, and nutrition along with efficient, economical management practices were taught in colleges, universities, and public schools. Even though the larger effect of the home economics movement was to keep women fully occupied within the home, the movement was supported by many feminists who used it as a way of justifying higher education for women.

By the 1930s, sex and sexuality became increasingly acceptable for married women. For example, although people at the turn of the century thought that a woman who wore makeup was promiscuous and beyond the pale of respectable society, ordinary housewives adopted it after makeup was used by the semi-respectable flappers of the 1920s. In general, as the Victorian dichotomy between good (asexual) and bad (sexual) women blurred, sexuality and sex appeal became something the middle-class woman could strive for. Women were (and still are) encouraged by advertising not only to have the cleanest floor in town, but also to look glamorous (for their man). Thus, being beautiful and buying products to make them beautiful became a part of women's jobs and one that women were encouraged to work at in order to maintain their husbands' interest. Also, a good-looking wife became a new way for a man to symbolize his own status; a glamorous wife was as much a status symbol as a shiny car. From a feminist standpoint, however, the glamour pattern increased gender differentiation ever further because men were not encouraged to be attractive, only occupationally successful. Moreover, it defined women largely in terms of their specifically sexual qualities as opposed to their more general humanistic qualities.[16]

An alternative pattern at this time was for the middle-class housewife to play the role of good companion to her husband by emphasizing this common humanistic element in their relationship.[17] Actually, the humanistic element was usually not shared, because middle-class men tended to be totally immersed in their occupations. Essentially, this role is an updated version of the cultural interests, moral activity, and charity work that were seen as part of a good wife's duties in the 19th century. But as services became increasingly professionalized, the work of volunteers, no matter how useful, tended to be downgraded. The "club woman" was the butt of many cruel jokes in the 1940s.

During World War II, as many men went off to war and as the economy boomed with the opening of shipyards, aircraft plants, and munitions factories, many women, even those with small children, entered the labor force. Although gender segregation persisted in the jobs in these plants, women took over many jobs that were previously held by men or were newly created. They were paid better wages than women had ever received, and employers needed their services so much that many were willing to provide child-care facilities. This wartime experience probably helped break down attitudinal barriers toward married women's employment.[18]

After the war, however, the men returned and took over the high-paying jobs. Although the proportion of married women working outside the home continued to climb, images in popular periodicals showed an almost compulsive return to images of domesticity after the war. Many couples had children that they could not have had during the war, and large families became fashionable for the middle class. Although the idea of sex appeal and motherhood were at opposite poles during the flapper era of the 1920s, by the 1950s more and more people were getting married and at younger and younger ages. In the 1950s couples were buying single-family dwellings and having more children. The divorce rate was rising, but so was the rate of remarriage.

Betty Friedan, in her now-classic *Feminine Mystique*,[19] criticized the situation of middle-class married women in the 1950s from a feminist standpoint. The book came at a time when feminism (as opposed to the feminine mystique) had never been less popular. As Friedan has said, words like career and emancipation were embarrassing in the 1950s. Nevertheless, she found that the women she interviewed and talked with informally all shared "a problem that had no name." They spoke of feeling "incomplete . . . as if I don't exist," of meaninglessness. Many went to psychiatrists to see what was wrong and were told that what they needed was to enjoy being feminine. Advice columns told women who complained of accomplishing nothing that their successful husbands and children were their accomplishment. It seemed that all the weight of the culture argued that women should rejoice in their femininity. Essentially, being feminine in the 1950s implied getting all one's life satisfaction from being a wife and mother, of not wanting to do the things males did, of not wanting to be strong, independent, or personally accomplished, of being grateful for the luxury of not having to work outside the home.

The feminine mystique had influenced the entire class spectrum. Although middle-class men's work was overly demanding, working-class men's work was likely to be deadening. In both cases, however, men saw home as offering the psychological solution to the problems generated in the work world. By the 1970s, working-class wives whose families had followed the middle-class move to the suburbs also began to be faced with the problem that had no name:

> I don't know what's the matter with me that I don't appreciate what I've got. I feel guilty all the time, and I worry about it a lot. Other women, they seem to be happy with being married and having a house and kids. What's the matter with me?[20]

The main exception to the ideology that married women should not work outside the home was African-American wives, especially in the South, who worked in the homes of whites as domestic servants. Perhaps out of necessity African-American wives have tended to see outside work as part of their family role. African-American families were often too poor for mothers not to work, and earning money for the children became part of the mother role.

One of the reasons that Friedan's book could strike a responsive chord in middle-class women was that it articulated the contradiction between their level of education and the actual life the feminine mystique required them to lead. Even though middle-class girls were very oriented to getting married, they were also being trained to do other things. Women were told to look on their education as a contingency plan to be put to use if something went wrong; nevertheless, they were being educated. In college, they learned to value personal achievement; yet they were only allowed vicarious achievement through their husbands and children. For many women, vicarious achievement proved not to be enough.

Women and Men in the Contemporary Family

By the end of the 1980s the typical family in the United States was vastly different from one in the 1950s. In fact, the differences are so great that a present-day family might be called a "postmodern" family.[21] The rate of marriage has declined precipitously, and young people now are much more likely to delay marriage. In 1950 less than one-third of all women between 20 and 24 years of age had never married; by the late 1980s, over 60% of the women in this age bracket were still single.[22] At the same time, marriages that do occur are much more likely to end in divorce. Although the divorce rate was relatively high immediately after World War II, it fell almost to the prewar levels in the 1950s. The rate then began to rise rapidly during the late 1960s and 1970s. Between 1960 and the late 1980s the number of divorces calculated for each 1,000 married women aged 15 and over more than doubled, going from 9.2 to over 20.[23]

Women are also having fewer children. The fertility rate began to decline in the late 1960s and remained well below the levels from the 1950s to the 1980s. This fertility decline has been attributed to the older age at marriage, delaying child bearing once marriage occurs, and the use of more effective contraceptive methods.[24] Children are more likely to be born outside of marriage now than in the 1950s, and the number of births to unmarried women has risen more quickly than the number of single women.

African-Americans are much more likely than whites to delay marriage or to be divorced or separated from their spouses. They also tend to remain separated longer than whites. Although differences in total fertility have narrowed in recent years, African-American women are still less likely than white women to delay childbirth and much more likely than white women to have children outside of marriage.[25] In 1987 over 60% of all births to African-American mothers, but only 17% of all births to white mothers, occurred outside of marriage.[26] The differences are especially large among young women, but are much smaller among African-American and white teenagers from upper-status backgrounds.[27] These different experiences of African-Americans and whites can be largely traced to the extremely high unemployment rate of young African-American men noted in Chapter 2, as well as their higher mortality rate from infancy through adulthood and their higher rates of incarceration and institutionalization. These unemployment rates have increased dramatically in the last few decades. Because most marriages are racially homogomous, African-American women of marriageable age face a shortage of potential partners.[28]

Taken together, these trends result in household compositions that contrast strongly with those of the 1950s. Young adults are much more likely to live alone or with a member of the other sex prior to marriage. Older adults, especially women, are also more likely to live alone, as a result of higher divorce rates, fewer children, and lengthening life spans. Given the high divorce rate and the growing number of children born out of wedlock, families with children are much more likely to be headed by women. The number of female-headed households with children more than doubled between 1960 and 1980, and African-American children are much more likely to be affected by this trend.[29]

These changes in the family along with women's increased participation in the paid labor force have resulted in many fewer women being totally economically dependent on their husbands. Similarly, women are spending much more of their adult lives outside the traditional, husband–wife nuclear family.[30] At the same time, these changes have not eliminated the strains and tensions experienced by women in the family. Although both men's and women's roles in the family and economy have changed, women's roles appear to have changed much more than men's. Moreover, basic assumptions about the gender-based division of labor within the home appear to have altered very little.[31]

These assumptions appear among couples who are married and among those who are cohabiting. Even though we use the terms *husband* and *wife* below, most of the discussion that follows also applies to heterosexual partners who are not married.

Paid work and housework Fewer women identify themselves as housewives today than in the 1950s. In addition, relatively few women today view housewifery as a lifetime vocation. Nevertheless, more women identify with this role than with any other single occupation. In addition, women who are employed outside the home also spend a great deal of time working within the home, and housework is critical to the maintenance and well-being of families. These activities include not just the mundane tasks of cleaning and cooking, but also maintaining the emotional well-being of family members and planning and administering areas of family life as varied as meals, child care, and social activities. Although these tasks are essential for the family, and thus for the society as a whole, women who have been housewives for many years usually have a very difficult time entering the paid labor force if they desire or need to do so. In addition, they accumulate no pension or retirement benefits from their labor in the home apart from those they gain from their husband's employment. Given the current high divorce rate, the job of housewife may be seen as a fairly high risk occupation. If they divorce they generally lose their husband's economic support and find it extremely difficult to enter the paid labor force.[32]

Neoclassical economists, writing in the tradition of the New Home Economics, have tried to explain why families would choose to have wives, rather than husbands, devote their energies to housework instead of work in the paid labor force. They suggest that families need commodities that can come from both time in the paid labor market and from time spent in domestic or home labor. They also suggest that one spouse will often have a comparative advantage in one or the other of these markets. Most commonly, husbands command higher wages than wives; wives are assumed to be more skilled at household activities. A rational choice for families would then be for husbands to specialize in paid labor and wives to specialize in domestic labor. If both husband and wife could command high wages, a rational choice would be for both to specialize in paid labor and to purchase goods and services they would otherwise produce at home, such as meals, child care, and cleaning.[33] In a sociological extension of this model, Valerie Oppenheimer suggested that families try to maximize not just economic rewards but the family's status. In her model wives are more likely to work if their jobs do not detract from, but enhance, their families' social standing.[34]

One major shortcoming to the New Home Economics model as formulated by economists is that it often ignores the fact that an individual's comparative advantage may change over the life cycle. Domestic needs may be highest when children are young, and it might be beneficial to a family to have a wife at home at that point. Yet earnings in the labor market tend to increase with greater experience and decline if a woman is not employed. When the children are older and the wife wishes to reenter the labor force, she may not be able to command the wages she could have earned if she had been employed in earlier years. Thus, a family's decision to have the wife specialize in home work, although rational at one stage of the life cycle, may not be advantageous to either the family or the wife as an individual over the long run.[35]

Socialist and Marxist feminists have taken a different view of the housewife role. They see the housework women do precisely as work—socially necessary work that is not paid for by capitalists but by workers as a hidden cost. These authors suggest that regardless of whether women work outside the home their household labor, including child care, constitutes a huge amount of socially necessary production that is not considered real work under capitalism. Women's work in the home is seen as reproducing the labor force, both by caring for those who are currently employed and by nurturing future generations of workers. Women provide these goods and services without economic compensation and at a much lower cost than they could be purchased on the open market. Thus by assuming the costs associated with the reproduction of the labor force women's work as housewives saves capitalists money, increases their profits, and helps maintain the economy.[36]

Power in the family and housework Most feminist scholars would agree that a major fault of the New Home Economics model is that it ignores the reality of male dominance and the relative power of husbands and wives within marriage. Many sociologists have studied power within the marital relationship, using a wide variety of methodologies, and virtually all have concluded that wives have less power than their husbands and that this differential increases when the wife is not employed outside the home.[37]

Two major explanations have been used to account for this phenomenon. The first focuses on the different economic resources that husbands and wives bring to their relationship and suggests that working wives enjoy greater power because of their economic contribution to the household.[38] Even though many wives now work outside the home, they rarely earn as much as their husbands, and they have less economic leverage in the marital relationship. The other explanation adds a focus on how husbands' and wives' specialized roles within the family affect their interactions. Women, even when they work outside the home, tend to specialize more than their husbands in expressive roles—those oriented toward maintaining and enhancing interpersonal relationships within the family—such as child rearing. Men tend to specialize in instrumental roles and activities, such as providing economic resources. Whereas men's activities and skills are easily transferred to other relationships, women's tend to be more tied to their current relationship and are generally less valued in the occupational world. Thus, women have fewer alternatives outside their current family, and this gives them less bargaining power than their husbands. According to this perspective, increasing women's power within the family will require not just decreasing gender inequities in pay, but also a greater valuation and sharing of women's roles within the family.[39]

The gender-based division of labor within the family appears to be very strong even as more women have entered the labor force. The norms governing both who takes responsibility for various household tasks and the kind of work that she or he generally does are strongly gender typed, both for adults and children. For instance, wives are very likely to be responsible for cleaning the house, cooking, and child care, whereas husbands are more likely to be responsible for household repairs and sometimes yardwork and care of pets. Daughters are more likely than sons to be assigned housecleaning responsibilities, whereas sons are more likely to be assigned yardwork.[40] Wives who work outside the home still bear almost all the responsibility for housework and essentially have a double workload.[41] Even though the media occasionally report on men who choose to stay home and care for their families while their wives work, such "househusbands" are actually very rare. One extensive study of predominantly middle-class, married couples found only 4 husbands out of over 3,600 surveyed who could fit this description.[42] The gender-based division of household labor is found with both cohabiting and married couples, even though the former group tends to hold more egalitarian ideologies. This suggests that it is not norms inherent in marriage, but those related to gender and the system of male dominance in heterosexual interaction, that underlie these patterns of unequal household labor.[43]

Of course, some husbands do devote more time to household chores than others. The amount of time that the wife works and the number and age of children in the family all appear to affect the husband's participation. Yet the greater participation of fathers primarily involves providing greater time in which they are available to their children, rather than doing more housework or narrowly defined child-care tasks. In general, greater participation of the husband seems to be in response to household demands and especially the unavailability of the wife rather than a large-scale alteration of gender roles.[44] Since the 1970s, women's "double work load" seems to have decreased, but not through husbands' increased participation. Instead, women have decreased the time they devote to these efforts, leading to somewhat less total time that families devote to housework.[45]

Although greater power in the marriage relationship tends to enhance wives' self-esteem,[46] couples' attempts to share household labor do not automatically produce greater satisfaction. For instance, in families where husbands do a lot of housework, marital conflict is more common.[47] Similarly, increased involvement of the father in household tasks, and especially his solo participation in child-care tasks and interactions, does not decrease the wife's conflicts and tensions, but instead seems to engender her guilt and self-blame. Fathers in these families tend to feel more involved and competent, but devalue their wives' parenting.[48]

These results probably appear because there have been no widespread changes in societal norms regarding gender divisions of household labor, even though individuals have altered their behavior in some circumstances. Generalized attitudes toward the division of labor and power in the family have continued to become more egalitarian.[49] Yet husbands often continue to hold traditional views of their own marital roles, even when their wives hold very responsible positions in the labor force.[50] Women are often reluctant to diminish their overall responsibility for housework and child care, for this is often the one area where they have the greatest authority. Thus, husbands' and wives' definitions about what they *should* be doing in the family, despite what they may be doing in the world of work, appear to be unaltered and very difficult to change. Sarah Fenstermaker has suggested that the division of household labor produces not only the goods and services that the family needs for survival, but also produces gender itself.[51] The day-to-day gender-typed activities in which virtually all households engage continually reinforce and reproduce both gender roles and male dominance.

Family violence The ultimate expression of male power within the family is probably physical abuse against women and children. Common law from the earliest periods of recorded history allowed husbands to beat their wives, and it was not until the late 19th century that such abuse was outlawed in the United States.[52]

Today, even though it is illegal, spousal abuse is relatively common. Estimates based on a variety of sources, ranging from official crime reports to anonymous surveys of representative samples of adults indicate that from 25% to

50% of all women in the United States will be beaten at least once by their intimate partners.[53] Cohabitors appear more likely to report spousal abuse than married couples.[54]

Women may also be violent against their husbands and children. Yet women's actions are probably more often defensive in nature. Moreover, given men's greater physical size and strength, women are many times more likely than men to sustain physical injuries.[55]

One in-depth study of couples' experiences with violence indicated that men were most likely to batter their spouses when they perceived that their wives' behavior challenged their power or control.[56] Using a variety of methods, other scholars have determined that men are more likely to abuse their partners when they hold very traditional views of appropriate gender roles, when they are unemployed or facing other economic hardships, when their wives are pregnant, and when their wives have higher educational levels and occupational status than they do.[57] Thus, in one way or another, all of these results point to the centrality of male power in explaining spousal abuse. Men more often abuse their wives when their traditional expectations of control and authority within the family are challenged by their own economic failure, especially in relation to their wives, and even when their central role in the family is challenged by the expected appearance of a new member.

Female-headed families The recent rapid increase in female-headed families could suggest that women are much more likely now than in the past to leave relationships that they find unsatisfactory. For many years, most female-headed families resulted from the death of the husband. Today, however, the major reason for their existence among white women is divorce. Among African-American women the sharp increase results from a greater incidence of both childbearing outside of wedlock and informal separation, usually because divorce is too costly. To some extent the increase reflects women's increasing options in the economy and their ability to provide at least a minimal level of subsistence for their families without the aid of husband or other relatives.[58] For some, however, especially African-American women in urban ghetto areas, the changes are also related to a substantial decrease in the availability of jobs for men whom they might marry.[59]

Even though the rising divorce rate may be related to an increase in women's earnings relative to men, female-headed families, especially those with children, are much more likely than other families to live in poverty and to depend on welfare. Divorced women are much more likely than divorced men to face financial difficulties.[60] In addition, women's poverty tends to be long term. For many families, poverty is only a temporary state, lasting only 1 or 2 years. For others, poverty is a persistent condition, and of these families, over three-fifths are headed by women.[61]

Although this pattern occurs within all racial-ethnic and socioeconomic groups, it is most apparent among African-American families where the mother has never married. These mothers are much more likely than others to be less than 20 years old and thus least likely to have job skills or employment opportunities needed to support a family. Although a minority of all women who head families receive child support, given the high unemployment rate of young African-American males, these young women are even less likely to receive assistance.[62]

The lack of money is only one problem single mothers face, for it is extremely difficult for one person to take care of all of a family's emotional and physical needs. Both the mothers and children in these families have poorer than average mental health and more often must use community mental health services. The children are much more likely to drop out of school, have out-of-wedlock births, divorce or separate, and be dependent on welfare themselves.[63] One study of African-American single mothers found that they faced levels of stress in their daily lives that would typically predict impending physical or emotional illness within a short period of time. Mothers who coped with the stress better than others were those who had extended kin who could help maintain the family through not just money, but also advice, emotional support, and child care.[64] Another study of middle-class, white single parents found that mothers who had experienced less traditional divisions of labor while married coped best with the stresses of single parenthood. These earlier experiences provided them with skills and confidence, which they could carry over into their new, more demanding parental roles.[65]

Love

Despite gender inequalities that pervade the family, it is still viewed in Western societies as our major source of intimate love relationships and of nurturance and emotional support. Since the 1920s the ideal marriage in the United States has been one in which husbands and wives are good companions, with both partners expected to be affectionate and understanding toward the other.

Yet even though both husband and wife love each other, their views of what this love involves and their ways of expressing love generally differ a great deal. Wives emphasize emotional expression and talking about their feelings, whereas husbands emphasize physical activities such as providing help with daily chores, sharing leisure activities, and sexual relations. Both popular discourse and scholarly discussions of love tend to focus on the aspects that women emphasize, leading to what Francesca Cancian has called the "feminization of love" within our culture. She has suggested that this feminization of love helps maintain male dominance, with women overspecializing in interpersonal relationships and men overspecializing in the work activities that are more highly regarded in the larger society.[66]

In recent years, this orientation toward love relationships has been altering somewhat, at least among some segments of the middle class. Since the 1970s various therapeutic movements have emphasized the importance of self-development and self-actualization for individuals, rather than the fulfillment of traditional role-linked obligations, such as those for husbands and wives. Several scholars have decried this orientation, suggesting that it has led to an overemphasis on the needs of individuals, undermining the possibility of continued committed relationships.[67] Others, such as Cancian, have suggested that the contemporary emphasis on self-development can be combined with committed relationships that emphasize the interdependence of husband and wife. As partners in these relationships expand their views of love to envelop aspects traditionally emphasized by members of the other sex, the traditional association between love relationships and male dominance could lessen.[68]

Sexuality

Over the years, ideas about sexuality, especially women's sexuality, have changed considerably. Researchers have found that women's sexuality is far more like men's, at least in terms of physiological response, than was previously thought. The Kinsey report on women, based on interviews with almost 6,000 white nonprison women from a wide range of classes, was published in 1953 and was an important factor in changing beliefs about women's sexuality. Kinsey and his associates noted the importance of the clitoris to women's orgasm[69] and clearly stated that a vaginal orgasm was a "biologic impossibility."[70] The Kinsey group also reported that some 14% of their female subjects had multiple orgasms[71] and that women could climax quickly when they masturbated.

The work of Masters and Johnson, which involved the direct observation and physiological measurement of women's sexual responses in masturbation and intercourse, was published in 1966.[72] Their findings regarding women's sexual capacities confirmed those of Kinsey and were given wide publicity. They indicate that women who achieve orgasm in intercourse do not do so through passivity and compliance, but by feeling free to seek their own pleasure. Feminists have used these findings concerning women's capacity for multiple orgasms and the greater effectiveness of masturbation over intercourse in producing orgasm to point out the extent to which male-dominated intercourse has worked against women's gratification.[73]

Love is related to sexuality, but more so for women than for men. An extensive comparison of heterosexual couples, married and unmarried, and homosexual couples, gay and lesbian, indicated that both men and women tend to value monogamy within their relationships. Yet men are more likely than women to be nonmonogamous and to have more outside partners than women do. Moreover, when women do have outside relationships, they are much more likely than men to be emotionally involved with their partners.

The comparisons also indicate gender differences in sexual practices and in power relationships. Gay men engage in genital sexual relationships most frequently, lesbian couples least frequently. Lesbians are most likely to stress the importance of kissing; gay men are least likely to do so. In both comparisons heterosexual couples fall in between the lesbian and gay men. Within heterosexual couples, some men and women try to share the initiation and refusal of sexual relationships equally, but in the majority of couples men are more likely to be the ones who initiate sexual relationships, whereas women refuse. Many heterosexual women also indicate that their reluctance to initiate relationships stems from their belief that it would offend their partner, challenging his ultimate authority in the relationship.[74]

Some scholars contend that these differences, especially those related to initiation and refusal, evolved over the years because women have a much greater burden to bear should the sexual relationship result in a pregnancy.[75] Other scholars, although not denying the direction and nature of these variations, stress the importance of situational norms. For instance, men in general seem more inclined than women in general to desire nonmonogamous relations. Yet married men are much more likely than those who are cohabiting with women or those who are in homosexual relationships to actually be monogamous. The norms of marriage clearly constrain their behavior.[76]

Much of the advice to women that came out of the sexual revolution, then, has encouraged women to be sexual, but in a context in which male dominance is essentially unchallenged.[77] Yet there is considerable evidence that sexuality and dominance feelings go together in women as well as men. Kinsey's findings[78] of greater frequency of orgasm among highly educated women support Maslow's earlier argument that self-esteem, dominance feelings, and sexuality positively correlate in women.[79]

In saying that dominant women with high self-esteem tend to be sexual, we do not mean to imply that women wish to dominate in the sexual situation. Rather, what women probably want is truly egalitarian sex—mutual pleasuring that would emancipate men from the demands of dominance and women from the demands of compliance.[80] In fact, evidence suggests that couples are happier with their sex lives when they are more egalitarian.[81] Now, however, ideas about sexuality imply that the male should be in control and the female should help give him the feeling that he is.

Men, Women, and Child Care

Much of the literature on the family has focused on male–female relations rather than on parent–child relations. This focus may reflect the fact that we have been assessing changes in the family and creating changes in the family in terms of a masculine paradigm. Alice Rossi has contended that we have been designing women's lives, including their motherhood, to meet the needs of men and the economy, which men dominate, rather than to meet the needs of mothers and children.[82] This occurs partly because the family is geared to the economy rather than vice versa.

Rossi has contended that efforts to produce male–female equality will not succeed in the long run unless we consider that men and women view children differently. She has argued that although children are of central importance to women, men tend to view them as consequences of or appendages to mating and tend to "turn their fathering on and off to suit themselves or their appointments for business or sexual pleasure."[83] Rossi believes that the masculine way of viewing motherhood has led to practices that add stress to the lives of young mothers and impoverish the quality of their relationship with their children.[84] Solving these problems will require altering the roles of mothers and fathers and increasing attention to child care outside of the home.

Altering husband and wife roles As more women have entered the paid labor force some writers have predicted that men will gradually decrease their commitment to work and increase their participation in the home. This would result in a *symmetrical family.*[85] In this type of family, both husband and wife would work outside the home and both would share responsibility for work within the home more or less equally. Currently, within the majority of two-parent families, both the mother and father are employed and contribute to the family income. Attitudes toward fathers' family roles have also changed a great deal since the early 1970s, with fathers now expected to be active, nurturant, caretaking parents.[86] Thus, it is not surprising that more families appear to be developing arrangements where mothers and fathers, husbands and wives, share household duties to a greater extent than in earlier years.[87] Arrangements where mothers and fathers try to share household duties equally actually are quite rare, for, as noted earlier, even when wives work outside the home, they still do far more than one-half of the domestic labor.

Some couples, when both have well-paying, demanding jobs, hire people from outside the family to perform domestic chores. The domestic helpers are, of course, almost always women. Moreover, the wife, not the husband, in these *dual-career families* remains responsible for the household. She normally finds, hires, and supervises the help, and is the one who maintains a flexible schedule to be available to deal with household crises. If couples pool their money for household expenses, the costs for child care and housework are usually deducted from the wife's salary, presumably because it is her area of responsibility. Wives in such dual-career families are much more likely than their husbands to report stress and conflicts because of the dual demands of home and work.[88]

Although such dual-career families may become more common as more women enter professional fields, it is doubtful if many families will follow this pattern. Studies of male professionals indicate that their wives play a critical role in their career advancement. It is unclear how women can enjoy similar career success if they lack the functional equivalent of a supportive wife, especially if they have children.[89] Moreover, only a small minority of workers hold very high paying positions. The maintenance of the dual-career lifestyle requires the existence of a low-paid, almost exclusively female, workforce to ensure the family's domestic well-being.[90] These low-paid women workers clearly cannot hire household help like their employers do and must find some other solution to the problems of child care and domestic chores.

Other families, who usually are not as financially well-off as the dual-careerists, develop various ways of *role sharing* with relatively little outside help. Some couples are forced into this arrangement because they work different shifts and child care is difficult or expensive to obtain. Others, however, choose this pattern because they believe that role sharing in the home is fair and that it is important for both mothers and fathers to be involved in their children's care. Even among these ideologically committed couples, however, inequities and role segregation appear. The wives are more likely to be the organizers and managers and to keep track of and assign household duties. They also hire and supervise domestic help when it is used. If one parent is assigned primary responsibility for child care, it is almost always the mother. Moreover, mothers are much more likely than fathers to feel guilty about leaving their children for work or other activities.[91]

Child care Even if role-sharing families become more common, the need for child care outside of the home will remain high, for it is unlikely that either mothers or fathers will be able to or would want to cease work outside the home. Moreover, single mothers often do not have a partner or other kin who can help with child care.

The United States is far behind most modern industrialized countries in providing child-care facilities outside of the home. Much of the opposition to public support of day care has centered on the notion that such practices would destroy the family and remove children emotionally and even physically from their parents. These charges seem ironic in view of the desperate need of many families for adequate care. Such care would seem only to strengthen the health and security of children as well as relieving worries of parents. The parents, then, could give their children better attention, and the children as recipients of quality and consistent care would be better parents when they have their own families.

Even when a mother does not work outside the home, child care benefits both the mental health of the mother and the health and education of the child. To be a loving and caring mother, one must also be a fulfilled adult. A mother cannot devote all of her waking hours to the care of a small child, especially when she herself is isolated from other adults, and hope to maintain a separate adult identity. Thus, some time in which others take over the child's care is essential for both the well-being of the mother and the assurance of good care for the child. Middle-class mothers have long recognized this necessity and have been able to afford the luxury of baby sitters and private nursery schools. Public nursery schools, however, except for the very poor, are almost unknown in this country.

Care outside the home is important for children. Specialists in early childhood development stress that group experiences are very desirable for children at the age of 3 and over. This applies not just to only children or to those with special problems or a working mother, but appears to be a developmental need of all children to expand their realm of significant others beyond the immediate family at that age. Experiments with quality group care for infants also show that with a good staff/child ratio, this experience can also be beneficial to children.[92]

The Current Family and the Need for Change

During the 19th century, the family as we know it today began to emerge. Households became smaller as nonfamily members were gradually excluded, and the family itself came to be viewed as the seat of personal life, "a haven in a heartless world,"[93] sharply different from the world of paid work outside. Women were defined as the moral core of the family, and on this basis feminists fought first for property rights and later for legal and educational rights. In the 19th century, very few married women worked outside the home, but the number of married women working has increased steadily in the 20th century, especially since midcentury.

Today, the vast majority of all women, including those with preschool children, work outside the home. Fewer women are getting married, divorce is more common, and women tend to have fewer children. However, gender inequalities still persist within the family. Women are much more likely than men to bear the major responsibility for household duties and to have less power than men in the family, even when they are employed in prestigious jobs outside the home. An alarming number of women also experience physical abuse from their partners. Because of the rising rate of divorce and childbearing out of wedlock, the number of female-headed families has increased rapidly in recent years. These families are extremely likely to experience poverty and other stresses. Although love relationships are still viewed as the basis of family relationships in Western societies, both love and sexuality tend to be viewed differently by women and men. Although the patterning of men's and women's sexuality has changed considerably in recent times, women's greater sexual participation continues to be defined in ways that do not threaten male dominance.

Various attempts to alter the family division of labor, so far at least, have not equalized the sex groups, and problems have been particularly acute with regard to child care. As things stand now, with more and more women entering the work force, the problem of child care looms large. So far, attempts to increase women's equality have largely taken the form of increasing women's work-force participation without compensating provisions for child care by fathers or day-care centers, or reducing women's work load in the home. In other words, there has been more assimilation of women's roles to men's in the economy than assimilation of men's roles to women's roles in the family. If gender stratification is to end, family roles must also change.

THE EDUCATIONAL SYSTEM

Women and men have generally been treated more equally in education than in other areas of society. In general, individuals' educational attainment and achievement are more influenced by class status than by gender. Men and women usually have equal scores on intelligence and standardized achievement tests; indeed, women have higher grades than men at all levels from grade school to college. For many years, women have been more likely than men to finish high school. Yet, when families must make decisions concerning who receives post-high-school education, men are favored. Women attain less education than would be expected given their qualifications and may face discrimination in secondary and higher education.

Influences on Educational Attainment

Over the years, men have been more likely than women to drop out of high school before graduation, largely because working-class men could get jobs without a high-school certificate and women often needed such certification for clerical work.[94] Reflecting this relative freedom, men are more likely to say that they have dropped out because they dislike school or, for groups such as Hispanics, because they must help support their families. Women are more likely to report that they dropped out because of pregnancy and early marriage. In addition, male dropouts are more likely to have found work and to have participated in job training and high-school completion programs.[95] In recent years, the importance of formal education has been increasingly stressed, and educational requirements for employment have risen. As a result, more people graduate from high school, and the proportions of men and women finishing high school have become more nearly the same.[96]

A much larger percentage of both males and females in the total population are also going to college now, as job requirements change and community colleges burgeon. As shown in Table 3-1, institutions of higher education have continually grown in size since the mid-19th century. Yet the proportion of women enrolled or receiving degrees has fluctuated over the years, rising gradually to a peak in the 1920s and 1930s, dropping during the Great Depression and especially the post–World War II years, rising again to this historical peak in the late 1960s and 1970s, and reaching near parity at the predoctoral levels by the mid-1980s.

These trends reflect cultural and class-specific definitions of the importance of a college education as well as specific economic conditions and educational policies. For instance, they show how the sexes are generally given the same education, unless specific economic or political circumstances require that some people be denied access to schools. The economic problems of the depression caused a sharp decline in the rate of growth of total college enrollment. Although the number of both men and women enrolled in college continued to rise during the depression, the number of women enrolled rose much more slowly than the number of men. This trend probably resulted from the decisions of families to invest more heavily in the college education of their sons than of their daughters. The even greater difference between the percentage increase of enrollment of males and females at the end of World War II probably reflects specific national educational policies as colleges set quotas limiting the admission of women in order to absorb men returning to school on

Table 3-1 Total enrollment and representation of women in institutions of higher education in the United States, 1969–1986

		WOMEN AS A PERCENTAGE OF ALL STUDENTS			
Year	*Total Enrollment (in 1000's)*	*Enrolled in Resident Degree Programs*	*Receiving Bachelor's or 1st Prof. Degrees*	*Receiving Master's Degrees*	*Receiving Doctoral Degrees*
1869–70	52,286	21.3	14.7	0	0
1889–90	156,756	35.9	17.3	19.1	1.3
1909–10	355,213	39.6	22.7	26.4	9.9
1929–30	1,100,737	43.7	40.0	40.4	15.4
1949–50	2,659,021	30.3	23.9	29.2	9.6
1959–60	3,639,847	35.3	35.5	31.6	10.5
1969–70	8,004,660	41.0	41.5	39.7	13.3
1979–80	11,569,899	50.9	47.3	49.4	29.7
1986–87	12,504,501	52.9	50.4	51.2	35.2

Source: Adapted from Thomas D. Snyder, *Digest of Education Statistics, 1989.* (Washington, D.C.: National Center for Education Statistics, 1989), p. 166.

the GI bill.[97] As a result of these quotas, the proportion of students enrolled in 1949–50 who were women was 30% lower than the rate of enrollment in 1879–80! The vast enrollment growth after World War II altered the social class distribution of college students, as men of lower-middle-class and working-class backgrounds were able to attain education beyond high school. The rising representation of women in higher education in those years parallels the changes in the late 1800 and early 1900s as it became accepted by not just the upper middle class but also by a greater proportion of the population that both men and women should have a college education. Although men were first sent to college, when families could afford to do so, daughters were also sent.[98]

Today, women represent a slight majority of all students enrolled in colleges and universities, primarily because of a large influx of older returning women students, many of whom attend school part time and are enrolled in community colleges.[99] Women are just as likely as men to receive bachelors, first professional, and masters degrees. Although the disparities have somewhat declined in recent years, gender stratification is most apparent with doctoral degrees. By the late 1980s only about a third of all doctoral degree recipients were women.

Enrollment in degree programs, especially at the graduate level, is also segregated by gender.[100] For instance, in the late 1980s, women received 58% of the doctorates in the humanities, 53% of the doctorates in education, and 33% of the doctorates in social sciences. But only 17% of the doctorates in mathematics and in the physical sciences and 7% of the doctorates in engineering were awarded to women.[101] An increasing number of women are receiving graduate professional degrees. For instance, although less than 1% of all dentistry degrees were awarded to women in 1950 and only 4% in 1976, 24% of all dentistry degrees were earned by women in 1987. In 1950, 10% of the medical degrees were awarded to women, and 6% in 1960, but this figure rose to 32% by 1987. Similarly, the percentage of women law graduates rose sharply from 5% in 1970 to 40% in 1987.[102] Even with these recent increases, however, women are still far from achieving parity within these professions. They are still underrepresented in graduate programs, and the increase in their representation has occurred only recently. Thus, the vast majority of practicing professionals in these fields are still men.

As shown in Table 3-2, differences in educational attainment tend to be larger between racial/ethnic groups than between the sex groups. Both men and women of the white majority have higher median levels of education and are much more likely to have graduated from college than members of racial/ethnic minorities. Yet, to some extent, the pattern of gender differences in educational attainment varies among racial/ethnic groups in the United States. Among both whites and Hispanics, men have higher median levels of education because they have historically more often graduated from college than have women. Among African-Americans, however, women and men have similar levels of education and are more similar in patterns of college attendance than women and men in other groups. This probably reflects race discrimination in the economy, where African-American women are better rewarded—in terms of eventual income—for attaining more education than are African-American men.[103] Decisions of African-American men to go to work rather than further their education may

Table 3-2 Median years of school completed and college completion rates by gender and race/ethnicity for persons 25 years and over, 1987

RACE/ETHNICITY AND GENDER	*MEDIAN YEARS OF SCHOOLING COMPLETED* [a]	*PROPORTION OF POPULATION AGED 25–29 WITH 4 OR MORE YEARS OF COLLEGE*
White		
Total	12.7	20.5
Men	12.8	24.5
Women	12.6	16.9
African-American		
Total	12.4	10.7
Men	12.4	11.1
Women	12.4	10.5
Hispanic		
Total	12.0	8.6
Men	12.1	9.1
Women	12.0	8.2

a. Data are from U.S. Bureau of the Census, *Current Population Report, series P-20, No. 428, March 1987 and 1986* (Washington, D.C.: U.S. Government Printing Office, 1987), pp. 3–9.

be economically rational; even if they attain higher education they will often not be rewarded with better jobs in the same way white men are.[104] Since the early 1980s Hispanic women have been more likely than Hispanic men to enroll in college, perhaps indicating a change in the traditional educational patterns and patterns of economic rewards for that ethnic group.[105] Asian-Americans have traditionally had high levels of educational attainment, despite discrimination in the occupational world, and both men and women have generally enjoyed these educational advantages.[106]

A number of social scientists have examined influences on eventual educational attainment. Although most of these studies have involved only men, in recent years some have also looked at the educational attainment of women.[107] They have found that women's educational attainment is highly influenced by family background status, whereas for males academic ability is a stronger influence. Moreover, after controlling for variables generally found to relate to educational attainment, including academic ability, status background, performance, educational goal orientations, academic self-concept, curriculum enrollment, and the influences of significant others such as parents, teachers, and peers, women have lower expected educational attainment than men do.

Gender Discrimination in Access to Education

Gender segregation occurs in both academic and vocational curriculum areas. Males and females train in vocational education programs for very different jobs. Women are usually in the clerical or home economics areas, whereas men are more evenly distributed throughout the various possible fields and are most highly concentrated in trades and industry. Very few of the students in agriculture and technical education are women. Notably enough, the areas with more men have much higher wages than the areas for which women are trained. Moreover, women overwhelmingly teach the courses in home economics, health, and office skills, whereas men tend to teach the trades and industry, technical education, and agriculture courses.[108]

This gender segregation also appears in academic areas. Women are more likely than men to take foreign languages and more than 2 years of English in high school. Men are more likely to take advanced mathematics and science. Among college students, men are much more likely to major in areas such as architecture, physical sciences, and engineering; women more often major in areas such as education, foreign languages, and home economics, both at the gradute and undergraduate levels.[109] In general, the areas in which women are likely to graduate are those leading to occupations that have lower levels of income and are judged to be less powerful.[110]

These discrepancies do not reflect women's lack of interest or potential skills in these male-typed areas. For instance, similar numbers of men and women enroll in premedical programs as college freshmen, but about twice as many men as women eventually apply to medical school.[111] Similarly, 46% of all people who receive bachelors degrees in mathematics are women. Traditionally, most of these women have entered high-school teaching, which is not strongly gender typed. Women are much more underrepresented in prestigious, high-paid, male-typed fields that apply mathematics, such as physics, engineering, and economics.

Women tend also to be underrepresented in more prestigious colleges and graduate programs.[112] It is not clear, however, that these discrepancies result from overt discrimination against women in the admission process. Laws now explicitly prohibit such discrimination, and few overt discriminatory practices appear to continue.[113] A historical study suggests that gender discrimination in the admissions process cannot explain women's continuing underrepresentation in medical schools. Since 1929, women have been admitted to all medical schools in the United States in proportions that would be expected given their rate of application and qualifications.[114] Somehow, during their undergraduate years, many women decide not to apply to medical school.

Women's underrepresentation in more prestigious and costly programs may reflect fewer financial resources. An extensive study of graduate programs in sociology found that women graduate students are less likely than men to receive financial support. Minority women receive support more often than white women, but less often than minority men.[115] Similarly, even though women undergraduates are more likely than men to receive financial aid, the dollar amounts awarded to men are higher.[116] Scholarship programs that rely on test scores may also discriminate against women. Women consistently have higher high-school and college grades than men, even though they tend to have slightly lower Scholastic Achievement Test (SAT) scores than men.[117] High-school grades predict college success more accurately than scores on tests such as the SAT.[118] Yet some scholarship programs, such as the New York State Regents scholarships and the National Merit scholarships, have based their awards on SAT scores, rather than grades, thus unfairly eliminating a disproportionate number of women.[119]

Although discriminatory regulations have virtually disappeared from most schools and women are more often entering male-typed areas, subtle discouragement of women may also persist. Faculty may make comments in class that disparage women and their intellectual ability and may encourage men more often than women to pursue their intellectual interests.[120] A retrospective study of students who received their doctorates in the 1970s found that women more often felt they were not taken seriously during their graduate careers, had more difficulty than men in finding mentors to guide their work, and, in the arts and natural sciences, were more often given teaching assignments rather than prestigious research assistantships. None of these areas is typically addressed by policies aimed at reducing gender inequities.[121]

Although this lack of encouragement for women can be seen in individual interactions, it can also be reflected in organizational policies. On many campuses only minimal child-care facilities are available. A study of women who were not attending graduate school but planned to do so indicated that they considered the availability of child-care facilities the most important condition for their graduate study.[122] Many older women who have returned to school also have children, or even parents, who need care. In spite of this need, universities have consistently resisted providing support for such facilities. Jo Freeman has contrasted the concern universities showed for young men during the Vietnam War by providing letters and jobs to help them retain their draft-exempt status with the lack of concern shown pregnant women who must often leave school, lose a fellowship, and get medical care outside the university facilities.[123]

It is important to note that the lack of child-care facilities and provisions for maternity leave becomes most important for women when they are in graduate and professional schools. It is widely accepted that middle-class women will attend and graduate from college, and because they usually major in different areas, they rarely compete directly with men during those years. When, however, they enter graduate and professional schools, they encroach more on traditional masculine territory, and it is here that they receive even less personal and institutional support, even though they are at an age where it is probable that they will want or already have children and be in need of such services.

Institutional Linkages

Institutional explanations of gender stratification in education generally focus on the relationships between education, the economy, and the family. A great deal of work has examined how students' social class and racial-ethnic background influence their experiences in education. This work shows that the limited opportunities working-class and nonwhite people face in education reflect the limited resources and opportunities for them in the occupational world. This correspondence can also help account for gender stratification in education. While upper-middle-class boys become doctors and engineers, their sisters most often become teachers or social workers as well as wives and mothers. Thus, they have different majors in college and graduate school, and males more often go to graduate and professional schools in male-dominated areas. Although working-class men may enter skilled trades, their sisters probably enter much lower paying clerical and service occupations.[124] The exclusion of women from the male-dominated areas in vocational training reflects their absence from those areas in the occupational world.

Because students generally choose their college majors and their vocational course work themselves, these patterns may appear to persist because of voluntary decisions by the students. Yet students do see the gender segregation in the occupational world and are aware of what is considered women's work and men's work.[125] Although the laws and regulations that once enforced this segregation are now banned, more subtle and covert means discourage women from entering the highly rewarded male fields. Unofficial norms among both teachers and students support the maintenance of gender-segregated classes. These are reflected in expectations individuals hold and communicate to students and in organizational patterns including even the physical structures of school buildings. For instance, women's bathrooms are much less commonly found in shop, vocational education, and other buildings used mainly by men. The absence of these facilities can then be used as a reason to discourage women from classes. Thus, although it may appear that women voluntarily avoid entering male-dominated areas in education, this may often be motivated by a realization of the actual barriers to their entrance into these fields in the occupational world.[126]

Besides this gender segregation in educational programs, women may face discrimination in financing their education. This involves an assumption that men's education is more important than women's and reflects the cultural assumption that men's major social role is in the economic world, whereas women's major social role is in the family. Thus, traditionally, families will invest in their daughters' education to ensure that they find suitable husbands and thus provide them with a secure future. Families will invest in sons' education to ensure directly their occupational and economic success. Because the male's economic role is central, families and educational organizations tend to invest more heavily in his education. Explanations of gender stratification in education rest upon families' decisions to allocate resources to males rather than females and on females' views of the nature of the opportunity structure in the adult world.

People in our society tend to see education as the key to success in adulthood, and indeed, schools do help prepare people for their adult roles. Many people, especially liberal feminists, believe that if we change boys' and girls' experiences in school, they will have greater equality as men and women. Programs designed to end gender stratification then focus on education and promote developing new curriculum materials and new training programs for women. To some extent, this focus occurs because it is probably easier to affect school policies than those in other institutions.* Yet, given that males' and females' experiences and performance in education have always been at least relatively similar, especially when compared with other areas of society, it is ironic that so many change efforts focus on education. Moreover, because gender inequalities in education largely reflect those in other institutions, changes in education are probably neither the most efficient nor the most effective way to alter gender stratification in the total society.[127]

If women are to enter male-dominated occupations, the most effective strategy is for business firms to hire them in these posts. Even today, men and women with identical training are hired for different jobs and then paid vastly different wages. Simply giving women additional training is not going to alter the practice of businesses. In addition, if it ever became true that employees in a given field were not chosen on the basis of gender, then a major reason for the

---

*This approach has also been used in attempting to combat poverty in general as well as the discrimination that racial-ethnic minorities face. The discussion that follows also applies to these attempts.

different representation of men and women in training programs would have been removed and students could make different choices. Similarly, schools do not encourage families to invest more heavily in their sons' education than in their daughters'. Families make that decision themselves, and they are prompted by the belief that men's major social roles are in the work world and women's in the home. This belief, of course, is buttressed by the fact that men are paid more for their work. Changing this balance of family and work roles is probably the most direct way, then, to alter gender differences in investment in higher education.

Much research shows that increased education promotes tolerance for the roles of others and support for greater equality between women and men.[128] That women generally have as much education as men in the United States also no doubt promotes strains for women when they are placed in a subservient role to men and has been an important impetus for the feminist movement. Thus, education is an important tool for promoting equality, but it cannot be the sole answer. If gender stratification in social institutions is to end, changes must be made in each of the institutional areas.

SUMMARY

As institutions, both the family and the educational system prepare people for and maintain them in the occupational world. Women generally are highly visible in both of these institutions. Women's major social role is viewed as anchored in the family, and this idea gained currency in the 19th century as industrialization progressed. Even if women work outside the home, as well over half of all married women now do, their roles as wives and mothers continue to be perceived as central. In contrast, men's roles as husbands and fathers mainly involve providing for the family through work. Many analysts put women's family roles at the heart of their secondary status.

Both women and men attend schools in the United States in almost equal numbers through the master's level. Women usually receive better grades than men and women teachers predominate, especially at the beginning levels. What gender stratification there is in education reflects the gender stratification in the economy. Change efforts that focus on education alone, then, may not succeed unless the economy itself can be changed. On the other hand, educational curriculum that sensitizes individuals to the gender stereotyping and gender stratification in the economy may stimulate efforts to change the system.

SUGGESTED READINGS

Blumstein, Philip, and Pepper Schwartz. 1983. *American Couples: Money, Work and Sex.* New York: Morrow. An analysis of the relationships of heterosexual and homosexual couples, with specific focus on decisions and conflicts regarding finances, employment, and sexual relations.

Chamberlain, Mariam K. (Ed.). 1988. *Women in Academe: Progress and Prospects.*

New York: Russell Sage Foundation. An extensive examination of the historical and current status of female students, faculty, and administrators in higher education.

EHRENSAFT, DIANE. 1987. *Parenting Together: Men and Women Sharing the Care of Their Children.* New York: Free Press. Explores family relations for couples who choose to share child rearing.

FERREE, MYRA MARX. 1990. "Beyond Separate Spheres: Feminism and Family Research." *Journal of Marriage and the Family.* 52:866–884. A review and synthesis of recent theoretical work on gender stratification in the family.

GERSTEL, NAOMI, and HARRIET ENGLE GROSS. 1987. *Families and Work.* Philadelphia: Temple University Press. A collection of articles dealing with women's role in the family and in the economy.

STOCKARD, JEAN. 1985. "Education and Gender Equality: A Critical View." Pp. 299–326 in Alan Kerckhoff (Ed.). *Research in Sociology of Education and Socialization* Volume 5. An extensive discussion of the extent of gender inequality in education and the implications of this for social change.

THOMPSON, LINDA, and ALEXIS J. WALKER. 1989. "Gender in Families: Women and Men in Marriage, Work, and Parenthood." *Journal of Marriage and the Family.* 51:845–871. Reviews research on gender in three domains of family life—marriage, work (both paid and in the family), and parenthood.

chapter 4

Gender Stratification in Contemporary Societies

The gender stratification in institutions in the United States is not an exception, but part of a general pattern found in all contemporary societies. Gender stratification appears in and affects women's position in the economy, in education, the family, and the polity in all countries. This gender stratification may be seen in countries that have been industrialized for many years and in those that are just beginning to develop industrially. It may be seen in countries with widely different political forms, in countries with different religious and cultural beliefs, and in countries in all parts of the world. In this chapter, we explore gender inequality in these societies.

THE ECONOMY

Since the first years of this century, and especially in the past few decades, more and more women have entered the paid labor force in the United States and in other industrialized nations. Yet the proportion of women working outside the home varies from one country to another. This variation appears to be influenced by a number of factors, and we cannot make simple generalizations about their impact. In all countries, however, capitalist or socialist, West or East, with or without specific nondiscriminatory policies, the labor force is segregated by gender and men as a whole earn more than women do.

The Labor-Force Participation of Women

A large number of women participate in the labor force, both in fully industrialized and in developing countries. Several variables appear to influence the amount of participation. First, if there is a relative shortage of available male workers, as may happen after years of warfare, the demand for workers may lead to women's greater inclusion in the paid labor force. Second, in some countries official policies strongly support women working outside the home, and this generally produces a larger labor-force participation rate. Third, ideology or attitudes regarding women's proper roles also influence whether women work. Fourth, apart from official policy and individuals' attitudes, a country's level of development influences the number of available jobs and thus the number of women who are employed outside the home in formal wage work. Finally, the pattern of male dominance in a society may affect the options open to women and their tendency to work outside the home.

No simple generalizations can be made about the impact of these variables, for their influence may vary from one society to another. For instance, countries with similar levels of development or similar ideologies may have quite different rates of women's participation in the labor force as a result of different official policies or different patterns of male control over women's lives.

Table 4-1 gives the percentage of all women over age 15 who are employed in several contemporary societies and the female proportion of the total labor force in each country. The first figure indicates how common it is for a woman to be employed in that country; the second figure indicates how large the female labor force is in that country.*

Table 4-1 Labor-force participation of women ages 15 and over in selected countries[a]

COUNTRIES	WOMEN'S LABOR-FORCE PARTICIPATION RATE	PROPORTION OF THE LABOR FORCE THAT IS FEMALE
North America, Western Europe, and Oceania		
Australia (1989)	51.2	41.0
Austria (1988)	41.8	40.5
Belgium (1988)	28.6	39.1
Canada (1989)	57.9	44.3
Denmark (1986)	60.4	45.8
Finland (1989)	58.4	47.2
France (1987)	45.8	43.3
Germany, Federal Republic of (1988)	42.7	39.7
Ireland (1988)	31.1	30.5
Italy (1989)	35.8	36.9
Mexico (1988)	35.3	30.0
New Zealand (1989)	52.5	42.7
Norway (1989)	62.3	44.4
Spain (1989)	32.8	34.5
United Kingdom (1986)	48.2	42.0
United States (1989)	56.5	44.8
Africa		
Algeria (1987)	7.8	9.2
Egypt (1984)	18.0	19.0
Nigeria (1986)	34.8	32.3
Zimbabwe (1986–7)	70.4	47.8

*It should be noted that cross-national comparisons are less exact than those within one country because countries may vary in the way they define labor force participation.

Table 4-1 *(Cont.)*

COUNTRIES	WOMEN'S LABOR-FORCE PARTICIPATION RATE	PROPORTION OF THE LABOR FORCE THAT IS FEMALE
Asia		
Bangladesh (1985–6)	9.7	9.4
Hong Kong (1989)	47.1	36.4
Israel (1989)	41.3	40.4
Japan (1989)	49.5	40.4
Korea, Republic of (1989)	46.5	40.4
Pakistan (1989–90)	11.3	11.1
Singapore (1989)	48.4	39.3
South and Central America		
Argentina (1989)	29.1	27.8
Brazil (1986)	41.1	33.9
Chile (1989)	31.6	30.8
Columbia (1989)	46.4	41.4
Costa Rica (1989)	32.0	28.6
Cuba (1988)	41.2	36.1
Ecuador (1989)	32.7	29.5
Paraguay (1989)	53.4	43.7
Peru (1989)	48.2	40.5
Venezuela (1989)	34.8	29.8

a. The crude labor-force participation rate in the first column is the percentage of employed women in the total population of women. The figures in the second column give the percentage of women in the labor force, the proportion of all employed people who are women. Figures in parentheses give the year data were gathered.

Sources: Yearbook of Labour Statistics, 1989–90 (Geneva: International Labour Office), Table 1, pp. 17–44.

The labor-force participation rate, or the proportion of women employed in each country, varies widely from under 20% in traditional Muslim countries such as Algeria, Egypt, Bangladesh and Pakistan to close to one-third in countries such as Ireland, Mexico, Spain, Argentina, and Costa Rica to close to one-half and even larger in Australia, Canada, Denmark, Finland, the United Kingdom, Paraguay, and Zimbabwe. Women are now less than half the labor force in all countries. However, they once were more common than men workers in the U.S.S.R. and East Germany because of the huge number of men killed in World War II as well as official policies promoting women's work.[1]

The proportion of married women in the labor force better reflects the extent to which women are a stable part of the labor force. Other data indicate that in the Western European countries, married women in Sweden and Finland have relatively high participation rates, whereas participation rates for married women in the Netherlands, Italy, and Luxembourg are much lower.[2] As in the United States, however, the proportion of married women with young children who are working has risen rapidly during the past 20 years in many industrialized countries as economic opportunities have expanded.[3]

Because the Eastern European countries explicitly encourage and expect women to participate in the labor force, the percentage of employed women found in Western European countries generally is lower than in Eastern European nations. Because official policies in Eastern and Western Europe have differed, other variables are required to explain variations in labor-force participation within each set of countries. Among the Western European countries, those with lower birthrates, higher divorce rates, a lower cost of living, and a higher standard of living have a higher labor-force participation rate for women. In the Eastern European countries, these family and economic variables are not important. Instead, demographic variables related to development, such as greater urbanization, greater per capita growth rate, and greater population density, influence increased employment of women. The only variable that correlates with greater participation of women in the total labor force for both the Eastern European and Western European countries is the greater participation of women in the professions.[4]

Ideology and attitudes regarding women's behaviors also affect women's labor-force participation. For instance, the Netherlands has historically been one of the world's most advanced countries in tolerating social and political diversity and is bordered by countries in which many women participate in the labor force. Yet, compared to neighboring countries, married women in the Netherlands, especially those with children, are much less likely to be employed, and both men and women express less support for women working outside the home.[5] Similarly, both the Soviet Union and Poland have official policies that support women's participation in the labor force. Yet women in Poland are less likely to be employed and far less likely to report that working outside the home is very important to them.[6] Women in Islamic countries are much less likely to be employed than women in countries where other religions predominate. Yet various Islamic cultures have interpreted the Koran in differing ways, often in response to pressing needs for labor, with the result that the labor-force participation of women can vary substantially from one Islamic nation to another.[7]

Most nations are now developing industrially. The labor-force participation rates in Table 4-1 tend to underestimate the economic activity of women, especially the poor, in these developing countries. Poor women in rural areas may not to be counted as officially employed, because they work in family enterprises, such as family farm plots. Poor women in urban areas may not be counted, because they work in an informal economic sector, doing work such as domestic service, street vending, or sewing or crafts in the home.[8]

With industrialization and economic development, the proportion of the labor force engaged in agriculture shrinks drastically and the proportion of the labor force in manufacturing or industry grows. Women's participation in the economy also tends to change, but the pattern tends to vary with the type of agricultural production typical of the area, the availability of work within the formal sector, the extent to which men or women migrate to take advantage of this work, and the extent of industrialization within the society. In general, as agriculture becomes more mechanized and less labor intensive, men tend to take over the mechanized farming jobs. Women may be displaced or relegated to routine tasks associated with agriculture, such as the sorting of coffee beans. As women lose jobs in the agricultural sector, there are generally few employment opportunities for them in the industrial sector, as men are preferred.[9]

Historical trends in industrialized countries such as the United States and France suggest that the decline in women's labor-force participation that follows the mechanization of agriculture will reverse as the expansion of other economic sectors opens new employment opportunities.[10] Yet much of the industrial development in developing countries today is not internally financed, but is sponsored by multinational corporations, whose primary aim is maximizing global profit rather than investing in specific nations.[11] Thus, although the labor-force participation of women in developing countries does seem generally to increase over time, caution must be taken in applying historical patterns from the developed Western countries to the developing countries.

Cultures with equally restrictive ideologies may institutionalize male dominance in ways that allow different access for women to alternative work patterns, even when the levels of industrialization are similar. Latin America has had a marked increase in women's labor-force participation, whereas the Middle East, at a similar point in economic development and with similar restrictive attitudes toward women, has had no comparable increase. These differences in labor-force participation appear to come not from differences in fertility or marriage rates, but from differences in the institutional structures that enforce male dominance. In the Middle East, the family and kinship system retains total control over women's lives, an arrangement supported by the judicial and religious systems. In Latin America, both the church and the family maintain sway over women, and their demands may not always coincide. This divided control in Latin America may actually provide more options for women and a greater probability of their joining the labor force, even though the ideology is as restrictive as that in the Middle East.[12]

Finally, it is important to realize that in countries where people approve of women's working, the overall status of women may not be necessarily improved. Although a larger proportion of women in Finland work than in most other Western European countries, both Finnish men and women appear to hold more traditional attitudes toward gender roles in the family and in leadership roles in the society than do either the Swedes or Norwegians. Moreover, household tasks are divided more traditionally in Finland than in the other Scandinavian countries, where women may work less.[13] Similarly, even though economic development has meant that many more women in developing countries are working outside the home than in previous years, this has often only added to their total workload. For poor women in developing countries simple survival activities such as obtaining water and firewood and preparing food are very time consuming. Because women add their agricultural activities or informal economic activities to their normal household duties, they spend many more hours at work than women in developed countries or men in their own countries.[14]

Gender Segregation of the Labor Force

The evidence strongly suggests that gender segregation of the labor force persists in industrial societies cross-culturally. There is some evidence that what we consider in our country to be traditionally masculine occupations, such as pharmacy and dentistry can be transformed. Indeed, they are generally female occupations in other countries. Yet this transformation involves only a change in the sex of the dominant occupants and not a mixture within the occupation. How people view the profession also differs. For instance, "In country after country, medicine is regarded as an acceptable extension of women's interest in caring for people. Even in Czarist Russia, many girls studied medicine."[15] In most European countries, about one-fifth of the physicians are women. Approximately three-quarters of the physicians in the U.S.S.R. are women, compared to only about 16% in the United States. Similarly, female dentists and pharmacists are much more common in European countries than in the United States. Notably enough, however, medical personnel enjoy extraordinarily high incomes as well as extensive control over the profession only in the United States.[16]

Gender segregation in other occupational areas appears to be similar in most countries. For instance, an extensive study of 12 industrialized countries found that women are overrepresented in clerical, service, and low-prestige sales and professional areas. Men are more often employed as administrators and managers and in production work.[17] As in the United States, even when women enter atypical fields, such as administration, they tend to be segregated. For example, few women in Great Britain are employed as managers or administrators, and those who are tend to be in female-typed fields and rarely at the highest levels.[18] Throughout the world, women are generally heavily represented in teaching, although, as in the United States, they are more commonly found in the elementary schools and in the less prestigious areas of more advanced education.[19] This occupational differentiation persists in nonprofessional areas. For instance, in Sweden, 95% of the practical nurses, 100% of the domestic helpers, and 98% of the counter clerks and cashiers are women, but only 4% of the drivers, 8% of the machine repairers, 6% of the electricians, and virtually none of the carpenters are women.[20] In Finland, 98% of the charworkers and 94% of the clerical workers but only 2% of the transport workers and 1% of the construction carpenters are women.[21] Similar patterns are found in all countries, and gender segregation tends to be more severe in countries with higher participation of women in the labor force.[22]

Because the Soviet Union has explicitly encouraged the participation of women in the labor force, almost 90% of able-bodied women are employed or in school, generally full time.[23] In contrast to the United States, many Soviet women are found in scientific, technical and industrial fields. Yet they predominate in economic sectors and occupations that have low status and pay, and are underrepresented in more prestigious, highly rewarding occupations. This cannot be explained by lower levels of education or by less experience in the labor force than their male counterparts.[24] Just as in the United States, women are found disproportionately in the service sector, as secretaries and bookkeepers, and in the garment and textile industries rather than in mechanical engineering or metallurgy. Over 90% of all nurses, kindergarten teachers, librarians, telephonists, typists, and secretaries in the Soviet Union are women.[25]

Both medicine and education are dominated by women in the Soviet Union, yet gender segregation also occurs within these areas. Women are much more likely to teach younger children than they are to direct schools. Over three-quarters of the teachers of grades 1 to 10 and directors of primary schools are women, yet less than one-third of the directors of 8-year and secondary schools are women. Even fewer women teach and administer at higher levels of education. Similarly, although women predominate in medicine, the chief physicians and supervisory personnel are frequently men.[26]

Gender segregation also appears in occupations held by men and women in developing countries. Both men and women may work in agriculture, but when both are present, they perform different activities. If men migrate to cities to obtain wage work, women may simply add the men's duties for family production to their own, creating an even greater workload. In urban areas women are much more likely to be employed in the informal sector, engaging in small-scale marketing or cottage crafts, work that allows them greater flexibility in meeting their extensive responsibilities for child care and domestic labor, but that is poorly paid and not generally subject to legal regulations. In developing countries some women, especially the young, are increasingly employed in industrial settings, usually manufacturing component parts for export. These women are overwhelmingly found in gender-segregated jobs.[27]

Wage Differentials

Gender differentials in wages are also consistently found cross-culturally.[28] Almost every European country has ratified the International Labor Office Convention 100, which assures women "equal pay for work of equal value." Many countries have also passed equal pay laws of their own. But, just as in the United States, the net effect of both the convention and the laws has been very small. These laws generally have little effect because the gender segregation of the labor force ensures that few men and women are really employed in the same job. Even among those doing similar work, men may be given one job title and women another. Their unequal pay may then be "officially legal." Women may also be prohibited by law from engaging in some work areas or from working at night and receiving overtime pay.[29]

Some European countries have lessened the gender gap in wages by minimizing the overall variation in income between job categories.[30] All socialist countries effectively do this when they minimize the wage gap between all workers. This is not a direct attempt to deal with gender segregation of jobs and gender inequalities, but an indirect attempt to lessen the gender gap in wages by minimizing overall inequalities in wages earned, thus minimizing class inequalities. Gender segregation of jobs persists in these countries, and women consistently predominate in lower-paying jobs.

These facts are shown by the experience of the Soviet Union. Although the nature of Soviet statistics and available data make it difficult to calculate wage gap information that can be directly compared to information from the United States, it is apparent that women in the U.S.S.R. do earn less than men do. Soviet wages are based on the economic sector of employment. Table 4-2 shows the average monthly earnings and the percentage of women in each of these sectors. It is clear that even though there is much less total inequality than in many other countries, the sectors with fewer women tend to have higher salaries and those with more women have lower salaries. Numerous scholars have concluded that the gender discrepancy in wages in the U.S.S.R. cannot be explained by various

Table 4-2 Female participation in the labor force and average earnings by economic sector in the Soviet Union

ECONOMIC SECTOR	*WOMEN AS PERCENTAGE OF LABOR FORCE*	*AVERAGE MONTHLY EARNINGS (RUBLES)*
Construction	28	236.6
Transport	24	220.3
Science and scientific services	52	202.4
Industry (production personnel)	49	210.6
Apparatus of government and economic administration	67	166.2
Credit and state insurance	86	180.9
Education	75	150.0
Agriculture (state sector)	44	182.1
Communications	68	159.5
Housing and municipal economy, everyday services	51	146.6
Trade, public catering, materials and equipment, supply and sales	76	149.2
Arts	50	145.3
Public health, physical culture, and social welfare	82	132.8
Culture	82	117.3
Nationwide average	51	190.0

Source: Gail Lapidus, "The Interaction of Women's Work and Family Roles in the U.S.S.R.," in Barbara Gutek, Ann H. Stromberg, and Laurie Larwood (Eds.), *Women and Work: An Annual Review, Vol. 3.* (Newbury Park, Calif.: Sage, 1988).

Data on women as a percentage of the labor force are for 1983, data on earnings are for 1985.

human capital variables and have suggested that discrimination is at least partly to blame.[31]

EDUCATION

As nations industrialize, more and more people learn to read and write, and both males and females attend school. Yet gender stratification appears in the sense that educational advantages are given first to men and then to women. When the illiteracy rates of males and females are compared, those of females are almost always higher. In a comparison using data gathered by the United Nations in 143 countries, only 5 countries had a higher illiteracy rate for men than for women.[32] In many developing countries boys are much more likely than girls to be enrolled in school. Girls often must leave school to help care for the home and for younger siblings while their mothers work.[33]

Gender stratification also appears cross-culturally in higher education. When choices are to be made, men are almost always the ones allowed the opportunity for a higher education. Far less than half of the students in higher education in Switzerland, Turkey, Japan, and Luxembourg are women,[34] yet when societies can afford to do so they tend to invest in women's higher education as well as men's. Just as in the United States, men and women in highly industrialized countries such as the Soviet Union, the Scandinavian countries, and Germany now receive approximately equal years of schooling, including higher education.[35]

Even though males and females around the world may increasingly have equal years of education, gender segregation appears both in vocational training programs and higher education. Women are much more likely to be trained for relatively low paying clerical, nursing aide, and service positions; men are much more likely to enter training programs that prepare them for high-paying crafts and trades.[36] In universities, women much more often enroll in traditional fields such as education, whereas men are much more often found in programs such as law and engineering.[37] Thus, even in countries such as France, where women and men have similar educational levels, they tend to enter widely different occupational fields and have vastly different economic opportunities in adulthood.[38]

Gender segregation sometimes begins much earlier than at the university level. Many countries have separate schools for males and females from their earliest years. Although these schools generally teach the same curriculum, some authors have charged that the girls are channeled more into traditionally female fields, whereas the males receive more training in the traditionally male and more lucrative areas.[39] In support of this, an extensive cross-cultural study of mathematics achievement in schools found the largest gap between males and females in countries with extensive patterns of gender-segregated schooling.[40] This suggests that girls' schools simply do not provide the rigorous training boys' schools do, even though this may be required by law.

The reasons why this stratification occurs cross-culturally parallel those in the United States. Families tend to invest more heavily in the education of boys than in that of girls, partly because boys can earn more in the future from their advanced education than girls can. Also, however, in many cultures boys, but not girls, are expected to support their parents in their advancing years. A girl is expected to marry, to leave the family home, and to devote herself to her husband's family.[41]

Even though extensive gender stratification can be seen cross-culturally, education has been a key factor in promoting women's greater equality. For instance, in recent years in Italy the disparity in educational attainment between men and women has greatly diminished. These similar experiences of males and females in adolescence counteract the repression young girls experience in the family and promote similar aspirations and interests in both sexes. Yet marriage still gives men almost total control over their wives.[42] This contradiction between women's heightened aspirations and their subordinate status may have contributed to the recent feminist activism and successes in Italy.[43]

Similarly, after World War II, Japan established coeducational schools and compulsory education. Although this move ran contrary to the traditional patterns of the society, it is now widely accepted. About as many females as males are enrolled in senior high schools, although there are still more men than women in universities, even though many older women participate in educational programs outside the traditional university setting. This growing education of women is seen as an important reason for women's increasing participation in the economic and social world as well as their increasing political involvement.[44]

The most dramatic changes related to education probably have been in the Islamic countries, with cultures that totally segregate males and females after puberty and severely restrict women's public lives. Some countries such as Turkey have had compulsory education for women since the 1920s, but others such as Saudi Arabia and Tunisia did not follow such practices until well into the 1950s and early 1960s. With the increase in women's education, the birthrate has declined, polygamy has often been abolished, laws require the consent of the bride before a marriage can be contracted, and women have gained many important political rights and are increasingly entering the labor force.[45] Generally, then, as women become as educated as men, their aspirations change and they are likely to perceive status inequalities with men more sharply.

THE FAMILY

Women in all countries balance their work and family roles differently from the way men do. Just as in the United States, perhaps even more so, women in other countries are responsible for the life of the home. Even though they often work outside the home, their work is generally seen as subservient and supplementary to their roles of wife and mother. Moreover, because of male dominance, men retain greater overall power in the family, and there is no indication that the man shares equally in home chores even when the woman works.

That work is seen as subservient to the family and that women often define their role as a wife and mother as central may influence participation in the labor force. For instance, women in Holland appear to lessen their labor-force participation when children are born.[46] In many other countries, including Sweden, Denmark, Great Britain, and Poland, women are far more likely than men to work part time.[47] In some countries, such as Czechoslovakia and Poland, women work because national policies urge it and because two paychecks are needed for the family's survival. Yet surveys of women in these countries indicate that they would quit if they could and that their only motivation for working is to fulfill the material needs of their families.[48] These patterns may occur at least partly because women value their family roles. But they also may be prompted by the realization that a job outside the home does not mean that their responsibilities for housework will decline.[49]

Extensive cross-cultural studies of family work patterns show that even when women work outside the home, men do not generally increase their participation in household tasks.[50] This occurs even in countries with official policies that call for women's participation in the workforce. For instance, even though many women in the U.S.S.R. work outside the home, they are still responsible for the day-to-day duties of cleaning and washing.[51]

Similarly, the 1949 Communist revolution in China brought enormous changes in women's status. Although traditionally marriages were arranged and wives and their children were under the total authority of the husband's family, women are now granted a voice in marriage and in the political sphere. Yet housework and child care are still viewed as women's work, and it is seen as natural that only women work in the day-care centers.[52]

Although non-Communist countries generally do not have policies that explicitly promote women's labor-force participation, women often work and again hold two jobs instead of one. For instance, in Finland the vast majority of women work outside the home. Nevertheless, employed women spend twice as much time as employed men doing domestic chores. Women are almost totally responsible for such tasks as baking, care of clothing, and child care.[53] In some societies, such as those in Islamic countries, men's power has been almost absolute. In others, such as some African countries, women have traditionally had certain property and legal rights. Greater industrialization and urbanization changed both situations. Women in Islamic countries have generally gained rights;[54] those in other regions may, however, have lost power. For instance, although in some areas of Africa women traditionally owned the land, the European colonists brought the notion that men controlled the land and eventually this right was taken from women.[55] Similarly, some authors have suggested that women's increasing participation in spheres outside the family in Latin America may actually decrease the formal power women hold within the family.[56]

Care for young children becomes especially important as more women enter the labor force. Many countries have well-planned centers with varied activities and extensive care as part of an overall policy of child development.[57] Yet countries vary considerably in the extent to which day care is available, and no country appears to have fully met the large demand for adequate facilities. Some highly industrialized countries, such as Japan, have no well-developed institutionalized means of child care, even though many women are active members of the paid labor force.[58] Other countries such as Norway, Sweden, and France, have had legislation promoting child-care facilities for a number of years. Even though their programs of child care are much more extensive than those found in the United States, the demand for child care still exceeds the supply.[59] Although official policy has strongly promoted women's labor-force participation in Eastern European countries, the Soviet Union, and China, none of these countries has yet met the need for child care. One study estimated that 25% of the children needing child care in Yugoslavia did not receive it, because of lack of facilities.[60] Although showplace factories in China may have model child-care facilities, most workplaces have minimal services or none at all.[61]

Finally, it is important to realize that governmental policies that are favorable to women, such as the provision of child care, are always vulnerable to political decisions. For instance, even though the Eastern European countries have encouraged women's participation in the labor force, government officials became alarmed about the dropping fertility rates in the 1950s and by the 1960s had cut back on provisions for day care. Mothers have been encouraged to take leaves from work, and the availability of abortions and, at times, even the availability of birth control have been drastically limited.[62] Western European countries have also been concerned with falling birthrates. Although abortion is now legal in most of these countries, many have instituted or are considering substantial child allowances to encourage women to have more children and to leave the paid labor market.[63]

THE POLITY

Even though almost all countries now grant women the right to vote and have legislation supporting equal rights, gender stratification appears in the polity. New Zealand granted women suffrage in 1893, Norway in 1913, Denmark in 1915, the Netherlands in 1917, and Sweden in 1919. Other countries, however, such as Iran, Kenya, Monaco, Paraguay, and even Switzerland, did not grant women suffrage until the 1960s.[64]

Women may often engage in political activities from voting to peaceful protests and even revolutionary movements. Yet, as in the United States, women in other countries are noticeably underrepresented in elective offices and are only rarely found in the highest levels of political life.[65] One extensive study of political leaders in 138 countries since the the end of World War II found that only slightly more than 1% of the ministers or cabinet members had been women. Even fewer had been leaders of their countries.[66] Women almost never compose more than 30% of national legislative bodies and most often are far less than 10% of the legislators. Even in Israel, Great Britain, and India, which have all had women prime ministers, women have not been well represented in legislative bodies and cabinets.[67]

In general, even though they are rarely found in the highest positions, women tend to hold political office somewhat more often in Western Europe and North America than in other countries. They are most common in the Nordic countries of Finland, Denmark, Sweden, and Norway and are less often found in political positions in Eastern Europe and the Soviet Union, despite official ideology. The Islamic countries of the Middle East and Northern Africa are least likely to have women political officers, undoubtedly because of severe cultural restrictions on women's public activities.[68]

The nature of a political system and the responsibilities associated with a position may affect the probability of women's involvement in the polity. Women seem to fare less well in countries that elect legislators from "single-member" districts, than in those that have a "proportional" electoral system with several representatives for given geographical areas. In other words, if a woman is just one of several representatives she may be more acceptable to the electorate.[69] In addition, no matter how they are elected or what country they live in, women tend to specialize in gender-typed areas, such as child and family welfare and education. Women cabinet members are typically responsible for these areas, and women in parliament tend to serve on committees dealing with these issues.[70]

These gender differences in political participation occur despite legal guarantees of equal status for men and women in most countries. Some laws do, of course, support the maintenance of male dominance. This is probably most apparent in Islamic countries, which typically allow religious law, rather than secular law, to prevail in matters such as marriage, divorce, guardianship of children, and inheritance rights. Notably enough, these are the areas that are of utmost concern to women, and the reliance on traditional religious law reinforces men's ultimate control and authority within the family.[71]

Yet other laws do promote equality between men and women and have drastically changed women's lives. The passage of divorce laws has been extremely important in some countries in helping women terminate painful marriages[72] and in other countries in protecting women from economic ruin and separation from their children.[73] Similarly, some countries, such as India, did not recognize the right of a widow to inherit her husband's property until specific laws were passed.[74] China's Marriage Law, passed in 1950, brought enormous changes to women's lives. This law gave women new divorce and property rights. Concubinage, bigamy, child betrothal, and the bride price—all practices that virtually guaranteed men's dominance over women—were abolished.[75]

These legal reforms have drastically altered systems of male dominance, but they have not yet ended gender stratification. Most European nations have adopted some form of a law calling for equal pay for equal work, but the gender segregation of the labor force ensures that men and women work in different areas and the wage gap remains. Women are guaranteed free and equal access to the political arena in most countries, but their unequal participation remains a reality.

Some countries, however, most notably the Nordic countries, have also adopted specific policies that promote the lessening of gender segregation and changes in men's as well as women's roles. For instance, all the Nordic countries now grant paid leave from work for new parents, ranging from only 3 months in Iceland to a full year in Sweden. Other provisions in these programs typically allow parents of preschoolers to work shortened weeks at little loss in pay and to take time off to care for sick children. Although women generally are the ones to use these leaves, about a fifth of all fathers in Finland and Sweden participate. Unfortunately, however, such official policies that promote institutional changes are not widespread. Neither Great Britain nor the United States, both highly industrialized countries, has a national policy that promotes the granting of paternity leave.[76]

SUMMARY

As in the United States, gender stratification exists in other contemporary countries. Because it is assumed that women should devote their energies to the family, they may face discrimination in the economy and in the polity. Women's lower participation in higher education and their lower literacy rate also reflect the assumption that their major role is supportive and familial. Yet women's lack of higher education and political power also influences their lack of economic power. The various patterns of institutional gender stratification are obviously mutually reinforcing.

It does not appear that increasing women's labor-force participation guarantees less gender stratification in a society. Instead, if men do not increase their participation in family roles—and they usually do not—then women simply assume two heavy jobs instead of one. Neither does socialism, at least as it is currently operating, seem to guarantee women's greater equality. Although policies that minimize the wage gap among all workers may indirectly affect women by lowering the overall variance in income, gender stratification appears in both the economy and polity of Communist countries and countries with governing democratic socialist parties. The increasing education of women does appear to promote women's equality to at least some extent.[77] With higher education, then, women are more likely to hold professional jobs and laws promoting women's equality become more common. Furthermore, when women are as well educated as their husbands, there will be increasing strain if they are required to submit to his authority. This may have influenced the recent development of feminist movements in some countries. Finally, laws may promote women's equality, and many countries have governmental mechanisms designed to promote the equality of males and females.[78] Yet, despite this legal basis, gender stratification remains in social institutions. In general, the particular pattern of gender stratification within a society appears to be influenced by many variables, not just those within particular social institutions such as education, family, or the polity, but also by the linkages between these institutions and cultural and religious traditions.[79]

SUGGESTED READINGS

The following edited volumes contain articles written by scholars from around the world. The first three volumes focus on industrialized countries; the latter four primarily concern gender roles in developing countries.

Davidson, Marilyn J., and Cary L. Cooper. (Eds.). 1984. *Working Women: An International Survey.* Chichester, Eng.: Wiley.

Farley, Jennie. (Ed.). 1985. *Women Workers in Fifteen Countries: Essays in Honor of Alice Hanson Cook.* Ithaca, N.Y.: Cornell University.

Iglitzin, Lynne B., and Ruth Ross. (Eds.). 1986. *Women in the World: 1975–1985 The Women's Decade* (2nd rev. ed.). Santa Barbara, Calif.: ABC–Clio.

Beneria, Lourdes. (Ed.). 1982. *Women and Development: The Sexual Division of Labor in Rural Societies.* New York: Praeger.

Buvinic, Mayra, Margaret A. Lycette, and William Paul McGreevey. (Eds.). 1983. *Women and Poverty in the Third World.* Baltimore: Johns Hopkins University Press.

Nash, June, Helen I. Safa, and contributors. 1986. *Women and Change in Latin America.* South Hadley, Mass.: Bergin & Garvey.

Ward, Kathryn (Ed.). 1990. *Women Workers and Global Restructuring.* Ithaca, N.Y.: Cornell University Press.

chapter 5

A Cross-Cultural and Evolutionary View of Gender Stratification

Although gender stratification is widespread in industrial societies, could it possibly be missing from other, less complex societies? Anthropologists do not totally agree on whether male dominance characterizes all human cultures. Although the majority probably do believe that some aspects of male dominance and the devaluation of women are universal, the nature of gender inequality and the way in which gender is defined can vary a good deal from one society to another.

Below we first use evidence gathered by anthropologists in many societies to assess similarities and differences in conceptions of gender in human groups. We then use an evolutionary perspective beginning with our nonhuman primate relatives to explore how patterns of male dominance developed and changed as human society became more complex.

A CROSS-CULTURAL VIEW OF GENDER

Gender symbolism is basic to all cultures. However, the way gender is symbolized varies cross-culturally in many ways, often in fashions that are extremely difficult for the Western mind to fathom.[1] Some cultures have highly elaborated complex notions of gender, regulating virtually all aspects of social life, whereas others have less elaborate conceptions of gender, which are somewhat less important in defining everyday activities and social roles. Many cultures conceive of males and females as opposites to each other, much as our own culture does; others have highly elaborated notions of only one sex group.[2] Also even more variable are definitions of basic social institutions such as the family, which vary widely from one culture to another, so that some anthropologists are reluctant to make any broad generalizations about cross-cultural patterns.[3]

Although recognizing the unique characteristics of any one culture, other anthropologists, often influenced by sociological traditions, have examined cultural variations in hopes of finding common patterns. Most anthropologists agree that all cultures devalue women to at least some extent. Religious rituals and myths embody cultural symbols and illustrate this devaluation. A survey of 93 preindustrial societies found that cultures with only female gods are rare, only one society had solely female mythical founders, and the majority of cultures more often assigned powerful religious roles to men.[4] Rituals also reproduce and legitimate gender relations. The sociologists Karen Paige and Jeffery Paige have suggested that reproductive rituals, those associated with puberty, birth, menstruation, and circumcision, may be especially important in determining control over women's labor and offspring. The particular form that the rituals take varies from one culture to another, but all implicitly involve negotiations or competition by men over the loyalties of women and their children.[5]

Social Roles

Every known society has a gender-based division of labor, and the separate tasks of both women and men seem essential for the society's survival. This division of labor is clearly an efficient procedure for cultures to adopt, for not everyone needs to learn to perform all tasks.[6] As the classic sociologist Emile Durkheim pointed out, the division of labor also serves to bind a society's members together by making the contribution of each sex group essential for survival.[7]

Even though all cultures have gender roles, activities are not always gender typed in the same way. For example, in some societies women tend fowls and small animals, and in others men do. In some societies, men carry out dairy operations, and in others women do. On the other hand, there are general tendencies reversed in only a few societies. Generally, men are assigned to such tasks as trapping, herding, fishing, and clearing the land for agriculture, whereas women are more frequently assigned to jobs such as gathering and preserving food, cooking, carrying water, and grinding grain.

A few distinctions seem to be virtually universal. Childbearing, and responsibility for child nursing and its caretaking extensions are universally assigned to females, and hunting has been assigned to males. Among the 224 societies studied by George Murdock, an anthropologist who started the Human Relations Area Files, 166 assigned hunting to "men always." Thirteen assigned it to "men usually," but in no society was it open to "women usually" or "women always." In addition, metal working and weapon making are exclusively male activities. Although women may participate in warfare, war making is male dominated in all societies that make war.[8]

Some authors suggest that these different role assignments may be based on physical sex differences. Perhaps warfare can be explained by men's greater strength and size and women's childbearing. But the manufacture of musical instruments is also almost exclusively a male prerogative, which can hardly be explained by sex differences in physical characteristics. Furthermore, in many societies, women, not men, carry the heavy burdens.[9]

Whatever the basis for these different role assignments, the most important phenomenon in the sexual division of labor is that masculine activities of any and all sorts tend to be defined as more worthwhile and necessary than feminine activities. For example, in some parts of New Guinea, where women grow sweet potatoes and men grow yams, yams are the prestige food distributed at feasts, whereas sweet potatoes are nothing very special. Among the Iatmul of New Guinea, both men and women fish for food, but women's fishing is considered merely their work, whereas men's fishing is viewed as an exciting expedition.[10] In many societies, women actually provide the bulk of a group's nutrition; but whatever men's contribution to the food supply is, it is considered the more important and valuable.[11] In addition, women may often influence political and economic activities of a group, but their participation is rarely formally acknowledged.[12]

Women's Status

There is no evidence, historical or contemporary, of any society in which women as a group have controlled the political and economic lives of men. (Even the mythical Amazon society excluded men; the Amazon women did not directly rule over or dominate men.) Yet the extent to which men dominate women varies a great deal cross-culturally. Some societies are relatively egalitarian; others embody extensive differentiation and inequality.

It is important to realize, however, that the concept of women's status in a culture is multidimensional. It is impossible to point to one or two indicators to determine women's position in a society. As Naomi Quinn and Martin King Whyte have pointed out, women's status cross-culturally should be viewed as a composite of many different variables.[13] Within a given society women may have relatively high authority in the domestic arena, but have little value placed on their labor. The extent to which women control property may be totally independent of the extent to which they have power within kinship groups. Women's political participation, economic autonomy, sexual freedom, and prestige are all indicators of women's status, but vary independently of one another from one culture to another.[14]

As anthropologists have recognized the complexity of women's status, attempts to find key variables that can explain cross-cultural variations in women's position have become increasingly problematic.[15] For instance, in one of the more sophisticated of these arguments, Michelle Rosaldo once suggested that the key social factor underlying the universal cultural devaluation of women may be that human societies have two primary types of institutions: domestic and public. Domestic institutions are organized around one or more mothers and their children, whereas public activities and institutions are broader and generally organize or relate particular mother–child groups. Rosaldo suggested that males' greater prestige is based on their extradomestic or public activities. Ultimately, women's association with childbearing connects them with domestic institutions and underlies their lower status.[16]

Although this distinction remains a valuable descriptor for many societies, it probably does not correctly describe distinctions between men's and women's roles in all societies.[17] Thus, scholars have increasingly begun to examine variables that are associated with various aspects of women's status, rather than key variables that can explain the totality of male dominance from one culture to another. One of the major areas of concern has been kinship, in part because kin relations and especially marriage are often associated with men's maintenance of prestige within a society.[18]

Kinship Systems and Women's Status

All known societies have incest taboos that prohibit marriage among certain kin. This prohibition forces people to seek mates outside their immediate circle of relatives. There are wide variations with regard to which kin come under the taboo. For example, in some societies, a male can marry a first cousin on his father's side but not on his mother's side because kin are counted only through the father.

We tend to think that our own society's kinship system is normal and obvious and reflects the biological facts of kinship. Actually, however, there are many different ways of counting kin, and all of these, including our own, are primarily social, rather than biological designations. All kinship systems stress some biological facts and ignore others, and all serve mainly to organize the social relations of people in that society. For example, in our society, an adoptive father is still a father and has the same duties and obligations as natural fathers. In addition to different ways of counting kin, there are also wide variations in how marriages are contracted, where married couples live, the permissible number of spouses, and even whom one may talk to. Many societies have kinship systems of such subtlety and complexity that they defy analysis, at least in Western terms. Certain generalizations can be made, however, about the relative prevalence of different types of kinship systems and their implications for the status of women. Although generally women gain less from a society's kinship arrangements than do men and although kinship systems reflect male dominance, some kin arrangements give women relatively more authority than others.[19]

Ways of reckoning descent may be roughly categorized as patrilineal, matrilineal, and bilateral. When descent is determined through the father, the society is patrilineal. When descent is figured through the mother's line, the society is matrilineal. When descent is figured through both the father's side and the mother's side, the society is bilateral. Our own society is bilateral, although names are inherited patrilineally. Cross-culturally, children are linked with their ancestors exclusively through males at least five times as often as they are linked exclusively through females.[20] Furthermore, in matrilineal societies, males often still retain authority over kin and domestic affairs. However, this authority over the family is vested more in the mother's brother(s) than in the mother's husband. Inheritance of lore and valuables passes from the mother's brother to his sister's children rather than to his wife's children. The opposite pattern does not occur in patrilineal societies. In no patrilineal society does the father's sister control his children.

Residence patterns may be roughly classified into patrilocal, matrilocal, or neolocal, that is, unrelated to either spouse's parents' residence. Again, the most common residence pattern is some version of patrilocality, where the bride moves from her own family to live with her husband's family. In only one-tenth of all societies does the husband go to live with the wife's family. Rarer still is the pairing of matrilineal descent with matrilocal residence. In such societies, women tend to have greater control over property, somewhat more domestic authority, more equal sexual norms, more ritualized female solidarity, and perhaps more value placed on their lives,[21] although these associations are far from universal.[22]

Patterns of plural marriage also suggest male dominance. Polygyny (plural wives) is much more common than polyandry (plural husbands) and is often associated with the capture of women through warfare.[23] Furthermore, although having more than one wife is ordinarily associated with high status and wealth in a society, the pattern of women having more than one husband is associated with female infanticide. It is a way of ensuring that at least one male is at home to assume reponsibility for the household in societies where war or hunting require males to travel long distances.

Overall, then, the formal structure of kinship systems more often than not gives greater weight to the male line and to patrilocal residence. Even in the relatively rare situations where kinship is matrilineal and matrilocal, male authority still prevails but is vested in the mother's brother rather in the mother's husband. Plural wives are more common than plural husbands, and male dominance is still found in societies that practice polyandry.

Women as Wives

It is significant that among the various kinship roles that adult women play, it is the role of wife that tends to be least powerful. Within the larger kinship group the roles of mother and mother-in-law may be quite powerful. For example, in the polygynous Tiwi society, where the recruitment of women to the local group is important, the relationship of mother-in-law and son-in-law is particularly critical. In order to obtain a virgin wife (the daughter of his prospective mother-in-law), the prospective son-in-law must provide food on a long-term basis for the mother-in-law and live in her camp. This pattern can be viewed as expressing how a male's hunting prowess allows him to buy wives. On the other hand, in certain real respects, the mother of the bride is the beneficiary of and gains considerable power in this transaction. The mother-in-law's power does not derive from her age status either, because she may be a generation younger than her prospective son-in-law, who can be contracting for a daughter not yet born.

In contrast to the mother role, in which women have control over their children, women's role as wives places them under the institutional control of men. This may even be seen in relatively egalitarian societies such as the !Kung, a group that lives in the Kalahari Desert. Here the little gender inequality that exists seems to be associated with marriage. Drawing on a description of !Kung women's lives written 30 years ago, Lamphere described the situation:

> Young girls were betrothed to older boys at a time when they were still prepubescent and would rather have remained playing in the bush. Although many of these early marriages break up, there is considerable pressure on the girl from her parents to accept the new responsibilities of cooking and gathering for her husband and pressure (and even aggressiveness) from the new husband to accept his sexual advances. It is the 13–14 year old !Kung woman who is in the most vulnerable and unequal situation, and it is perhaps in the husband–wife pair bond that domination is a reality.[24]

Similarly, among the African Yoruba, women are relatively powerful because of their trading activities. Yet, as wives, they must feign ignorance and obedience, and in approaching their husbands they must kneel to serve the men.[25]

In many societies, if a woman is expected either to exercise power or symbolize power in her own right, she is not allowed to hold the status of wife. The reason is that the role of wife implies low status. For instance, over 40 African populations, especially the Bantu peoples, have the phenomenon of "female husbands." In these groups when a woman moves into an extradomestic status of high prestige, such as political leader or diviner, she must take on the social role of male by becoming "husband" and head of a household. This phenomenon of female husbands shows that the combination of high power and wife is anomalous. The idea that a political leader cannot be a wife is not limited to Africa but can also be seen in England and on the European continent.[26] Although the word *queen* in English most often denotes the wife of a king, it may also refer to a woman who rules in her own right. When *queen* does refer to a woman who actually rules, however, the husband of this woman is not called a king, but is a prince or a prince consort. This prevents the ruler from being a wife by rendering her mate a prince consort rather than a husband. Thus, at a deeper level, it seems that it is not women's role as mothers but their role as wives that relates to their secondary status in all cultures. Through marriage mothers become wives, and this basic element of kinship systems places men in control of women.

Matrifocal Societies

If then, it is being a wife, more than the fact of mothering, that is related to the secondary status of women, would we find less gender typing and more gender equality in societies in which the wife role is little stressed? This does, in fact, seem to be the case in the so-called matrifocal societies studied by Nancy Tanner.[27] These societies do, in fact, tend to be equalitarian, as we shall see. Matrifocal societies, regardless of their particular type of kinship system, stress the mother role and not the wife role. In these societies, women play roles in the public sphere and define themselves less as wives than as mothers. Tanner quoted Raymond Smith, who coined the term "matrifocality" in 1956, as saying that "priority of emphasis is placed upon the mother–child and sibling relationship, while the conjugal relationship is expected to be less solidary and less affectively intense. It is this aspect of familial relations which is crucial in producing matrifocal family structure."[28]

Tanner described five societies whose kinship systems are characterized by matrifocality: the Javanese, Atjehnese, and Minangkabau (all Indonesian groups), the Igbo of West Africa, and black African-Americans. In all of the societies, relationships between the sexes are relatively egalitarian and there is a minimum of differentiation between the sexes. For example, Tanner reported "little difference between women and men with regard to initiative, assertiveness, autonomy, decisiveness."[29]

Although matrifocal African-American families in the United States have generally been analyzed as pathological, there is evidence that this may simply reflect the patriarchal or phallocentric bias of our culture. What pathology may exist in the African-American ghetto may be a result of poverty, not of matrifocality. Diane K. Lewis has argued that, in contrast to much that has been written concerning African-Americans in the United States, "Afro-Americans share a distinct sub-culture in American society and that 'the hard black core of American is African.'"[30] With regard to gender she stated:

> Not only is behavior considered appropriate for males in white culture displayed by both women and men in black culture, but behavior which is associated with females in white culture is characteristic of both men and women in black culture. For example, in black families, both males and females display similar styles of child care; they are nurturing and highly interactive physically with children. Both men and women value personal relationships and are expressive emotionally.[31]

It is significant that "mothering" is a characteristic of both fathers *and* mothers and is deliberately fostered in both male and female children.

EVOLUTIONARY PERSPECTIVES ON MALE DOMINANCE

Over the years, anthropologists have looked at many societies in different stages of technological development and complexity. From these studies, they have developed an understanding of how women's status and roles have changed through time with changes in work and the methods of survival in the environment. These analyses are either implicitly or explicitly evolutionary in nature, assuming that human societies evolved through several stages: hunting and gathering (or foraging), horticultural, agricultural and/or pastoral, and state societies. Adaptations to each of these situations have different implications for the status of women, but it is extremely difficult to generalize about just what these implications are.

Anthropologists[32] and sociobiologists[33] have extended the evolutionary perspective on human development to include the nonhuman primates and the transitional hominids. Although humans are primates, they are not directly descended from the nonhuman primates now in existence. Instead, we share a common ancestor with our closest relatives, the chimpanzees, and evolved over the same historical era beginning perhaps as recently as 5 million years ago.[34] Humans are very similar in genetic makeup to the chimpanzees, with one calculation of the genetic difference being equal to that between two "nearly indistinguishable" fruit flies.[35] Nonhuman primates and humans are also similar in various social characteristics, including a long period of dependence of the young on the mother.

Of course, humans do differ physically in many important ways from their nonhuman primate relatives, including posture, locomotion, reproductive physiology and behavior, brain size, and intelligence.[36] More importantly, the nonhuman primates lack the elaborate cultural symbol systems, most notably language as well as religious rituals and the elaborate kinship systems of humans. Thus, we cannot directly infer from their social lives to our own and must guard closely against simplistic applications of the results of studies comparing nonhuman primates to human beings. Yet, because primates do have many physical and social characteristics that are similar to those of humans, we can perhaps gain some idea of the starting point for our own earliest social patterns.

Prehuman Groups

Although the field of primatology has expanded rapidly in recent years, many species have not yet been studied and new findings will undoubtedly continue to appear. The most important results in this field have come from long-term observations of nonhuman primates in natural settings. These studies provide important observations about the division of labor in these early relatives of humans and provide evidence for deducing the basis upon which human groups developed and elaborated their systems of gender roles and male dominance.

Nonhuman primates such as chimpanzees have basic cognitive capacities that are similar to those of humans. They have been taught to use sign language and computers to communicate with humans, to the extent that they can even create new words. They live in social groups, and, like human children, nonhuman primates have a long period of dependency upon their mothers. There is no evidence, however, that as a group they have, as humans do, any type of developed symbol system or social institutions.

Nonhuman primates exhibit wide variability in sex-related physical and social characteristics. Some, such as tree-dwelling monkeys, are very similar in size and other physical characteristics; whereas others, such as baboons, show marked dimorphism, with the males almost twice as big as the females. In a few species males are actively involved in all aspects of infant care except lactation; in others males have much less day-to-day involvement with infants. In most, but not all, species females usually defer to males in direct confrontations over access to resources such as food. Finally, social organization and mating patterns vary a great deal from one group to another, from species with long-term monogamous pairings with both parents intimately involved in infant care to those with a wide variety of polygynous and promiscuous arrangements and less involvement of males in care of the young.[37]

These differences among species seem to be influenced both by their physical characteristics and their environment. In general, species with large sex differences in size tend to live in situations where predators are a large problem and males are needed for defense. In addition, lactating females in these groups generally need to consume so much food to produce milk for their infants that additional size would only add to their energy needs.[38] Those with monogamous pairing, less male dominance in male–female interactions, and greater male involvement in infant care tend to be species in which the mother must feed almost continually to produce enough milk for her offspring. Deference to females in feeding and greater involvement of males in infant care help the young to survive by ensuring that the mother can get enough energy to feed the infant.[39]

For a number of years, based on studies of baboons, it was popularly assumed that early human life involved a pattern where males bonded together to protect females and young. A rigid dominance hierarchy among the males was seen as a basic component of the social structure of these groups.[40] Today, this model has been widely criticized, both because it does not accurately reflect the intricacies of baboon societies, but also because baboons are not as closely related to humans as other primate species. Because chimpanzees are more closely related to humans than any other primate, studies of their traits can probably provide the best clues about possible evolutionary antecedents for human behavior.[41]

The bond between mothers and offspring is the core of chimpanzee social groups. Chimpanzee mothers nurse their young until they are about 4 years of age and remain physically close to them until they reach sexual maturity at about 10 to 12 years. As mothers forage for food they are accompanied by their suckling infant and older offspring. Generally females leave the group at sexual maturity to join other groups, but mature sons may continue to forage with the mother. Both males and females avoid mating with close relatives.[42]

Chimpanzee social organization beyond the matrifocal unit appears to be relatively fluid and complex.[43] Two levels of chimpanzee social organization have been identified: small groups that tend to travel, sleep, and forage for food together and larger communities that recognize one another, are not antagonistic when they meet, and may join together to defend their community from others. The size of foraging groups tends to vary depending upon the availability and distribution of food resources, with the mother–offspring bond being the only constant element in social organization and interaction patterns.[44]

Chimpanzees have been observed making and using tools, with the nature and use of the tools varying from one community to another. Although males have occasionally been observed using tools in aggressive encounters with others, most tool use has been observed among females, presumably because they are more likely than males to eat insects such as termites and thus use more probing or fishing instruments than males do. The hunting of small animals is primarily conducted by males and is done without tools.[45]

Some early descriptions of food sharing among chimpanzees emphasized the role of hunting by males and sharing of the meat with older males and related females.[46] Later studies have shown that most food sharing involves plant foods, such as hard-to-open fruits, and occurs within the matrifocal unit, primarily from mothers to offspring. In contrast to implications from some early formulations, there is no indication that females and their offspring must depend upon males for food provisions. In contrast, both chimpanzee females and males are very mobile and primarily gather food for themselves.[47]

Long-term observations of baboons have documented extensive friendships between males and females, with reciprocal grooming and assistance, including males helping with infant care.[48] Although chimpanzees do not exhibit as much male involvement with infant care as baboons do, male and female chimpanzees do establish long-term relationships with reciprocal benefits for each sex group. In contrast to baboons and macaques, where these relationships tend to be dyadic, among chimpanzees the relationships occur between one individual female and an entire group of males. Female chimpanzees exhibit friendly gestures, such as grooming, hugging, or kissing, toward males when they associate at food sources and can either choose or reject members of the group as mating partners and associates. Males not only sire the young, but help protect females and their young from aggression by strange males or females who have recently entered the group. Females' choice of male associates and mates appears to be related to the males' relative sociability as well as their ability to defend the group.[49]

Knowledge about early hominids that were the ancestors of contemporary people comes from paleontological and archeological records, primarily fossilized skeletons and artifacts, and the environment in which these records are found. From this evidence scientists try to piece together ideas about physical behaviors and characteristics of the beings, including their intelligence and walking patterns as well as knowledge about home life such as patterns of group living and permanent campsites. The earliest hominid fossils that have been unearthed come from about 3.5 million years ago. Although these creatures were much smaller than contemporary humans and had much smaller brains, skeletal evidence indicates that they walked erect, the primary criterion for being classified as a hominid.[50]

Although some accounts of hominid life speculate that females remained in some sort of base camp and were provisioned with food by hunting males,[51] most scholars now suggest that the early hominids were timid scavengers who did not know about fire and probably slept in trees to protect themselves from predators.[52] Many anthropologists have argued that the characteristics of chimpanzee social life, including the intense matrifocal unit at the center of a relatively fluid social organization that adapts to changing environmental situations, would also have appeared in hominid and early human societies.[53] Some also suggest that the earliest tools might have been developed for food gathering and carrying infants, rather than hunting, and that females practiced selective mating, choosing males more like themselves as partners, thus eventually reducing large physical and behavioral sex differences and integrating more males into the social group.[54]

In general, these studies of nonhuman primates and speculation about the transitional hominids suggest that the matrifocal unit was at the core of social organization. Although sex-differentiated behaviors appear in the nonhuman primate groups and males usually dominate over females in individual interactions about resources, there is great variability in these behavior patterns, largely as a result of environmental pressures. Systems of male dominance that embody the devaluation of women's activities are documented only in human societies, with their elaborate cultures, kinship structures, and ideologies.

Hunting and Gathering Societies

The vast majority of evidence about the cultural lives of paleolithic peoples indicates that they obtained their subsistence from various hunting and gathering activities.[55] After the last Ice Age, about 10,000 to 15,000 years ago, societies with hunting and gathering technologies were widespread.[56] This has been the main adaptation of *Homo sapiens*.

Societies with this economic form are still found today, primarily in areas where agricultural or pastoral economies are impractical. It is sometimes difficult, however, to know whether a given social pattern represents an adaptation to culture contact or whether the pattern existed before the society was influenced by the outside world. Anthropologists have studied these groups for a number of years, and from their observations we may get clues about the nature of the earliest human divisions of labor between sex groups. Yet hunters and gatherers constitute only about .01% of the world's population, and all have had some (and usually considerable) contact with modern culture.[57]

To the extent that we can infer from these contemporary hunters and gatherers what the earliest humanoid social organization was like, it is clear that the "man the hunter" model, which posits that men provided for the women, is far from the truth. An extensive study of 90 hunting and gathering societies in various parts of the world found that in the majority of these societies, gathering, not hunting, is the primary activity. Women are almost wholly responsible for gathering. Even in societies where hunting is important, it is always the less predictable activity; therefore, the products of gathering usually compose the dietary staples. Thus, women make a very substantial contribution to production and subsistence in these societies.[58]

Neither do the kinship systems of hunting and gathering societies reflect the male dominance that the "man the hunter" hypothesis would posit. Hunters and gatherers usually live in small, loosely structured bands consisting of several married couples and their dependents. The organization of these groups is very simple, and institutionalized leadership and hierarchy are minimal. Apart from age, generally the only major permanent social division is between men and women. Most of these societies have a rather sharp division of labor between the sexes, with women gathering and men hunting.

A common explanation for men as hunters and women as gatherers is that males are physically suited to hunting in that they are larger and stronger, can run faster, and have greater lung capacity and a hormonally based aggressiveness. Ernestine Friedl has suggested that this explanation is too simplistic.[59] Most local hunting and gathering bands are small and contain fewer than a dozen women of childbearing age. In addition, the infant mortality rate is very high. Thus, in order to maintain the population, which is already low, all the women need to be pregnant or nursing, throughout their childbearing years. Freidl has maintained that the sex-based division of labor in hunting and gathering bands comes from the fact that women cannot hunt large game and carry or tend to children at the same time. It is hard enough to gather while carrying small children, much less hunt. The need to maintain the group size pretty much rules out the possibility of some women hunting some of the time while other women bear and care for children. Thus, the necessity for reproduction seems to preclude (at least under these circumstances) women hunters, not their inherent unsuitability for the task.[60]

Observational studies tend to confirm Friedl's theory. The societies in which women, as well as men, hunt for game are those in which hunting does not interfere with their ability to care for their children. For instance, Agta women, in the Philippines, regularly hunt for meat, even while caring for young children. They live in a tropical area with abundant game near their camp and can easily return home with their catch in less than an hour.[61]

Many authors have concluded that in hunting and gathering societies relationships between the sexes are relatively egalitarian.[62] On the other hand, most of these researchers still find some gender inequality. The locus of males' authority may vary. For instance, it may be embedded in political patterns of authority or, it may appear in religious rites and rituals. Nevertheless, some type of gender inequality always seems to appear.

Upon what does this inequality rest? According to Friedl, it is related not simply to the fact that men hunt, but rather to the advantages related to the distribution of the products of the hunt. In hunting and gathering societies, kinship and kin roles define the basis for exchanging the products of hunting and gathering. Theoretically, it would be possible for a group of brothers and sisters along with their parents to constitute the group that both collected and then exchanged food among themselves. The progeny conceived outside the group by the sisters in each group would be considered to belong to the group, but not the progeny sired outside by the brothers. So far as we know, however, no human society follows this arrangement. Rather, humans have invented the idea of marriage, which not only unites two individuals from differing kin groups but also serves to unite the two separate kin groups in a network of reciprocal obligations. In terms of subsistence itself, marriage enlarges the network of kin from whom food can be received and to whom it will be given. Thus, marriage reduces the risk of starvation for any given individual.[63]

Although the bulk of vegetable foods and small animals that women collect are rarely shared outside the household, big game is distributed more widely throughout the community. Friedl suggested that this extradomestic and public exchange of meat accounts for the dominance of men in hunting and gathering societies. This ability to act publicly as generous hosts also binds others to repay and gives men the edge over women. Women's gathering activities are absolutely essential to the existence of the society, but they are generally confined to the domestic sphere of the society. The extradomestic exchange of meat coupled with the male monopoly of individual and small-group hunts give men the ultimate advantage. It places men in the public sphere and binds them to other men in ways that women are not bound.[64]

Friedl classified hunting and gathering societies into four basic types according to the relative importance of hunting and according to the way in which hunting activities are organized. Each type has distinct implications for the status of women. The four types are as follows: (1) Societies in which both men and women engage in gathering—men usually for themselves and women usually for themselves and for their children—and in which males hunt rather little and have little to distribute. The !Kung Bushmen of the Kalahari Desert, whom we discussed earlier, are of this type. (2) Societies in which both sexes from several households engage in collective hunts in which the men actually kill the animals, but the women actively participate in the entrapment. The sexes may also gather collectively. The food is usually shared immediately, and the male advantage in meat distribution is minimized by the collective methods. (3) Societies in which men hunt alone or in groups separately from the women, who gather nearer the camp. (4) Societies in which large game provided by men is virtually the only source of food for the society. Women depend on men for food.

Relationships are much more egalitarian in societies of types 1 and 2, where men hunt less or have less control over the distribution of the products of the hunt than in types 3 and 4. This egalitarianism extends to sexual freedom as well as influence in other kinds of decision making. In the first two groups, men and women are equally free to choose spouses, to take lovers after marriage, and to separate when they wish. In type 4, where men totally control the food supply, women have very little control over their own personal destinies.[65] Friedl used the Eskimo as an example of this type of society; among these peoples, both wife-lending as an act of hospitality and female infanticide are practiced.

Hunting and gathering societies, then, are relatively egalitarian. Their very lack of structure may allow both men and women to become personally powerful, the men through hunting expertise and the women through attracting married offspring to live with them as adults. On the other hand, males do enjoy greater dominance than females even in these societies. This dominance seems to derive not from their subsistence activities so much as from their control of the extradomestic exchange of the products of these activities. Thus, if we can deduce the earliest human adaptation from these societies, we may conclude that the male advantage arose not as a result of biological superiority or greater role in production but of greater control of exchange outside the domestic sphere, involving ties with other men. This includes not just exchange of meat and material goods, but also control over the kinship system and particularly over women as wives.

We also learn from examining the variations in these societies that the greater the society's dependence on the products of the hunt for survival, the greater the likelihood that males will exert considerable control. Thus, even though there is imperfect correspondence between women's contribution to subsistence and their status, the contribution of males to subsistence does enhance their status, at least under these arrangements.

Horticultural Societies

In contrast to hunting and gathering societies, horticultural societies depend for their subsistence on domesticated plants cultivated with hand tools. Horticulture probably developed as a gradual elaboration of the gathering activities of women. It made sedentary communities, increased population density, and more complex sociopolitical arrangements possible. These societies stress kinship lineages more than do either hunters and gatherers or the later agriculturalists. Most of the "tribal" peoples anthropologists have studied have been horticulturists.

Martin and Voorhies examined a sample of 104 horticultural societies and found both patrilineal and matrilineal systems of kinship, although patrilineal descent and patrilocal residence predominated.[66] They found that matrilineal descent and matrilocal residence increase the status of women. The combination of matrilineal descent and matrilocal residence seems to appear where there is little necessity for economic competition among local communities.[67] The pattern loses its adaptive value "in the face of expansive competitive or more intensely exploitive techno-economic systems."[68] These latter conditions put pressure on the society to keep related males together for potential warfare, always a masculine specialty.

According to Martin and Voorhies, matriliny coupled with matrilocal residence represents one possible adaptation to horticulture, but is only adaptive under rather limited circumstances. Thus, it was probably never a major stage in cultural evolution. These matrilineal and matrilocal societies are intriguing to study, however, because they do allow women to obtain considerable authority as well as power. The Iroquois Indians of New York, who fascinated early theorists such as Frederick Engels,[69] are a good example of a matrilineal, matrilocal horticultural society. In this group, women of the same matrilineage lived together in different compartments of a long house with their children and imported husbands. They were exclusive cultivators and also controlled access rights to seeds and to land. Iroquois women were not only producers, but were also collectively the owners of the means of production. Thus, women controlled the dispersal of food to men and children both within and outside their domestic units. This right of women to determine how the products of work were to be allocated gave them real political power in the society.[70] On the other hand, even this society cannot be considered matriarchal, because formal political control and authority were vested in men. Even though men gained and held office only with female approval, the council of chiefs that headed the Iroquois League was male.

The status of women is more variable and less predictable where descent is patrilineal, but generally speaking, women in these types of horticultural societies are under more rigid sexual controls and have less formal authority. Polygyny, the system where a male has more than one wife, is often associated with horticultural societies, but again it is difficult to make a blanket statement about its effect on women. It sometimes gives women advantages and sometimes reduces their status.

In spite of the much greater diversity in the status of women in horticultural societies, it is possible to find some consistencies: Although there is considerable variation in who does the cultivating—one or the other sex or both—clearing land and making war are virtually exclusively male tasks. Friedl speculated that men's monopoly on land clearing is related to their monopoly on war. New lands are likely to be on the border of the territories belonging to others and may be in dispute, thus making war possible. She speculated that war is a male activity because a population can survive the loss of men better than it can the loss of women because women are the childbearers. Men, in turn, by virtue of their control of warfare and land allocation (as between populations) become more involved than women in extradomestic economic and political alliances. Thus, men have greater control than women over the extradomestic distribution and exchange of valued goods and services. This, in turn, enhances their power.[71]

Thus, in both horticultural and hunting and gathering societies, it appears that men dominate women because they have greater control over extradomestic distribution and exchange. Among hunters and gatherers men obtain this control through their monopoly on hunting large game. Among the horticulturists, they gain it through monopoly on the clearing of land and its allocation. Behind this pattern, in both kinds of societies, lies women's childbearing. It allows men to hunt game in hunting and gathering societies and to participate in warfare in horticultural societies. The relative power of women increases among hunters and gatherers and among horticulturists if both sex groups contribute to subsistence and also have opportunities for extradomestic distribution and exchange of valued goods and services.[72]

Agricultural and State Societies

The development of agriculture depended upon the use of manure, the plow, and irrigation. These farming innovations were developed separately and in combination at different times and locations throughout the world. The immediate spur to their invention was probably the necessity for increased productivity to meet the needs of a particular population. Agriculture did indeed allow for greater productivity, greater population density and political centralization. Furthermore, in contrast to hunting and gathering and horticultural societies, the majority of agricultural societies have relatively distinct social classes.[73]

Agricultural societies have a higher incidence of neolocal residence and bilateral descent than hunting and gathering and horticultural societies. Kinship and domestic groups are smaller, and the incidence of polygyny is much lower. Both the matrilineal and patrilineal adaptations to horticulture give way, as families become less lineage conscious. The main effect of the shift to agriculture on men's and women's roles is the removal of women from production. As a society adopts intensive techniques of cultivation, males consistently tend to take them over. The extent to which women are excluded from agricultural production varies, of course, from one society to another, and seems to be related to cultural traditions, environmental pressures, and the nature of domestic responsibilities including the care of animals, which often falls to women.[74] Martin and Voorhies have argued that the male-provider/female-domestic division of labor first arose in agricultural societies.[75] In many hunting and gathering and horticultural societies, even though men generally have public kinship and religious roles, women are very much involved with production. But with the advent of agriculture, the main responsibility for large-scale economic production shifts to men.

In general, the development of agriculture is associated with greater societal complexity, including the appearance of larger settlements, more complex tools, larger political units with specialized offices, and the declining influence of kin groups. In these more complex societies women are more likely to exercise influence only indirectly and informally, often through their relationships with men who hold formal authority.[76] The shift to agriculture is also accompanied by the development of an ideology that supports a more rigid distinction between domestic and extradomestic labor. Sometimes the ideology has been carried to extremes where women have meaning only in terms of work directly connected with the home. For example, the Islamic religion, which began in an agricultural society, places a value on keeping women within the confines of the home and on severely restricting their sexual freedom. Although the seclusion of women in Islam may increase women's solidarity with one another,[77] male dominance was definitely enhanced as the domestic–public split was sharpened. This further legitimized men's public role and their claim to formal authority.

A number of theorists have stressed the association of women's secondary status with the development of state societies, with complex political structures, as well as divisions between social classes. Modern industrialized societies, such as our own, are, of course, state societies. Theorists do not yet agree on precisely why women's status is consistently lower in state societies than in less complex groups, and the exact patterns undoubtedly vary from one society to another. It is clear, however, that state societies rely upon political authority much more than kinship authority in developing group decisions, and women are generally excluded from high-ranking political positions. In addition, the development of the state involves the codification of status, so that ideologies and traditions regarding women's roles are often written into laws rather than simply enforced by group norms.[78]

SUMMARY

Gender symbolism is basic to all cultures, and all societies differentiate between activities that are assigned to men and women. Although the content of these symbols and the nature of role assignments vary a good deal from one society to another, hunting and warfare have almost always been assigned to or controlled by males. The nature of women's status also varies a good deal cross-culturally, although no society has been found where women control men's political and economic lives. In fact, women's status must properly be seen as a composite of many different variables, and women may have relatively high status in some areas but low status in other areas within the same society.

Women's positions in kinship systems are important in maintaining men's authority. All societies have some type of marriage and some way in which men may control particular mother–child units. These men may not necessarily be the mother's husband, because power over children may reside with the mother's brother. Yet this societal requirement is an important means for linking mother–child, or domestic, units to men. In all cultures, the status of wife appears to be understood as incompatible with the exercise of independent authority. Matrifocal societies, which emphasize the mother–child bond, tend to be relatively equalitarian.

Evolutionary stages of societies depend upon the development of new technologies that prompt changes in the means of subsistence. Each advance allows societies to become more populous and more complex. Hunting and gathering societies have the smallest role differentiation, whereas modern industrial societies have a wide proliferation of special roles and hence far greater complexity. There is no perfect correspondence between kinship systems and economic systems. For example, matrilineal and matrilocal principles are found only in special circumstances where lack of competition for land allows groups of related males to be dispersed. On the other hand, the isolated nuclear family consisting of mother, father, and children is stressed in both the simplest and the most complex societies, whereas matriliny and patriliny are most often found in horticultural societies, midway in complexity.[79] In state societies, kinship recedes in importance and the family is pared down to the smallest possible unit.

Although prehuman groups have sex-differentiated behaviors, devaluation of females is a cultural phenomenon unique to humans. In the earliest human adaptations, the distinction between domestic and public activities is not very salient because both sexes are usually involved in providing food. Men do have superior status, which comes from their roles as husbands and from their control of the extradomestic distribution of meat. In horticultural societies, kinship relations are highly elaborated, extended, and defined in the public sphere. Only in rare circumstances are these extended kinship systems matrilineal and matrilocal, and even then men maintain authority in their roles as brothers rather than as husbands. In all these horticultural societies, male dominance seems related to males' extradomestic roles, particularly in their monopoly on obtaining and clearing new lands.

The agricultural adaptation greatly sharpens the domestic–public dichotomy, and women are for the first time clearly assigned to domestic roles almost exclusively. Men's sexual control over women increases, and men and women engage in clearly separate spheres of activity. To some extent, women use the rules and symbolic conceptions that set them apart and circumscribe their activities as a basis for forming extradomestic bonds with other women and creating their own public sphere. On the other hand, kinship itself is male dominated, and men's formal authority is great.

Complex state and class societies have the most elaborate political structures and legitimate women's inferior status through written laws. With industrialization, production in the home becomes less important, but married women continue to be largely identified with the home, not as producers but as consumers. As industrialization advances from producing goods to producing services, more jobs outside the home tend to become available to women. Now many married women work outside the home in most advanced industrialized societies. As we saw in Chapter 4, legal guarantees of equality are found in many of these countries, but these have not been sufficient to end male dominance.

SUGGESTED READINGS

COLLIER, JANE FISHBURNE, and SYLVAI JUNKO YANAGISAKO. (Eds.). 1987. *Gender and Kinship: Essays Toward a Unified Analysis.* Stanford, Calif.: Stanford University Press. A collection of articles that see gender and kinship as socially constructed in relation to each other and is based on the premise that neither can be understood as a biological phenomenon.

COONTZ, STEPHANIE, and PETA HENDERSON. (Eds.). 1986. *Women's Work, Men's Property: The Origins of Gender and Class.* London: Verso. A collection of theoretical articles that consider women's status cross-culturally and historically.

FEDIGAN, LINDA MARIE. 1986. "The Changing Role of Women in Models of Human Evolution." *Annual Review of Anthropology.* 15:25–66. A review of work by primatologists, anthropologists, paleontologists, and archeologists.

MORGEN, SANDRA. (Ed.). 1989. *Gender and Anthropology: Critical Reviews for Research and Teaching.* Washington, D.C.: American Anthropological Association. Articles review anthropological research on gender in all sub-areas of the field.

MUKHOPADHYAY, CAROL C. and PATRICIA J. HIGGINS. 1988. "Anthropological Studies of Women's Status Revisited: 1977–1987." *Annual Review of Anthropology.* 17:461–495.

QUINN, NAOMI. 1977. "Anthropological Studies on Women's Status." *Annual Review of*

Anthropology. 6:181–225. Extensive review articles citing most of the relevant materials in the field.

SMALL, MEREDITH F. (Ed.). 1984. *Female Primates: Studies by Women Primatologists*. New York: Liss. Reports of research on female primates in natural settings.

WHYTE, MARTIN KING. 1978. *The Status of Women in Preindustrial Societies*. Princeton, N.J.: Princeton University Press. A quantitative analysis of the various dimensions of women's status in a wide variety of preindustrial societies.

PART TWO

GENDER DEVELOPMENT

chapter 6

Biological Influences on Gender

With this chapter we begin our analysis of how individuals develop gender identities, gender differences, and their views of appropriate gender roles. Here we examine the influence of biology on gender. We describe the range of differences between the sex groups that may be affected by biological factors, and we argue that although biology clearly influences many aspects of human behavior, these influences do not make that behavior inevitable or immutable. Biology may provide cues, but what is done with those cues is a social decision. We begin by discussing how sex differences develop in utero and how sex of assignment (based on genital differences) leads an individual to develop a consonant gender identity. As a way of understanding physiological sexual development and the development of gender identity more fully, we also discuss how these processes can go awry. We then describe the nature of physical differences between the sex groups before and after pubescence and what the meaning of these differences might be. Finally, we discuss the influence of biology on psychological traits.

Popularized biologistic theories claim that one biological factor or another determines other psychological and social phenomena.[1] Usually, these analyses try to justify male dominance and the traditional gender division of labor on the basis of some male capacity or female incapacity. This misuse of biology has understandably led many feminists to be extremely leery of any biological perspective on gender differences. Actually, biological data need not, and in fact do not, imply that women are inferior to men nor that societal systems of male dominance or female mothering are inevitable.

As feminists and as social scientists, we believe it important to understand as much evidence as possible relating to gender development and discrimination. Just because biology has been misused, we cannot hide our heads, ostrichlike, from all the controversy and gender evidence about biological influences. Biological evidence, carefully interpreted, needs to be incorporated into a feminist analysis.

The cultural patterns of male dominance discussed in earlier chapters influence how humans interpret biological differences. Some of this involves gender *stereotypes,* unexamined and oversimplified mental pictures of what women and men are and how they differ. Scientists are not immune from the influence of stereotypes, for, like everyone else, scientists live in a male-dominated world. Thus, most scientific investigating and reporting occurs within a masculine paradigm and is likely to have a built-in masculine bias. This masculine paradigm assumes that what is related to males is somehow better than what is associated with females. It may influence what scientists choose to study, the questions they ask, and the interpretations they make. For instance, Alice Rossi noted that the familiar description of the union of the sperm and ovum is permeated with masculine fantasy. Even scientific descriptions portray the powerful active sperm swimming strongly toward the passive female egg that is waiting to be penetrated. Actually, the transport of the sperm through the female system cannot be accounted for purely by the movement of the sperm, as the transition is far too rapid. Completely inert substances such as dead sperm and particles of India ink reach the oviducts as rapidly as live sperm do![2]

There are obviously biological differences between females and males. There also probably are some psychological gender differences that have a biological base. However, because many studies of these differences have been based on a masculine paradigm, it is important to try to analyze these differences without a masculine bias. At the same time, we must avoid a possible feminist bias, a tendency to distort findings or overlook contradictory evidence because we want to believe certain "congenial truths."[3] For instance, many feminists have resisted biological evidence concerning the influence of hormones on behavior, preferring to believe that all gender differences in behavior are learned. Our own view is that it is biased to ignore biological findings.

Few people now would argue for the exclusive importance of either nature or nurture in explaining sex gender differences. Biology by no means fully determines what happens to individuals or to social groups. Although physiological variables may prompt individuals to move in certain directions, the social situation, including economic factors, cultural, or individual desires, may overrule or drastically alter these biological predilections. As Alice Rossi put it: "A biosocial perspective does not argue that there is a genetic determination of what men can do compared to women; rather, it suggests that the biological contributions shape what is learned, and that there are differences in the ease with which the sexes can learn certain things."[4] In other words, biology can help define potential behavior, which can then be influenced to a greater or lesser extent by other factors.[5]

Because of the obvious difficulties of biological experimentation on human beings, much of the evidence we use comes from studies of animals, especially the higher primates. Although humans are not the direct descendants of any of them, these higher primates are closest to humans in the evolutionary schema, both physiologically and sociologically. Although it is always hazardous to make inferences from animals to humans, certainly the most reliable ones are those made from animals most closely related to humans. Most of the information regarding humans that we use comes from studies of people who have experienced some type of genetic, hormonal, or physiological accident related to gender assignment. Although we cannot experiment on humans, we can examine the gender development of people with physical anomalies of one kind or another and thus gain insights into the role these factors play in development.

THE DEVELOPMENT OF SEX DIFFERENCES IN UTERO

When a baby is born, its external and internal genitalia are fully developed. This differentiation occurs because the sex chromosomes direct the differential development of the sex glands (gonads). These, in turn, produce different hormonal mixes that influence the genital structures of the two sex groups. Some evidence suggests that hormones secreted in utero may also affect sex differences in nurturance and aggression by influencing structures in the brain. Below we describe how these differentiating processes normally take place and how they are sometimes altered.

Normal Prenatal Development

Biological gender is first determined when the male's sperm unites with the female's egg to form the zygote. Both the sperm and the egg cell have 23 chromosomes. These chromosomes are then paired in the fertilized egg, yielding 23 pairs of 46 individual chromosomes. One of these pairs of chromosomes determines genetic sex. The egg contributes an X sex chromosome; the sperm contributes either an X or a Y chromosome. If the embryo has two X sex chromosomes, it is a genetic female; if it has an X and a Y chromosome, it is a genetic male. Because the female always contributes an X chromosome, it is the male's sperm that determines a child's sex. Scientists estimate that almost 140 XY conceptions occur for every 100 XX conceptions. However, more XY conceptions fail to develop and so, at birth, the ratio of males to females is about 105 to 100.[6]

The embryo that develops from the zygote has a bipotential structure. This original structure and the differentiation for females and males are shown in Figure 6-1. For the first 6 weeks after conception, embryos with either an XX or an XY sex chromosome structure appear the same, although they can be differentiated microscopically.[7] All embryos have "growth buds" that can develop into male or female organs. Differentiation takes place in stages, starting first with the gonads or sex glands (the ovaries and testes), moving then to the internal reproductive structures, and finally to the external genitalia.

If the embryo has XY sex chromosomes, at about the 6th week after conception the bud of the gonads begins to develop into testicles, the male gonads. If the embryo has XX chromosomes, nothing will happen for about 6 more weeks, when the buds begin to differentiate into ovaries. These will contain many egg cells for reproduction in later life. Scientists now think that the sex chromosomes never again influence sexual development after the testicles and ovaries develop, even though people carry the sex chromosomes in all cells of their bodies for the rest of their lives.[8]

The testicles then begin to produce sex hormones: progesterone, androgen, and estrogen. Although we normally think of estrogen as the female hormone and androgen as the male hormone because of the relative proportion of the hormone each sex group produces, it is important to remember that both males and females have all three hormones in their bodies. The proportion of hormones varies both between men and women and between individuals within each sex group and over the life cycle. Testicles produce more androgen than estrogen, and ovaries produce more estrogen than androgen.[9]

Many scientists believe that only the hormone mix normally secreted by males is important for prenatal development. At around the 3rd to 4th month after conception, hormones produced by the testicles cause the wolffian structures, which are present in all fetuses, to develop as seminal vesicles, the prostate, and the vasa. These are the internal male genitalia. During this time of prenatal life, the testicles also produce a substance that inhibits or stops the mullerian structures, also present in all fetuses, from developing into female organs. If testicles have not developed and none of these hormones has been produced, female internal genitalia develop. Much less research has been conducted on female differentiation than on male differentiation. No hormones appear to be needed to prompt the mullerian structures to develop into the uterus, fallopian tubes, and upper vagina, the internal female genitalia.[10] It is possible, however, that hormones from the placenta and the mother, as well as even the ovaries, may influence the development of female genitalia.[11]

Although the male and female internal genitalia develop from different structures, both present in all fetuses, the external genitalia develop from the same preliminary structure. Again, the hormonal mix determines how the preliminary genital tubercle will develop. If hormones normally secreted by males are present, the tubercle becomes a penis and a scrotum to hold the testicles when they descend. If hormones generally secreted by the testicles are not present, the tubercle stays small to become the clitoris, and the two folds of skin, instead of joining to form the scrotum, stay separate to become the labia minora and head of the clitoris, separating the vagina from the urethra, which connects to the bladder.[12]

To summarize, the sex chromosomes influence only the development of male and female gonads. From then on, it is the hormones secreted by the testicles, or male gonads, that determine the development of male genitalia. Without these hormones, in fact without any hormones at all, female genitalia develop. Problems in the process of gender differentiation occur with boys much more often than with girls, probably because masculine development has many more chances to be sidetracked.[13]

One of the most important differences between males and females is the cyclic nature of female hormonal activity. In all female mammals, hormone

Figure 6-1 Sexual Differentiation in the Human Fetus

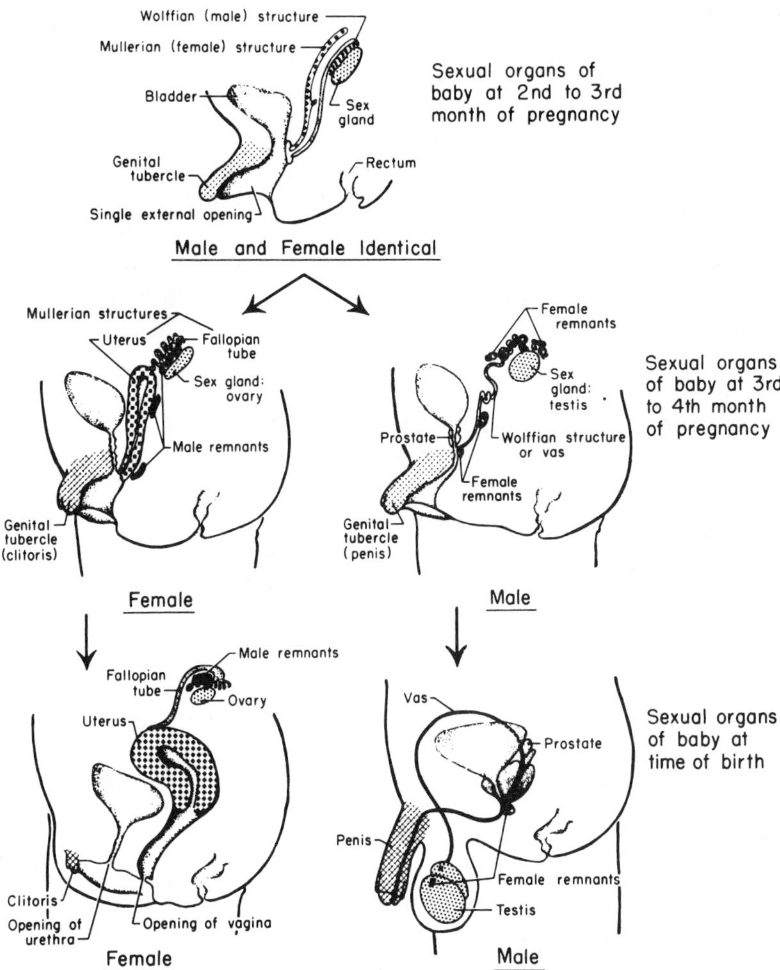

The diagram shows the three stages in the differentiation of the sexual system, both internal and external. Note the early parallelism of the mullerian and wolffian ducts. Eventually the one becomes a vestige and the other develops. (*Source:* John Money and Anke A. Ehrhardt, *Man and Woman, Boy and Girl* [Baltimore: Johns Hopkins University Press, 1972], p. 41. Copyright © 1972 by the Johns Hopkins University Press.)

production follows a regular cycle. Estrogen production is higher from the menstrual period to the time of highest fertility, and progesterone levels are higher after that. These cycles are controlled by the pituitary gland. Males do not have such specific or regular patterns of hormonal activity. Scientists have concluded from experiments on animals that prenatal secretion of androgen by the testicles influences how the pituitary gland will behave later. If the androgen is lacking in prenatal life, the female pattern of cyclical secretion develops in later years.[14] Other aspects of the brain are also affected by the prenatal hormone mix including, perhaps, as we discuss below, some aspects of personality and behavior.[15]

Abnormal Prenatal Development

Much of our knowledge about the normal development of sex differentiation comes from studies of cases where problems have arisen. These conditions may stem from the chromosome structure or from problems with the introduction of hormones throughout the development period. Study of these atypical cases has led to much of our knowledge about the influence of biology on gender development. Although we cannot give a detailed explanation of the many possible abnormalities, we will briefly outline some of the possibilities.[16]

The embryo may have either too few or too many sex chromosomes. In some cases, the second sex chromosome is either missing or defective, and the embryo has an X0 chromosome mixture—or in scientific language, a 45, X, signifying 45 chromosomes plus the X sex chromosome. Children with this mixture develop as anatomic females, but they lack ovaries. Because there are no testicles that secrete hormones, the genitalia develop as feminine. But because no ovaries develop, the child will be sterile in adulthood and will develop secondary sex characteristics only if supplementary estrogen is given at puberty. The condition is known as Turner's syndrome.[17]

In other cases, the embryo has one or more extra sex chromosomes. The most common cases are XXX, XXY, and XYY, although other combinations can occur. XXX children are anatomically female and can bear children. Both the XXY and XYY people are anatomically male.

Even if the sex chromosome combination is a normal XX or XY, several anomalies in sex differentiation can occur before the child is born. These may affect the gonads, the internal and external genitalia, and the changes in brain development. Sometimes a fetus will have the normal XX or XY chromosome mixture, but the gonads fail to develop properly. More frequently, the gonads differentiate normally, but the influence of the hormones alters genital or brain differentiation later in prenatal development. Masculine fetal differentiation encounters more problems because not only are male hormones needed to stimulate masculine development, but also an additional hormone is needed to suppress female development. Sometimes the mullerian-inhibiting hormone is not present, and the boy develops a uterus and fallopian tubes along with his functioning male genitalia. The uterus and fallopian tubes will not function, because the child lacks ovaries.

In other cases, the embryo has the XY chromosomes and develops testicles, which produce androgen and the mullerian-inhibiting hormone, yet it cannot use the androgen. This is called androgen insensitivity, and it is a hereditary trait passed through females and affecting their male children. Because development of the mullerian structures is repressed and the male genitalia cannot develop due to the inability to use androgen, the child has neither male nor female internal genitalia. The mullerian structures are not involved with the external genitalia, and so the child looks like a normal female externally. The child can respond to estrogen, normally secreted by the testes, so at puberty the secondary sex characteristics of a woman will appear. However, the child does not menstruate and as an adult cannot become pregnant, although she can have sexual intercourse. The lack of menstruation often leads to discovery of the condition.[18]

Sometimes the child will be only partially sensitive to androgen, and the external genitalia will be ambiguous in appearance. In such cases, doctors and counselors recommend rearing the child as a girl. Surgery and hormone therapy can make the external genitals feminine in appearance and suitable for penetration, but the woman cannot bear children. Corrective surgery to produce male external genitalia is much more difficult, and because the boy will never be fully sensitive to androgen, he will never fully develop male secondary sex characteristics such as facial hair, masculine body shape, and a deep voice.[19]

Because prenatal female differentiation apparently requires no prompting or suppressing hormones, the problems that arise with females involve accidental overdoses of androgen. This may come from tumors of the ovaries or the adrenal cortex, which produce a product closely related to androgen and having the same effects. Other problems can arise from overstimulation from progesterone. Cases of this occurred in the 1940s and 1950s when doctors used progestin, a synthetic form of progesterone, to prevent miscarriage.

The exact effect of these hormones depends on the amount received by the fetus and at what developmental stage. At birth some babies will look like girls, others will look like boys, and some will have fairly ambiguous genitalia. With surgery and hormonal therapy, these children can usually function as their assigned sex. Unlike the androgen-insensitivity syndrome, XX babies with an androgen excess who look like boys at birth can be raised as boys. They are sensitive to androgen and, with hormone therapy, can develop masculine secondary sex characteristics. With their prenatally masculinized external genitalia, they can function sexually as normal males, except that they are sterile.[20] There are no known cases of male XY fetuses exposed to excessive amounts of estrogen because large prenatal doses of estrogen almost invariably produce miscarriage.[21]

THE FORMATION OF GENDER IDENTITY

Remarkable as it may be in view of the complexity of the process of differentiation, the vast majority of individuals have unambiguously male or female genitals at birth. Ordinarily, too, the vast majority of people develop in the first few years after birth an unambiguous *gender identity*, a gut-level conviction that one is male or female. No one is quite sure yet how this gender identity develops, and the current literature is filled with controversy.[22] We do know that a very important factor is the assignment of a gender to an individual by others at birth. Children who have been assigned to a sex group that is not consonant with their biological or chromosomal sex usually grow up thinking and feeling that they belong to their assigned gender. Although one is assigned to a sex group by the appearance of the genitals, it is not just biology that produces the cognitive phenomenon of feeling masculine or feminine. Rather, it appears that communications of the parents and others in the child's environment also have a very important effect on the child's gender identity.

The Plasticity of Gender Identity

The earliest and most publicized work on gender identity has been conducted by John Money and his associates.[23] They have emphasized the central role of gender assignment in determining gender identity, suggesting that this identity is firmly established by about the age of 2½. Examples of children matched with regard to the nature of their biological abnormalities support this thesis. These stories also illustrate the deep-seated nature of gender identity and that it develops relatively early in life.

Money and Ehrhardt presented cases of matched pairs of genetically female individuals with congenital adrenal hyperplasia, that is, a malfunction of the adrenal glands that causes excessive male hormones to be secreted. At birth, both members of each pair had ambiguous external genitalia, but one was assigned to be a female and the other a male. The assignment was usually a function of the judgment of the professional personnel attending the birth and counseling the parents shortly thereafter.[24]

In one matched pair, the child raised as a girl had corrective surgery at the age of 2 but was pronounced a girl and seen as such from the age of 2 months on. She had a fairly normal girlhood, although as is typical of girls with this syndrome, she exhibited "tomboyish" traits. She also projected her romantic interests with boys into the future, concentrating on her academic interests during adolescence. The member of this pair assigned as a boy had an unhappier experience. A series of operations designed to masculinize his genitalia ended in failure. At the age of 3, he was again admitted into the hospital and was terrified by his thought "that a nurse would cut off his wee wee."[25] It was decided to let the child continue to live as a boy, and surgery succeeded in making masculine genitalia. His family life was not happy, he was an underachiever at school, and he tended to be rebellious later. All his romantic interests were directed toward girls, even though he was continually afraid that his penis would be too small for intercourse.

The two children in the second pair experienced hormonal sex changes at age 12 that did not correspond to their gender identity. The child who thought herself a girl found her body masculinizing with her voice changing and facial hair appearing; the boy found his body feminizing with enlarging breasts. Both children were extremely upset with their condition, and after diagnosis they underwent surgery and hormonal therapy to bring their bodies in line with their gender identities. Both children reported romantic interests in the sex group other than their assignment, and they engaged in activities typical of their assigned gender. Clearly again, the sex of assignment outweighed biological factors in determining gender identity.

Some cases are not as clear-cut. This most often occurs if the parents are at all ambiguous about the child's gender. The results are extremely unpleasant for the children involved. A third matched pair that Money and Ehrhardt discussed involves two children who requested a sex reassignment in their 10th and 11th years.[26] In both cases, the parents had not been clearly told the sex of the child at birth. Furthermore, there had been no corrective surgery at that time, follow-up treatments, or counseling. Both cases were referred to Johns Hopkins when school authorities became alarmed about the children's refusal to communicate with others. In each case, medical and psychiatric personnel conferred with the children and their parents both separately and together. The possibility of sex reassignment was openly discussed with the children. Each child opted for a sex reassignment, both choosing to write notes rather than verbalize their desires. The note of the child wishing to change to a boy dramatically illustrates the urgency these children felt. She wrote, "I got to be a boy." After the sex reassignments and corrective surgeries, both children blossomed. They began to talk to others, became much more proficient both academically and socially, and began to date. The boy is sexually interested in girls exclusively, and the girl is married.

Other authors suggest that Money and his associates have overstated the extent to which gender identity is fixed in the early years of life. The most widely cited challenge to Money's formulation involves a group of chromosomal males from a small village in the Dominican Republic with a genetically inherited deficiency for a certain androgen. At birth, because of their ambiguous genitalia, they were, according to the researchers, unambiguously raised as females. At puberty, these "girls" developed male secondary sex characteristics, including a deep voice and adult-size male genitalia. Of the 18 for whom full information was available, 16 then assumed a male gender role, married, and fathered children.[27] Other case studies indicate that Money and his associates may have underestimated the possible influence of prenatal sexual differentiation in the brain and hormonal changes occurring with puberty on the process of gender identification.[28]

Clearly the last word has not been spoken in this area. Because cases of ambiguous genitalia are so rare and most children with these conditions receive auxiliary hormonal and surgical treatment, it will undoubtedly be many years before clear answers are developed. The evidence available to date, however, indicates that both biological variables and social variables probably influence the development of gender identity.[29]

Transsexuals

The puzzle surrounding the origins of gender identity becomes more complex when the experiences of transsexuals are considered. Transsexuals are people who have no physical abnormalities in their genitalia and are unambiguously assigned to and reared as members of one sex group. Yet, in spite of this assignment and usually harsh opposition by peers and family members, they have a different gender identity. This usually appears at very early ages and persists into adulthood.[30] Unless they are psychotic or delusional, transsexuals recognize their assigned gender and often can act successfully in that role. They feel that they are "women trapped in men's bodies" or, more infrequently, "men trapped in women's bodies." They typically have a body characteristic of their assigned sex group, but are extremely unhappy with it.[31]

James Morris, a famous and daring reporter who once climbed Mount Everest, elected to become Jan Morris. He wrote a book describing this experience. He said, "I was born with the wrong body, being feminine by gender but male by sex, and I could achieve completeness only when the one was adjusted to the other."[32] Richard Raskind, a top-notch men's tennis player, a well-respected opthalmologist, and a married man with children, shocked the sports world when he became Renée Richards and sought to play tournament tennis as a woman. Richards also reported the agony she felt in her presurgery dilemma. "As a child . . . I would pray every night that I could be a girl. I knew then I wanted Renée as my name. It means reborn."[33]

Richards and Morris along with several thousand other people were medically given new female bodies. Although the transition from a female to a male body is more difficult, it too is possible. Before agreeing to a professed transsexual's request for a sex-change operation, reputable medical centers require many hours of psychological examinations and counseling. The individual is required to live successfully for at least a year as a member of the desired sex group before final changing surgery is performed. For male to female transitions, feminizing estrogens are administered, and the masculine external genitalia are transformed surgically to feminine genitalia. Surgeons, of course, cannot create the uterus and ovaries, but they can form a vagina. Although the process is surgically more complex and less satisfactory, female to male transsexuals follow the same pattern by receiving male hormones and transforming surgery. As the phenomenon of transsexualism has become more widely known, the incidence of females requesting reassignment has increased. By the mid-1980s, one major clinic reported a ratio of about two females for every three males in their assessment process.[34] Although the sex-change operations do not solve all of the transsexual's problems, most transsexuals who have the operation are reported to be happy over the results and few regret their decision.[35] Yet evidence from follow-up studies indicates that transsexuals who have a sex-change operation do not differ significantly in their life adjustment from those transsexuals who weather an identity crisis without having an operation.[36]

Scientists still do not know why transsexuals develop gender identities contrary to their biological sex. A number of people are examining physiological, psychological, and sociological explanations. We do know that transsexuals are not unique to our culture and that there have been examples of such people throughout the ages. Some authorities stress the importance of early family relationships, especially ties with the mother, in influencing the development of transsexualism.[37] Others are exploring possible influences involving genetic, hormonal, and central nervous system abnormalities.[38] Although a definitive answer must depend on further research, Susan Bradley, an expert in the area, has suggested that biological or constitutional factors may induce a vulnerability to gender identity disorders, but that the critical factors in eventual development of transsexualism involve interactions within the family.[39]

A great deal of anguish accompanies a gender-related condition such as transsexualism. Although the incidence of cross-gender behavior among children is quite rare, children with these characteristics tend to encounter many social problems with their peers.[40] Psychiatric help appears to counter some of these symptoms and to help the children live happier lives.[41]

Some feminists suggest that transsexualism is simply "the result of the stereotyped sex roles of a rigidly gender-defined society"[42] and that "transsexualism is most basically the result of normative definitions of masculinity and femininity."[43] Raymond has suggested that "counseling which incorporates elements of 'consciousness-raising'" is preferable to sex-change operations.[44]

Yet because gender identity forms a core part of self-identity, it is likely that neither sex-change operations nor counseling can totally undo its importance to individuals. The basis of male dominance probably does not lie in the fact that people have a gender identity tied to biology, but rather in the identification or association of greater power and prestige with males. The solution to male dominance, then, lies more with changing this valuation than with eliminating gender identity itself. In later chapters, we will show that, in fact, a secure gender identity—not the elimination of this identity—will be most important in eliminating male dominance.

THE NATURE OF PHYSICAL DIFFERENCES

Physiological differences between the sex groups continue to appear and develop after birth. Some of these differences, primarily involving traits such as skin sensitivity and strength, first appear at birth. Others become important only at puberty, when sex differences in hormonal levels again occur. Below, we discuss differences in size and strength, susceptibility to illness and disease, perception and postpubescent development.

Size and Strength

At birth, boy babies tend to be slightly longer and weigh slightly more than girl babies. Females' lungs and hearts are proportionally smaller than those of males, and females have a lower percentage of their body weight in muscle, but a higher percentage in fat.[45] Despite these size differences, females mature more rapidly than males. This difference first appears 7 weeks after conception. By the time of birth, the female is 4 weeks ahead of the male baby. Females learn to walk and talk and are toilet trained more quickly than males. They also reach puberty and full physiological maturity earlier.[46]

At birth, male metabolism is faster than female, although the difference may not be statistically significant. From the age of 2 months, males consume more calories than females. Adult males also have a lower resting heart rate, higher blood pressure, greater oxygen-carrying capacity, and more efficient recovery from muscular activity.[47] These physiological characteristics are one basis of male superiority in strength. Females may certainly develop their strength and endurance through exercise programs. In recent years as more funds have been devoted to training women athletes, they have rapidly improved their athletic performance.[48] However, it is not yet known whether they will match men athletically in all endeavors.

Illness and Disease

A well-known sex difference that appears even prenatally is the male's greater susceptibility to illness and death. As we noted in the previous section, many more male than female fetuses are conceived, but the sex ratio is almost equal at birth. After birth, males also tend to be more susceptible to both disease and death. In this country, one-third more males than females die before their first birthday. Even as life expectancy in a society lengthens, the benefits accrue faster for women than for men, although this may result from the decline of female deaths associated with pregnancy and birth.[49] Figure 6-2 shows the change in the relative death rates of females and males during this century. Since 1900 the female death rate has become consistently lower than the male rate. This drop is especially noticeable in the childbearing years, a result of the rapid advances in maternal health care.

Males are susceptible to physical difficulties that pass females by. Such well-known problems as color blindness, hemophilia, and even baldness result from the males' XY chromosome structure. These inherited conditions arise from genetic information on the X chromosome that the child receives from the mother. Girls may also receive this condition-carrying X chromosome. But because the gene related to hemophilia or color blindness is recessive, the corresponding gene on the girls' other X chromosome can prevent the appearance of the condition in the female. The boy has no other X chromosome to block this effect and thus exhibits the defect. The girl remains a carrier and can pass the characteristic on to her offspring.[50]

Some disorders may develop more often in males than in females because males are developmentally behind females. These problems include greater proneness to speech defects such as stuttering and language disorders, reading disabilities, limited vision, impaired hearing and deafness, and mental retardation.[51] Studies of school children consistently note that boys are much more likely than girls to be referred for almost all learning disorders.[52]

The incidence of other disorders may be influenced by our culture. Both males and females have physiological reactions to stress. But in our culture men

Figure 6-2 Female Death Rate as Percentage of Male Death Rate by Age Group in 1900, 1940, and 1987

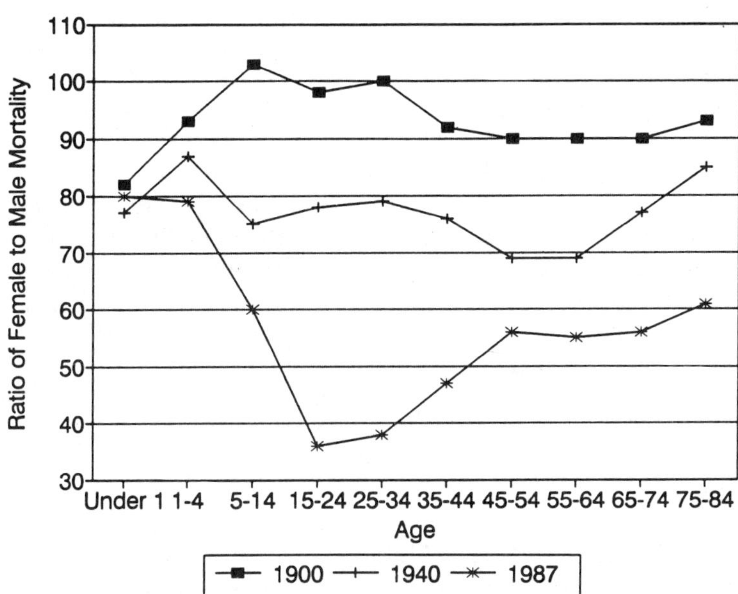

Source: National Center for Health Statistics, *Vital Statistics of the United States: Mortality, Vol. 1,* 1950, pp. 191–192; and National Center for Health Statistics, *Advance Report of Final Mortality Statistics, 1987, Monthly Vital Statistics Report,* vol. 38, no. 5 supp. Hyattsville, Maryland: Public Health Service, 1989. Graph designed by Walter T. Martin, Department of Sociology, University of Oregon.

more often develop peptic ulcers and skin disorders, and women exhibit headaches, migraines, backaches, and insomnia. Sex differences also appear in the incidence of many other diseases and conditions, although the reasons underlying all of these differences are not yet clear. For instance, women develop diabetes, phlebitis, and diseases of the thyroid gland more often than men, whereas men more often develop most forms of cancer and cardiovascular and immunodeficiency diseases.[53] In middle age, women more often develop nonfatal chronic diseases, and men more often develop fatal diseases.[54] Differences also occur in the incidence of mental illness. Women more often suffer from depression; men more often suffer from substance abuse and personality disorders that include problems with aggression and impulse control.[55] Although nonwhites have higher mortality rates than whites, gender differences in the incidence of illness and disease are similar in various racial/ethnic groups.[56]

Finally, some sex differences in physical vulnerability may come from environmental and activity differences. A higher proportion of male deaths than female deaths results from accidents and injuries. Males also smoke cigarettes more and die from lung cancer more than females. However, as women become more involved in dangerous activity and as they increase their smoking, their death rate in these areas also rises.[57] Although it is popularly assumed that the stresses men face in the occupational world contribute to the higher number of heart attacks, there is now some evidence that women's hormonal secretions somehow protect them from heart disease. When these secretions diminish at menopause, women's susceptibility to heart disease rises.[58] Females' lower death rate may also be promoted by their tendency to seek medical help more quickly than men.[59]

Not all male–female differences in disease and susceptibility can be attributed to differences in activities or environments. The differences in susceptibility appear before any differences in activity occur. Studies of men and women in similar controlled environments, such as religious communities where men and women have similar work tasks and related pressures, sleep patterns, diet, and medical care, also find longer life spans for women.[60] Even so, the different environments and roles of men and women before entering the cloister may have influenced these differences, and it is hard to ever fully rule out environmental influences.[61]

Perception

There is evidence of sex differences in sense perception. Some of the evidence is contradictory, however, and some differences appear only in adulthood, indicating that adult hormonal levels may contribute to their development. Females do appear to be more sensitive to tastes, with female infants perhaps responding more to sweet tastes and female adults discriminating bitter tastes more readily than males. Although there seem to be no sex differences in the sense of smell in infancy, by adulthood women are more sensitive to odors. This seems to be related to the increased estrogens in the body after puberty. Although the evidence is contradictory, there is some indication that female infants are more sensitive to touch than male infants. In adulthood, women can detect painful stimuli more quickly than men. The two sex groups do not tend to differ in responses to auditory or visual stimuli in infancy or for the most part in later life.[62]

There does appear to be a sex difference in visual–spatial ability. Numerous reviews of studies in this area conclude that more males have this ability than females. Tests used to measure spatial ability usually involve comparing one object with a number of others rotated in different planes and matching the two that are alike, looking at systems of gears and finding which gear moves a specific part, or looking at a two-dimensional picture of a three-dimensional surface and telling how many surfaces are on the figure.[63] For many years, psychologists thought that spatial perception was a psychological trait linked to analytic reasoning skills. They now realize that it is a simple perceptive ability unrelated to intellectual capacity (see discussion in Chapter 7).

Some authors suggest that boys' greater spatial ability may have a biological base. Two theories that purport to account for this are currently considered most plausible. The first involves hormones, and the second involves hemispheres in the brain. Neither of these theories has yet been disproved, and further research is needed to understand the physiological source of spatial perception.[64]

Although there is considerable evidence that biological factors are involved in visual–spatial ability, several researchers have shown that the ability can be improved by training, especially in girls.[65] That training helps girls' scores more than boys' suggests that boys may already have been trained in some way for this ability. For instance, activities such as model construction and block building may encourage the development of spatial visual skills.[66]

One interesting finding in this area is the negative association of males' "masculinity" with their visual spatial ability. Boys with more masculine physical characteristics, including large chest and biceps along with pubic hair, tend in these studies to have lower scores of spatial ability. Conversely, boys with less masculine bodies have higher spatial ability. Similar results have come from various personality measures of masculinity. Obviously, masculinity is a complex phenomenon. Even though biology may influence both processes, what makes a good football player is not necessarily what makes a good mechanic.

Postpubescent Differences

At puberty, physical differences between the sex groups triggered by hormones appear for the first time since before birth. From birth through about 8 years of age, boys and girls have similar hormone levels and they grow at about the same pace. Boys are slightly, but insignificantly, bigger than girls until age 5. From then until females begin to grow as they enter puberty, around 11 years of age, boys and girls grow at about the same pace. At puberty girls only initially grow faster than boys.[67]

Scientists do not yet understand exactly why or how puberty begins when it does. They do know that at around 11 years of age in girls and 13 years in boys, the pituitary gland secretes gonadotropic hormones that prompt the gonads to secrete sex hormones. Pubescence is accompanied by a growth spurt and the development of secondary sex characteristics such as female breast development, male voice changes, and the growth of pubic hair in both sexes.[68] It is at this time that females' distinctive pelvic shape develops.[69]

Although genetics influences the age at which puberty occurs, the major influence for both boys and girls is body weight. Several studies have shown that girls with different timings of puberty all had the same body weight when it began, whether menstruation and the growth spurt were early, on time, or late.[70] The age of puberty has steadily declined over the past 150 years as better nutrition and public health has resulted in both boys and girls growing faster and bigger than in earlier years.[71]

Many sex differences in body shape and proportion come from the differences in growth at puberty. Males continue their growth spurt longer than females and end up taller than females. Women have lighter skeletons, wider pelvises, different shoulder and pelvis proportions, and different socket shapes at the shoulder and pelvis than men. These differences are, of course, functional in childbearing. They also contribute to the different throwing and running styles of men and women, and to women's greater endurance and men's greater strength.

Summary Comment

In general, sex differences in physical characteristics appear at birth or develop at puberty. Males are larger and stronger, and they have well-developed visual–spatial ability more often than females. Females mature more quickly, are less susceptible to disease, live longer, and may be more sensitive to taste, smell, and touch than males are. Although women have a regular pattern of hormone secretion after puberty, no regular pattern has yet been found in men.

Although these physical differences generally appear cross-culturally, the meaning given to them varies from one society to another. For example, in this society, we have tended to stress women's relative lack of strength and men are expected to be the burden carriers. In other societies, relative strength is apparently unimportant and women carry the heavy loads. Biological differences are also used to justify differential evaluation of the sex groups, but here again the connection is by no means obvious. If one focuses on endurance and freedom from physical defect, one could argue for the natural superiority of women. If one focuses on size and strength, men might be called naturally superior.

PHYSIOLOGY AND PSYCHOLOGICAL GENDER DIFFERENCES

In Chapter 7, we thoroughly review psychological gender differences that seem substantiated by research evidence. Some of the differences we think of as "psychological," however, may have a physiological base, including gender differences in nurturance, aggression, and mood change.

Nurturance

We use the term *nurturance* to describe the "giving of aid and comfort to others."[72] Nurturant behavior often involves responding to bids for help and comfort from others who are younger, weaker, or for some other reason, such as illness or old age in a dependent position.[73] Nurturant care of the young is essential for the survival of the human species, for human young depend totally on others for their care for a number of years.

Sex differences in the propensity to nurture appear in studies of adolescent animals and in studies of humans. Field studies show that young male langurs and baboons mainly play with other males and that young females spend a great deal of time with adult females and help take care of infants.[74] Similar results have also been observed with human children in a wide cross-section of cultures.[75] Similarly, experimenters who gave young monkeys to preadolescent pairs of male and female monkeys found that the preadolescent females were four times as likely as the males to act maternally toward the young monkeys. The males were 10 times as likely as the females to exhibit hostile behaviors.[76] Both males and females exhibit nurturant behaviors; females simply seem more likely to show an interest in learning to do so.

Both prenatal and postnatal doses of hormones appear to affect the amount of nurturance males and females exhibit. Prenatal hormones are generally said to have an "organizing" effect on behavior, affecting a person's propensity to learn certain behaviors, whereas postnatal doses, such as those associated with pregnancy and parturition, are said to "activate" behavior or facilitate gender-associated responses.[77]

The major studies involving the relationship of abnormal prenatal hormone doses to nurturant behavior in humans have been conducted by Anke Ehrhardt and her associates.[78] These carefully planned and well-supervised studies match groups of young women, and sometimes men, with various genetic or prenatal hormonal abnormalities with one or two normal young people of the same sex group. The matching variables generally include age, race, socioeconomic status of the family, intelligence, and medical conditions unrelated to the hormonal abnormality. From these studies one can assess the extent to which either excessively high or excessively low prenatal exposure to androgen is associated with nurturant behavior in childhood and later life. Although the relationships are not large, they indicate a tendency for girls exposed to higher levels of prenatal androgens to exhibit less interest in doll play and parenting, to be somewhat less likely to marry, and to be less likely to attempt parenthood in adulthood. They are not more likely, however, to have male-typed career aspirations. Genetic males with androgen insensitivity syndrome (genetic males whose bodies do not respond to androgen at all, have female external genetalia, and have been raised as females) are more likely to be interested in young children and marriage than matched comparators. However, genetic males who can respond to androgen but have, for some reason, been exposed to lower than usual prenatal doses, do not appear to exhibit more nurturant behavior than matched controls.[79]

The hormones produced during pregnancy and parturition also enhance nurturant behavior. Although the precise effect varies from one species to another and care must be taken when generalizing from animals to humans, results with animals generally indicate that administration of hormones associated with pregnancy to nonpregnant animals leads to behaviors commonly associated with nurturance, such as nest building, retrieving, and care of young.[80] Other studies with animals suggest that a female's responsiveness to young increases during pregnancy. This does not occur if her ovaries, which produce most of the hormones, have been removed. As the hormones associated with the pregnancy and parturition gradually diasppear after birth, the nurturant behavior diminishes. When postparturient females are continually given new young litters, their amount of "mothering" behavior lessens.[81]

Although biological factors influence nurturance, other factors also play an important part. Some authors emphasize the importance of physical contact in the postpartum period in cementing maternal–child ties.[82] Similarly, however, greater contact between fathers and children appears to increase fathers' nurturance.[83] Attachment and nurturant behaviors appear to develop as parent and child interact and communicate with each other. Although the prenatal hormone doses males receive may hinder their interest in nurturing young children, they by no means eliminate their capacity for nurturing as shown by experiences of fathers of newborns. Even among young boys, those with younger siblings at home show more nurturance in doll play than other boys. Girls show nurturance whether or not they have younger siblings.[84]

Although hormones secreted during pregnancy may help prompt women's nurturant behavior, the social experience of birth and childrearing also may enhance women's and men's nurturance. Thus, hormonal influence helps prompt the appearance of and interest in nurturant behavior, but social situations and interactions also exert an influence, making it possible for males as well as females to nurture. Thus, just because research findings on animals and humans indicate some hormonal basis for nurturance, we need not conclude that this means women must nurture and that men cannot.

Aggression

Males exhibit more aggressive behavior than females in all known societies. Children exhibit these sex differences early in life, and there is little evidence that adults have "socialized" or encouraged males to increase these behaviors. Male nonhuman primates also exhibit more aggression than their female counterparts.[85] Certainly, aspects of these differences are socially learned. Most important, the patterns of aggressive behavior that individuals exhibit depend on the social and cultural context. For instance, young boys may wrestle and fight during school recess, but they know that such behavior is not permitted in the classroom. Brawls and fights may occur regularly in some areas of town, but almost never in others.

Yet there is evidence that physiological influences also affect this difference between the sex groups. This evidence comes both from studies of nonhuman mammals and from studies of human beings. As with influences on nurturance, this may involve both the prenatal influence of hormones and postnatal hormonal differences. Studies have examined gender differences in the more typical rough-and-tumble play style that is often a precursor to aggression as well as fighting behavior and more direct indicators of aggressive behavior.

Prenatal influences As with nurturance, prenatal hormone doses are believed to have an organizing function on aggressive behavior. Evidence from research with animals indicates that males receiving lower than normal prenatal doses of androgens tend to exhibit less aggressive behavior in later life, whereas females who receive higher than normal prenatal doses of androgens exhibit more fighting in adulthood.[86]

Although one may generalize from such animal studies to humans only with caution, studies with humans do suggest some connection between prenatal hormone doses and later aggression. Some direct evidence comes from the studies reported in the previous section of people who received abnormal hormone doses in prenatal life. These studies indicate that boys and girls who received unusually high doses of androgen were more likely to have a higher level of energy and prefer boys' toys and activities. This was not unfocused hyperactivity; it involved a high degree of rough, outdoor play.[87]

The increased activity of the children with excessive hormonal doses may not be the same as aggression, which is usually defined as action with intent to hurt another (see discussion in Chapter 7). It may be that in acting out a female gender identity, these girls learn to pattern their activity in nonaggressive ways. This finding suggests that because the feminine role does not include aggressiveness, hormones cannot produce it. The hormones do influence the young women, but the influence is expressed in ways compatible with a feminine identity.

It is important to realize that the girls with excessive prenatal hormones had relatively normal hormonal dosages in postnatal life. They look like other girls, they are no bigger than other girls, and they have definite female gender identities. The boys with adrenogenital syndrome also experience excessive prenatal androgen doses, but look like other boys at birth. The subjects in these studies were generally given cortisone treatments to prevent the early onset of puberty and generally had corrective surgery to their genitals. Some authors have suggested that these medical treatments, rather than the prenatal doses of androgen, may be seen as influencing the results.[88] However, a study of children with abnormal prenatal hormone doses, but no abnormal genital development, revealed significant differences in aggressive tendencies.[89] Such findings have led researchers in this area to continue to suggest that the behavioral differences between the studied groups are influenced by the prenatal influences of hormones on the brain.

Ehrhardt and Baker did not find that the genetic boys who had received unusually large doses of androgen during fetal life were behaviorally different from their unaffected brothers except for the increased energy level.[90] This suggests that a certain level of prenatal male hormones is needed for "masculine" behavior but that excessive amounts will have little effect.[91]

Postnatal influences At puberty, the differences in hormone levels of the two sexes widen greatly. Girls begin to secrete more estrogens, and boys to secrete more androgens. Some studies of animals link the level of androgen in the body with the level of aggressive behavior although the causal direction of this link is not yet clear. These studies generally show a relationship between testosterone (an androgen) levels and various types of aggressive behaviors for males and females in a variety of species, including nonhuman primates.[92]

Yet, for both animals and humans, hormonal levels can fluctuate markedly as a result of changes in the social environment. Studies on humans that try to link the level of testosterone within individuals' bloodstream with their level of aggressive or criminal behavior have yielded conflicting results. The relationship may be stronger with certain types of aggressive behaviors and with younger men, but more evidence is needed.[93] Testosterone levels do appear to be associated with positions of dominance. Evidence from studies of nonhuman primates indicates that the more dominant animals have higher androgen levels than the less dominant animals,[94] and some have suggested that this model may apply to human groups as well.[95]

Under certain conditions, females are aggressive. Maternal aggression is found in many different species.[96] This behavior, whether involving attacks toward strangers or just general irritability, is usually directly related to pregnancy, parturition, and lactation. Among the primates, this aggression appears to be elicited largely by the distress of the young and is shown by others as well as the mother. Males in a primate troop and other females besides the mother may display strong defensive reactions for the young.[97]

In some cases animal mothers kill their young. However, this probably arises from a different endocrine base than maternal aggression, including an abnormally high level of androgen.[98]

Mood

Advertisements of medications to combat women's "premenstrual syndrome," or "PMS," and summaries of research on this syndrome commonly appear in magazines, newspapers, and on television.[99] Almost 60% of all women report that they experience discomfort or changes with their monthly menstrual period.[100] Some of the shifts in mood that women experience may result from negative attitudes toward the bodily functions, but some may result from the influence of different hormonal levels within the body. All living creatures experience cyclic changes. Sleep, pain tolerance, and cell division all appear to vary in regular cycles. Yet, among humans, women's mood changes during the monthly menstrual cycle have usually received the most research and popular attention.[101] Women secrete hormones in a fixed pattern, corresponding with the menstrual cycle. During the first half of the menstrual cycle, after menstruation, the secretion of estrogen rises. Midway through the cycle, ovulation occurs, as an egg is released from a follicle in one ovary. Estrogen secretion then drops, but begins to rise again about the 20th day of the cycle and finally drops quickly just before menstruation. Progesterone, also called the pregnancy hormone, increases after ovulation and peaks around the 20th day of the cycle. Its function is to prepare the body for pregnancy in case sperm fertilizes the egg. Just before menstruation the level of progesterone production falls markedly. There is some evidence that testosterone, a type of androgen, is secreted more heavily just before menstruation and also at ovulation.[102]

Hormones travel through the bloodstream and thus can potentially affect all parts of the body.[103] A number of studies have examined how women's periodic hormonal cycle affects mood fluctuations. Measures have included women's self-reports of moods, analyses of the content of their conversations, and observations of their behavior. Although some women have much wider mood changes than others, a good deal of evidence indicates that hostility, anxiety, and depression appear more during the premenstrual stage than in other parts of the cycle. Self-esteem and self-confidence seem to be highest in midcycle at ovulation.[104] Yet, as research in this area accumulates, it has become clear that no simple generalizations can be made about the incidence, symptoms, or source of PMS. Only a relatively small percentage of women experience the extremely debilitating symptoms associated with a clinical definition of this syndrome. Moreover, cultural beliefs about menstruation and women's cycles are extremely widespread, and hormonal secretions are influenced by environmental variables such as stress. Thus, any kind of complete understanding of premenstrual syndrome will need to understand its multiple dimensions and the interaction of hormonal, cultural, and social influences.[105]

Some evidence suggests that men as well as women experience cycles of hormonal secretions and mood. Several studies have documented relatively regular fluctuations of emotions or moods of both sex groups over a variety of time periods.[106] Other studies have noted fluctuations in the testosterone levels of males, with over half experiencing repeating cycles.[107] Even though men may have cyclical changes in mood and other bodily functions, it is not known if individual fluctuations in hormones are related to these changes. Relatively little research has examined this issue, and almost no work has compared women's mood fluctuations with men's.[108]

Whatever may eventually be found with regard to hormonal and mood fluctuations in men, we can say now that the attention given to these matters in women has often been used to disparage them. Both women and men have fluctuations in mood from one time to another. Yet, to say that women should not hold responsible positions because their monthly changes in hormonal secretions affect their moods is akin to saying that men should not hold responsible positions because of their biologically based aggressiveness!

Avoiding a Masculine Bias

In general, biological influences appear to affect psychological traits by increasing the likelihood that certain behaviors such as aggression or nurturance will appear. It is probably easier to prompt women to nurture and men to be aggressive because of prenatal hormonal influences and hormonal changes later in life. Yet, under certain circumstances, both women and men can nurture and both women and men can be aggressive. Hormones are neither necessary nor sufficient for these behaviors. Thus, that nurturance and aggression are influenced by biology does not mean that the social assignment of mothering to women and warfare to men is inevitable.

Although both men and women are subject to changes in mood, women's moods are somewhat more predictable than men's because they are more clearly influenced by cyclic hormonal changes. It is a masculine bias to assume that these cyclic changes are in themselves bad.

THE INFLUENCE OF BIOLOGY ON GENDER ROLES

Social scientists and feminists have often avoided biological explanations of gender differences. Yet, in actuality, the findings concerning biological differences between the sex groups do not degrade women and, in fact, indicate little or no basis for the patterns of male dominance found in human societies.

The findings reported in this chapter, as well as in Chapter 5, indicate that there may be biological influences on gender differences in social roles, including child care and food gathering; on psychological traits, such as nurturance and aggression; and on physical differences, such as strength, susceptibility to disease, and perceptual ability. From an evolutionary viewpoint these differences have been functional for the preservation of the human species. For example, women's hormonal impetus to nurturing is functional because extended periods of nurturance are vital for the development of the child's ability to relate to others. On the other hand, the physiological prompting of this nurturant response in women does not mean that men should not nurture. In fact, the power of infants themselves to evoke nurturant responses in both sex groups means that men, too, can nurture, and this provides additional guarantees for the well-being of the child.

Because they cannot lactate and physically provide milk for the young, males are not essential for the care of infants. Thus, men could be biologically prepared to fight off intruders and to capture game to supplement the regular food supply. The physical prompting of aggressive tendencies as well as males' greater strength and visual–spatial perceptual ability could enhance their skills in this area. As we saw in Chapter 5, however, the basic reason why males were the warmakers and hunters in the earliest human societies was most likely that they were simply more expendable than women.[109] Even females' lower susceptibility to illness and death may help contribute to group survival, because the presence of females who can nurture and bear children is more important to the group's ultimate survival.[110] It does not follow from all this, however, that a greater division of labor between the sex groups indicates better life possibilities.

Many popular writers who point out the biological impetus behind certain gender differences imply that this can explain all social phenomena. They also imply that these differences cannot be altered and that the status quo is inevitable and immutable. In contrast, social scientists and feminists correctly argue that humans are quite capable of structuring social situations and social roles to minimize the impact of physiological sex differences. Certainly, too, members of one sex group can learn to perform roles usually assigned to members of the other sex group. Biology may give cues for social roles, but it does not determine them.[111]

Some writers also contend that male dominance itself can be explained by biology. Yet the activities and roles toward which females are biologically prompted are more important to the long-term survival of the group than those of males. For example, the affectional bonds between mother and young and between female members of primate groups promote group cohesion and survival much more than dominance and aggression. Although biology can help explain the social role divisions between women and men, it cannot explain why men's activities are valued more highly than women's. In order to explain this, one must look for theories that take into account the unique capacity of humans to imagine, to interpret, and to create meaning from their physical and social world.

SUMMARY

Physical differences between females and males first develop before birth. Although all embryos have a bipotential physical structure, the presence of either the XY or XX sex chromosomes prompts the development of the testes or the ovaries. In males, the testes produce the sex hormones that prompt the development of male genitalia. Without the hormone mix normally secreted prenatally by males, the fetus will develop female genitalia.

At birth, a child is pronounced female or male. This social decision is based on gender identity, a person's conviction that he or she is a male or a female. This gender identity develops very early in life and is virtually impossible to change after a young age. Transsexuals form a gender identity that does not match their genitalia. Although this condition is very rare, some transsexuals have had surgery to transform their bodies to match their gender identity.

Males and females do differ physically. Differences occur in size, strength, incidence of illness and death, perception, and of course reproductive functions. Physiological differences between males and females may also be related to sex differences in nurturance, aggression, and changes in mood.

Although some of these physical differences have probably been important in the maintenance of human society and the preservation of the species, none of the physical differences can account for the maintenance of male dominance.

SUGGESTED READINGS

BLEIER, RUTH. 1984. *Science and Gender: A Critique of Biology and Its Theories on Women.* New York: Pergamon Press.

FAUSTO-STERLING, ANNE. 1985. *Myths of Gender: Biological Theories About Women and Men.* New York: Basic Books. Critical reviews of the literature on biological influences on gender roles.

HALL, ROBERTA L., with PATRICIA DRAPER, MARGARET E. HAMILTON, DIANE MCGUINNESS, CHARLOTTE M. OTTEN, and ERIC A. ROTH. 1985. *Male–Female Differences: A Bio-Cultural Perspective.* New York: Praeger. A collection of essays reviewing the literature on the influence of both biological and social variables on gender differences.

MONEY, JOHN, and PATRICIA TUCKER. 1975. *Sexual Signatures: On Being a Man or a Woman.* Boston: Little, Brown. Well-written explanation of the development of physical gender differences and gender identity.

TRAVIS, CHERYL BROWN. 1988. *Women and Health Psychology: Biomedical Issues.* Hillsdale, N.J.: Erlbaum. A review of research on many aspects related to women's health.

chapter 7

Psychological Gender Differences

In part because of the feminist movement, psychologists' interest in gender differences was rekindled. Fortunately, now there is a new awareness of gender stereotyping and of the relationship of these stereotypes to male dominance. We are also more aware of the ways in which some research findings of difference have been exaggerated and how differences that do exist have been conceptualized in terms of a male bias.

In this chapter, after discussing gender stereotyping, we will review cross-cultural research and work that focuses on the United States to assess similarities and differences between the sex groups in personality characteristics and abilities. We shall also review evidence concerning the causes of these differences.

In the last part of the chapter after a discussion of attempts to measure individual gender differences, we shift our focus from specific differences in traits and abilities to a discussion of attempts to generalize about how traits are organized in the personalities of the two sex groups. Here we discuss qualitative typologies that seek to capture in a global way basic differences in orientation between the sex groups.

In discussing the ways in which the sex groups are psychologically the same and the ways in which they are different, we are not trying in any direct way to explain male dominance, but simply to get a picture of what exists. Getting that picture is an ongoing process, and all the evidence is by no means in. Nevertheless, although the sex groups probably differ less than we once thought, they do differ, and in order to construct a more egalitarian society we need to take these differences into account. So far, our society has tended toward the view that women should be more like men. Some of the findings and interpretations in this chapter suggest the reverse.

GENDER STEREOTYPES AND MALE BIAS

In the early 1970s a group of researchers in the northeast United States conducted a series of studies on gender stereotyping of personality characteristics.[1] These researchers began their work by asking a group of undergraduate men and women to list all the ways they thought men and women differed psychologically. They then listed all the traits that the students mentioned at least twice, placing them in a bipolar form on a continuum ranging from one extreme to the other with 60 points in between. Using a number of other samples of men and women from 17 to 60 years of age, they asked respondents to indicate the extent to which each item characterized adult men and adult women. For instance, on the item ranging from "not at all aggressive" to "very aggressive," respondents would indicate the closeness of the typical adult man or typical adult woman to each pole.

The researchers found extensive agreement on the nature of these stereotypes and on the values attached to them. Men were consistently characterized as more aggressive, independent, objective, dominant, active, competitive, logical, worldly, and ambitious than women. Men were also stereotyped as less emotional, excitable, and dependent than women. Women were stereotyped as more talkative, tactful, gentle, religious, neat, and sensitive to others than men. These researchers suggest that, in general, males are perceived as more competent than females and females as more warm and expressive than males. The researchers also found that more of the traits stereotyped as masculine than those stereotyped as feminine were perceived as desirable; that is, both male and female respondents considered the masculine poles of the various items socially desirable more often than the feminine poles. In later years many other studies replicated these results, both in the United States and, to a large extent, cross-culturally.[2]

Work in recent years has focused on how gender stereotypes affect people's interpretations of men's and women's behavior. Most of the studies have focused on interpretations of achievement and success. Because people hold gender stereotypes, they often attribute one meaning to behavior exhibited by a man and a different meaning when the same behavior is exhibited by a woman, even in tightly controlled and carefully devised experimental settings. In other words, even when men and women behave the same, people interpret their behavior in different ways. In general, these studies suggest that men's achievements are more likely to be attributed to their ability, whereas women's achievements are more often attributed to either effort or luck.[3]

Information about the roles that men and women hold can affect the nature of the stereotypes that people express. One study compared subjects' beliefs about the characteristics of women and men with various levels of paid employment. The results suggest that housewives are perceived in more stereotypically feminine ways than working women, and men who work full time are seen as more stereotypically masculine than those who work only part time.[4] Yet social roles are only one characteristic that appears to affect stereotypes. In general, the way in which gender stereotypes affect attributions and attitudes is very complex, and psychologists are just beginning to understand more about this process.[5]

Because of the evidence suggesting that gender stereotypes strongly influence how we interpret males' and females' behavior, it is important to recognize that social science professionals as well as the general population are likely to evaluate any differences in favor of males. Even when the differences themselves cannot be readily interpreted as favoring males, the author's exposition may make it seem that males "win out." As an example, J. E. Garai and Aram Scheinfeld, in a review of findings concerning gender differences in verbal and mathematical abilities, displayed a systematic male bias in their interpretation and reporting.[6] Mary Parlee documented their bias by calculating that in the 76 comparisons Garai and Scheinfeld made between the abilities of females and males, they used some form of the word *superior* ("male superiority has been shown on . . .") to characterize 46% of the comparisons where males scored higher but used it in only 27% of the cases where females' scores were higher. This gives the impression that males performed considerably better than females in the experiments reviewed, whereas actually a simple count of the findings shows that females scored higher in the majority of the comparisons.[7]

In this instance, male bias does not show up in the appraisal of traits but in overuse of such terms as *superior* and *surpassed* to characterize male scores. Recent attempts to summarize findings on gender differences are much more sensitive to male bias in the assessment of differences and have moved to correct them. Several articles in the field provide guidelines for researchers hoping to avoid a male bias.[8]

CROSS-CULTURAL STUDIES

The work of Margaret Mead, especially her *Sex and Temperament in Three Primitive Societies* (1935), is the classic refutation of the idea that gender differences are the same the world over.[9] In comparing the Arapesh and the Mundugamor peoples in New Guinea, Mead showed that many of the characteristics Americans classify as typically male or female are classified differently in these cultures. Among the Arapesh, both men and women are nurturant, gentle, and compliant. Relations of husband and wife are patterned after those of mother and child, and the Arapesh husband speaks of "growing" his much younger wife. According to Mead, the personalities of males and females in this society are not sharply differentiated by gender. Both boys and girls learn to be cooperative, unaggressive, and responsive to the needs and demands of others.[10] In contrast, the Mundugamor are headhunters and cannibals, and both males and females are aggressive, highly sexed, and nonnurturant. Thus, among the Arapesh, both sex groups would seem feminine to us, whereas both sex groups among the Mundugamor would seem exaggeratedly masculine. Neither the Arapesh nor the Mundugamor makes aggressiveness or nurturance specific to one sex group. These sharp contrasts with our society indicate that culture may play a powerful role in shaping the personalities of both sex groups.

Perhaps the most interesting group Mead studied was the Tchambuli. This society virtually reverses our own gender roles and stereotypes. The women are brisk, efficient, managerial, impersonal, and unadorned whereas the men are decorated and vain and spend their time carving, painting, and practicing dance steps. This marked contrast again shows the power of culture, "that a culture can select a few traits from the wide gamut of human endowment and specialize these traits either for one sex or for the entire community."[11]

Even though male and female personality traits are similar among the Mundugamor and Arapesh and reversed among the Tchambuli, gender roles and status are differentiated in all three societies. Among the Mundugamor, the women provide the food, whereas the men are the much admired headhunters. Among the Arapesh, during certain rituals, the wife is required to act like an ignorant child, clearly subordinate to her husband. Finally, even though Tchambuli women are traders and have considerable economic power, they still must engage in a tribal ritual that marks them as inferior to men in knowledge and morality. All societies have some cultural mechanism, whether it be religious, political, or economic, that marks females as inferior to males.

Although gender typing takes different forms and may be maximized or minimized within a given culture, some fairly constant gender-linked characteristics appear in children in a wide variety of cultures. Some knowledge about cross-cultural variations in personality gender differences comes from reviewing ethnographic observations of anthropologists in many different cultures over the years.[12] Other more systematic knowledge comes from careful observations of children in different cultures such as those described by Beatrice and John Whiting and Carolyn Edwards.[13] These authors and their associates observed boys and girls from 13 cultures who were under the age of 11. They observed them in carefully chosen time sequences at home, at play, and at assigned tasks.

In their latest analysis of these data, Whiting and Edwards examined five major areas of interpersonal behavior: nurturance, dependency, prosocial dominance, egoistic dominance, and sociability.[14] Gender differences appear consistently in two of these areas among children old enough to walk. On the average, girls are more nurturant than boys. They more often interact with younger children, care for them, and respond to their needs. Boys are more often egoistically dominant than girls. That is, they more often try to change others' behavior to satisfy their own desires, without consideration of the needs or wants of the other person. There are no consistent gender differences in dependency, sociability, or prosocial dominance behavior, designed to persuade others to act in a socially approved manner.

Although Whiting and Edwards did not dismiss the possibility that these differences may have a physiological base,[15] they suggested that they more likely reflect different interaction situations, different role expectations, and also different behaviors of the children themselves. As a result, girls come to develop and prefer different interpersonal habits and skills.

The others with whom one interacts help influence behavior. Infants evoke nurturance, and parents tend to inhibit aggressive behavior and evoke more intimate touching and help-seeking behavior. The reason for the greater nurturance of girls and their lesser egoistical dominance may be that they interact with infants and parents more than boys do. On the other hand, this cannot explain all the gender differences in personality, because some remain in all interactional settings.[16]

At least some of these differences seem to be prompted by children's own actions. Boys may tend to avoid adults because adults usually squelch aggressiveness, at least toward themselves. By avoiding adults and largely participating in same-sex play groups, boys may reinforce their propensity for their own dominance. By staying closer to adults and adult women in particular, girls may develop nurturant skills and minimize egoistically dominant tendencies as they participate more in interactions with an older generation. This may also involve an element of role modeling as the girls try to emulate their mothers' behaviors.

Finally, assignment of responsibilities or social roles also helps explain gender differences in behavior. The Whitings and Edwards found that in all cultures studied, girls care for infant siblings more often than boys. Girls, then, are expected to be nurturant. Herbert Barry, Margaret Bacon, and Irvin Child's large study of gender differences in socialization practices in 110 cultures also found differential role expectations for boys and girls.[17] Pressures toward nurturance, responsibility, and (less clearly) obedience are most often stronger for girls, whereas pressures toward achievement and self-reliance are most often stronger for boys. The Whitings' and Edwards' findings suggest that the sex groups do not differ on prosocial behavior that may be similar to acting responsibly, but they do differ with respect to nurturance. If one can equate the seeking of dominance and attention with achievement, then boys in the studies do, in fact, emphasize these behaviors, and perhaps socialization pressures influence this emphasis. On the other hand, these behaviors appear early and do not change with age, suggesting that socialization may not be a major influence.

Clearly, more cross-cultural studies are needed if we are to increase our confidence in our knowledge about gender differences. Most of what we know comes from data collected on middle-class white children in the United States and Great Britain. But as we shall see, the cross-cultural findings on social behaviors parallel quite closely those obtained from the large number of studies done in the United States.

SIMILARITIES AND DIFFERENCES IN TRAITS AND BEHAVIORAL TENDENCIES

Eleanor Maccoby and Carol Jacklin's *Psychology of Sex Differences* was a path-breaking work.[18] They took on the time-consuming and painstaking task of summarizing, categorizing, and interpreting approximately 1,600 studies concerned with psychological gender differences. They reported not just some but, insofar as was possible, all of the findings, both those showing differences and those showing no differences between the sex groups in a given area. Since their book appeared, other authors have followed in their footsteps, often using sophisticated statistical techniques called meta-analyses to summarize the results of many studies.[19] This complete coverage is an extremely important safeguard against the tendency to accept "congenial truths," that is, to examine and note only the findings compatible with one's biases.

Looking at all the studies in an area also helps combat what Maccoby and Jacklin call the "primacy effect" in beliefs about scientific truths. It may take an overwhelming amount of negative evidence, not just a preponderance, to refute an original erroneous impression, especially if it involves an exciting positive finding. For example, a study on 13-month-old infants' behavior in the face of an obstacle indicated that although girls tended to cry, boys tended to try to move the barrier or go around it.[20] This was obviously a truth congenial to those with a masculine bias. A number of feminists also tended to accept it and explained the behavior differences in terms of socialization: Mothers must have somehow encouraged their daughters in dependency and their sons in active mastery. At any rate, all assumed that findings from this one study settled the matter. Actually, Maccoby and Jacklin found a number of studies that contradict these findings, and they concluded that there was insufficient evidence concerning gender differences in dependency for a clear-cut answer at that time.[21] Although it is tempting to cite a study in detail and then generalize about the findings, it is clearly better to look at the total array of relevant studies before coming to conclusions.

But this procedure, too, involves some difficulties. In the first place, not all of the studies are equally well designed or even accurate. For example, observations of actual behavior may contradict self-ratings of behavior. Findings of no difference between the sex groups are also less often reported than findings of statistically significant gender differences. On the other hand, in studies not specifically dealing with gender differences, a difference that appears may not be reported, simply because the editor of the journal publishing the research cut the article to its stated essentials to save space. In fact, many of the findings that Maccoby and Jacklin and others have used are accidental or incidental to other scientific concerns.

Frequently the nature of gender differences varies with age. Maccoby and Jacklin restricted their survey to studies of the early childhood years, although they included some data on college students. In general, the younger the child, the less likely differences are to be found. When one studies young adults, one is likely to discover a great many differences in social roles revolving around work, marriage, and child care rather than basic differences in orientation and capacities. If one is interested in understanding gender differences in basic orientations and capacities, it is probably best to observe young children.

Finally, we must remember that when we speak of psychological gender differences, we are never dealing with categorical differences, but with central tendencies. Individuals from each sex group will always overlap considerably, and the within-group differences may be greater than the between-group differences. For instance, the difference between the most aggressive girl and the least aggressive girl in a group may be much larger than the difference between the average aggressiveness of the girls and the average of the boys.

Furthermore, the most aggressive girl will probably be more aggressive than a large number of males.[22]

Using Maccoby and Jacklin's categories, but primarily reviewing newer studies, we examine gender differences and similarities in four major areas: temperament, social approach–avoidance, power relationships, and mental abilities and achievement. Because most of the studies in these areas used middle-class whites as subjects, we are usually unable to make generalizations about variations in these findings across social class and racial-ethnic groups.

Temperament

Temperament refers to both general activity level and emotionality. Activity level is not a consistent characteristic of individual children from one time to another during the preschool years. Rather, it responds to a number of emotional states and to other people in the environment. Nevertheless, a careful and extensive review of 205 results in this area found that males tend to be more physically active than females. These differences appear with all age groups, in various types of settings, and with different forms of research observation. The differences tend to be smaller with younger subjects and in settings that are unfamiliar, more stressful, and more restricted. They are larger, however, when peers are present.[23]

Although on the average girls are less active than boys, the findings do not justify calling girls passive. Helene Deutsch defined female passivity as "activity turned inward," and it would seem that only in this sense could girls be called passive.[24] Although boys are running around, girls may be concentrating.

In contrast to the stereotype of women as emotional and easily frustrated, the sex groups probably do not differ in the first year of life in the frequency and duration of crying. There is some evidence, however, that boys after the age of about 18 months have more outbursts of negative emotion in reponse to frustration. This does not necessarily lead to constructive action and may in some cases impede such action. A little later, it appears that the gender differences in frustration responses are caused not so much by boys increasing the frequency and intensity of their emotional reactions as by girls decreasing theirs at a faster rate than boys.[25] Thus, the differences found here contradict the stereotype, with boys displaying more frequent and intense emotional outbursts than girls.[26]

With respect to fear and timidity, teacher ratings and self-reports indicate that girls are more timid and anxious than boys. In contrast, observational studies usually do not show such a difference, especially when young subjects are studied. The self-report and teacher-rating data may simply indicate differences in willingness to admit to certain behavior and gender stereotypes. Because most of the data on fear and timidity come from self-reports and because researchers have used few physiological measures of these responses, researchers generally feel that they can reach no firm conclusions on this subject, and they speculate that the answer may turn out to depend on the particular stimulus situation. Girls may be more afraid of some things and boys more afraid of others.[27]

In summary, these findings indicate that there are gender differences in temperament, yet they do not create a picture of generalized masculine activity, impulsiveness, or bravery or feminine passivity.

Social Approach–Avoidance

Perhaps no stereotype of females is as pervasive as the belief that women are dependent. No one questions that many females are economically dependent on males, but does economic dependence mean psychological dependence? Much work on gender roles assumes that it does, and then argues that women are somehow socialized to be dependent. However, dependency, defined as seeking nurturance, help, or care, does not represent a single identifiable cluster in the social behavior of young children. Rather, there are proximity-seeking behaviors and attention-seeking behaviors, as well as sociable behaviors and social skills. Furthermore, the tendency to direct these behaviors toward adults is relatively independent of the tendency to direct them toward age mates.[28]

Maccoby and Jacklin suggested, then, that dependence may involve proximity-seeking behaviors and a broader category of behaviors that include social responsiveness, social interests, and social skills. They included here also attention-seeking behaviors (which boys engage in more than girls).

Proximity seeking Using both experimental data and some cross-cultural data, Maccoby and Jacklin concluded that there are no firm gender differences in the tendency to seek out contact with others. This conclusion holds whether the objects of attachment are adults or other children.[29] Based on their extensive cross-cultural work, Whiting and Edwards suggested that gender differences in proximity seeking and dependency do not appear, because all human infants have a common genetic heritage and common needs.[30] All young children, both boys and girls, need and seek help from caregivers, and adults respond to these needs with nurturance toward both male and female young.

Sociability One of the more firmly entrenched ideas about gender differences has been that girls are more social than boys. Yet extensive reviews of studies in the United States and cross-culturally suggest that this broad social–nonsocial distinction does not differentiate the sex groups in infancy or even in later years.[31]

As proximity-seeking behaviors give way to more complex forms of sociability, boys and girls remain very similar in the amount of friendly interaction they have with nonfamily adults. Girls have no greater sensitivity to social cues and are not more "empathic" than boys.[32] In fact, Maccoby and Jacklin suggested that the social judgment skills of males have been "seriously underrated."[33]

Even though boys and girls do not differ in sociability when seen as an individual personality trait, they do differ in *patterns* of social relations. One of the most striking differences is the gender of those they seek out. Boys overwhelmingly prefer to play with other boys; girls prefer to play with other girls. These preferences appear by the age of 3, remain strong until preadolescence,[34] and are found not just in the United States, but cross-culturally.[35] The other major difference involves style of interaction. Boys are much more likely than girls to engage in a rough-and-tumble play style.[36] When trying to influence others in play settings, girls more often use "polite suggestions," whereas boys more often use direct demands.[37] Maccoby suggested that girls tend to find interactions with boys who prefer rough-and-tumble play and are unresponsive to polite suggestions so aversive that they begin to avoid them as play partners, thus reinforcing the tendency to select same-sex playmates.[38]

The finding that members of both sex groups are equally social, but differ in their patterns of interaction, provides an important conceptual clarification. It can counter stereotypes that suggest that women are motivated externally by a desire to please, are more dependent on social rewards, and lack inner motivation for action. Men, by contrast, sound principled, autonomous, and even immune from social constraints. In fact, neither sex group is exempt from the rules governing social interaction, neither is free from the effects of social rewards or social punishment, and neither is unsocial.

Nurturance There is much evidence on older children and adults to suggest that women and girls do nurture others more than men and boys. Yet, in their classic review of the literature, Maccoby and Jacklin left open the question of whether the sex groups differ with respect to nurturance, primarily because there were so few studies concerning nurturant behavior in young children. The more recent extensive cross-cultural work of Whiting and Edwards concluded that from the age of about 2 years, girls are, on average, more nurturant than boys. This difference need not be seen as biologically based, but can be accounted for by the greater amount of time girls interact with younger children in all of the cultures studied.[39]

Both men and boys are nurturant when given the opportunity. In addition, men are more likely than women to display helping behavior toward strangers in field studies and laboratory settings.[40] Thus, although men's nurturing may be impeded by both male hormones and by definitions of proper masculinity, there is every indication that men and boys have the capacity to be nurturant. In addition, when social roles prescribe such behavior, they are more likely than women to exhibit caring and helpful behavior toward others.

It is interesting that those who consider women to be passive usually fail to consider that the nurturance they often also attribute to women has a very active character. As Maccoby and Jacklin suggested in another context, "Training a girl to be 'feminine' in the traditional nonassertive, 'helpless' and self-deprecatory sense may actually make her a worse mother,"[41] because, in caring for the child, she has total control over the child's well-being. In fact, dependency needs are likely to be the greatest danger to successful motherhood.[42]

In summary, from all of the studies relating to the issue of social approach–avoidance, it appears that both groups are highly sociable and responsive to social cues. The difference does not lie in degree of sociability, but in the specific patterning of the social interactions. One important difference in these patterns is that boys tend to play in larger groups, whereas girls tend to have more intimate friendships in twos or sometimes threes. Large groups more often have a dominance hierarchy, whereas twosomes can easily function on an egalitarian basis. This leads us to a discussion of how males and females differ in power relations, both in same-gender and in cross-gender groupings.

Power Relationships

War has always tended to be the province of men. Both the seizing of territory, possessions, or governments by force and the forceful resistance to such attempts have been male activities. Males also engage in person-to-person combat much more than females do. There is much to suggest that males are naturally aggressive. In this section, we explore the research evidence on gender differences in aggression, competition, and dominance and try to understand the complex relationships among them.

Aggression In contrast to many traits studied by psychologists, aggression is generally defined as consisting of both actions and motives whose central theme is the intent to hurt. In essence, aggression is the expression of hostile feelings.[43] Actually, it would be almost impossible to define aggression without taking intent into account. For example, even some very careful behavioral studies employ an operational definition of aggression that is designed to measure intent. D. R. Omark, M. Omark, and M. Edelman defined aggression as "pushing or hitting without smiling." Not smiling (unless, of course, the push was accidental) would indicate the individual was not kidding and intended to hurt. These researchers have done extensive observations on school playgrounds in the United States, Switzerland, and Ethiopia and found a greater incidence of hitting without smiling among boys in all three countries.[44] Their findings are typical. Extensive meta-analyses of gender differences in aggression strongly indicate that boys are more aggressive than girls.[45]

Although almost everyone is convinced that boys are physically more aggressive than girls, some argue that girls are more verbally aggressive than boys and that although boys aggress directly, girls aggress indirectly. According to this hypothesis, the two sex groups are equally aggressive in their underlying motivation, but characteristically show aggression in different ways. Although gender differences in physical aggression tend to be larger than those for verbal and psychological aggression, males are more likely than females to display both kinds of aggression.[46] In addition, there is evidence that verbal aggression is not so much an alternative to physical aggression as it is a prelude to it. Anyone who had heard boys shouting insults to one another before the fists start flying can attest to this possibility. Even the studies that treat girls' propensity for "tattling" and "excluding" as evidence for aggression do not provide clear-cut evidence that girls make up for more overt aggression by these means. For example, in a study often cited in support of the hypothesis that girls and boys express aggression in different modes, girls in two-person groups tended to ignore, avoid, and exclude a third person initially more than boys. However, this behavior only lasted for about 4 minutes before the girls warmed up.[47] Maccoby and Jacklin also questioned whether it is legitimate to call initial lack of acceptance of a newcomer aggression in the sense of intent to hurt, especially because girls usually play in two-person groups and boys do not.[48]

It is true that girls have more anxiety about aggression than boys. Some have interpreted this to mean that girls have aggressive tendencies equal to those of boys, but repress them out of fear of punishment or retaliation. Maccoby and Jacklin suggested, however, that if this were so, surely the aggression would come out in some attenuated form. What actually happens, though, is that males act out aggressive impulses in play and fantasies as well as in reality.[49] In addition, boys are more likely than girls to aggress in the presence of weakness in another male. Girls do not respond to weakness in either boys or girls with aggression. Surely, if girls were repressing great amounts of aggression, they would take it out in a disguised form or on a nonthreatening person. But they do not. In summary, then, the evidence, both from the United States and cross-culturally, suggests that males really are more aggressive than females—both physically and verbally, directly and indirectly, and in a wide variety of settings.

Even though meta-analyses and narrative reviews of the literature indicate that gender differences in aggression appear at all ages, they are smaller with adults than with children.[50] The largest differences appear with preschoolers.[51] Clearly, then, aggression is socially patterned and affected by role expectations;[52] boys learn to control their aggressive desires as they grow older.

Role expectations also affect women's aggression. Reviews of the experimental literature on aggression argue that women may act as aggressively as men under certain conditions. These conditions generally involve situations where the women do not empathize with the victim and in which they feel the aggression is justified.[53] One such justification that cannot be very well tested on humans is a threat to their offspring. It is possible that we rarely see aggression in human females simply because they are rarely faced with a direct threat to their children. On the other hand, of all the traits discussed, aggressiveness does appear to be most clearly a generalized trait that characterizes males far more than females and that probably has a biological base. (See also Chapter 6.)

To say that aggression is biologically based, however, does not explain its social patterning—how it appears in social roles—nor does it in itself explain the greater prestige given to males. It is important that readers be aware of their own biases regarding the value of aggressiveness. In a society governed by a masculine paradigm, aggression is likely to have desirable connotations. In the public mind, it is often associated with competitiveness, single-mindedness, or strong will. Steven Goldberg, in his *The Inevitability of Patriarchy*, used the assessment that males are more aggressive than females to construct a theory to explain the universality of male dominance. Goldberg argued in effect that because of their innate aggressiveness, males "try harder." Goldberg argued that feminists agree with him that aggressiveness explains male dominance and said that the only difference between him and feminists is that the latter claim that masculine aggressiveness is learned and not innate and that, therefore, women could learn it too.[54] Some feminists might take this position, but they are operating within a male paradigm that sees aggression as a desirable characteristic. In contrast, many feminists today do not define aggression as a positive trait and argue that it is as likely to interfere with constructive activity as it is to underlie it. In fact, the common definition of aggression as the intent to hurt can be seen as emphasizing its antisocial nature.

Competition The evidence regarding gender differences in competitiveness is not as clear-cut as the evidence on masculine aggressiveness. Almost all the research on competition has involved situations contrived to make competitiveness maladaptive to eventual success.[55] For example, research using the prisoner's dilemma game for measuring cooperation has not consistently shown males to be more competitive. It is likely that if studies were designed so that competitiveness led to individual success or dominance, males would more clearly show up as more competitive than females. Although masculine aggression may reinforce greater masculine competitiveness, this does not mean that females are born to lose because they are less motivated to compete. Rather, it seems that although constructive behaviors among males may be motivated by aggressive competitive motives, constructive behaviors among females may have different underlying motives.[56] As we shall see in a later section, boys' achievement efforts and imagery in many spheres are enhanced in a competitive situation, whereas girls' are not. Girls are motivated to achieve, but not necessarily by competitive or aggressive motives.

Dominance As in other areas, the findings concerning gender differences in dominance behaviors depend in part on how one defines the concept of dominance. If toughness (giving out and taking physical abuse) is the criterion, then boys win hands down. Although there is some overlap, boys are considered tougher than girls as early as nursery-school age. On the other hand, if dominance is defined broadly enough to include moral leadership, behavior that is in fact controlling, or behavior in which one resists the control of others, then women too may dominate others.

As with aggression, dominance struggles tend to occur between males, not between males and females. In childhood, boys and girls tend to play in gender-segregated groups, thus preventing direct confrontation. In the adult occupational world, much the same thing seems to happen. Occupational segregation prevents direct competition between males and females and indirectly between husbands and wives.

Gender differences in dominance behavior are most apparent when all-boy and all-girl groups are studied. All-male groups are more concerned with egoistic dominance. Boys more often interrupt one another, use commands and threats, refuse to comply with others' requests, and call one another names. In contrast, girls more often take turns speaking, give polite directives, and express agreement with one another.[57] Whiting and Edwards documented similar patterns in their extensive cross-cultural work.[58] These gender differences in interactive style continue into adolescence and adulthood, with men more often using what has been called a *restrictive* style that seeks to inhibit partners, and women more often using an *enabling* or facilitative style that tries to support partners and maintain an interaction.[59] Perhaps reflecting these different styles, meta-analytic studies of persuadability and influence indicate a small to moderate tendency for women to conform to and be persuaded by others more than men.[60]

Despite these differences, it should be stressed that girls are not unassertive or that they lack a goal orientation. They simply pursue goals at the same time that they try to maintain group cohesion.[61] Similarly, boys' interactive style does not prevent group functioning; instead, the dominance-oriented interactions may be central to some of their group activities, such as team sports.[62]

Although young boys often use direct aggression in their dominance attempts, they do so less and less as they grow older. The status hierarchy in human societies seldom reflects prowess in physical aggression. Nowadays it is brains not brawn that is rewarded, and there remains only a symbolic connection between fighting and success. Raw aggression is more of an impediment than a help to making it in the higher circles of power. Thus, if aggressive and dominance needs motivate adult males to work and achieve, these needs must undergo considerable socializing in the life history of the individual. Like aggression, the term *dominance* tends to have a positive meaning in a society controlled by a masculine paradigm. Such a paradigm defines the issue as "dominate or be dominated." A feminine paradigm, on the other hand, might deny the necessity for either dominance or submission. Resistance to domination would be desirable, but not domination itself.

Mental Abilities and Achievement

There are no differences in measured intelligence between boys and girls, in part because test items that differentiate between males and females are discarded in establishing norms for these intelligence tests.[63] There are some gender differences in special academic skills, and girls generally receive better grades than boys. This appears in the early years of school, continues through junior high and high school, and still appears in college. On the other hand, as earlier chapters also showed, men are more often found in the prestigious and lucrative occupations and are more likely to obtain graduate and professional degrees than women. It would be easy to assume that women's failure to attain these positions is related to deficiencies in their mental capacities, but this is not supported by the evidence.

Analytic ability Analytic ability involves the ability to break a problem down into its component parts in order to reach a solution. It requires a capacity to restructure and to inhibit a previously established set toward a problem.

Although there may be other ways to solve a problem than through analytic ability and there may be kinds of problems that do not lend themselves to solution through analytic ability, in modern Western society analytic ability is highly valued and is ordinarily thought to be more characteristic of males than of females.

Actually, the question of gender differences in such abilities cannot be answered with a simple yes or no, because different kinds of tests measure what appear to be different facets of this ability. We do know with considerable certainty that at a very general level it is not true that girls are better at rote learning and simple repetitive tasks and that boys are better at tasks requiring higher-level cognitive processes and inhibition of previously learned responses.[64] We also know that although men are better than women at tests measuring visual–spatial ability, such as the Rod and Frame Test and the Embedded Figures Test,[65] these are not tests of any general ability to think analytically, but measures of a much more specific perceptual skill.[66]

A better measure of analytic ability may be tests that measure the ability to break set or restructure. Males are rather clearly better than females on such tests when they involve set breaking in a quantitative context. On the other hand, Maccoby and Jacklin argued that females may be slightly more adept than males at set breaking in a verbal context where the task is to recombine letters to make words, as in anagrams.[67] Jeanne Block argued, however, that anagram studies are not true measures of insight, because the subjects are explicitly instructed to make as many words as possible from the letters, whereas in the other insight tests, subjects are not explicitly instructed on how to proceed, and thus must arrive on their own at the insight that restructuring is needed.[68]

While Block is technically correct that the test instructions are different in anagrams than in other insight tests, Maccoby and Jacklin are correct in arguing that there may be different kinds of insight and that all kinds need to be considered before coming to the conclusion that males are better at set breaking in general. In fact, there are so many aspects of intelligence and analytic ability that formal tests can only begin to tap a few of these.[69] For instance, "behavioral intelligence" may be seen as "the capacity to interpret and to respond accurately and appropriately to behavioral cues."[70] Even though early studies found that females did better than males on tests of this type of behavior,[71] the concept has been virtually ignored by scholars.

Verbal and mathematical ability Girls consistently indicate that they are more interested in and like the language arts and other verbal activities more than boys,[72] and for many years studies indicated that girls have greater verbal ability than boys.[73] Boys are more likely than girls to stutter, and males appear to have more language impairment and more difficulty recovering language ability following strokes and brain surgery.[74]

In this country girls' better reading skills usually appear by the first grade.[75] Although boys and girls with equal scores on reading readiness tests appear to achieve equally well in reading in the first grade,[76] more girls than boys seem to be ready to read. Careful analyses of the process by which children learn to read indicate that this difference in readiness stems from girls' greater overall verbal fluency in areas directly related to reading skills.[77] Because boys develop these skills more slowly, they tend to take somewhat longer to learn to read, although by high school gender differences in reading ability have disappeared.[78]

Females' greater verbal fluency begins to appear strongly at about age 10 or 11 and continues through high school and college.[79] Sex differences are most apparent in measures of specific skills. These include spelling and punctuation, but also high-level skills such as "comprehension of complex written text, quick understanding of complex logical relations expressed in verbal terms, and in some instances, verbal creativity."[80] There is some evidence that girls' greater verbal skills may help explain their higher grades, even in traditionally male areas such as the sciences.[81] Nevertheless, gender differences in verbal ability are relatively small. In addition, they appear to have declined in recent years to the extent that some psychologists conclude that gender differences in this area no longer exist.[82]

Gender differences in quantitative ability also appear most strongly after puberty. Girls learn to count sooner than boys do[83] and do better than boys in computational tasks at all ages. By the upper grades boys tend to do better in various types of problem solving,[84] even though girls continue to receive better grades in all areas. Meta-analytic studies indicate that, as with verbal ability, gender differences in quantitative ability have declined in recent years. The only area in which males continue to do better is in tests of problem solving at the high-school and college levels, especially in highly selective samples of precocious youth. Although news articles often highlight males' higher scores on the Scholastic Aptitude Tests (SAT), these results appear to be idiosyncratic.[85]

Boys also begin to show more interest and better performance in science areas at adolescence. Females' generally greater interest in verbal areas and males' greater interest in science continue into college and adult occupational lives as males and females major in different academic areas and enter different occupational fields.

Even though gender differences in quantitative ability are quite small and appear only with specific skills and specific subgroups, they have received a great deal of attention. Several explanations for these differences have been suggested. Three of these involve characteristics of students: Boys and girls may have different achievement patterns because they take different courses, because they have different skills, or because they have different interests including an interest generated by the gender typing of an area as masculine or feminine.

Differential course taking does not seem to account for gender differences in mathematics ability that appear on tests such as the SAT among intellectually gifted students,[86] but does seem to account for differences that appear among other students.[87] Gender differences in visual–spatial ability may help account for some aspects of mathematical ability, perhaps especially those related to geometry,[88] although meta-analyses suggest that the association is questionable.[89] Students' interests appear to account for more of the variation in test scores and course taking. Analyses of the content of test questions with large gender differences indicate that females generally do better on items that deal with aesthetics, interpersonal relationships, and traditionally female tasks such as typing and sewing. Males do better on questions with content that focuses on science, practical affairs, and sports.[90] Perceptions of the gender typing of career areas linked to mathematics, perceived interest in the fields, feelings of self-confidence in mathematics, and self-perception help account for females' lower scores on mathematical tests and participation in areas requiring quantitative skills.[91]

It must be stressed that gender differences in achievement are much smaller than the popular media would lead one to believe. Within the general population, differences in mathematical ability are virtually nonexistent. Women college students are just as likely to choose mathematics as a major as they are to choose to major in the social sciences. Even though small gender differences persist in SAT scores, these are unrepresentative of other results and are extremely small when compared to differences in the income and occupational status of adult men and women.[92]

Adult achievement None of these findings concerning gender differences in abilities, however, can directly account for the fact that, in comparison to women, adult men hold the prestigious jobs and make achievements that are recognized and rewarded. A number of researchers have explored the possibility that women are not psychologically motivated to achieve, that they have less achievement motivation than men do. Although the original works tended to focus on psychological motivations underlying achievements, later reinterpretations have used social role analyses.

The classic work in this field was done over 30 years ago by David McClelland and his colleagues.[93] Most of their work was with men, but a few of their studies did include women. They tried to measure achievement motivation with a projective test by showing subjects a picture, asking them to tell a story about it, and then counting the number of achievement-related themes in the story. Sometimes, the picture was shown under an arousal situation supposedly designed to make the subjects want to achieve even more. Usually, the arousal situation involved tasks that the subjects were told would measure their leadership potential. Usually, boys were shown pictures of boys and under the arousal situation (but not the normal situation) would show high achievement motivation. Girls were usually shown pictures with girls and gave fewer achievement-related themes in their responses in both conditions. Based on these results, McClelland and his associates concluded that girls have a lower achievement motive than boys.

Building on the work of McClelland and his associates and hoping to clarify the findings regarding gender differences, Matina Horner introduced the notion of "the motive to avoid success" and devised a technique to tap women's conflicts regarding success.[94] She hypothesized that because women "expect negative consequences (such as social rejection and/or feelings of being unfeminine) as a result of succeeding" they may expect more negative consequences from success than men would.[95] To test this she asked subjects to write stories about members of their own sex group who were described as being successful in the traditionally male area of medical school. She then used the number of unpleasant themes in these stories as a measure of the subject's motive to avoid success. As she expected, the females in the study showed much more of this motive to avoid success than the males did.

Both McClelland and associates' original work and Horner's later work had respondents tell stories only about people of their own sex. When more complete research designs are used, the conclusions regarding gender differences in achievement motivation are questioned. For instance, when shown pictures of males, both girls and boys show a high level of achievement imagery. Neither females nor males show as high a level of achievement imagery when shown pictures of females.[96] Similarly, both males and females tend to give more negative responses, indicative of the motive to avoid success, to stimuli regarding women and fewer negative responses to stimuli regarding men.[97] The fact that an individual's measure of achievement motivation or motive to avoid success may vary with different stimuli suggests that achievement themes reflect not just inherent psychological motives but also actual social roles.

Contemporary studies of achievement motives stress both the multidimensional nature of achievement motivation and the importance of understanding its association with gender roles and expectations. Women appear to score higher on some aspects of achievement motivation, such as wanting to work hard and well, whereas men score higher on others, such as enjoying competition.[98] Typically the areas emphasized by men have received more research attention.

Moreover, achievement motivation appears to be related to gender-role-consistent activities and attitudes. For men, but not for women, high achievement motivation appears to be related to greater adjustment to work. For women, high achievement motivation is related to leisure-time activities and family life.[99] Elyse Sutherland and Joseph Veroff have suggested that achievement motivation can predict behavior only when gender-role ideals are taken into account.[100] Males' achievement is expected to reflect their roles as competitive, individuated people; females' achievement is expected to reflect their roles as competent, but socially concerned individuals. Thus, females may see the successful use of social skills as achievement in and of itself. Studies have shown that women, but not men, increase their achievement (not affiliation) imagery with arousal treatments that stress social acceptability and skill. This is especially true for women who value women's traditional roles. Also females are more responsive than males to social approval when the task is nonsocial.[101]

It may well be, then, that females express achievement motivation in activities that are culturally defined as feminine. They attempt to resolve the conflict between achievement desires and prescriptions for the feminine role by transferring achievement to a feminine context.[102] In the same way that we suggested in Chapter 1 that women respond to male expectations of role segregation and devaluation, women may deal with conflicts regarding achievement by staying only within traditional female areas or redefining an achievement activity as feminine.[103] Males have been traditionally seen as having higher achievement motivation than women because the research in this area defined achievement in a masculine context. Ultimately, then, the explanation for the relative absence of women in prestigious adult roles does not lie in dependency or lack of motivation for high attainment, but in the masculine definition of what constitutes high attainment, and in definitions of appropriate gender roles that support occupational achievement for men and work against it for women.

The Impact of Social Expectations

Psychological studies generally show few gender differences, especially among young children in psychological traits and behavioral tendencies. With regard to temperament, although many studies show males to be more physically active, females cannot be called passive. The findings also cast doubt on the idea that girls are more emotional than boys.

Studies relevant to social approach and avoidance yield no clear-cut gender differences. The bulk of evidence indicates that the two sex groups are remarkably similar in dependency by almost any definition: attachment, affiliation, sensitivity to and interest in social cues, interpersonal relations, or empathy. Both boys and girls are highly sociable, and the cliche that boys are task oriented and girls are people oriented is simply false. Striking differences do appear, however, in patterns of sociability. Females also appear to be more nurturing than males, but evidence suggests that, if given an opportunity, males can nurture almost as well as females.

In contrast, with respect to power, the evidence suggests that males are more aggressive than females—both physically and verbally, directly and indirectly, and in a wide variety of settings. This aggressiveness, defined as the intent to hurt another, may be rooted in biology but is socially patterned. Although males may not be more dominant than females in all ways, boys clearly make more overt and direct attempts to dominate others than girls.

With regard to intellect and achievement, there is no evidence that males have more general analytic ability than females, although males do have greater spatial ability and are better at most nonverbal insight problems. Although many studies over the years have noted females' greater verbal skills and males' greater quantitative skills, these differences have declined dramatically in recent years to the point where they often appear with only specific tasks and in small subgroups. Gender differences in adult achievement patterns cannot be explained directly by differences in talents and capacities or motivation, but must be explained in terms of differing adult social-role expectations.

These findings of relatively few gender differences have often been reached by reconceptualizing some of the key dimensions psychologists use to interpret the available data. At the same time, however, by focusing on individual personality traits, rather than on clusters of behaviors and interaction patterns, the nature of gender differences in behavior may be somewhat understated. Thus, in more recent writings, Eleanor Maccoby has tempered her earlier statements regarding males' and females' similarities in sociability by stressing the different *patterns* of social behavior and interactions that they seem to prefer. This more global and inclusive view that focuses on patterns of gender differences is reflected in attempts to develop summary measures of masculinity and femininity.

MEASURING MASCULINITY, FEMININITY, AND ANDROGYNY

Sometimes researchers try to measure individual differences in entire groups of psychological traits considered characteristic of males and females. They have devised so-called M-F tests to rank individuals in terms of the degree of their masculinity or femininity. These tests are constructed empirically rather than theoretically; that is, by choosing the test items on the basis of whether they actually do differentiate between males and females, regardless of why they might do so. For example, Gough's Femininity Scale, a widely used M-F test on the California Personality Inventory, is an empirical scale of 58 items chosen because women typically answer the items differently from men.[104] The items were selected from batteries of other test questions that were not originally intended to measure masculinity–femininity, but these items did tend to differentiate the sex groups. An individual's score on the test is based on the number of items answered in the manner most typical of women. The following three items are illustrative:

> "I become quite irritated when I see someone spit on the sidewalk."
> "I always like to keep my things neat and tidy and in good order."
> "I like to go to parties and other affairs where there is lots of loud fun."

Women tend to answer yes to the first and second items and no to the third. Although the feminine answers to these may seem obvious once they are pointed out, it is doubtful if anyone would have made up these items in an effort to tap masculinity–femininity. Even within a given item, it is difficult to know what element makes it feminine. For instance, the word *tidy* in item two is a word that men tend to avoid. Perhaps simply the presence of this word, rather than a lack of neatness among men, accounts for their answering no.

Other well-known M-F tests besides Gough's include Terman and Miles's Attitude-Interest Analysis Test, a 1936 test that set the pattern for subsequent tests; Strong's M-F scale of the Vocational Interest Blank; the M-F scale of the Minnesota Multiphasic Personality Inventory (MMPI); and the Guilford Masculinity Scale built on a factor-analytic technique. Another frequently used test is the Franck and Rosen Drawing Completion Test. In contrast to the other tests, this projective test purports to measure unconscious masculinity–femininity. It was also developed by empirical methods, by assessing how the drawings of most men and most women differ. Finally, there is the It Scale for Children. This is a gender-role preference test, but it is often used as if it measures psychological masculinity–femininity.

Criticisms of M-F Tests

Although M-F tests do to some extent differentiate between men and women and some tests even do so cross-culturally, it is hard to interpret the meaning of an individual's score. In the first place, to the extent that M-F tests are based on gender stereotypes, it is possible for individuals to fake their answers or to simply fall into stereotypic responses. To complicate matters, only some items are based on stereotypes. R. C. Nichols analyzed items drawn from M-F tests and concluded they are of three types: subtle items that do differentiate between the sexes, obvious items that differentiate, and stereotypical items that in fact do not differentiate. All of this complicates enormously the meaning of the scores obtained.[105]

Another questionable aspect of M-F measures is that the scores vary by the social class, education, geographic location, and age of the subjects. For example, more highly educated males score more feminine than less highly educated ones, whereas more highly educated females score more masculine than less educated women. This systematic variation certainly calls into question the assumption that the tests are measuring some stable personality trait.

A more important problem with M-F tests, however, is that they imply that masculinity–femininity is a single bipolar dimension and that an individual can be ranked on this dimension in terms of a single score. In fact, considerable evidence suggests that on all of the M-F tests, more than a single dimension is involved. Thus, for example, both high-school boys and adult engineers may receive a rather high masculinity score, but the test items that cause these high scores are different for the two groups.[106] In addition to the different dimensions within each test, the tests themselves do not all measure the same dimensions.[107]

Another criticism of M-F tests is that they tend to distract us from the more important fact that the traits and interests making up masculinity–femininity constitute a relatively small proportion of all personality traits and interests. Furthermore, there is some evidence that the personality traits that do differentiate between the sex groups are on the average relatively secondary.[108] Finally, attempts to measure masculinity–femininity imply that somehow it is "good" to be high in the characteristics of one's own sex group. In the 1970s psychologists challenged this assumption explicitly.

Androgyny Scales

Sandra Bem was the first psychologist to devise a test, the Bem Sex-Role Inventory (BSRI), to measure the degree to which an individual is both masculine and feminine, that is, androgynous.[109] Another widely used measure of psychological androgyny is the Personality Attributes Questionnaire (PAQ) developed by Janet Spence and Robert Helmreich.[110] These scales treat masculinity and femininity as two unrelated dimensions rather than as two ends of a single dimension. The tests consist of a list of stereotypically masculine characteristics (e.g., "independent," "assertive"), stereotypically feminine characteristics (e.g., "childlike," "tender"), and neutral characteristics (e.g., "happy," "sincere"). Subjects are asked to indicate how well each characteristic describes themselves. A person who has the masculine items to a high degree and the feminine items to a low degree would be said to have a masculine gender role. A person who has the feminine traits to a high degree and the masculine traits to a low degree would have a feminine gender role. A person who scores high in both stereotypically masculine and stereotypically feminine traits is considered androgynous.[111]

These tests can hardly be called subtle because the items used are blatant stereotypes, but they do provide a simple and understandable argument against the bipolar assumption of most M-F tests. They also attack the implication in the bipolar assumption that women should be feminine and men should be masculine.

Bem suggested that scores on the BSRI reflect individuals' cognitive processes and specifically the extent to which gender stereotypes affect the way they see the world.[112] Although she originally hypothesized that individuals who appear to be androgynous based on their BSRI scores would exhibit the most behavioral flexibility and greatest mental health, the literature generally indicates that high masculinity, rather than androgyny, is most highly associated with positive adjustment.[113] Similarly, work with both the BSRI and PAQ has produced inconsistent correlations with a wide variety of variables generally associated with gender typing or psychological adjustment.[114]

The tests did not meet the early expectations of their developers and Spence and Helmreich, and Bem, have, to a large extent, questioned their earliest works in the area and especially the way others have used their scales. Bem has decried the widespread use of the BSRI and stressed that it should only be used to examine the extent to which individuals incorporate gender-based schema or typologies in the ways they view the world.[115] (See discussion of schema theory in Chapter 8.) Spence has more directly rejected the utility of these measures, suggesting that the PAQ and the BSRI, as well as the conventional M-F tests, cannot adequately tap masculinity or femininity, gender typing, or even gender schemas.[116] She suggested that individuals' concepts of their own masculinity and femininity are too complex and multidimensional to be captured by such simple scales.

One of the problems of the PAQ and the BSRI is that they were both developed in a theoretical vacuum, relying on stereotypical views of men and women and utilizing descriptors that empirically and quantitatively differentiate men and women without a theoretical underpinning. Theorists who have explored more qualitative aspects of masculinity and femininity provide a different perspective.[117]

QUALITATIVE DESCRIPTIONS OF MASCULINITY AND FEMININITY

Efforts to assess systematically gender differences in traits and tendencies do not consider possible gender differences in patterns of relationship between traits. Many of the studies Maccoby and Jacklin report as showing no gender differences in a certain behavior have actually found striking gender differences in the pattern of relationships between a certain trait and other personality variables.[118] For example, a study might conclude that there are no differences between the sex groups in helping responses but might also find that helping behavior correlates positively with several other variables in boys and correlates negatively with those same variables in girls. Indeed, the differences in the linkages between traits in the personalities of males and females may be more important than the differences in average scores.[119]

Some scholars have sought to understand these gender differences in patterns and linkages of traits by using qualitative typologies that delineate broad differences in orientation between the sex groups. By using broad, qualitative descriptions, they hope to capture the principle of organization by which specific traits may be patterned within each sex group. Some hope that the qualitative approach may help us see femininity in a more positive way and overcome the tendency for researchers to study males more than they study females.[120] This final section reviews some of the theories that attempt to delineate the essence of masculinity and femininity including our own argument for the instrumental–expressive distinction.

Transcendence and Immanence

A number of years ago, Simone de Beauvoir sensitively discussed a distinction between masculine and feminine orientations that was based on the existential notions of transcendence and immanence.[121] She believed that people attain liberty and meaning in life through exploits and projects, an acting on the world that leads to transcending one's immediate situation. Even though women as human beings are free and autonomous, de Beauvoir explained that they live in a world where men have defined them as objects, as the Other, as a group apart. Because of this, women find it difficult to transcend their situation. Thus, although men's situation is one of transcendence, where they may act on and move beyond their present state, women remain in immanence, a situation of restriction and confinement that they are unable to transcend.

Although de Beauvoir recognized how a male-dominant society can constrain women's actions, her descriptions of feminine nature are always colored by her dedication to transcendence. She saw this latter as the morally superior stance involving not so much self-interest as self-determination and autonomy. She saw immanence as static and unfree. As a result she tended to define femininity only in relation to masculinity and did not see positive aspects in femininity itself. More recent attempts to theoretically distinguish masculinity and femininity have tried to counter this masculine bias and see positive aspects in their conceptions of both masculinity and femininity.

Allocentric and Autocentric Ego Styles

David Gutmann, a psychoanalytically oriented theorist, directly attacked the masculine bias in the concept ego strength.[122] He argued that the criteria used to assess ago strength, such as impersonality and objectivity, are masculine in nature and irrelevant to women's situation and their ego development in this society. He used the terms *autocentric* and *allocentric* to describe feminine and masculine ego styles. For Gutmann, the allocentric masculine ego tends to objectify others and to experience its own separateness from others. With the autocentric feminine ego, the distinctions between self and others and self and environment are blurred, and thus, ego boundaries are more permeable. For example, males characteristically approach the Thematic Apperception Test (TAT cards depict ambiguous figures and situations about which the subject must tell a story) by distancing themselves from the cards and making it very clear that they are imagining the story, using the pictures as cues. Women seem to experience the pictures they see in the cards as real events and get into their stories more than the men.

Gutmann also suggested that the autocentric (feminine) and allocentric (masculine) ego states differ in their perceptions of space and time, constancy and change, self and others. An empirical test of this formulation that analyzed the words, approaches, and constructs used by college students in written exercises supported Gutmann's theory. The researcher found that "males represent experiences of self, other, space, and time in individualistic, objective, and distant ways, while females represent experiences in relatively interpersonal, subjective, immediate ways in responding to a range of common tasks."[123]

Agency and Communion

Although Gutmann's formulation helps portray differing qualities of masculine and feminine ego functioning, it does not allow for both masculine and feminine qualities in one individual.[124] David Bakan's more generalized concepts of agency and communion offer this possibility.[125] Bakan saw these concepts as dynamic principles interacting with each other. The terms are defined at a very high level of abstraction and characterize

> two fundamental modalities in the existence of living forms, agency for the existence of an organism as an individual, and communion for the participation of the individual in some larger organism of which the individual is a part. . . . Agency manifests itself in the formation of separations: communion in the lack of separations. Agency manifests itself in isolation, alienation and aloneness; communion in contact, openness, and union. Agency manifests itself in the urge to master; communion in noncontractual cooperation.[126]

Bakan believes that both agency and communion are necessary qualities within any organism. If societies or individuals are to be viable, agency must be combined with communion.

Jeanne Block used Bakan's agency and communion to describe gender role changes over the life cycle precisely because it allows for one principle to be tempered with the other.[127] In Block's view, the earliest stage of development for children of both sex groups is unmitigated agency. At this impulse-ridden and self-protective level, children are concerned with "self-assertion, self-expression, and self-extension." In a slightly later stage of development when gender roles diverge, communion is emphasized for girls and discouraged for boys. At the adult level, as their emotional maturity increases, members of both sex groups may eventually arrive at an integration of both orientations, although males will specialize in agency and females in communion. Empirical work supports the thesis that males express slightly more agentic themes than females in reporting significant emotional experiences. Moreover, females have been found to have both agentic and communal orientations more often than males.[128]

Bakan's distinction is important in defining overall orientations, yet it can also be confusing. The concepts involved are so global and all-inclusive that their specific meaning is difficult to pin down. For example, the term *agentic* describes highly disciplined, self-oriented striving in the occupational world as well as the impulse-ridden self-assertion and self-extension of the infant. Such a remarkable equation may more confuse than clarify.

Autonomous and Relational Morality

The most popular qualitative gender distinction in recent years was developed by Carol Gilligan.[129] Gilligan, a developmental psychologist, contends that women tend to construct the moral domain differently from the way men do. Whereas men tend to think of morality in terms of individual rights and noninterference with the rights of others, women are more prone to think in terms of interdependence and the balancing of conflicting responsibilities in making moral decisions. Gilligan was careful to point out that she was not talking just about the cliche between male "justice" and female "mercy" or male "thinking" and female "feeling."[130] Rather, she was describing two different ways of constructing the moral domain. Women are more likely to think in terms of equality, process, conflict resolution, not hurting, and caring for others. In masculine conceptions, these considerations may appear to be weak-minded or "unprincipled," but to women they may constitute an alternative perspective, not an unprincipled one but one that balances a complex variety of "principles."

Gilligan's focus on moral decisions arose from her work with Lawrence Kohlberg and his analysis of the development of moral reasoning through a series of increasingly complex stages. Much of his earlier work suggested that women were less likely than men to exhibit moral reasoning typical of the higher stages of his model. By suggesting that women's moral reasoning was not inferior, but simply different, Gilligan attempted not only to counteract the masculine bias in Kohlberg's work but also to affirm the positive and constructive aspects of women's moral thinking.

This perspective has not been immune from criticism. Extensive reviews of the literature on gender differences in moral reasoning challenge the assumption that males and females approach moral issues differently. Studies that do find differences have been confounded by different educational and occupational statuses of the men and women. Moreover, women pass through the stages outlined by Kohlberg in the same order as men, and the type of moral dilemma discussed appears to be as important as gender in influencing the reasoning process used.[131] Despite this lack of empirical support, Gilligan's formulation has been intuitively appealing and has inspired a good deal of work that seeks to elaborate the qualitative differences in the ways men and women approach not just moral decisions,[132] but also epistemological issues, or the question of how we know what we know.[133]

The popularity of Gilligan's work, despite the relative lack of empirical support, illustrates a seeming need of both scholars and the public to understand more about the qualitative nature of masculinity–femininity.[134] Yet Gilligan's formulation, like that of the others reviewed here, is overly broad and difficult to operationalize or incorporate into other theories.

Instrumental and Expressive Orientations

A less global formulation that also allows for both masculine and feminine orientations in the personality and does not denigrate women is Talcott Parsons's instrumental–expressive distinction. The instrumental–expressive distinction is not a single dimension. Rather, it refers to two aspects of behavior, both distinctly social, each with a positive and negative pole. Drawing on distinctions running throughout several of Parsons's theoretical works, we define an action as expressive if it involves an orientation toward the relations among the individuals interacting within a social group.[135] Instrumental action involves an orientation to goals outside the immediate relational system. Instrumental actions are directed toward attaining some product as a means to a desired objective; expressive actions are concerned with the emotional quality of the group, controlling tensions, and motivating other group members. Individuals employ both instrumental and expressive modes of relating and within a given situation may act in both an expressive and an instrumental manner at different points in the interaction.

Although both instrumental and expressive actions are socially rewarded and emotionally gratifying, the rewards differ. The rewards for expressive actions are more reciprocal and emotionally direct. For example, someone responds to a friend's support with gratitude and love, and the reward for loving is often being loved in return. The rewards for instrumental action, on the other hand, tend to be impersonal. For example, a student who successfully explains a difficult topic to a seminar is probably rewarded with respect and approval by the instructor, symbolized by a high grade. Both rewards for instrumental and for expressive behavior might be socially and emotionally meaningful to the recipient. Thus, the instrumental and expressive distinction is not between nonsocial and social behavior or between nonemotionality and emotionality. Instead, it involves distinctions in role behavior and goals of action.

Both instrumental and expressive actions are necessary for social systems to function, and both kinds of orientations are present in both sexes. Instrumental actions relate individuals and groups to the wider environment; expressive actions relate individual units within a group.

Many feminists and social scientists have avoided attributing expressiveness to women for fear that it will be used as a scientific justification for keeping women in the home and implying that they are emotional, incompetent, and dependent. However, these characteristics are not inherent in the definition of expressiveness, and a derogatory view of women need not result from use of the term. In fact, the distinction can point to the very positive aspects of women's roles and personality organization.

Although expressiveness does engage socioemotional skills, it is misleading to view it as simply being emotional. It is true that women are penalized less for expressing emotion than men; indeed, women are even expected to express it on occasion. But more generally, women are expected to understand and deal with emotion, more than simply being subject to it. Women may resonate with, respond to, cope with, and even define emotions for others, but it seems incorrect to equate these acts with being emotional. Men are potentially as emotional as women, but they are discouraged from expressing emotion and from being sensitive to their own or others' emotions on pain of being considered unmasculine.[136] Expressiveness, then, is an interactive capacity, not a subjective state.

The contention that expressiveness implies lack of instrumental competence results in part from the unnecessary assumption that the instrumental–expressive distinction is a single dimension. This implies that a woman who is a pleasure to be with must be incapable of instrumental competence and the woman who is a success in instrumental terms must be an unpleasant person in interpersoanl interactions. Actually, the instrumental–expressive distinction is two dimensions, each with a positive and negative pole.

The assumption that women are more passive and dependent than men is so pervasive that it has often been either explicitly or implicitly read into the instrumental–expressive distinction. As we noted earlier, everyone clearly depends on the responses of others; we all ultimately seek social rewards. In this respect, men are no more independent than women. The instrumental–expressive difference lies, then, not in autonomy versus dependence, but in the nature of the rewards sought. Expressive rewards are direct and personal; instrumental rewards are indirect and impersonal. Neither is expressiveness tied to passivity. Expressiveness does not mean doing what others want one to do; it may just as well involve getting others to do what one wants *them* to do.

Empirical studies have demonstrated the usefulness of this conceptualization. For instance, our study using self-ratings of college students found that men and women differed considerably more in their scores on the expressive dimension than they did in their scores on the instrumental dimension. Women saw themselves as more positively expressive (e.g., sweeter and kinder) and less negatively expressive (e.g., quarrelsome and unfriendly) than men saw themselves. On the other hand, women did not see themselves as any more dependent or negatively instrumental (lazy or quitting) than men.[137] Replications of this work with men and women of varying ages and occupations indicate that "the major differences in the self-concepts of the sexes is that women conceive of themselves as being much richer in the positive qualities of social warmth and empathy."[138] Men define themselves in terms of not being too warm and empathetic or, in our terms, of not being too positively expressive.

Studies of group process suggest that these self-concepts are reflected in the style of interaction men and women typically use. A meta-analysis of studies of gender differences in interaction styles found a consistent tendency for women to engage more often in behaviors we would term expressive, such as agreeing and acting friendly, whereas men more often engage in instrumental task behaviors such as giving opinions and information.[139] Similarly, observers of boys' and girls' patterns of social behavior document differences that correspond to the expressive–instrumental distinction. Girls are much more likely to use and prefer play styles that emphasize cooperation with others and deference to the feelings of others, whereas boys more often engage in rough-and-tumble play and are concerned with interpersonal or egoistic dominance.[140]

Empirical evidence also shows that expressive behaviors in females do not correlate with passivity. Our studies with various samples of high-school students and adults generally indicate that expressiveness and measures of active/independent traits (the opposite of passivity) are positively correlated.[141] Similarly, studies of children indicate that even though girls prefer an expressive interactional style, their play could not be termed passive or non–task oriented.[142] These different patterns of traits in the two sexes support the theory that the development of masculinity involves the rejection of femininity. Males express independence by not being too expressive. It may be that male aggressiveness, especially as it appears in younger boys, reinforces negative expressive behavior as boys display hurting rather than helping behavior and disrupting and disobeying behavior rather than integrating tendencies.

Because men reject femininity, women as well as men have sometimes questioned the value of expressiveness. This probably reflects the masculine bias that influences our thinking. Our own view is that expressiveness is a common human orientation that one might hope could be fostered in both sexes. Certainly, the pressure men are under to eschew positive expressiveness in order to prove their masculinity is no reason to devalue it. Many feminists fear that if women lay claim to expressiveness, it will be used against them in the job market to justify assigning them helping and other low-level jobs. To some extent, these fears have been justified. However, the answer for women is probably not to deny expressiveness in their fight for inclusion, but to insist that an expressive orientation can operate along with instrumental orientations and that expressiveness might, in fact, enrich instrumental activities.

SUMMARY

This chapter has canvassed attempts to specify gender differences in generalized traits and behavioral tendencies; to measure individual differences in masculinity, femininity, and androgyny; and to define gender differences in orientation and in the organization of traits within the personality. There are almost no gender differences among infants, and the major psychological difference between the sex groups that appears to be biologically based is that males are more aggressive than females. However, this greater male aggressiveness by itself cannot explain male dominance or male achievement. It is essentially an antisocial trait that may reinforce males' greater negative expressiveness. A number of theorists discuss orientational differences between the sexes. We argue that the most useful distinction suggests that males see themselves as less expressive than females and tend to relate psychological independence to negative expressiveness. Females, on the other hand, relate expressiveness to independence and instrumentalness. These findings support the theory that the development of masculinity involves the rejection of femininity.

SUGGESTED READINGS

GILL, SANDRA, JEAN STOCKARD, MIRIAM JOHNSON, and SUZANNE WILLIAMS. 1987. "Measuring Gender Differences: The Expressive Dimension and the Critique of Androgyny Scales." *Sex Roles*. 17:375–400. Discusses the theoretical basis and development of a scale to measure expressiveness.

HYDE, JANET SHIBLEY, and MARCIA C. LINN. 1986. *The Psychology of Gender: Advances Through Meta-Analysis*. Baltimore: Johns Hopkins University Press. A collection of meta-analytic studies of gender differences in psychological traits.

MACCOBY, ELEANOR E. 1990. "Gender and Relationships: A Developmental Account." *American Psychologist*. 45:513–520. A readable summary of the current literature on gender differences and the theoretical perspective of one of the major figures in the field.

O'LEARY, VIRGINIA E., RHODA KESLER UNGER, and BARBARA STRUDLER WALLSTON. (Eds.). *Women, Gender, and Social Psychology*. Hillsdale, N.J.: Erlbaum, 1985; and

SONDEREGGER, THEO B. (Ed.). *Psychology and Gender: Nebraska Symposium on Motivation*. Lincoln: University of Nebraska Press, 1984. Both of these books are collections of articles by well-known psychologists on various aspects of gender differences and psychological development.

WHITING, BEATRICE BLYTH, and CAROLYN POPE EDWARDS. 1988. *Children of Different Worlds: The Formation of Social Behavior*. Cambridge, Mass.: Harvard University Press. A summary of systematic research on gender differences in children from a wide variety of cultures.

chapter 8

Becoming Gender Typed: Theories from Psychology

Even though one can find few gender differences in infants, behavior is clearly gender typed in some respects by the time children reach nursery-school age. Boys are more disruptive, and boys and girls play with different toys and engage in different types of activities. By the age of 4 children's play choices clearly reflect adult activities. Furthermore, from about the age of 4 boys become increasingly more gender typed than girls, more often avoid gender-atypical activities, and more often prefer activities associated with their own sex group.[1] These differences appear even in nursery schools where the personnel try not to encourage gender typing.[2]

How do these differences come about and why do they persist even in neutral environments? Although biological factors may play a part, learning is paramount. But how does this learning occur? Are parents and other adults important in this process through rewarding or serving as models of gender-typed behavior? Or does gender typing arise from children's own understandings of their sex group and its expected behaviors? These two views roughly represent the theoretical positions in psychology of social learning theory and cognitive theory. In this chapter we investigate these theories. In recent years many psychologists have advocated a synthesis of social learning and cognitive perspectives. We also examine the outlines of this developing synthesis and show how it can be used to help understand various aspects of gender development.

The theories were generally not specifically developed to explain gender-typed behavior. Rather, they are general theories about human learning and development that should be applicable to gender-typed behavior as well as other kinds of behavior. Although the differences among them are more than just a matter of emphasis, the theories do not represent absolutely different perspectives. For instance, proponents of social learning theory recognize that cognitive understanding is distinctly involved in learning. For their part, cognitive theories recognize that reinforcement and modeling take place but see them as secondary to cognitive processes.

We will evaluate each of these theories in terms of their adequacy in explaining gender-typed behavior. We use the word *evaluate* advisedly. There is no way that one can actually empirically test a theory. All one can do is examine the evidence for and against certain hypotheses that one might develop on the basis of a particular theory. When a particular hypothesis fails to hold up, one may question the theory itself. Yet frequently the fault does not lie with the underlying theory, but with the particular hypotheses derived from it. The phenomena predicted by the theory may indeed exist, but not exactly in the way specified in a concrete hypothesis. If we fail to see evidence, for example, of reinforcement of gender-typed behaviors, two explanations are possible: Either reinforcement does not adequately account for typing (in which case one must look for other explanations), or gender-typed behavior is actually being reinforced, but in a way different from that stated by the particular hypothesis.

Beyond assessing the theories in terms of how well they can explain gender typing, we will also be concerned with their adequacy in dealing with the phenomenon of male dominance itself. Each of these theories implies something about why males have greater prestige and power than females.

SOCIAL LEARNING THEORY

Social learning theory has a number of variations. The two aspects that have been most widely used in discussing gender development are the influence of reinforcements and modeling.

Reinforcements

Social learning theory originally grew out of stimulus–response theory, or behaviorism. The original idea of behaviorism was that a behavioral repertoire is built into the individual on the basis of the rewards or lack of rewards coming from the external environment. Because rewarded behavior is repeated and nonrewarded behavior is extinguished, behavior is shaped in terms of a schedule of reinforcements. Behaviorists, then, are not primarily concerned with the internal mental states of individuals, in part because these are subjective and cannot be objectively observed. They are more concerned with the individual as an organism who can be conditioned to behave in a certain way.

Social learning theorists modified the extreme forms of this behavioristic view considerably and do not say that each and every little bit of behavior has to be directly rewarded to be learned.[3] Social learning theorists such as Walter Mischel, and Albert Bandura and R. H. Walters, also recognize that cognitive processes do intervene between stimulus and response and that individuals are capable of generalizing from a specific case to other similar cases.[4] They are also capable of observational learning, such as perceiving what happens to others who display a certain behavior and inferring what the consequences of such an action would be for themselves. They can remember past outcomes and therefore predict future outcomes and act accordingly. Thus, although social learning theorists continue to believe that behavior patterns are maintained through reinforcement, they have moved away from the view that cognitive processes are irrelevant.

Social learning theorists also believe that the reinforcements that maintain behavior patterns are primarily social, and many of them share with psychoanalytic theory a belief in the importance of early childhood experience. Because of its dependency, the infant is especially sensitive to the mother's reactions. As the primary nurturer, she becomes an important shaper of the infant's behavior.

There is considerable variety in the reinforcement variables examined by social learning theorists. Investigations of naturalistic antecedents or causes of gender typing have tended to involve very general parental variables such as permissiveness, affection, and punitiveness. Researchers who study behavior in the laboratory usually examine more concrete reinforcement contingencies. Regardless of the level of abstraction at which they study reinforcement, though, social learning theorists assume that the sex groups are treated differently by parents and other socializing agents and that this differential treatment produces or maintains gender-typed characteristics.

Both experimental studies, in which a child's gender label is manipulated and parents' reactions are observed, as well as naturalistic studies of parents interacting with their own children provide some support for hypotheses derived from social learning theory. Although the differences are not large, adults tend to promote gender-typed toy choices, especially girls' exclusive use of dolls, and to encourage boys' gross motor activities more than girls'. Some studies indicate that parents are more likely to encourage girls than boys to show affectionate and tender emotional behavior. Although girls are often seen as more competent than boys and given more autonomy, they are more likely than boys to be chaperoned, undoubtedly because of fears of sexual molestation.[5] Parents do not directly reward or seek to encourage boys' aggressive behavior. In fact, boys are punished more than girls. Yet parents are more likely simply to respond to boys' aggressive acts, while ignoring girls' aggression. This may inform boys, but not girls, that aggression produces responses from others.[6]

A fair amount of evidence suggests that fathers are more likely than mothers to differentiate their treatment of the sex groups. When compared to mothers, fathers tend to perceive more gender differences, exhibit larger differences in play styles with boys and girls, be more concerned with the gender appropriateness of toy choices and play behavior, and show more differences in interaction styles with sons and daughters and larger differences in achievement expectations.[7]

Yet it is clear that social learning theory is not sufficient to explain the variety of gender-differentiated behavior nor its continuance. Children, but especially boys, persist in gender-typed behaviors even when they are not reinforced or when they are given negative feedback for these behaviors.[8] Although it is possible to produce changes in children's gender-typed behaviors through altering reinforcement schedules, this learning does not seem to generalize or persist much beyond the experimental setting.[9]

In addition, several processes besides direct reinforcement might explain the specific differences in the treatment of boys and girls. It may be that the greater punishment administered to sons can be explained by boys' greater resistance to complying with commands. Girls may receive more gentle handling because they "elicit" it by their own qualities and responses. In these cases differential treatment might arise because of differing eliciting qualities of girls and boys. It may be that the child differentially reinforces the parent rather than vice versa or at least that the parent and the child both differentially reinforce each other.

We must also consider the possibility that some of the reinforcement contingencies manipulated by parents actually inhibit rather than produce gender-typed behavior in children. Many parents do not attempt to gender type their children, but rather assume that their children's behavior is already gender typed and attempt to socialize children of both sex groups in terms of the same major goals.[10]

None of the above considerations should necessarily make us abandon the notion of reinforcement as a viable explanation for gender typing. However, many further specifications will have to be made beyond simply saying that parents develop masculine and feminine behavior in their children.

Modeling Theory

The second major social learning explanation of how we acquire behaviors is modeling, imitation, or identification. Social learning theorists suggest that through these processes, complex and elaborate behaviors, which are not directly and specifically reinforced, come to be part of the child's behavior.

Given their power and well-developed skills relative to their children, as well as their relatively high availability, parents should be powerful models to children.[11] Certainly we could strengthen our confidence in the modeling hypothesis if we had some evidence that a child does actually resemble the same-sexed parent. Although finding similarities between a parent and a same-sex child would not prove that they occurred through modeling, finding little similarity would give us reason to seriously question the modeling hypothesis as an explanation of gender typing. In fact, correlation studies of parent–child similarities find that children are not especially similar to their own parents, and that it is not at all clear that girls are more like their mothers and boys are more like their fathers. This is true for both young children and young adults, and for both non-gender-typed and gender-typed behavior.[12]

Similarly, with regard to gender-typed preferences, several studies have found that the femininity of girls is not related to their mother's femininity.[13] One study also found that girls who showed the most "feminine" preferences on the It Scale for Children were no more likely to have very feminine mothers than other girls. Interestingly enough, what this study did find was that the fathers of the most feminine girls "tended to be more masculine in interests and orientations (score lower on the Femininity Scale) than the fathers of the other group."[14]

This finding would suggest that sex typing may be learned through role complementarity or role complementation; in other words, one may learn a role by playing opposite someone rather than by copying. Other studies have found no relation between the masculinity of boys and that of their fathers, nor between the masculinity of boys and the masculinity or femininity of their mothers.[15] It may be that complementarity works best with fathers and daughters.[16] At any rate, correlational studies give little support to simple interpretations of modeling theory regarding the influence of parents.

David Lynn has modified modeling theory by arguing that it is easier for a girl to acquire her gender-typed characteristics by imitating her mother than it is for a boy to get his gender-typed characteristics by copying his father.[17] The reason is that mothers are both more salient and more available than fathers. As Lynn put it, the father as a model is an outline lacking most details, whereas the mother as a model is a detailed map. In testing this hypothesis Lynn found that about as many boys imitated a male stranger as their own father and the number of boys imitating the father was not greater than those imitating the mother, whereas twice as many boys imitated the male stranger as the female stranger. Lynn interprets these findings to mean that boys are motivated to imitate a masculine figure over a feminine one, but that the mother is not perceived by the boy as representing femininity. Rather, she is seen as a generally competent person with whom the boy is familiar. The conclusion would have been further strengthened if he had included a fourth group involving a choice between the child's mother and a female stranger. Lynn asserts that when a boy chooses to imitate his mother over his father, it "represents motivating factors other than masculinity and femininity." Lynn's findings imply that the mother identification is a less gender-typed identification than the boy's father identification.

Lynn within academic psychology and many others with a more psychoanalytic orientation[18] stress the importance of the mother as an object of identification for both sexes in early infancy. One hypothesis from modeling theory is that children identify with the more nurturant parent. Another is that children will more readily model those who are available to them. Both of these hypotheses would lead us to expect that children of both sex groups would initially model the mother rather than the father, for she is generally the more nurturant and more available to infants. If indeed this happens, it poses a problem for modeling theory alone as an explanation of gender typing. If boys initially imitate their mothers and then switch to male figures, girls (who do not have to switch models) should be more gender typed than boys. In fact, quite the opposite is the case. Existing research using behavioral measures indicates that boys of preschool age are more clearly gender typed than girls.

Boys may be more gender typed than girls precisely because they are "leaning over backward" to counteract their initial identification with, or disposition to model, the mother. Once they recognize that the mother is of a different sex and that they as boys are expected to be masculine, they begin to react against femininity. Some of the negative expressiveness characteristic of boys may stem from this reaction.

Although modeling theory in and of itself when applied to children and parents does not explain the acquisition of sex typing very well, it may be more effective when applied to the mass media and especially to television. Here, larger-than-life stereotypes are presented for children to copy. Studies of the association between the amount of television children watch and their gender stereotypes and gender-typed preferences show only weak or nonexistent associations.[19] However, extensive exposure to a television series with gender-typed portrayals that are counter to cultural stereotypes can appear to influence children's stereotyped beliefs and attitudes regarding appropriate behaviors for males and females. Such programing appears to have a much smaller effect on children's own interests and preferences.[20]

In an interesting and unique study of adolescents conducted in the 1970s, Cynthia Quattelbaum explored exactly what characteristics of television characters young people consciously model.[21] She found that over half of both the boys and girls in her sample reported that they modeled television characters and that they would like to be similar to a television character when they grew up. The boys mentioned 13 characters they would like to resemble in the future with Starsky (of "Starsky and Hutch," a detective show) receiving the most votes. The females identified 16 characters, with Mary Richards (Mary Tyler Moore) the most popular choice. Interestingly enough, both the boys and girls said that they wanted to be like these characters because they "helped people." The girls also wanted to model Mary Richards because she was independent and had a career. In this case, then, the modeling may counteract traditional sex stereotypes in some respects.

Although modeling does provide children with a wide repertoire of potential behaviors, exactly how children come to display gender-typed behavior is not directly explained by modeling theory without additional assumptions. One reason that modeling theory does not seem to adequately explain how young children acquire gender-typed behaviors is that it assumes that children copy specific individuals or specific behaviors rather than social roles. The sociologist John Finley Scott pointed out that if one looks at the acquisition of gender typing in the child in terms of the learning of appropriate age and gender roles, the modeling of specific persons, especially the parents, becomes totally inadequate as an explanation.[22] After all, mothers are not 6-year-old girls, yet it is the role of child and girl that must be learned. Although Scott does believe role learning entails reinforcement and modeling, he sees it as involving "less the modeling of persons [and] more the learning of roles."[23]

Contemporary psychologists have also downplayed the notion of modeling individuals. For instance, David Perry and Kay Bussey found that children do not as much imitate or model individual people as look at how males and females as *groups* perform various activities.[24] Although children may not model individuals of the same sex, they do model behaviors they consider typical or appropriate for their sex group by looking at the frequency of behaviors displayed by males and females.[25] These perspectives suggest that the traditional reinforcement and modeling theories need to be supplemented by cognitive theory and more sociological theory focusing on family roles (see Chapter 10).

COGNITIVE THEORIES

Cognitive theories of gender typing emphasize the child and its understanding rather than parents and their reinforcements. The two major perspectives in this area are Lawrence Kohlberg's developmental approach and gender schema theories, developed by several different psychologists.

Developmental Theory

According to Kohlberg, the child categorizes himself or herself as a male or a female and then seeks to act and feel like one. Thus, a girl does not act like a girl because she is rewarded for doing so, but because she knows she is a girl. Kohlberg described the difference between his theory and social learning theory this way:

> The social-learning syllogism is:
> "I want rewards,
> I am rewarded for doing boy things,
> Therefore, I want to be a boy."
> The cognitive developmental syllogism is:
> "I am a boy,
> Therefore I want to do boy things,
> Therefore the opportunity to do boy things (and to gain approval for doing them) is rewarding."[26]

Although social learning theory stresses the learning of specific gender-typed behaviors, Kohlberg's theory emphasizes the acquisition of gender itself. For Kohlberg, gender identity is a cause of gender learning rather than a product of it.

Gender stereotyping in terms of physical differences Kohlberg's theory of gender development derives, in part, from Jean Piaget's work on general processes of cognitive development in children. Basically Kohlberg thinks that gender identity or self-categorization as a boy or a girl is the primary organizer of gender attitudes and that basic universal gender stereotypes develop from the child's conceptions of body differences, which are given further support by visible social role differences. Only after masculine and feminine values have been acquired on the basis of these stereotypes does the child tend to identify with same-sex figures, especially the parent of the same sex.

For Kohlberg, gender identity formation is essentially based on the cognitive capacity to perceive objects as constant, independent of their surroundings. Understanding that one is a girl or a boy and that this cannot be changed is fundamentally the same process involved in the general stabilization of constancies of physical objects that Piaget described. The ability to grasp these constancies is related to mental maturity. By the third year the child usually knows its own sex and later learns to label the sex of others correctly.

After forming this identity and learning that gender and genital differences cannot change, the child wants to adopt gender-typed behavior. Kohlberg argued that this gender typing is not obtained directly by adopting the actual behaviors of parents and siblings, because the ideas of young children about gender typing are more, not less, stereotyped than those of adults. He thinks children build up these ideas mainly from perceiving gender differences in bodily structure and capacities that are usually supported by clearly discernible differences in the social roles the sex groups play. For example, they perceive that mothers take care of children and that fathers are often away. He cited studies indicating that although children aged 4 or 5 remain confused about genital differences, they clearly stereotype the sex groups in terms of size, strength, aggression, and power at this age.[27] According to Kohlberg, "the stereotype of masculine aggressiveness has a body-image basis because it is linked to the child's belief that males are physically more powerful and more invulnerable than females."[28] In this connection he reported that almost all the 24 children in a first-grade class agreed that boys fight more than girls. When they were asked why girls don't fight like boys, the most frequent response was that girls "get hurt" more easily than boys.[29] Children are also exposed to masculine aggression through learning that it is males who usually play potentially violent roles such as police officer, soldier, or robber.

In the child's concrete thinking, social power derives from physical power, which derives from physical size. A number of studies indicate that by the age of 5 or 6, children of both sex groups attribute greater power, strength, competence, and status to males. Although children do award a number of superior values to females, including nurturance, attractiveness, and niceness, basic power and prestige values are primarily awarded to males. Kohlberg feels these tendencies to attribute superior power and status to the male role are universal. As we saw in Chapter 5, the greater prestige given to males does appear to be universal, but this does not necessarily prove that it is based on body image.

Children from 5 to 8 increasingly view gender-stereotyped behavior as morally required even though it may not be stressed by their middle-class parents. At this stage children do not distinguish between conventional social expectations and moral laws and duties. They see acting out one's gender identity as a moral obligation. For example, a child of 5 to 7 is likely to say, "'God made her a girl and she has to stay a girl, that's what God meant her to be.'"[30]

Children usually exhibit gender-typed behaviors and attitudes before cognitive developmental theory would predict. For instance, gender-typed toy choices have consistently been found by the age of 2. In addition, children appear to differentiate males and females by hairstyle and length rather than by body size.[31] Although few dispute Kohlberg's developmental notions, psychologists now generally believe that Kohlberg overestimated the age at which children understand gender labels and achieve "gender constancy," the belief that their own gender cannot change, and did not fully tap the reasoning underlying children's concepts of gender. This probably occurred because the tests Kohlberg used require a fair amount of verbal competency. Young children just learning to talk can understand much more than they can say, and tests requiring relatively little verbal skills have demonstrated that children can correctly discriminate boys and girls by the age of 2 and can discriminate adult men and women at even younger ages.[32]

Identification phenomena In Kohlberg's view, the specific attributes of the child's own parents may inhibit or facilitate gender typing but do not cause it. "There seem to be 'natural stereotypes of paternal power which facilitate the boy's competence-motivated identification with masculine and father-role attributes. If family reality is extremely or grossly discrepant from these stereotypes, the boy's masculine values do not develop strongly.'"[33] In support of this he cited studies that show less gender typing in boys from homes in which the mother is dominant. In addition, he concludes that although maternal warmth has no effect, paternal warmth facilitates masculine gender typing because it helps reduce the "naturally threatening" aspects of the father image and makes it easier for the boy to identify with masculinity.

Kohlberg summarized his discussion of 4- to 8-year-old boys' modeling of their fathers with the following bedtime conversation of a 5-year-old boy and his father:

> "Oh, Daddy, how old will I be when *I can go hunting* with you? We'll go in the woods, you with your gun, me with my bow and arrow. Daddy, wouldn't it be neat if *we could* lasso a wild horse? Do you think we could do it? Do you think I could ride a horse backward if someone's leading me like you?"[34]

Here we see the boy clearly motivated to be competent in concrete stereotypical masculine activities. He is getting support from his father in carrying out these activities, definitely feels his father could do these activities, and categorizes himself with his father. This fantasy "has little to do with the father's actual interests and abilities [the man was a college teacher], and much to do with the concrete masculine sex role stereotypes of children."[35]

As usual, the research findings with respect to identification or modeling behaviors in girls do not neatly parallel the findings in boys. Although modeling the father goes along with boys' developing gender-typed behavior, it is not at all clear that modeling the mother goes along with girls' developing gender-typed behavior. In the first place, mother identification does not positively correlate with measures of general social adjustment in girls, whereas father identification correlates with measures of social adjustment in boys. Also, girls who come from mother-dominant homes are not more identified with the feminine role than girls from homes where the mother is not dominant. Finally, girls as well as boys at about the age of 4 become more father oriented. Thus, girls do not simply remain tied to the mother, but turn away from her and seek a relationship with the father.

According to Kohlberg, identifying with or modeling parents does not itself create gender-typed behavior, but the quality of a child's relationship to the parent can affect gender typing, especially the quality of the relationship to the father. The quality of the relationship of a boy with his father causes him not so much to model him as to use him as a supportive figure in learning to become masculine. The quality of the relationship of a girl with her father causes her not to copy him but to use him as a sounding board as she figures out what it means to be feminine.

Cognitive stages On the basis of interviews with children from 6 to 18, Dorothy Ullian suggested that as children grow older they qualitatively shift their views of gender roles.[36] Although children at first see gender differences as coming from biological and physical differences between the sex groups, as they get older children move into a societal orientation rather than a biological orientation toward gender. They do not challenge the role definitions of the social system, but simply believe "that a proper match exists between one's acquired traits and abilities, and one's future role in the familial, occupational, and social system."[37]

For instance, Ullian asked a 10-year-old boy the question, "Would it be wrong if (a) man wore jewelry?" The boy responded, "Well, women wouldn't just go wearing men's things. You could, it would be right, but everyone would say, 'look at him,' and he would not get a job if he wanted to and nobody would accept him; they would think he was a weird guy."[38] Although adolescents are aware that gender roles are to some extent arbitrary, they tend to elect to stick with them for psychological reasons related to their anticipation of heterosexual dating.

Ullian's work suggests that although children's notions are grounded in biological differences at first and tend to be strongly stereotyped, these ideas are clearly modified (not merely elaborated) as children mature.[39] Older children stop basing their conceptions of gender on physical differences and explain them in sociological and psychological terms, which leads them to see that gender-role conceptions can be modified by individuals and groups. Kohlberg noted that although strong gender typing is associated with high intelligence in young children, it is associated with low intelligence in adolescents.[40] Thus, later on, less stereotyped conceptions of gender appear to be part of cognitive growth. As children grow cognitively they have greater knowledge regarding the actual association between gender and various activities and can more easily discriminate among situations to determine how relevant gender is to a new setting. These more complex cognitive associations are reflected in their more flexible gender-related attitudes.[41]

Kohlberg's theory is a stage theory in the sense that an individual must develop one mode of understanding before proceeding to another. Several other investigators have also used the stage theory approach and concluded that less rigid and more flexible and adaptive ideas concerning proper gender roles are associated with greater moral or ego development. For example, Jeanne Block sees the highest stage of ego development as involving an integration of both masculine and feminine traits and values.[42] The rigid gender typing of young children then may be merely a phase rather than an end product. Meda Rebecca, Robert Hefner, and Barbara Oleshansky suggested that gender development proceeds through three main stages: an undifferentiated conception of gender; a polarized, stereotyped, either-or view of gender roles coinciding with Kohlberg's "conventional" stage; and, finally, a flexible dynamic transcendence of gender roles.[43] They believe that most people and institutions, including social scientists today, are at the second or conventional stage and that this is a major cause of gender discrimination. All of these models are hierarchic; they imply that at any one time there is only one characteristic level for each person. They also imply that not all people will reach each stage; some will be less "mature" or "developed" than others.

Ullian's and Kohlberg's cognitive approach and Block's and Rebecca and her associates' ego psychology approach focus on different correlates of gender development. Ullian and Kohlberg stressed the relation of cognitive development to views on conformity to gender roles, whereas Block focused on the association between personal maturity and conceptions of gender roles.

Although Kohlberg's theory does imply that all humans need and must have a sense of gender identity to function at all, his theory predicts that children will become less rather than more rigid concerning gender roles as they mature. In fact, a secure gender identity may actually be associated with being less rigid about what one's gender identity means for what one can do and be in the world. If one is very certain that one *is* a male, then one might not fear breaking the rules about what males are supposed to be like.

Schema Theories

In the early 1980s several psychologists proposed theories of gender typing that use information-processing models.[44] Central to these models is the notion of "schema," a cognitive structure that involves expectations or associations that guide individuals' perceptions of the world. A schema provides a structure by which people can understand new situations and information by incorporating the new information into categories already present within the cognitive model. Schemas are anticipatory, in that people tend to look for and assimilate information in ways that correspond to them. They then provide an efficient means for people to integrate new knowledge and information while at the same time maintaining consistency and predictability for individuals as they enter new situations.

Gender schemas are cognitive structures that organize information on the basis of gender-based categories. Carol Lynn Martin and Charles Halvorson suggested that there are two types of gender schemas: an "in-group/out-group" schema that children use to categorize objects and information as either for their own sex group or the other, and a much more detailed and involved "own-sex" schema that involves the information children have about characteristics of their own sex group.[45] Children use these schemas to help them choose toys and behaviors and also in attending to new information. Activities are chosen on the basis of their correspondence to gender schemas, and new information is more often recalled if it is consonant with one's gender schema. When children (or adults) encounter information that is contrary to their established gender schema, they tend to either ignore it or interpret it in ways that correspond to their existing schema.[46]

Sandra Bem has focused on the detrimental aspects of gender schemas and the possibility that they could become less salient to individuals. In an explicitly feminist analysis she has suggested that individuals possess elaborate gender schemas because we live in a society that emphasizes differences between the sex groups. She has also suggested that if parents and the culture at large deemphasized gender-based distinctions, gender schemas should become less central as a means of organizing and processing information. Most of Bem's work has focused on variations among adults in the extent to which gender schemas guide their information processing, and this work has indicated that individuals can vary a great deal in the extent to which gender schemas are salient when they encounter new information.[47]

Yet it is clear that children tend to develop elaborate gender schemas as part of the process of developing their gender identities. Both cognitive developmental and schema theories take the issue of gender identity as a given and do not explicitly explore how children come to learn that there are males and females in the world and to identify and associate with their own sex group.[48] To address this issue and to compensate for the shortcomings of social learning theory, most psychologists now advocate a synthesis of these approaches.

COGNITIVE LEARNING THEORY: A SYNTHESIS

Clear gender differences in children's behavior appear in three areas: choice of toys and play activities, choice of playmates, and aggressive behavior.[49] These differences appear earlier than Kohlberg's developmental approach would suggest and before clear gender schemas might be expected to be established.[50] In addition, the behaviors seem quite resilient and resistant to change through modeling and various reinforcement schedules.

Gender labeling, the ability to identify correctly the sex group to which oneself and others belong, appears to be a major milestone in gender development. Children appear able to distinguish males and females from early infancy, but only as verbal skills become more developed can they accurately label others and themselves as either male or female. Once children understand gender labels they can deliberately adopt behaviors that they see as gender appropriate and interpret experiences in light of their gender schema.[51] Although gender differences in toy choices appear before children exhibit accurate gender labeling, once children have established this skill boys decrease their incidence of doll play, girls are less likely to exhibit aggressive behavior, and both boys and girls are more likely to play with children from the same sex group.[52] In other words, the major hallmarks of childhood gender typing become most clearly established once children understand gender labels.

The development of gender labeling and gender identity is primarily a cognitive process and one that all children eventually attain. Yet an extremely well designed observational study illustrates how parental behavior influences when children learn to apply gender labels correctly and illustrates how parents' gender schemas can influence their behavior toward their children and their development. Beverly Fagot and Mary Leinbach observed a number of children in their homes from the time they were 18 months to 4 years of age.[53] The children did not differ in scores on an ability test given at age 4, indicating that at least at that age they did not differ in measured intelligence. At 18 months of age they did not differ in their incidence of gender-typed behavior, even though their parents did exhibit different behaviors. By the age of 27 months some of the children could correctly assign gender labels and some could not. Parents of children who were able to correctly label gender earlier than other children were more likely than parents of late labelers to have given positive and negative responses to gender-typed toy play. The parents did not report large differences in how they thought children should be taught about gender-typed toys; they differed in the way they reacted to the children's toy choices. Fathers of early labelers were also more likely to have traditional attitudes toward women and child rearing. Fagot and Leinbach suggested that these different *affective* responses of the parents served as markers to the child of the importance of gender. Children who experienced such affective responses were more likely to perceive gender as important and thus devote more energy to understanding it, leading to their earlier acquisition of gender labeling skills.

Cognitive theories, such as gender schema theory and Kohlberg's developmental theory, help explain why children more often attend to models that they believe are typical of their own sex group. Children appear to imitate others when they can identify with them; they need to have some knowledge of their gender identity and attach a value to it before they begin to model.[54] Yet it is also possible that, just as early parental reinforcements influence the development of gender labeling, early imitations, before a child is aware of her or his own gender identity, may also influence gender role behaviors.[55]

The development of gender segregation also illustrates the importance of both cognitive and social learning processes. At a very early age children prefer to play with others of their own sex group. Although reinforcement schedules can alter this preference temporarily, the behavior quickly returns in other settings and after the special reinforcements cease. Although these behaviors appear with nonhuman primates, suggesting that there might be some type of biological bias toward the practice, preferences for same-sex companionship become extremely strong once gender labeling has appeared. No matter how feminine or masculine children's individual personality characteristics tend to be or how strong or weak their individual preference is for gender-typed toys, once they see themselves as male or female they gravitate toward others of their own sex group.[56]

Girls tend to exhibit this same-sex preference earlier than boys. Eleanor Maccoby and Carol Jacklin suggested that girls begin to avoid boys because they find boys' play style and interaction patterns, described in Chapter 7, as aversive.[57] Thus, they choose to play with other girls or stay near adults. If girls are forced to interact with boys in teacher-structured groups, they actually become less willing to have boys as partners in the future. After the age of 3, when gender schemas are more established, boys are just as active, if not more so, than girls in maintaining gender segregation.

No matter how gender segregation begins, once it is established, processes inherent to groups such as those that define in-groups and out-groups help perpetuate the phenomenon. Children themselves serve as powerful reinforcers and models of "appropriate" gender-typed behavior. D. B. Carter was careful to point out, however, that children do not just blindly imitate others' behaviors, but first compare the behavior of the other to what they consider typical of other same-sex individuals.[58] Moreover, the patterns of reinforcement appear to differ from all-boy to all-girl groups. Both boys' and girls' peer groups provide positive feedback to members when they play with their own sex group. But boys also give negative feedback to boys who engage in behavior that is not male typical. A study of children aged 21 to 25 months found that boys, but not girls, were very likely to give negative feedback to boys who engaged in female-typical behavior.[59] As a consequence of this high level of negative feedback, boys seem very likely to drop participation in female-typed activities.[60]

Parents and teachers do not appear to actively reinforce gender segregation, and many adult models of interaction available to children are actually cross-gender typed. Fathers are seen in nurturant, not work roles; both male and female teachers behave in largely similar ways. In fact, less gender segregation appears among children when adults are present. Adults appear to mitigate the behaviors of boys that girls find most aversive, even though boys tend to be less responsive than girls to teachers' feedback.[61]

A SUMMARY INTERPRETATION

In general, these findings illustrate the complex ways in which both cognitive and social learning variables, as well as affective qualities of parental reactions, influence children's adoption of gender-typed behaviors. Parents' affective responses to children's gender-typed behaviors appear to influence the age at which they understand gender labels. The cognitive understanding of gender labels seems to be important in influencing gender differences in toy choice, aggression, and peer associations. This cognitive understanding also appears to influence the ways in which children interpret reinforcements and models, with children choosing to attend to and model behavior that they perceive as appropriate for their sex group. As children become older, this learning process is largely automatic in nature because children rely on their more developed gender schemas to guide their assessment of new information and situations.

Using this more complex analysis allows one to see how gender-typed behaviors develop even when parents or other adults do not directly reinforce them. Social expectations communicated in the form of attributions may serve as powerful reinforcers. If a child knows he is a boy, he tries to act like one, and confirmation that he is doing so will be a positive reinforcement. For example, if a male child resists the commands of adults and overhears that he is "all-boy," even as he is punished for his disobedience, he is likely to be pleased and conclude that he has been successful in finding out and displaying the attributes really expected of boys. Thus, even though parents do not reward behaviors such as dependency and aggression that they see as gender typed, parents (especially fathers) do indeed think the sex groups differ. Children pick up on this and act accordingly.

Similarly with modeling, children see others as representing gender roles and thus get their ideas of how men and women, boys and girls, are supposed to act by observing the roles they play. Precisely because the cognitive development of young children is too immature for subtleties, their notions of what behaviors are appropriate to each sex group may actually be more stereotyped than those of their parents. In general, modeling theory may work better with respect to television models than parental models. In television, children can see gross images of the masculine model, larger than life as it were. Although a middle-class child may not know what his father does at his law office, he does know that cowboys are always males. Although television does offer readily available stereotypes, children would probably create them by themselves because cognitive immaturity causes children to simplify and concretize the phenomena they see.

The findings concerning reinforcement and modeling do suggest that fathers play a stronger part in typing their children than do mothers. As we saw, fathers are more likely to reinforce gender-typed behavior than mothers. Some of the evidence suggests that both boys and girls may model the mother as a person in terms of general competence, but that fathers and other males are more relevant where gender typing is concerned. David Lynn has suggested that boys view their fathers and other men as representing masculinity and that their identification with them is a positional rather than a personal identification. The findings that a girl's femininity is more closely related to her father's masculinity than to her mother's femininity suggests that girls may learn about at least the flirtatious and directly male-oriented aspects of femininity (as opposed to the motherly aspects) more from playing a role complementary to their fathers than by modeling their mothers. Thus, although these findings suggest that more than parental modeling is involved in gender typing, they also suggest that fathers, more so than mothers, are the focus of this gender typing.

The psychological theories reviewed in this chapter cannot account for the intensity that children, but especially boys, attach to gender typing and to gender segregation.[62] Moreover, it is difficult to see how the theories can account for male dominance. There seems to be little evidence that male dominance occurs because women are reinforced in passivity and dependence and, thus, are rendered incapable of competing with men. In the first place, there is little evidence that women are passive and dependent (although, as adults, women may admit to self-doubts more than men). There is also little evidence that reinforcement of passivity and dependence as such takes place, even though girls may be more restricted in their movements than boys. There is little evidence, too, that women become passive and dependent by modeling their mothers, especially as they model the mother role, which can hardly be called passive. These explanations of male dominance seem more than anything else to blame the victim and are unjustified by the empirical evidence.

Similarly, little in cognitive theories allows us to explain male dominance. Cognitive developmental theory tells us that children think males dominate because they are bigger and stronger, but these are the views of children and change as children become more sophisticated. Gender schema theory simply says that children reify an emphasis on gender differences that is present in the culture, but does not explain why inequality exists. In human society, where culture dominates biology, there must be other reasons why we tend to be governed by a paradigm that tells us males are better. In order to explain this, we turn in the next chapter to psychoanalytic theory and its several interpretations.

SUMMARY

Theoretical approaches from academic psychology have been used to explain how children acquire gender-typed behaviors. Social learning suggests that boys and girls are rewarded for different behaviors by their parents. Modeling theory is a variation of social learning theory that suggests that children learn gender roles by imitating their parents and others. Cognitive developmental theory posits that children first understand that they are boys and girls and then adopt the behaviors that they believe are appropriate for their sex group. Gender schema theories suggest that children use cognitive models, called schemas, that are based on gender categories to make decisions and interpret new information in their environment.

A combination of these approaches, which we have termed cognitive learning theory, appears to have the most support. Empirical evidence suggests that social learning occurs within a cognitive framework and that the development of the cognitive framework may be affected by social learning. Once the cognitive framework or gender schema is in place, social learning is selective, as children attend to reinforcers and models that they preceive are behaving in ways appropriate for their sex group. Although these theories can help account for how gender-differentiated behavior is learned, none of them can directly explain the higher valuation all societies give to males.

SUGGESTED READINGS

BEM, SANDRA LIPSITZ. 1981. "Gender Schema Theory: A Cognitive Account of Sex Typing." *Psychological Review*. 88:354–364. Describes gender schema theory from an explicitly feminist perspective.

BLOCK, JEANNE H. 1984. *Sex Role Identity and Ego Development*. San Francisco: Jossey-Bass. A collection of essays by this late psychologist covering psychological theories on gender differences as well as the possibility of social change.

FAGOT, BEVERLY I., and MARY D. LEINBACH. 1989. "The Young Child's Gender Schema: Environmental Input, Internal Organization." *Child Development.* 60:663–672. An example of empirical and theoretical work that illustrates the synthesis of cognitive and social learning theories.

HUSTON, ALETHA C. 1983. "Sex-Typing." Pp. 387–467 in *Handbook of Child Psychology: Vol. 4. Socialization, Personality, and Social Development* (4th ed.). Paul H. Mussen (series editor), E. Mavis Hetherington (volume editor). New York: Wiley. An extensive review of the literature on gender differences and psychological theories regarding gender role development.

MACCOBY, ELEANOR E., and CAROL NAGY JACKLIN. 1987. "Gender Segregation in Childhood." *Advances in Child Development and Behavior.* 20:239–287. Extensive discussion of literature on gender segregation and why it occurs.

chapter 9

Psychoanalytic Explanations of Gender Development and Male Dominance*

Although biological influences can explain some gender differences in psychological traits and social roles, they cannot account for the greater value given to male roles. Similarly, theories from academic psychology help explain how children learn gender roles and self-conceptions, but they cannot account for the importance of gender in people's lives, the intense feelings people have about gender roles and gender differences, or the greater value accorded male roles. To help account for these phenomena and for male dominance itself, we turn now to psychoanalytic theory.

This field, more than any other discipline, is explicitly concerned with gender differences, sexuality, gender identity, sexual preference, and their development. Although academic psychologists accustomed to controlled experiments have generally rejected psychoanalytic theory, it has been used by some anthropologists and sociologists concerned with the family, kinship, socialization, and the perpetuation of cultural patterns.

THE PSYCHOANALYTIC PERSPECTIVE

Psychoanalysis was founded by Sigmund Freud and remains an active discipline. Although a number of Freud's theories have been modified, challenged, and even dicarded by his followers over the years, the basic concepts and ideas that he introduced are still central to the discipline and have been widely accepted by others in the social sciences. These include his concept of the *unconscious*, the idea that we have thoughts and ideas not available to our conscious selves that affect our behavior, feelings, and physical well-being. This unconscious mental activity is not something simply unnoticed but something actively *repressed* (although not consciously so) because it is too threatening, painful, or unmanage-

---

* Parts of this chapter originally appeared in Jean Stockard and Miriam M. Johnson, "The Social Origins of Male Dominance," *Sex Roles*, 5 (1979), pp. 199–218, and are included here with the permission of Plenum Publishing Corporation.

able. Furthermore, psychoanalysis postulates that we unwittingly carry over, or *transfer*, attitudes born in old relationships into new relationships.[1] Psychoanalysis, then, explicitly acknowledges that people attach meaning to their experiences. In infants and young children these meanings are very primitive and global. The basic themes of these early fantasies and interpretations, which may later be repressed, reflect or represent relatively consistent themes in human sociosexual relations. A central theme that Freud focused on was the conflict set up in individuals between the near universal social taboo on incest and children's natural love for their parents. The psychologist Gardner Lindzey attributed the great impact that psychoanalysis has had in the behavioral sciences to the fact that it grounds itself on this universal human conflict.[2]

The original intent of psychoanalysis was to understand how people's experiences and interpretations could create neuroses or mental illnesses. Psychoanalysts believe that when people understand the reasons for their obsessions and delusions they can then deal with their illness. Freud reminded his readers "that psychoanalytic investigations have no more bias in any direction than has any other scientific research. In tracing back to its concealed source what is manifest, psychoanalysis has no aim but that of disclosing connections."[3] In exploring people's psychic lives psychoanalysts developed complex theories concerning the nature of masculinity and femininity, why most men become masculine and most women feminine.

The terms used by psychoanalysts have changed over the years. Freud built his theories from the assumption of certain underlying drives or instincts in human beings. Although he also discussed the importance of object relations—the soical associations of an individual with others—his writings tend to emphasize this biological basis. To a large extent other psychoanalytic writings through the 1930s shared this emphasis. By the 1940s, however, object relations theorists were arguing that the child's social relational experience from infancy rather than its fixation on various bodily zones determines psychological development and personality formation. These theorists interpret Freud's view that the personality is built up out of "precipitates of lost objects" to mean that the child internalizes representations of what a relationship meant emotionally and cognitively at a particular point in his or her early development. These internalized images, then, influence how the child perceives and responds to later events and people. These intermal representations "are neither the real person nor the whole person, but rather represent the meaning of a relationship to an individual" when they were emotionally and cognitively immature or inexperienced and thus unable to "process" or "evaluate" events as an adult might.[4] Thus, the images have great power.[5]

With a few notable exceptions, until very recently, most feminists have been hostile to psychoanalysis because "therapeutic" practices all too often try to reconcile women to femininity and male dominance.[6] Another reason for feminists' antipathy for Freud was the fear that he was a biological determinist. Although it is true that Freud put much stress on the anatomical differences between the sex groups and once made the statement that "anatomy is destiny," it is not true that he felt that gender typing came about completely automatically. That he made parent–child interaction so central suggests that he thought learning was involved. Although one may argue about the extent to which Freud thought gender-related behavior instinctual, it is very possible to view psychoanalysis as a theory of the social creation of masculinity and femininity.

More basically, many social scientists (both feminists and nonfeminists) have questioned psychoanalysis's claims of truth. These scientists argue that psychoanalytic ideas are not so much wrong as they are impossible to prove wrong, because the concepts and their connections with behavior are vague and untestable in controlled experimental situations. This is not a devastating criticism, however, because many of the phenomena that social scientists deal with are not amenable to experimental testing. The only appropriate way to refute psychoanalytic theory would not be in an experiment but by means of an alternative theory that more convincingly explained the behaviors it is concerned with.

In spite of the intense reaction against Freud by many feminists and experimental scientists, it is important to study his work and that of other psychoanalysts precisely because they, more than the members of any other discipline, deal with the very matters that concern feminists. As feminists themselves have delved deeper into the basic factors underlying the secondary status of women, they have concluded that Freud's analysis of the child's developing sexuality within the family and the consequences of the incest taboo is highly relevant. Even though Freud himself may have been guilty of sexism, a psychoanalytic perspective need not endorse male dominance. In fact, it can point toward important ways of altering that system.

Furthermore, even though psychoanalysis has been criticized for not being verified empirically, this does not mean that these theories do not have an empirical basis. Freud first developed his theories about psychosexual development by analyzing his own memories and dreams and those of his patients. Many of his patients were adults, but some were children. His students and followers added to the theories through their own observations and analyses of their patients. Some of these theorists, most notably Freud's own daughter, Anna, and Melanie Klein, extensively observed and analyzed children, often using play sessions in which they encouraged children to talk about their fantasies and imaginary creations. In more recent years, psychoanalysts through their observations of children have added much to our knowledge of how gender identity is formed.[7] Anthropologists have also observed the development of children in other cultures. Although the nature of the various developmental stages and processes psychoanalysts discuss may depend to some extent on who fills family roles (for instance, a maternal uncle may fill the functions in some matrilineal societies that a father does in patrilineal societies), these comparisons have also informed and generally confirmed the theories that we discuss below.

Despite agreement on basic concepts and purpose, psychoanalysis, like any ongoing discipline, has been rife with controversies and alternative approaches to various issues. The controversy regarding the development of masculinity and femininity began very early, and the two trends of thought that first appeared in the 1920s are still visible today. Although in our discussion we separate these two general approaches, they were first developed as a series of articles often written in response to each other.

Feminists have used insights derived from both schools of thought in their analyses of how gender identity forms and of how male dominance is reproduced. The phallocentric school, as we shall call it, is represented by Freud himself and stresses the Oedipus complex and the father in gender differentiation. The gynecentric school of thought corrects Freud's lack of emphasis on the impact of children's earliest relationship with the mother before the Oedipal period on the development of gender identity.

THE PHALLOCENTRIC VIEW

Although Freud began developing his phallocentric view early in his career, a number of other writers have also contributed to the approach. Helene Deutsch especially clarified the analysis of feminine development and modified some of Freud's most sexist views.* She also dealt more concretely with how the father influences the girl's adoption of some aspects of femininity. The work of Erik Erikson, a contemporary psychoanalyst, also fits into the phallocentric framework but modifies Freud's analysis by attributing more value to feminine orientations and traits than Freud did. Contemporary feminists have used Freud's phallocentric theory to analyze women's secondary status, and these analyses of the basis of male dominance are reviewed in the last part of this section.

Developmental Stages

Freud's theory of self-development is a theory of gender socialization because he recognized that males and females have different experiences in the parental family in their formative years. He suggested that childhood development occurs in several stages, each involving a different focus of sexual energy. These developmental stages are analytic concepts, and they may not be clearly demarcated in an individual child. Freud believed that they can overlap and in fact often occur simultaneously.

Only at the third developmental stage, after the so-called oral and anal stages, did Freud suggest that males and females begin to develop differently. In this stage children expand their awareness to the genital area of their body. Freud called this the phallic stage, and it is at this stage that children experience the Oedipus complex and become aware of the incest taboo.[8]

---

* Helene Deutsch's work shows elements of both perspectives that we discuss here. Although she was a student of Freud's (as was Ernest Jones) and followed his analysis of developmental stages, she also used some of the work of gynecentric theorists in discussing the nature of penis envy and in emphasizing the importance of the mother in development. This illustrates how much the two perspectives are part of the total discipline of psychoanalysis and how the writings show mutual influences.

Freud came to believe that even very young children have some idea of the nature of sexual acts. In his self-analysis of the late 1890s he found the core of the Oedipus complex. He discovered in himself and later in both his male and female patients an early desire to possess the mother and a corresponding jealousy of the father. For the boy this desire is thwarted when he perceives that he cannot possess her, for she belongs to the father. The boy also fears retribution from the father in the form of castration if he should act on his desires, so he gives up his desire for the mother in a massive act of repression and identifies with the father.

It is important to understand that Freud always assumed that both males and females have a bisexual potential. A male child not only has a wish to actively possess his mother, but he also has a feminine wish to be passively possessed by his father. When the boy becomes aware in the phallic period of the anatomical fact of having a penis, he increases the active masculine desire for the mother. At this point the boy also makes a strong connection between the degradation of women and their lack of a penis. The realization of the possibility of castration, the undesirable results (becoming like a woman), and the fear of this possibility lead to the resolution of the boy's Oedipus complex. He renounces his claim for the mother in deference to the father. His desires for the mother become sublimated and in essence destroyed. He also represses his jealousy of the father and identifies with him and takes over the father's prohibitions into his own psyche in the form of a conscience, or superego.

Freud did not see the girl's experience as a mirror image of the boy's and did not approve of Carl Jung's use of the term *Electra complex* to describe the girl's experience. Freud believed that the resolution of the phallic phase was different and more complex for girls than for boys. In the phallic stage, just as the boy discovers his penis, the girl discovers her clitoris. Because stimulation of the clitoris brings her pleasure, it functions for her like the penis does for the boy. Thus, Freud believed that her orientation at this point is masculine and that she too wants to actively possess the mother. But Freud assumed that in comparing herself to little boys, the girl feels that her organ is inferior, that she has been shortchanged. Although she believes at first that her clitoris will grow to match the boy's penis, she later decides that although she once had the larger appendage, it was removed. She has been castrated. This is the girl's castration complex. Freud believed that although the boy fears castration, the girl thinks that she is castrated and accepts the "fact" of her castration. Freud called the girl's hope that she could regain the penis *penis envy*.

As a result of her castration complex, Freud suggested, the girl gives up clitoral masturbation and enters the Oedipal phase. The realization that she does not have a penis makes her turn from the mother as her love object to the father in the hope that he can give her a baby to replace her lost penis. The girl transforms her desire for a penis into a desire for a child. The core of the Oedipus complex for the girl is the hope that the father will give her this child (penis). Because she gradually realizes the father will not do this, Freud believed that she abandons the Oedipus complex only slowly and always remains to a certain extent suspended in a dependent relationship with both her mother and father.

Later Modifications of Phallocentric Theory

Freud's idea that females are mutilated males and that females deeply envy males' genitalia is obviously sexist and unsupported by evidence. Both Helene Deutsch and Erik Erikson, although retaining major aspects of Freud's analysis, have tried to alter the concept of penis envy. Deutsch accepted the view of the gynecentric theorists (see below) that what appeared to be penis envy is not a deep-seated phenomenon, but simply a rationalization or defense mechanism against emotions regarding the mother. Deutsch also suggested that penis envy is only half of a genital trauma for young girls that results from giving up the clitoris without yet being in a position to use the vagina. In other words, Deutsch suggested that penis envy is only part of a larger genital trauma that arises because girls have no conspicuous genital organs on which to focus their energies.[9]

Erikson goes a step beyond Deutsch's formulation by focusing on the positive elements of both males' and females' genitalia rather than only on those of males. Erikson once asked a large number of children to create "an exciting scene from an imaginary moving picture" using a collection of toys and blocks. Through this method he hoped to understand more about how they saw themselves and the world around them. Both he and independent researchers observed that the girls tended to create peaceful interior scenes with people in sitting or standing positions. Their scenes had low walls and occasionally an elaborate doorway with dangerous intruders. Boys tended to build scenes with high towers, walls with protrusions, and people outside the enclosures and moving about. The boys' scenes often displayed accidents and dangers of collapse and ruin.[10] Using this play as an indicator of psychic life, much as Freud used the memories of free association, Erikson suggested that the scenes portrayed important characteristics of male and female development and outlook. Although not concentrating on the obvious interpretation of the males' displays of protrusions and activity, he explored the possibility that the females' constructions suggested a theme of inner space. Erikson proposed that psychoanalysis make "a shift of theoretical emphasis from the loss of an external organ to a sense of vital inner potential; . . . from a 'passive' renunciation of male activity to the purposeful and competent pursuit of activities consonant with the possession of ovaries, a uterus, and a vagina."[11] In short, Erikson modified Freud's view of penis envy by focusing on what he saw as the positive aspects of women's genitalia and psyche. He believed that this perspective can provide a new way of examining the development of women without necessarily seeing them as wounded men.

Development of the Superego

For Freud the different ways in which boys and girls resolve the Oedipus complex lead to important characterological differences between the sex groups.

In boys the castration complex promotes a prompt and sure resolution of the Oedipus complex and the development of the superego. The superego is the conscience, the moral authority, and arbiter within the individual. It enforces the rules of society on the individual, most especially the incest taboo. Freud believed that when the Oedipus complex succumbs to the threat of castration, the boy firmly establishes the superego. "This new psychical agency continues to carry on the functions which have hitherto been performed by people (the abandoned objects) in the external world: it observes the ego [the rational part of the self], gives it orders, judges it, and threatens it with punishments, exactly like the parents whose place it has taken."[12]

Freud believed that for the girl, however, the Oedipus complex can never be fully resolved. For Freud castration is a foregone fact that produces the girl's Oedipus complex instead of motivating its resolution. The Oedipus complex can only gradually disappear; and, because it cannot be totally resolved, Freud believed that women never develop the strong superego that men develop:

> Their superego is never so inexorable, so impersonal, so independent of its emotional origins as we require it to be in men. Character traits which critics of every epoch have brought up against women—that they show less sense of justice than men, that they are less ready to submit to the great necessities of life, that they are more often influenced in their judgments by feelings of affection or hostility—all these would be amply accounted for by the modification in the formation of their superego which we have already inferred.[13]

Obviously some feminists have been outraged and many psychoanalysts embarrassed by the devaluation of women implied in Freud's characterization of their weak superegos. Within the psychoanalytic community itself, Helene Deutsch, David Gutmann (Chapter 7), and Erik Erikson have tried to counteract Freud's view by giving women's characteristics the same value as men's.

Freud's theory of gender development obviously has a masculine bias that assumes the physical superiority of the penis and the moral superiority of males' psyches. Although he admitted that he could not fully explain female development and looked to the writings of others for explication, Freud never renounced the basic phallocentric nature of his work.[14] Women for Freud tended to be deprived males. He believed that their initial impulses were masculine and that motherhood for women was not a basic superiority or even an equivalent capability, but a circuitous route for women to get a penis for themselves. Deutsch and Erikson attempted to alter some of the more objectionable parts of Freud's work, but retained his general phallocentric emphasis.

EXPLANATIONS OF MALE DOMINANCE USING FREUD'S PHALLOCENTRIC THEORY

Juliet Mitchell and Gayle Rubin are feminist theorists who hold to Freud's own analysis because they see it as an essentially accurate description of the symbolic ideas held by both males and females in a male-dominated society. They look at the incest taboo that arises from the resolution of the Oedipus complex as the key element of kinship systems. Because kinship arrangements are made possible by the incest taboo and always seem to involve male dominance, Mitchell and Rubin suggest that somehow the source of male power may lie within the resolution of the Oedipus complex itself.

The Oedipus Complex and Male Dominance

Juliet Mitchell interpreted the girl's resolution of her Oedipus complex as representing "her acceptance of her inferior, feminine place in patriarchal society."[15] She sees Freud as documenting that women at first are active and masculine but are forced to give up and reconcile themselves to femininity. Mitchell does not accept Shulamith Firestone's notion that penis envy in the female child simply recognizes the social fact that males really do have power.[16] Neither does she think that women literally envy the male organ in an anatomical sense. Rather, both she and Rubin have suggested that women envy the penis because in male-dominated cultures the phallus (a term meaning the erect penis and which Freud used on occasion to mean the symbolic penis) is seen as a symbol for male dominance. In male-dominated cultures the phallus *is* considered to be of great value. According to Mitchell and Rubin, following the French psychoanalyst Lacan, the organ itself is neither good nor bad, worthy or unworthy, powerful or powerless, until it is given a cultural definition. The presence or absence of the phallus stands for both the categorizing of humans into two basic types and also for the dominance of the type with the phallus, namely males.

Mitchell and Rubin have suggested that the Oedipal phase is the time when gender identity is organized according to the kinship rules of the culture. If the boy gives up his mother to his father during the Oedipal crisis, his father will validate the phallus in his son (accept him as a male and not castrate him). The little girl lacks this symbolic token that can be exchanged for a woman. She never gets the phallus. She can get it in intercourse or in the form of a child, but only as a gift from a man. Thus, the resolution of the Oedipus complex for the girl means accepting castration, becoming feminine, and giving in to male dominance. Rubin and Mitchell have suggested that it is no wonder some women refuse to give up and envy the phallus, because accepting femininity involves accepting a secondary status.*

---

*Juliet Mitchell, especially, has tended to be almost totally uncritical of Freud's work. Her *Psychoanalysis and Feminism* suggests that Freud's own analysis is far superior to those theorists who have attempted to revise his work.[17] Nancy Chodorow took issue with Mitchell's unquestioning acceptance of Freud.[18] She argued that although sometimes Freud was describing how women do in fact develop in a patriarchal society, at other times he was simply making assertions about women's reactions that are not supported by clinical evidence. She argued that even though the phallus is a valued symbol, it is pure male fantasy to assume that the instant a little girl sees a boy's penis she wants one. According to Chodorow, it does a

Kinship and Male Dominance

Both Mitchell and Rubin use the arguments of Claude Levi-Strauss,[19] the noted contemporary French anthropologist. He suggested that men's dominance is reflected not only in the extradomestic exchange of gifts and goods, but more importantly in the extradomestic exchange of women themselves. According to Levi-Strauss the institution of marriage involves essentially the exchange of women by men. Levi-Strauss argued that the taboo on incest is a social invention that forces the exchange of women outside the immediate kin group to which they belong. This establishes social ties and obligations between kin groups. The incest taboo, then, is not simply a prohibition of marriage with close relatives for biological reasons. It has a social function: requiring that groups give marriage partners to outsiders. The act of exchange and the resulting reciprocal relationships create alliances between kin groups and make a wider community possible. Thus, the existence of society itself depends on the incest taboo.

More important, according to Levi-Strauss, it has always been men who exchange women and not vice versa. This can be seen in our own society in the custom of the father giving the bride away in marriage ceremonies. Thus Levi-Strauss notes:

> The total relationship of exchange which constitutes marriage is not established between a man and a woman, but between two groups of men, and the woman figures only as one of the objects in the exchange, not as one of the partners. . . . This remains true even when the girl's feelings are taken into consideration, as, moreover, is usually the case. In acquiescing to the proposed union, she precipitates or allows the exchange to take place, she cannot alter its nature.[20]

Rubin succinctly summarized the importance of this insight: "It suggests that we look for the ultimate locus of women's oppression within the *traffic in women*, rather than with the traffic in merchandise."[21] Levi-Strauss focused our attention on kinship structures rather than economic relations. Rubin stressed that Levi-Strauss's exchange of women thesis should not be taken too literally, however. She suggested that the term is "shorthand for expressing that the social relations of a kinship system specify that men have certain rights in their female kin, and that women do not have the same rights either to themselves or to their male kin."[22]

Neither Freud nor Levi-Strauss directly addressed the question of why men exchange women instead of women exchanging men or the more general question of why male dominance exists. Yet their theories suggest that the answer to the origin of male dominance in human societies may lie in men's roles in kinship systems rather than in their roles in the production and exchange of goods. Levi-Strauss went on to argue that because there are very few universal aspects of the division of labor between the sexes apart from tasks related to child

---

disservice to psychoanalysis as a theory of personality development to adopt Freud uncritically, even as a description of psychosexual development in a male-dominant society.

care, there must be some reason besides biological capacity for the sex-based division of labor found in every society. He proposed that the division of labor is a societal device to create "a reciprocal state of dependency between the sexes."[23] In essence, assigning sharply different roles to males and females makes them depend on each other and thus motivates marriage or relatively permanent bonding between the sex groups.

Rubin went beyond Levi-Strauss's idea that the division of labor between men and women necessitates marriage and has suggested that heterosexuality and gender identity itself are also socially imposed. She has suggested that "far from being an expression of natural differences, exclusive gender identity is the suppression of natural similarities. It requires repression: in men, of whatever is the local version of 'feminine' traits; in women, of the local definition of 'masculine' traits."[24] Even in societies that allow homosexuality under certain circumstances, heterosexuality is always the predominant norm, and homosexual relationships tend also to be defined in terms of mutual dependencies.

To illustrate Rubin's general point, a number of primitive societies provide for the possibility that some individuals find it very difficult to fit into the gender role prescribed for their biological sex. These societies create additional gender categories or statuses (supernumerary sexes) for those who cannot fit into the ordinary gender categories. Both the Mohave and the Chuckchee, for example, recognize only two biological sexes but generate four rather than two gender statuses. Among the Mohave Indians centered in what is now California, biological females were allowed to adopt a masculine-like role and were called *hwame,* and biological males could adopt a feminine-like role and be called *alyha.* Most individuals who chose to do this underwent a ceremonial initiation into their new status at puberty. Individuals in each category could marry persons of the same biological sex, but they took a role similar to that of the other sex.[25] Thus, the resulting union between two males or two females was socially defined as a heterosexual union of social female and male. These practices suggest that societies insist upon complementary gender statuses for reasons other than biological propensity, specifically as a way of defining social order. The presence of supernumerary sexes does not really challenge the division of labor between the sex groups, because there is always a tendency to assimilate the supernumerary sexes to one or the other sex group.

Thus, according to Rubin, human sexuality is organized in the interest of kinship organization, which rests upon the incest taboo and heterosexuality. The incest taboo forces marriage outside the immediate kin group, and obligatory heterosexuality reinforces marriage itself. Mitchell and Rubin have suggested that the Oedipal phase is the time when gender identity is organized according to the kinship rules of the culture.

Mitchell's and Rubin's analyses suggest that the secondary status of women is very deeply rooted indeed. They have argued that for change to occur the Oedipus complex itself must be attacked. Because the Oedipus complex rests upon the internalization of kinship rules, Rubin has claimed that "feminists must call for a revolution in kinship."[26] Neither Rubin nor Mitchell, however, has given a very clear picture of how this may occur. Rubin has suggested that males' sharing child-care responsibility with females may be important in that it could make individuals bisexual. She implied that somehow both gender identity and obligatory heterosexuality would have to disappear before the whole Oedipal structure that oppresses women could collapse. Mitchell has argued that the family is actually unnecessary in capitalist societies and has suggested but not developed the idea that the key for change may lie in the contradiction between the irrelevancy of kinship exchange in capitalist society and the societal demands that it be preserved.

In the last analysis, neither Mitchell nor Rubin offers much hope for change. The possibility or even desirability of eliminating human kinship systems altogether as a way of ending male dominance seems highly questionable. Also it is questionable if one can eliminate gender identity totally, as Rubin seems to imply, because it does have a body image basis. Mitchell and Rubin both repeated Freud's practice of including in the concept of gender identity not only the self-definition of a person as male or female, but also sexual preference. As we shall show later, it is important to keep these two factors separate because they may have separate sources.

Summary and Interpretation

For phallocentric theorists, femininity is problematic. Freud saw the route to masculinity as rather straightforward, ending with identification with the father. Girls by contrast arrive at what he called "mature femininity" by a very circuitous route in which they are induced to give up their active masculine strivings and become acquiescent and passive. Mitchell and Rubin, feminists who accept the phallocentric emphasis, have interpreted the difficulty of becoming feminine as referring to the fact that in a male-dominant society, women are oppressed by femininity and resist taking it on. Phallocentric theorists stress, however, that the phallocentric emphasis in our society and in all societies is a cultural, not a biological phenomenon. In male-dominated cultures the phallus is valued.

Although one must be extremely cautious in accepting their conclusions regarding anthropological studies, Mitchell's and Rubin's analyses seem important in focusing our attention on human kinship systems and on the fact that within them women are secondary to men. Their analyses can be linked to a theme we have stressed previously: Women's secondary status seems more related to their role as wives than as mothers. The wife role is a kinship role par excellence because it is marriage between unrelated individuals that makes kinship systems possible. In phallocentric cultures, women are defined in relation to the phallus. They are seen as wives, or sex objects, primarily and as mothers, or people, secondarily. They serve the kinship system.

The gynecentric theorists do not deny that we live in a phallocentric culture, but they ask why this occurs. Although phallocentric theorists focus on the phallic period and the Oedipus complex, gynecentric theorists focus on the pre-Oedipal period as the source of males' apparent need to dominate. They point to the universal phenomenon of women's mothering as the source.

THE GYNECENTRIC VIEW

In the decade from 1925 to 1935 psychoanalysis focused a great deal of attention on masculine and feminine development, and the different theories were first developed. Ernest Jones, Freud's student and biographer, gave the most definitive articulation of the different approaches and tried to arbitrate the dispute. The work of Melanie Klein and Karen Horney, two early feminists, was most important in Jones's formulation, and the later writings of Helene Deutsch, Ronald Fairbairn, and Nancy Chodorow have contributed further ideas. The various issues raised have never been fully resolved but have reappeared in different forms to the present day.

All the writers we discuss, although approaching the question of childhood development in a different way from Freud, accept his ideas of the unconscious, of repression, and of the importance of sexuality in human society. The changes in emphasis in the gynecentric perspective over the years involved a move from biological and physical descriptions by the early writers to an emphasis on social relations and the development of the ego in later years. Although the descriptive terms and emphases change, the gynecentric basis of the analysis remains the same.

The gynecentric position turns Freud's conception around and stresses that a feminine orientation predominates for both males and females in the first stage of life. The gynecentric basis of this position is obvious. The mother is the first person to whom the children relate. Moreover, the first primary orientation of children toward the world around them is seen as feminine. These theorists view castration anxiety as only a secondary manifestation. In contrast to Freud's own view, the gynecentric theorists do not see femininity as a secondary phenomenon, but as part of the child's first orientation toward the world.

The Pre-Oedipal Stages

For gynecentric theorists the first stage in life involves a feminine orientation. Based on her analyses of children, Melanie Klein emphasized the importance of the oral-incorporative stage and the child's close relationship with the mother in early infancy. Helene Deutsch also emphasized that children's first object relation is with the mother figure. She feeds, cleans, and directs them through the first years of life. Deutsch stressed that it is only natural that children develop not only intense affective attachments to the mother, but also dependencies.[27] The quality of this first-love relationship between the mother and child is the basis of all subsequent development.[28] The relationship is a "primary identification, the precursor of object love"[29] and is necessary for the formation of the ego, or self. It is not, however, a complete symbiosis or linkage, for observations of children indicate that children have at least a preliminary notion of themselves as separate from others.[30] This strong attachment applies to whoever cares for the child, but because the person is generally a female, this primary identification is feminine in nature in all known cultures.

Most of these theorists agree with Freud that this pre-Oedipal period is largely similar for boys and girls. But whereas Freud thought a masculine orientation predominates, the gynecentric theorists think a feminine orientation prevails. Both boys and girls identify with the mother, and "definitive differentiation" between the sexes occurs later.[31] Yet mothers, because they have once been the daughters of mothers, may identify more with their girl children than with their boy children. The tie between a mother and daughter may be stronger than that between the mother and son because the mother tries to repeat "her own mother–child history."[32]

The Girl's Oedipus Complex

Whereas Freud believed that the phallic phase represented a basic masculine orientation in girls, gynecentric theorists (both classical and contemporary) suggest that the phallic phase really only manifests attempts to deal with deep-seated anxiety about aggression against the mother and guilt associated with the Oedipus complex.[33] Karen Horney, for example, talked about a "fictitious male role" to which girls retreat in order to deny their incestuous desires for the father.[34]

Because the phallic stage or penis envy is not really a stage but a defensive position, it is never fully overcome. Instead, as the girl grows older, the need for this defense lessens. She develops other defensive postures and realizes that her wish for a penis is an unsatisfactory solution to her anxiety and desire to be separate from the mother. Her femininity, which has always been present, is then more visible. Thus, according to gynecentric theorists, the girl does not revert to femininity because she cannot have masculinity. Femininity is the basic identity.

The gynecentric theorists do not accept Freud's view that the resolution of the Oedipus complex leads to a weaker superego for girls than for boys. They agree with Freud that the superego is based on the incorporation of the parental figures. However, they suggest that this incorporation begins in the first stages of life.

The gynecentric theorists with an object relations orientation and interest in ego psychology stress that the Oedipus crisis involves breaking the primary identification and dependence on the mother that was established in earlier stages. The father assists in breaking these ties. Ronald Fairbairn suggested that the resolution of the Oedipus complex is a key element in the move away from infantile dependence on the mother. For him, "the 'overcoming of the Oedipus complex' . . . is clearly the struggle to repress an elaborate unresolved infantile dependence on parents, and ultimately on the mother, under the pressure of the need to adjust to the demands of outer life on an increasingly grown-up level."[35]

Resolution of the Oedipus crisis involves both transformation of the first primary identification with the mother and breaking the intense ties of dependence formed in early infancy. Helene Deutsch[36] and Nancy Chodorow[37] have noted how the father helps break the girl's dependent ties with the mother. They have suggested that older women also help widen the girl's social world and encourage her independence from the mother. The daughter has both strong affectional ties and also hostility toward the mother, especially as she grows older, because she sees her mother as keeping her as a child. This vacillation and dependence on the mother continue to at least some extent throughout life, and one can never fully break this dependent tie.[38]

Chodorow has stressed particularly the significance of the girl's pre-Oedipal tie to her mother in her resolution of the Oedipus complex.[39] Daughters, according to Chodorow, do not feel inadequate because they have no penis. Rather, they, along with boys, feel inadequate because of the mother's omnipotence. Unlike the male child, the girl does not have a penis to help her feel separate and independent from the mother, and also the mother herself feels differently toward her daughter from the way she feels toward her son. Penis envy in girls, then, according to this view, develops, not because girls wish to become men, but because they want to liberate themselves from the mother and become "complete, autonomous *women*."[40]

These authors have also suggested that a girl might develop penis envy because she needs the mother's love. This need coupled with her perception that the mother prefers men may cause the girl to feel she needs a penis in order to win her mother's love. Here it is the girl's love for her mother rather than her hostility toward her that explains penis envy.

Both these explanations have the advantage of not positing some biologically given heterosexuality in explaining the girl's turn toward the father. Both suggest that the girl's turn to the father is not because she already is heterosexual but rather because of the nature of her relationship with her mother and because of her mother's own attitudes. Although the father encourages the girl's male-oriented femininity, the girl's identity as a woman is developed in her first, early identification with the mother.

The Boy's Oedipus Complex

The early gynecentric theorists stressed that the first orientation of boys, as well as girls, is feminine. As with the development of girls, the gynecentric theorists see male castration anxiety (the fear of castration) as only a secondary manifestation of the resolution of the phallic phase. The theoretical explanation of the process is extremely complex and involves fantasies the boy creates to deal with his anxiety regarding his desires for the mother and his fears of both parents.[41]

Later writers in the gynecentric vein emphasized how changes in social relations prompt the resolution of the boy's Oedipus crisis. Helene Deutsch again saw the father as helping to promote the boy's independence from the mother. In a man-to-man relationship the father encourages the boy's independence from the mother and even supports his devaluation of the mother. The nature of this father and son relationship varies from one family to another and affects the boy's later life.

Although the father helps promote a boy's gender identity—his conviction that he is male—this process is more difficult for males than for females because their first and primary identity was feminine. The boy must replace his early feminine identification with the mother with a masculine identification, usually based on the father or other males. But adult males tend to be remote from the world of children and are not available for identification. The boy's identification with the masculine role then tends to be more diffuse, an identification with a position or a fantasized image rather than with a person. Because what he knows most intimately is feminine, the boy comes to define masculinity as that which is not feminine. Internally he rejects his early attachment to and dependence on the mother. Externally he devalues what is feminine and denies his attachment to the feminine world.[42]

Both because the male's identity is built upon a negative basis, only knowing what it is not, and because there are few actual males with whom the boy can identify, his sex role identity is more ambiguous and unstable than the girl's. Chodorow has suggested that boys' and girls' different experiences of identification contribute to their later life orientations.[43] The girl may continue her personal identifications with others, primarily with her children and other women. The boy, however, less often has personal identifications, having neither close relationships with children nor in many societies personal affective relationships with other men. Some work with transsexuals supports this thesis that males' first identification is feminine and that difficulties in breaking this tie produce problems in gender identification.[44]

Summary

In contrast to Freud's phallocentric approach, the gynecentric theorists assert that children's first orientation is feminine. The castration anxiety and penis envy Freud noted are seen by these theorists as secondary manifestations that result from anxiety regarding the Oedipus complex and hostility toward and fear of the mother. The Oedipus complex is seen as both the time at which children develop greater independence from the mother and the point at which their gender identity becomes fixed. Because the child's basic identity is feminine, the boy's gender identity is less stable than that of the girl, yet the girl may maintain a closer relationship to the mother. Based on clinical experience, most contemporary psychoanalysts support this gynecentric focus on pre-

Oedipal relationships rather than on Freud's phallocentric view that emphasizes the Oedipal period.[45] This perspective on gender development is also especially helpful in understanding motives underlying male dominance.

GYNECENTRIC EXPLANATIONS OF MALE DOMINANCE

Two basic themes, both of which arise from the emphasis on the pre-Oedipal period of intense mother–child contact, are important in the gynecentric analysis of male dominance. One involves the unconscious fear and envy children of both sexes, but especially males, feel toward the mother. The other concerns the problems males encounter in establishing a secure sense of masculine gender identity. The earliest gynecentric theorists tended to emphasize the fear-and-envy hypothesis. Later ones, who used an object relational analysis, emphasized identity problems of males. None of the early theorists was primarily concerned with explaining male dominance, but some did point to how the early primacy of the mother is related to a tendency of males to devalue females and femininity. Below we trace each of these themes and explore their implications for change.

Fear and Envy of Women

The early gynecentric theorists stressed how the mother's power over the child in its early years contributes to the child's unconscious fear and envy first of its mother and later of women in general. This stems from the child's total dependence on the mother and the child's hostility and ambivalence that arise at the Oedipal period. Although both female and male children experience this fear and envy, the female can counter it later with the fact that she herself is a female. The male child has no such relief, and the envy and dread may be repressed and later expressed collectively in legends, artwork, and ceremonies and sometimes individually in dreams and neuroses. Below we note examples of how this fear and envy are shown in the actions of individuals, in stories and art, and in collective ceremonies and customs and how they relate to individual and group efforts to devalue the activities and nature of women.*

Karen Horney reported a small experiment conducted in a children's clinic in Germany that she interpreted as confirming the strength of males' symbolic fear of the vagina:

> The physician [who conducted the experiment] was playing ball with the children at a treatment center and after a time showed them that the ball had a slit in it. She pulled the edges of the slit apart and put her finger in, so that it was held fast by the

---

*Freud himself noted men's dread of women's genitals in his analysis of "The Taboo on Virginity,"[46] but he later dropped this in favor of men's fear of castration by the father or his representatives. The gynecentric theorists, however, developed this idea in their own work. Ernest Jones suggested that the boy believes his own genitals are inferior in size to his mother's vagina and that this influences a boy's castration fears at the time of the Oedipus crisis.[47]

> ball. Of 28 boys whom she asked to do the same, only 6 did it without fear and 8 could not be induced to do it at all. Of 19 girls, 9 put their finger in without a trace of fear; the rest showed a slight uneasiness but none of them serious anxiety.[48]

Horney linked men's general fear of women to the boy's fear of being rebuffed by the mother and the subsequent loss of self-esteem. In turn she saw this fear as prompting men's compulsion to prove their manhood. This compulsion is linked to the desire to conquer or possess many women, "the propensity to debase the love object"—that is, to love only women who are seen as less than equal to them, and the tendency to "diminish the self-respect of the woman."[49]

Fear of women and of female genitalia may be seen in both myths and written history in widely varying cultures. This fear may be masked, however, by outward glorification of women. For example, a medieval statue when viewed from the front appears to be a peaceful serene woman, but from the back it is literally "covered with sores, ulcers, worms and all manner of pestilence."[50] Hays specifically argued that social institutions in societies from the most primitive to the most modern have been designed to defend men against their fears of women by circumscribing, regulating, and containing women.[51]

In addition to fear, however, there is an element of envy and even awe in men's attitudes toward women. Margaret Mead argued that men envy women's procreative powers and interpreted some initiation ceremonies and puberty rites of primitive tribes as attempts to give this mysterious power to men. In the parts of New Guinea she studied, "it is men who spend their ceremonial lives pretending that it was they who had borne the children, that they can 'make men.'"[52] According to Mead, men in New Guinea also tell stories about how their mythical man-making powers were invented by a woman and stolen from her by men.* Other groups in this area have initiation ceremonies in which boys are taught to make their noses bleed in imitation of female menstruation.[55]

Horney and Mead both suggested a probable link between men's envy of women and their cultural productivity, their creation of material and cultural goods,[56] and their need for achievement.[57] This may be seen in the biblical account of creation in Genesis, where the woman Eve is in effect born of the man Adam. Also, primitive initiation ceremonies of boys are conducted by older men, suggesting the idea of boys being reborn, this time of men. Thus, the initiation of males by males along with some of the symbolism can be taken as an acting out of the repressed male wish to give birth. "He [the boy] still carries his knowledge of child-birth as something that women can do, that his sister will be able to do, as a latent goad to some other type of achievement. He embarks on a long course of growth and practice, the outcome of which, if he sees it as not only being able to possess a woman, but to become a father, is very uncertain."[58]

---

*This idea has been attributed to Bruno Bettleheim, who devoted a chapter to it in his book *Symbolic Wounds*.[53] Mead noted that Bettleheim used her own discussion of these activities, which she published in *Male and Female* in 1949, without acknowledgment and then speculated on "why men said they had stolen their supernatural imitative feminine powers from women!"[54]

These writers focus on how males' fear and envy of women prompt their need to separate their activities from women's and to devalue women's role. Dorothy Dinnerstein argued that both women and men agree to let males have the power in the adult world because this power is less of a psychological threat than the power the mother had over them as infants. She emphasized that both males and females fear the power of the mother and suggested that we give males authority because it appears to be a refuge from female authority. Female rule is more threatening because it is more primitive and more all-encompassing—"the relatively limited despotism of the father is a relief to us."[59] Thus, "both men and women use the unresolved early threat of female domination to justify keeping the infantilism in themselves alive under male domination."[60]

Tenuous Masculine Identity

Although unconscious fear and envy of the mother's power may prompt men to separate their own activities from women's and to elevate their own power, the tenuous nature of males' gender identity also contributes to this motive. Cultural ceremonies illustrate men's need to break with the world of women when they enter adulthood. For men all initiation ceremonies signify passage into the adult male role. Cross-culturally initiation ceremonies are much more common for males than for females, suggesting that it is males who need an extra push into masculinity. Initiation ceremonies for young men are also more common in father-absent societies, whose sleeping patterns and residence arrangements emphasize and exaggerate the mother–son bond.[61] Other evidence from our own society indicates that in cultural groups where the father is only rarely involved in childhood socialization young males tend to develop their own initiatory rites, such as gang or club membership, to demonstrate their departure from the world of women.*

Moreover, just as Margaret Mead suggested that males' fear of women influences their achievement needs, so does their need to separate their own identity from women's. In a great number of human societies, men's sureness of their gender role is tied up with their right or ability to practice some activity that women are not allowed to practice. Their maleness, in fact, has to be underwritten by preventing women from entering some field or performing some feat. Here may be found the relationship between maleness and pride, a need for prestige that will outstrip the prestige accorded to any woman. There seems no evidence that it is necessary for men to surpass women in any specific way. Rather, men do need to find reassurance in achievement. Because of this connection, cultures frequently phrase achievement as something that women do not or cannot do, rather than directly as something that men do well:

---

*Clearly, initiation ceremonies have multiple meanings and functions. By discussing their possible psychological significance for masculinity we do not mean to imply that these are their only function.

> The recurrent problem of civilization is to define the male role satisfactorily enough—whether it be to build gardens or raise cattle, kill game or kill enemies, build bridges or handle bank-shares—so that the male may in the course of his life reach a solid sense of irreversible achievement, of which his childhood knowledge of the satisfactions of child-bearing have given him a glimpse. . . . If men are ever to be at peace, they must have, in addition to paternity, culturally elaborated forms of expression that are lasting and sure. Each culture—in its own way—has developed forms that will make men satisfied in their constructive activities without distorting their sure sense of their masculinity.[62]

In recent writings Evelyn Keller and Jessica Benjamin have suggested, using somewhat different theoretical arguments, that science (Keller) and Western culture itself, especially its erotic imagery (Benjamin) are structured in ways that reflect men's deep-seated concerns with maintaining dominance and control. Using D. W. Winnicott's version of object relations theory they have suggested that these overwhelming concerns with hierarchy and control are rooted in early childhood experiences.[63]

This tenuous identity influences males' devaluation of women. Nancy Chodorow stressed that the boy's "attempt to gain an elusive masculine identification . . . explains the psychological dynamics of the universal social and cultural devaluation and subordination of women."[64] The boy, in order to deny his attachment and deep personal identification with his mother, does so "by repressing whatever he takes to be feminine inside himself, and, more importantly, by denigrating and devaluing whatever he considers to be feminine in the outside world." Beyond this, Chodorow suggested that in the social world "he also appropriates to himself and defines as superior particular social activities and cultural (moral, religious, and creative) spheres."

Summary and Implications

Gynecentric theories suggest a psychological explanation of male dominance that rests on the universal social assignment of mothering to women. To escape from the power of the mother and the intensity of their first feminine identification, males create ways of coping that deny this identity in themselves and establish their own independent power. Societies value the phallus because it symbolizes males' separate identity from the mother and their greater power. According to this perspective, males' psychic need for individuation—that is, for separating themselves from the mother—requires that they devalue, and segregate themselves from, the activities that represent her world and the time when they were totally dependent on and identified with her. Females, because their first identity is feminine, have no such need to segregate and devalue the actions of males.

If the source of the fear and envy of the mother as well as males' tenuous masculine identity is the close mother–child contact in infancy, an obvious way to alter this would be for both males and females to nurture infants. In contrast to Rubin's suggestion that this would obliterate gender identity,[65] it would probably facilitate a less problematic gender identity for both males and females and minimize males' psychic need to disparage women. Such a move would also minimize the division of roles within the family. In contrast to Mitchell's suggestion that the family could be eliminated, the extension of child-care tasks to both males and females would facilitate a less oppressive family situation, for both adults and children.

If men were to become more involved in child care it would be important that this involvement occur within a "feminine paradigm," rather than the "masculine paradigm" critiqued by authors such as Keller and Benjamin. As we saw in Chapter 7, fathers are more likely to treat sons and daughters differently than are mothers. If male dominance were to lessen, men's nurturing of children would have to involve a more gender-neutral mode of interacting than it now does. In other words, fathers would have to behave more like mothers.[66] In addition, the culture as a whole would need to provide greater valuation to and support for nurturant interactions of all adults with children. (See the discussion in Chapter 12.)

Thus, although the phallocentric analysis describes how the male-dominant culture continues to be reproduced and stresses the role of phallic symbolism in feminizing women, the gynecentric perspective describes how the masculine motive to dominate is reproduced. The sociological analysis discussed in the next chapter clarifies these views and helps point toward change.

SUMMARY

A psychoanalytic explanation of gender development focuses on early associations within the family and can help account for the motivational bases of male dominance. Two threads of psychoanalytic thought may be distinguished. The phallocentric perspective follows Freud's early outline and assumes the basic superiority of males and that girls accept femininity only when they realize that they cannot be males. This analysis has been used by contemporary feminists to show how the maintenance of male dominance is linked to human kinship systems, the incest taboo, and the resolution of the Oedipus complex. The gynecentric perspective, although using basic concepts and understandings of Freud, stresses the early and basic feminine orientation of both males and females. Theorists with this perspective suggest that because of this early feminine orientation and early associations with the mother, it is more difficult for males than females to establish their gender identity. Femininist theorists use this perspective to analyze the origin of the psychological motive behind male dominance.

SUGGESTED READINGS

Chodorow, Nancy J. 1989. *Feminism and Psychoanalytic Theory*. New Haven, Conn.: Yale University Press. A collection of Chodorow's writings in this area.

Dinnerstein, Dorothy. 1976. *The Mermaid and the Minotaur: Sexual Arrangements and Human Malaise*. New York: Harper & Row. The author's version of the theory that male dominance is a result of women's mothering.

FREUD, SIGMUND. 1965. *Sexuality and the Psychology of Love* (ed. Philip Rieff). New York: Collier Books. An easily available volume that includes most of Freud's writings that deal with sex role development.

International Journal of Psychoanalysis. The best way to understand psychoanalytic writings is to read the original sources. Most of the early articles by such people as Ernest Jones, Helene Deutsch, Karen Horney, Melanie Klein, and Sigmund Freud and many later ones were published in this journal.

JOHNSON, MIRIAM M. 1988. *Strong Mothers, Weak Wives: The Search for Gender Equality*. Berkeley: University of California Press. Critical reviews of a wide range of psychoanalytic writings by a sociologist who integrates the material into a sociological analysis of gender development and inequality.

MITCHELL, JULIET. 1974. *Psychoanalysis and Feminism*. New York: Vintage. Reviews and interprets theories of others and presents Mitchell's own psychoanalytic view of the basis of male dominance.

STROUSE, JEAN. (Ed.). 1974. *Women and Analysis*. New York: Grossman. A collection of older and contemporary psychoanalytic writings on women.

chapter 10

Parents, Peers, and Male Dominance

In this chapter we attempt a more multileveled analysis to integrate findings and theories from academic psychology and psychoanalysis with a more sociological perspective. We focus on the interaction between parents and children in the family and the interaction in gender-segregated peer groups. From this we can see how institutionalized roles within these groups contribute to the development of gender-differentiated personalities and the reproduction of male dominance.* We begin with a discussion of how fathers and mothers affect the gender typing of their children, and then we turn to a discussion of adolescence and how the male peer group contributes to and reinforces attitudes of male dominance and female devaluation. We also discuss the deviant phenomena of incest and rape, as they are both consequences and distorted versions of family relations and male peer group relations, respectively.

PARENTAL ROLES AND GENDER TYPING

Although Talcott Parsons's model of gender socialization in the family does not attempt to analyze male dominance, his model of interaction in reciprocal roles is a useful starting point in analyzing the development of gender-differentiated personalities and male dominance in social systems.[2] In essence Parsons's model recasts psychoanalytic ideas on development into terms compatible with theories from academic psychology and puts them all into the framework of social role theory. He has suggested that through interactions in the family in reciprocal roles the child learns both what it is to be human and what it means to be male or female.

---

*We prefer the word *reproduce* to *transmit* because, as Christopher Lasch has pointed out, the latter implies a cultural determinism we wish to avoid.[1] The word *reproduce* implies that social relations produce social relations, and this more closely represents our meaning.

Parsons suggested that the processes Freud referred to as identification and social learning theorists refer to as modeling can best be understood not so much as learning to become like another as learning to play a social role with another person. A role defines the expected behavior for an individual in a given status. Roles are complementary or reciprocal because they make no sense without the related actions of others. For example, the husband role is complementary to the wife role, and the mother role is complementary to the child role. Social learning, then, takes place through interacting in complementary or reciprocal roles in terms of a shared system of meaning or values. Common meanings and understandings are established in the interaction. In learning to play social roles with their parents, children are not only integrated into a social interaction system, but also their personalities are in large measure formed by this social interaction. Gender-typed personalities, then, are reproduced in children by interacting in family roles.

According to Parsons, in spite of enormous cross-cultural variations in kinship systems and family structure, all societies have two basic structural regularities that underlie the uniformities we find in gender acquisition: A child's first human contact tends to be with a nurturing female or females; and the father or other male(s), who is not primarily nurturant, enters both male and female children's psychological world at a later time. This does not mean that fathers do not nurture, but that cross-culturally the mother role is more associated with nurturance than the father role. The concept *mother* may mean different things to different people and in different cultures, but cross-culturally nurturance is at least one of its meanings. Parsons's model does not refer to the structure of any particular concrete family; rather, he described the family in terms of gender and generational roles. Obviously many children can and do grow up without mothers or fathers, but they do not grow up without a conception of what mothers and fathers are supposed to be like.

Parsons suggested that through interaction with the mother in a dyadic role relationship infants of both sex groups learn to respond to the attitudes of others and to love. This first interaction of the infant with its mother is not gender typed. Both male and female infants learn how to feel nurturant as well as how to be nurtured in interaction with the mother.

According to Parsons's role-oriented version of Freud, the Oedipal stage has two functions: to promote the internalization of gender role categorization, and to break the child's dependent relationship with the mother and integrate him or her into the role system of the family as a whole. This is the meaning that Parsons gives to Freud's superego concept. In Parsons's view, both sex groups (not just males) must achieve independence from the mother and join the wider social system. As he put it, "The childhood level of dependency is just as unsuitable for either sex beyond a certain point."[3] Thus, although gender role adoption and breaking dependency ties with the mother occur closely in time, they are distinct conceptually. Parsons believed that Freud did not adequately distinguish the two.[4]

When the child moves into the larger social system of the family as a whole, two major differentiating axes—age and sex—become important. The boy learns that he cannot adopt his mother's role, because of his sex categorization; on the other hand, he cannot adopt his father's role with the mother, because of the generational difference. Like the boy, the girl breaks her dependent attachment to the mother and enters the wider social system of the family. In so doing she identifies again with the mother because of their common gender, but she cannot take over the mother's relation with the father because of the generational difference. In essence, Parsons sees the incest taboo as reflecting and preserving the difference between generations and of emphasizing the responsibility of the parent for the child as a person. Parsons himself did not explain how sex categorization is learned, nor did he give any special role to the father in the process other than noting that the father is the representative not only of masculinity but also of the family as a whole. In Freud's account, the boy acquires a superego when he identifies with, or introjects, his threatening father. The girl, by contrast, is left to acquire what superego she can through more gradual means. Unlike Freud, Parsons sees both sex groups as acquiring a superego by internalizing the role structure of the family, including its gender-differentiated roles and incest taboos.

Parsons's model is more a conceptual framework in whose terms further analyses can be made than an empirical analysis in and of itself. Because the model is so general, it can serve as a baseline for developing specific hypotheses to interpret empirical data on parental roles and the development of gender typing in children.

Miriam Johnson suggested as an implication of both Freud's and Parsons's theories that given women's earlier primacy for children, the father role might be more critical than the mother role in reinforcing masculine and feminine behaviors and orientations in children of both sex groups.[5] This view of the father as the focus of gender-differentiated behaviors has since received considerable empirical support (see Chapter 8) and can help specify more concretely how gender differentiation and male dominance are reproduced.

Much of the confusion about whether and how mothers and fathers might foster gender typing in their children can be clarified if we make a distinction within the so-called feminine role between its nurturant aspects and its heterosexual aspects. Both sex groups learn nurturance from being nurtured, usually by the mother. Acquiring the heterosexual aspects of femininity (and also of masculinity), on the other hand, appears to be more associated with interactions with the father and is also tied to male dominance. The heterosexual aspects of gender roles (the wife role for women and the husband role for men) involve an element of masculine superiority. As we discussed earlier, the husband role is culturally defined as more powerful than the wife role because of male dominance in the society. The term *feminine* in our culture more often refers to the heterosexual than to the nurturant or maternal aspects of the feminine role.[6]

The Mother Role and Learning to Be Human

In the maternal role as opposed to the wife role, the mother has considerable power over her offspring throughout their lives. The reciprocal of the mother role is the child role, and the mother is more powerful than the child because of the generational difference. The strong mother–child bonds developed in infancy continue throughout life, and mothers may retain emotional and psychological influence over their children until death.

In the first few years of life, infants learn in their interactions with their mothers to relate in nurturant and expressive modes—to respond to and be aware of the social needs of others. In the reciprocal role relation with the mother, children learn both their own responsive child role and that of the nurturant mother. Both boys and girls relate to the mother in this manner and develop their basic human qualities, their capacity to relate to other people, to care for and care about other people.

Research indicates that the degree of a child's self-control is related to the warmth and responsiveness of his or her early caretaker. For example, researchers have found that the development of obedience and then internalized controls in infants is related to the "sensitivity of maternal responsiveness to infant signals, but not to frequency of commands or forcible interventions."[7] One of the most consistently replicated findings in child-rearing studies is the positive association between ratings of maternal warmth and ratings of conscience in children of both sex groups.[8] (Unfortunately, we know of no studies that correlate paternal warmth and internalized control of infants. Such studies are undoubtedly rare because fathers spend little time in early child care.) All of this supports Parsons's view that the early influence of nurturant and maternal love helps establish internal controls.

Social learning and modeling theorists also suggest that the mother is the major source of moral learning. Lawrence Kohlberg (and to some extent the gynecentric psychoanalytic theorist Melanie Klein) has suggested (contrary to Freud) that the mother's moral role leads girls to have stronger consciences than boys. However, the relationship both boys and girls have with the mother comes before gender differentiation becomes salient and before the Oedipal period. Thus, we see no reason to assume that one sex group is more socialized or moral than the other. Both girls and boys learn to respond to social sanctions in connection with the pre-Oedipal mother relationship.[9]

Some authors in the psychoanalytic tradition suggest that this early emotional relationship with the mother is more intense for daughters than for sons. According to Nancy Chodorow, because the mother and daughter are the same sex the mother experiences and treats girls differently from boys.[10] She has contended that these differences are too subtle to be captured by the studies of academic psychologists. Chodorow has argued that on a deep emotional level, quite apart from a level of role expectations and even physical contact, mothers experience daughters as less separate from themselves than sons. In fact, Chodorow has suggested that these differences in maternal relations produce the gender differences in personality organization described in Chapter 7. She sees females as less separate and differentiated from others than males are.

In support of her argument that mothers experience and treat their pre-Oedipal girls and boys differently, Chodorow relies on evidence from psychiatrists treating patients rather than on the kinds of experimental and observational evidence that academic psychologists use. She noted that there are many more clinical accounts of pathological mothers who deny separateness and refuse to allow their daughters to individuate than accounts of mothers who do the same with sons. She has maintained that these cases reflect in exaggerated form the differences in normal tendencies. Hence, she says that girls retain their pre-Oedipal attachment to their mothers and continue to define and experience themselves as continuous with others.

Chodorow's description of women feeling more continuous with others and less individuated than men obscures several important distinctions. Her description implies that mothers' treatment of daughters makes them both more dependent and more expressive than males. We have argued that women are no more dependent on others' responses than men, but they are more expressive. Both males and females learn from the mother how to nurture and to deal with others in expressive modes, but men later deny this capacity in their effort to establish a separate identity. Chodorow has argued that mothers "mother" their female infants more than their male infants and thus reproduce mothering in females.

We argue that both boys and girls learn the maternal role from the mother but that boys are later constrained to deny this capacity. Both boys and girls must become more independent as they grow older.[11] Because of the early primacy of the mother in all societies, fathers or other males tend to represent independence from the mother to children of both sexes. The father helps both boys and girls achieve freedom from depending on and merging with the mother.

The Father Role and Learning Gender-Typed Interaction

Many accounts of the Oedipal period tend to assume a symmetrical process in which girls love their fathers and copy their mothers, whereas boys love their mothers and copy their fathers. In fact, from a psychological standpoint, the mother in the Oedipal period does not play a role toward her son that is symmetrical to the role the father plays toward his daughter.[12] In a male-dominant society the male's learning to be masculine by interacting with his mother introduces a contradiction, because in this relationship the mother is the dominant figure. The relationship between mother and son reverses the usual power position between the sex groups. As a consequence, the son cannot very well use the complementary relationship of mother and son as a model for learning adult heterosexual relations, for these involve the sexual control of women. Thus, although mothers and sons may interact sometimes in a way that mimics adult heterosexual relations, the mother–son relationship is not the prototype of these. In the father–daughter relationship, on the other hand, the father is dominant both because of his generation and because of his sex. Therefore, this relationship does mimic more closely adult heterosexual relationships.

The anthropologist Serge Moscovici has argued that because the mother–son relationship involves female dominance, the fundamental reason for the incest taboo is to end this relationship and install male dominance.[13] He says, essentially, that if sons were allowed to stay with (or marry) their mothers, women, not men, would be the dominant group. Moscovici has argued that the only true incest taboo is that between mother and son (and indeed this is by far the strongest and most universal taboo), and the fear of this type of incest is inspired by the fear of female dominance.

In a very different way, Eleanor Maccoby and Carol Jacklin in their discussion of how males learn masculinity also recognize that the mother–son relationship is not the prototype of adult male–female relationships:

> *Each parent transfers to his children some of the behavior he is accustomed to displaying toward adults of the two sexes.* In some cases this amounts to outright sexual attraction and seduction of the opposite sex child. . . . Most commonly, of course, there are simply discreet elements of flirtation with the opposite sex child. Dominance-submission relationships, as well as sexual ones, may generalize to children. If a woman is accustomed to taking a submissive stance toward her husband and other adult men, the hypothesis says that she will be more likely to behave submissively toward a son than a daughter. Clearly there are instances in which the role demands of parenthood (especially *motherhood*) are not consistent with habitual male–female interaction patterns.[14]

This emphasis on the mother role is needed as an important qualification to the assumption that males learn the heterosexual masculine role from interacting with their mothers as girls learn the heterosexual aspects of the feminine role from interacting with their fathers. Because the mother role carries more power than the son role, a seductive relation between mother and son, if not counteracted by some other factor, may actually be more of a threat than a spur to the son's masculinity with its overtones of male dominance.

The different feelings and emotions involved in the father–daughter and mother–son relationship in the middle class were once commented on by Mike Nichols in an interview: "Women, girls, live very comfortably with the fact that they want to sleep with their fathers. Right from the beginning they make jokes about it. They sit on Daddy's lap. Everybody knows it and it's sort of nice. Not us. Lots of edginess. Lots of 'Oh mother puhleeze!' I think the discomfort stays with us always."[15] Although Nichols is describing a middle-class phenomenon and may have exaggerated the overt sexuality in the father-daughter relationship, his perception that males somehow must resist their mothers seems correct. Males feel this uneasiness because the mother's dominance over the child is incompatible with the expected dominance of the male over the female. Although males may develop heterosexual urges as well as learn how to nurture and love from their mothers, they do not learn to view women as sex objects from their mothers. In a patriarchal world, growing up for the male involves overcoming the power of the mother and gaining independence. It also involves learning that males should be dominant over females and learning to take the sexual initiative with women. Males learn this largely through interaction with other males. They protect themselves from female dominance through their interactions with their fathers and within the male peer group.

Fathers and gender-differentiating behaviors Compared to children in many other societies, boys and girls in the United States are treated relatively similarly by both mothers and fathers.[16] As we saw in Chapter 8, generally researchers have found that mothers distinguish little in handling their male and female children. In contrast, the few studies on fathers all suggest that they do differentiate between the sex groups and have differing expectations for the future of their boys and girls.[17] Fathers also generally have much less contact with children than mothers do, and tend to engage in play activities more than routine activities with both boys and girls. Yet, within these parameters, fathers differentiate between the sex groups more than mothers do. Moreover, male and female children respond very differently to fathers from the way they do to mothers.

Miriam Johnson has emphasized that the greater differentiation that fathers make between their sons and daughters and the greater differentiation sons and daughters make in their responses to fathers have been found in experimental and observational studies and in unconscious and conscious behavior and statements.[18] These findings also seem to hold regardless of the age of the child. Although the associations are rarely strong and are not always found, the persistence of the trend in various types of studies cannot be ignored. These patterns even appear among fathers who consciously try to avoid stereotyped behaviors and who spend relatively more time with their children.[19]

Generally, the gender-differentiating behavior of fathers takes two forms: withdrawal from girls (or preference for boys) and a differentiated style of interaction with the two sex groups. Fathers explicitly state that they feel more responsibility toward a male child than toward a female child.[20] Generally, fathers want to have male offspring,[21] and in the event of divorce they are more likely to maintain frequent contact with their sons than with their daughters.[22] Fathers also appear more likely than mothers to differentiate in the amount of positive and negative feedback they give sons and daughters[23] and to vocalize and interact more with infant and toddler sons than daughters.[24] In addition, fathers also tend to have more gender-stereotyped attitudes toward newborns and reinforce gender-stereotypical behaviors in their children more than mothers do.[25] As children grow older fathers appear more likely to encourage cognitive competence in their sons than in their daughters; mothers are much less likely to make such differentiations.[26]

Yet, impressive as this evidence is, much of it comes from studies of the American middle class, and it is therefore difficult to generalize about all cultural settings or even about the working class in this country. Evidence does suggest that both working-class and middle-class fathers, as well as fathers in other cultural settings differentiate their behaviors toward the sex groups. However, the exact form of this differentiation may vary from one group to another.[27]

Although some of these findings may turn out to be specific to the middle class, we might predict that the father's role toward the girl, whatever its specific form, is more directly related to control over her sexuality and concern with it than is the mother's role toward the boy. In other words, the father affects the heterosexual, not the maternal aspects, of sex role behavior. The heterosexual aspects of the feminine role reflect and support male dominance, whereas the maternal aspects actually work against it. So when we say men are more concerned with gender typing than women, we mean that the core of this concern has the effect of creating and maintaining men's sexual dominance over women.

Fathers and the heterosexual aspects of gender roles If we maintain the distinction between the maternal and the heterosexual aspects of femininity, the data do suggest that males are more concerned with the heterosexual aspects of gender roles than females are and that the father role is more involved in the process by which individuals become heterosexual. Males are more likely than females to support the double standard of sexual behavior for males and females. Obviously, both fathers and mothers are concerned with the morality of their sons and daughters, and both fathers and mothers do tend to be more concerned for their daughters than for their sons. Yet studies of parents' attitudes toward sex education as well as young peoples' reports of their parents' attitudes show that fathers are more likely than mothers to want their sons to receive one message about sexuality and their daughters another. Research reports show fathers more concerned than mothers with controlling or curtailing their daughter's sexual activity.[28] Similarly, a survey of high-school students' occupational choices reported that females more often than males believed that having a "sexually moral" job was important to their parents. Many more young women attributed this concern to their fathers than to their mothers.[29]

Of course, this evidence does indicate that mothers also support the double standard, although less so than fathers. Both sexes are operating within the masculine paradigm, but because it *is* masculine its main tenets are held, under most circumstances, more strongly by males than by females. The ultimate form of this phenomenon might be seen in the traditional notion found in many cultures that a father, and often other male relatives, must protect the daughter's "honor." They must protect her from sexual advances from other males.[30]

Studies of parent–child interactions also indicate fathers' greater concern with the heterosexual aspect of gender roles.[31] Although mothers express physical affection equally toward both boys and girls, fathers tend to show more to daughters than to sons.[32] Girls report more often than boys that they would be embarrassed to be seen naked or in their underwear by their father, to tell him a dirty joke, or to tell him about a sexual experience. Boys and girls do not differ from each other, however, with regard to the mother, except that boys are more embarrassed than girls to be in the bathroom with her.[33] Fathers more often knock before entering girls' rooms than boys' rooms; mothers knock less often than fathers and make little distinction between sons and daughters in whether or not they knock.[34] An extensive study of families in which both mothers and fathers were extensively involved with child care found that fathers report that they are "in love" with their children and prefer girls; mothers simply "love" their children without a romanticized flavor to the relationship and without differentiating between sons and daughters in their feelings.[35]

All this suggests that fathers, more than mothers, see their daughters as potential sex objects for themselves or for other men. As fathers, they generally do not make their daughters into sex objects directly, even though there are elements of flirtation and mock courtship in the relationship. Johnson has suggested that these results illustrate how the father–daughter relationship is more nearly a paradigm for adult heterosexual relationships than the mother–son relationship.[36] Father–daughter intimacy does not pose the same threat to male power that mother–son intimacy does. In the father–daughter relationship, the father is in control; in the mother–son relationship the mother is in control.

Fathers and sexual preference Perhaps the clearest test of the hypothesis that the father is more involved in children's adoption of the specifically sexual aspects of gender roles than the mother comes from data on the factors influencing sexual preference. Sexual preference refers to whether individuals prefer to relate sexually to members of their own sex group or to members of the other sex group. Increasingly, sexual preference is coming to be seen as distinct from gender identity. Most homosexuals (individuals who prefer same-sex sexual partners) identify with their own biological sex. Although it is important not to dwell on the causes of homosexuality as if it were a disease, it is also important not to ignore existing data comparing the backgrounds of heterosexuals and homosexuals for what they can tell us about social factors affecting sexual preference.* Although clearly there are multiple routes by which an individual might arrive at a given sexual orientation, in contemporary society where families tend to be nuclear, isolated from each other, and privatized, the impact of parents on their children's sexuality might be expected to be great. As it turns out, data

* Much of the research on homosexuality is flawed methodologically because the subjects have come from patient populations and the findings cannot be taken as representative of normally functioning homosexuals. Even the studies on nonpatients do not represent the actual distribution of homosexuals in the population. Also the supposedly heterosexual controls in these studies may have actually contained some homosexuals or bisexuals because researchers usually assume heterosexuality if individuals do not explicitly define themselves as homosexual. Finally, these studies are retrospective rather than longitudinal, and we must assume that individuals' present perceptions of their past are accurate. Because of these difficulties, research on the causes of homosexuality is rightfully suspect. On the other hand, imperfect research is better than no research at all if it is used with discrimination.

concerning the parental relationships of both female and male homosexuals strongly suggest that the father relationship is more critical than the mother relationship.†[37]

Psychoanalytic theories concerning male homosexuality generally posit that homosexuals are likely to have had close-binding mothers and hostile or distant fathers who did not counteract the mother's seductiveness. This left the male child forever tied to the mother and unable to seek relationships with other women. In general, however, the studies of male homosexuals compared to heterosexuals (whether researchers used patients or nonpatients as subjects) have actually found a close-binding mother far less consistently than they have found a hostile or detached father.[39] Cross-cultural studies, which use societies rather than individuals as the unit of analysis, also indicate that among societies that officially disapprove of homosexuality the practice is more commonly found in groups where fathers are minimally involved in the care of infants and thus would be seen by children as distant and detached.[40]

Although many psychoanalytic theorists tend to relate homosexuality to an overly close mother relationship, Irving Bieber and others have theoretically accounted for why the father relationship might be especially important.[41] Bieber has argued that under ordinary circumstances all males would be heterosexual (especially in a world that values heterosexuality), but homosexuals have rejected heterosexuality out of fear not of women but of other men. Bieber's idea is that homosexuals fear that they will be in some way punished for showing an interest in women by aggressive males who "own" these women. They therefore turn away from heterosexuality and seek sexual relations with men who are perceived (perhaps because they are themselves not heterosexual) as non-threatening.

This fear of males develops during the Oedipal phase when the child fears the father's punishment for his sexualized attachment to the mother. Ordinarily, fear is resolved when the boy learns to relinquish the mother and joins the world of male peers, finally becoming sexually attached to another woman with his father's blessings. But when the father fails to form a solidary relationship with the child, the child continues to fear the father's intervention in his sexualized relationship with the mother. He finds it hard to join his male peers and repeats this fear in relations with other women in whom he may become interested sexually. Thus, to the extent that women may be phobic to male homosexuals, the women are perceived as belonging to a fear-inspiring man.

Bieber's analysis fits with Kohlberg's idea that adult men in general are perceived by boys and girls alike to be more threatening than adult women. These ideas are based on the gross physical differences between the sex groups such as men's greater size and strength, their deeper and louder voices,

---

†We do not wish to reject out of hand the possibility that sex object choice has a biological component.[38] But this biological component must be expressed and developed in a social context. Thus, the analysis of the relation to the father would not be invalidated if such a biological influence could be substantiated.

and their larger physical movements. Thus, men project a greater potential for violence than women do, and, in fact, men are more aggressive than women (see Chapter 7). It would follow that if the father or some other male does not ally himself with the child to mitigate this perception and to indicate to the child that men are not fearsome after all, the child (especially if he perceives himself to be unlike other males his age) will probably feel unable to join the world of males in general. This helps explain why some male homosexuals actually did have violent and frightening fathers, whereas many others simply had fathers who were passively hostile or indifferent to them. In both of these cases, there was no solidary relationship between father and son and no way to mitigate the sons' early impression that masculinity is formidable.

In arguing that the father is more critical than the mother with respect to influencing sexual preference, we do not mean to imply that many other factors are also not important or that Bieber's explanation covers all instances of homosexuality. Neither do we wish to imply that homosexuality is undesirable. We focus on parental relations not in order to cure homosexuality, but because it has significance for our general analysis of male dominance. Bieber's work is significant for us because it suggests that although superficially homosexuals appear to reject women, at a deeper (perhaps unconscious) level, it may be that many homosexual males are attempting to cope with male dominance. Certainly one important implication of this analysis is that it is not the supermasculine father that would be conducive to heterosexuality in his son (if heterosexuality remains a desirable goal), but a male who would mitigate the image of the threatening male who "owns" women.

With regard to lesbians some psychoanalytically oriented theorists posit a reversal of the male situation and suspect a hostile and distant mother and a close-binding father.[42] Other analysts argue that the quality of the mother relationship alone is central in the development of lesbianism.[43] Again, however, evidence supports the greater significance of the father relationship in differentiating heterosexual women and lesbians.[44]

Marjorie Leonard gave clinical examples of how fathers can deter daughters from being heterosexual in various ways—by not being there enough to provide a realistic image of men, or by being too overwhelmingly seductive and causing the daughter to flee from him and males in general.[45] Some feminists also see lesbianism as a rejection of male-dominated heterosexual relationships.[46]

Harvey Kaye and his associates in a study of lesbians modeled after the Bieber study found, contrary to their expectations, that the mothers of lesbians did not differ markedly from their counterparts in the control group. The authors reported that fathers, however, are "an alien breed in contrast to the control fathers."[47] They stated that the fathers "tend to be puritanical, exploitative, and feared by their daughters, although the fear is not that of being physically abused. He is overly possessive and is subtly interested in his daughter physically, yet tends to discourage her development as an adult."[48] Other studies comparing lesbians and nonlesbians have indicated few differences in how they see their mothers, but that the lesbians are significantly more likely than nonlesbians to see their fathers as fear-inducing, repressive, and especially as intolerant of their expressions of anger.[49] A very large nonclinical study also found that more homosexual women than heterosexual women thought their parents had little or no affection for each other and that these women were more likely to have negative relations with their fathers.[50] Thus, although the mother herself probably does affect the girl's perception of the father and men in general, the father image, however this image developed, appears to be most important in influencing the daughter's views of men and her later sexuality.

In our view, homosexuals in general do not constitute a vanguard against male dominance, because they may be as much involved in sexist role-playing as heterosexuals. On the other hand, many homosexuals, especially lesbians, are using their refusal of heterosexuality as a way of protesting male dominance in heterosexual relations. Heterosexuality per se does not necessarily have to involve male dominance, however; nor does heterosexuality explain male dominance. Fathers could help boys and girls survive in a male-dominant society, while also trying to change it by affirming the gender identity of each sex without defining male dominance and female submission as a part of sexual identity and heterosexuality.

Incestuous fathers Public awareness of incest, and especially of father-daughter incest, has steadily increased over the past 2 decades. Although both father–daughter and mother–son incest are tabooed in our society, incest between mothers and sons is extremely rare compared to incest between fathers and daughters. This fact is yet another indication of male dominance. As we noted earlier, mother–son incest would constitute a reversal of male dominance if the boy were young, whereas father–daughter incest fits the paradigm of dominant male and subordinate female. (Father–son incest is much less common than father–daughter incest. It may also be more unreported than father–daughter incest because the boy victim perceives it as a threat to his masculinity.)

Judith Herman and Lisa Hirschman interpret father–daughter incest as "an abuse which is inherent in a father dominated family system."[51] Using Freud's categories, they say that the taboo against father–daughter incest does not carry the same force as the taboo against mother–son incest, because there is no punishing father to prevent father–daughter incest as there is to prevent mother–son incest.[52] In the Freudian account of the Oedipus complex, the boy gives up his incestuous desires for the mother out of fear of the castrating father, who has rights in the mother. On the other hand, the mother does not have comparable rights in the father. Herman and Hirschman contend that for every family in which incest is actually consummated, there are likely many more with essentially similar if less extreme psychological dynamics, including such things as flirting and sharing of sexual secrets. Herman refers to this as an "incest continuum."[53]

Clinicians, social workers, and academicians who deal with incest cases generally find that the incestuous father is not crazy or otherwise deviant.[54] It often appears that fathers simply do not see anything seriously wrong with incest, because they conceive of themselves as owning the child. One mother of an incest victim whose husband is now in therapy said he had been a very authoritarian person: "He didn't see our daughter as a person. She was *his*. He didn't see it as incest."[55] Although the father himself is not an authoritarian in all cases, father–daughter incest does involve the exploitation of a dependent child, whom the father uses for his own gratification. Professionals in the field as well as the general public now understand that incest is not something a child imagines, or desires, or causes. It is something a father does to a child.

Father–daughter incest differs from rape because it occurs in the context of a family relationship in which the parent is supposed to care for and about the child. The victim of rape is not socially or psychologically dependent on the rapist and is thus free to hate the attacker. The daughter of an incestuous father, however, cannot hate her father, because she depends on him for protection and love. Although she may feel repelled in one way by his sexual demands, at the same time, she may feel that this is the only kind of love she can get and may prefer it to no love at all.[56] Thus, incest victims may be psychologically affected more deeply and adversely than rape victims because their own self-image and sense of worth are more involved.

The precise harm done to incest victims varies. Herman and Hirschman found that their cases almost uniformly reported an inability to feel and communicate. They tended to think of themselves as witches, bitches, and whores and as undeserving of love. They usually did not hate their fathers and in fact overvalued men and got into masochistic relationships with them. They tended to hate themselves and their mothers far more than they hated men.[57] In a larger study of women who had been outpatients in a mental health clinic, Karen Meiselman found that orgasmic dysfunction was strikingly more characteristic of the women who had been incest victims than of the women in the control group of patients who had not experienced incest.[58]

The mothers of incest victims have often been themselves blamed for colluding in the incest. This has in part come about because the victims almost uniformly report poor relations with their mothers. Generally, the mothers of incest victims have been weak in some way or other, did not respect themselves or their daughters, and thereby "allowed" incest to occur.[59] Both the behavior of the mother and the incest victim and the behavior of the father himself ultimately reflect a patriarchal system. The mother sees herself as not having the power to defend the daughter against the father, and the father sees himself as having a right to his daughter.

At several points we have argued that fathers should take a more nurturant role within the family. The problem of incest reminds us, however, that by nurturance we do not mean seductiveness. The nurturing father needs to form a genuine coalition with the mother on the basis of their equality, not on the basis of his authority in the family. In this coalition with the mother, the father cares for and about his children as children, not as sex objects.[60]

Summary

Children of both sex groups learn nurturant and maternal attitudes and behaviors in their earliest interactions with a maternal figure. In this relationship with the mother, both girls and boys learn to respond to the attitudes of others, to love and to be loved. This relationship is not the prototype of male dominance, and it is not markedly gender differentiated. Male dominance appears to be reinforced by fathers more than by mothers. Evidence suggests that fathers are more concerned about gender typing and are more differentiating in their behavior toward each sex group than are mothers.

The child's relationship with the father seems especially related to adopting the heterosexual aspects of gender roles. Studies of various aspects of heterosexual behavior indicate that the father relationship is a more important influence than the mother relationship. Our analysis suggests that heterosexuality in males is effected through minimizing the child's fear of other males. Thus, although males in general in a male-dominant society reinforce male dominance, individual male parents in a male-dominant world can help mitigate this fear.

The far greater prevalence of father–daughter incest than mother–son incest reflects male dominance. Fathers who do use their daughters as sex objects usually assume that this is their privilege as the father and that the mother will not interfere, because of her lesser power. Mothers are far less likely than fathers to make their male children into sex objects.

To some extent in this society, heterosexual relations are characterized by male dominance and are governed by a masculine paradigm, but heterosexuality itself does not necessarily have to imply or reflect male dominance even though it does in this society. The psychological motive that may underlie males' devaluation of women arises not as much from boys' assuming the heterosexual aspect of masculinity but more from their repressing the maternal aspects of femininity. This repression also occurs at the time of the Oedipus complex, when children begin to enter the world beyond the mother–child dyad and seek to become independent from the mother.

THE REVOLT FROM THE MOTHER

In Chapter 9 we reviewed the work of the gynecentric psychoanalytic theorists and their view that boys' and girls' first identification is with the mother, their primary caretaker. Because mothers or other females are the early caretakers of infants, it is more difficult for boys to establish masculinity than for girls to establish femininity. Talcott Parsons analyzed male gender development in the United States as the gynecentric theorists do by suggesting that in establishing masculinity boys must reject their first identification with and attachment to the mother.[61] He also noted that males in attempting to gain independence from the mother also tend to reject what they see as the goodness of the mother. The mother in the middle class tends to represent rules and conformity in her capacity as primary guardian and caretaker of the child. In revolting against the mother or rejecting his identification with her, the boy unconsciously identifies goodness with femininity and "being a 'bad boy' becomes a positive goal." Thus, Parsons suggested that the boy's need to reject the identification with the mother not only leads to an identification of himself as unlike her in a psychic sense, but in the tendency of boys toward antisocial role behavior.[62] This is also the source of the boy's rejection of positive expressiveness for negative expressiveness. Expressiveness represents the mother and goodness, and the boy fears retaining this if he is to be a "real male."[63]

Leslie Fiedler described what is essentially "the bad boy pattern" as a pervasive theme in American literature. He cited numerous works of fiction from Mark Twain's stories up to Ken Kesey's *One Flew Over the Cuckoo's Nest* as sagas in which men (or boys) seek to escape from a world dominated by female morality.[64] In almost all of this literature one's sympathy is with the bad boy. As Parsons pointed out, mothers themselves seem to love the bad son more than the good son who tries too hard to please her. Thus, it seems to be almost understood by all of us that somehow boys must be bad to be unquestionably masculine real boys. Girls, on the other hand, feel no need to reject the mother and establish alternative role patterns.[65]

John Whiting has suggested that males' rejection of their identification with the mother can be observed cross-culturally, especially in societies where fathers are generally not involved in early child care.[66] Less complex societies usually employ initiation ceremonies or endurance trials to help young men formally break their primary identification with the mother. Modern industrialized societies rarely have such ritualized rites of passage. Instead, individual men search for ways to signify their transition to manhood, both to themselves and to their peers, through means as varied as the military, sports, fraternal groups, and sexual adventures.[67]

Boys' tendency to resist what they perceive to be feminine can help explain the different attitudes boys and girls hold toward school. Many studies show that girls like school more than boys and usually make better grades than boys. Girls' greater liking of school appears to be associated with children's tendency to define school and school objects as feminine.[68]

Males' difficulties in becoming masculine not only play into the bad-boy pattern but also and more importantly are related to the devaluation of women. Studies of preadolescent boys indicate that they seem to bolster themselves in assuming expected masculine attributes by taking a very negative view of women.[69] They describe girls as limited and restrained and adult women as weak, afraid, easily tired, in need of help, squeamish, inadequate in emergencies, making an undue fuss over things, not very intelligent, and demanding and jealous of their husbands. Preadolescent boys tend to see the masculine role as extremely demanding, yet their very negative image of the feminine alternative impels them to assume masculinity. One must be masculine in order not to be such a pitiful specimen! In fact, the greater prestige of masculinity helps induce males to take on the responsibilities (and freedoms) that go with it.[70]

In contrast to males, females do not need to reject the first identification they have with their mothers, although they, like boys, do need to become less dependent. They do not have a need for greater glory as an inducement to be feminine. In fact, even though girls increasingly realize that males do receive more prestige, they continue to remain feminine. Kohlberg in surveying the research literature on this reported that "girls continue to prefer feminine objects and activities at all ages, and their own preferences seem to be even more feminine than their more objective and sterotyped judgments of value."[71] This strongly suggests that girls are feminine in a way that boys are not masculine and that they remain feminine in spite of the prestige that accrues to masculinity. It seems that in breaking their dependency ties with their mothers girls are more likely to become hostile toward their own mothers than to reject the maternal role itself.

As we discussed in Chapter 9, fathers are likely to form a kind of coalition against mothers with children of both sexes. In our society where the mother–infant tie is so exclusive, this coalition may help the child become less emotionally dependent on the mother, but it may also lead, in the case of the father–son relationship, to a devaluation of women.

PEER GROUP INTERACTION

One important way males handle the threat of being unable to separate themselves from women and femininity is through male peer groups. As we have seen, males very early show an interest in other males and tend to bond together in "homosocial" fellowship. Although there is competition in male groups, the basic ambiance seems to be one of solidarity based on being masculine. Hanging out with the boys, a male can be comfortable, protected from the judgments and the anger of women and most importantly from the danger of femininity itself. In doing this, however, the male peer group can also be a powerful promoter of the sex objectification of women, making women not human beings but objects to be possessed and used sexually. These attitudes toward women in fact are more likely to be fostered in the male peer group than by fathers.

Women also bond together, in some societies more than in others. In our society both girls' and boys' childhood and adolescent friendships are important in helping them develop their views of gender roles.[72] Yet, in adulthood, the emphasis on the nuclear family and the heterosexual bond paradoxically works against women's being close to one another. To the extent that women depend on men economically, they are in part constrained to give men their primary loyalty.

Growing Up Male

Cross-culturally, the solidarity among boys is ordinarily not duplicated among young girls, who tend to mix more with adults than boys do.[73] Male groups involve a mixture of both dominance struggles and camaraderie. Young boys in most societies tend to play in larger groups than girls, and, partially as a function of the larger size of these groups, they tend to develop dominance hierarchies in which boys jockey and compete for position.[74] These groups also involve a certain amount of friendly aggression such as bopping, tripping, wrestling, and exchanging of verbal insults. The intimate exchange of insults is epitomized by the practice called "doin' the dozens" among ghetto black adolescents.[75]

At first, the validation of masculinity involves avoiding what is feminine in the literal sense. Boys in elementary school are likely to exclude girls from their activities. Our concern here, however, is what happens in early adolescence as children begin to anticipate adult roles and boys begin to learn their heterosexual role in the context of both competition and solidarity within the male peer group.

Competition in sexual capacity In early adolescence, masturbation may become an occasion for exhibition and comparison among boys. Alfred Kinsey and his associates found that 60% of the preadolescent boys they interviewed had engaged in sexual exhibition or other sex play with other boys. Kinsey commented that this behavior in the young boy "is fostered by his socially encouraged disdain for girls' ways, by his admiration for masculine prowess, and by his desire to emulate older boys. . . . The anatomy and functional capacities of male genitalia interest the younger boy to a degree that is not appreciated by older males who have become heterosexually conditioned."[76]

Günter Grass in his novel *Cat and Mouse* graphically described an exhibition of masturbation among a group of young adolescent boys on a deserted ship monitored by a lone girl.[77] One particular male was acknowledged to be the clear winner of the rather disorganized competition not only on the basis of the size of his penis, but also on the basis of his speed (duly timed by a watch) in reaching ejaculation and on his ability to repeat this performance several times in rapid succession. The episode suggests how readily sexuality can be assimilated to a competitive format essentially unrelated to one's own sexual pleasure, much less that of a partner.

Competition in heterosexual prowess Although virtually all boys masturbate, intercourse with a female is usually considered far preferable, and among many groups of boys, especially in the working class, masturbation is considered positively unmanly. Thus, sooner or later, heterosexual prowess becomes the basis for competition. Today, both young men and young women are often sexually experienced. Yet the meaning of losing one's virginity is quite different for males and females. For men, these first encounters do not involve the idea of relating emotionally to a female so much as the idea of validating one's status as a male among males. To actually have intercourse with a girl becomes an important rite of passage (usually publicly affirmed) in the male group.[78] This demand may occur quite early. Bill Cosby in an article that first appeared in *Playboy* described how he, as a preadolescent, had no knowledge of the basic mechanics of intercourse, but did know that it was important to "get pussy" from a girl—however this was done.[79] After visiting a willing girl and doing very little, he was able to parry the questions of his friends concerning the details of his experience with the inspired explanation that they had "done it, the regular way." At the same time, he hoped to find out what the regular way was! This episode illustrates nicely how important in the male peer group it is to be sexually experienced, so experienced that one dare not reveal ignorance of basic sexual information.

The avoidance of anything that has the appearance of homosexuality is almost an obsession with boys, as if the denigration of homosexuality helps affirm their status as "true men." Gary Fine described how Little League baseball players insult one another with taunts of "faggot" or "queer," as well as "baby" and "girl."[80] This juxtaposition of insults demonstrates how boys identify masculinity as not being a baby, not being a girl, and not being a homosexual, all negative attributes in their peer culture.[81]

Adult males carry this attitude with them, and several analysts see homophobia as the linchpin of male dominance. As Joseph Pleck has pointed out, "Our society uses the heterosexual–homosexual dichotomy as a central symbol for all the rankings of masculinity, for the division on any grounds between males who are 'real men' and have power and males who are not."[82]

In our society fathers ordinarily do not give sexual information to their children. The heart-to-heart talk a boy is supposed to have with his father is indeed a myth. Most fathers' difficulties in talking to their sons about sex may stem from their own ambivalent attitudes toward women. Does the father talk to his son as the husband of his son's mother or as a fellow male who has had his share of fun chasing women? Are women equal partners in a marriage or are they sex objects? From whatever cause, all the studies that have been done on boys show that the vast majority learn about contraceptives, prostitution, and coitus from their peers, not their parents.

Male sexuality, then, develops in the context of status striving in the male peer group. The focus at adolescence tends to be on "getting it from" or "doing it to" girls, with the reactions of the latter of little concern beyond securing their minimal cooperation.[83] Many men, then, learn to become aroused sexually in a context in which sexual excitement is associated with defining women as objects of conquest.[84] Although men undoubtedly vary considerably in this respect, at least part of the explanation of why men are prone to consider women sex objects is that they become sexual in the context of competition with other males. John Stoltenberg has suggested that cultural homophobia keeps men's sexual aggression directed toward women, saying "for the most part . . . homophobia serves male supremacy by protecting 'real men' from sexual assault by other real men."[85] The major exception is homosexual behavior of males in prison (see below).

Sex as a direct expression of male dominance Although in the male peer group sex may become an occasion for competition, sex is sometimes also used by men as a direct expression of aggression or dominance. Men may use sex directly as a way of controlling uppity or threatening women. At a peace demonstration in Washington, D.C., in 1969, when an attractive radical woman was speaking concerning women, the male radicals expressed their resentment by sexualizing her and all that she said: "Take it off! Take her off the stage and fuck her!" They yelled and guffawed at statements such as "We must take to the streets," making her reference to a march into a reference to prostitution.[86]

The association between sex and dominance is seen even more clearly in situations where males use sexual relations to express dominance over other males. This appears most graphically in reports of male homosexual behavior in prisons. In prison, "fucking" another male is symbolic of establishing dominance over him, of humiliating him. Part of the explanation for the humiliation is that the one who is penetrated becomes symbolically like a woman. Men who sexually assault other men in prison do not define their behavior as unmasculine or homosexual, because it is understood as an expression of dominance associated with masculinity. This dominance is dramatically expressed in the movie *Deliverance,* where a trespasser from the city is humiliated by being sodomized (anally penetrated) at gunpoint in front of his friends by one of the local males.

Penetration as dominance is not confined to heterosexual males. Philip Blumstein and Pepper Schwartz quoted a bisexual male: "There are four kinds of men: men who screw women, men who screw men and women, men who screw men, and then there are the queers (i.e., the ones who get screwed)."[87] Many slang words used to describe sexual intercourse also connote dominance and aggression. To get "fucked," "screwed," "reamed," or "had" implies that one has been victimized. Although this is not the typical male view of intercourse, there is within the masculine paradigm a symbolic association between sexual initiative and aggressive dominance. The association of sex with love is more a part of a feminine paradigm, and males as they "grow up" and form long-lasting alliances with women begin to share this view.

It is significant that male homosexual behavior in prison contrasts sharply with homosexual behavior among female prisoners. In female prisons, homosexual relationships are usually patterned after traditional heterosexual marriages. Establishing these relationships between a "stud" and a "femme" involves no physical coercion, and the relationship resembles an ordinary heterosexual marriage with the partners calling each other sometimes "mommy" and "poppy" or "my old lady" and "my old man." This seems important evidence that women tend to assimilate sexuality to at least relatively egalitarian relationships more readily than men do. Whereas women without men assimilate sexuality to a family, men without women assimilate it to a dominance hierarchy.[88]

Male bonding and women as sex objects The competitive aspect of male sexuality should not be overemphasized. As Richard Udry pointed out, sexual competition among males, with females the objects of conquest, provides a set of experiences that cement them as a male group.[89] Boys may egg each other on to make sexual attempts with girls ("It's tonight or never"), but this is not so much competition as peer pressure to *be* heterosexual.[90] The male peer group's conception of heterosexuality, however, distinctly does not mean liking or loving girls in the sense of allowing girls to have power over them. Instead, it means making girls into objects.

Although women may emphasize their specifically sexual qualities in order to attract men, the making of women into sex objects has psychological roots within men themselves. If a male's self-doubts are related to his need to separate himself from his mother, who was to him as a child a powerful feminine figure, then what better way to quell those doubts than to define women as mere objects? Making women into sex objects becomes a way of reinforcing masculine gender identity by rendering women harmless. If a woman is a "cunt" a "piece," a "skirt," or if one looks at women as assemblages of "asses," "tits," and "beavers," then the male is in control of them, and not the reverse. Among male peers, becoming involved in a relationship with a woman is often explicitly condemned. For instance, in traditional Muslim societies, love has been thought to downgrade men because it robs them of their masculinity.[91] According to the testimony of some men, going steady was considered bad because it put one in danger of being "pussy whipped," of letting a woman get the upper hand. When a male does get married or forms a serious relationship with a woman, he is viewed somewhat as a deserter from the male group, or he may be commiserated with as having been hooked or trapped. Some homosexual males pride themselves on their supermasculinity, which, they feel, is attested to by the fact that they would never let themselves be trapped by a woman. Heterosexuality, then, as it is fostered in the male peer group, is of a sort that defines women as objects of male conquest who are not to be taken seriously. The pursuit of women becomes a game that knits heterosexual males together more than it divides them.[92]

This does not mean that men do not fall in love or become seriously emotionally committed to women. Such emotional involvement for men, however, may signify a sharp break with the male peer group that does not occur when women fall in love, mainly because women in their peer groups do not compare heterosexual encounters or objectify the other sex in the same way that men do.

The motive for rape To some extent the motivational dynamics behind rape can be explained in terms of male peer group phenomena. Feminist theorists argue that the motives of rapists primarily involve male violence and male bonding.[93] Sexual excitement for men can be fostered and reinforced by male bonding and dominance motives. The most clear-cut examples are the rapes that occur during wars. Men show solidarity against enemy males by raping their women. Even though women are the victims, to some extent they represent the enemy males. Rapes in war are usually gang rapes, which increase the solidarity of the males involved. In the United States, gang rapes or rapes by pairs of buddies are usually planned beforehand and have little or nothing to do with sexual seduction or temptation by a woman. The victim or the place of the attack is often picked in advance. Gang rapists are ordinarily not mentally disturbed; they are engaging in an act of violence and male solidarity at the expense of a woman. Here the idea of ownership by enemy males is transformed into the idea that all unprotected women are fair game.

Although the male peer group mentality supports rape, it is not necessarily rape by a group or rape by a single stranger that a women need fear but also acquaintance rape in casual dating relationships, and beyond this, of course, rape in committed relationships and the rape that occurs in marriage.[94] Several studies have indicated that male peers influence the likelihood of rape in these situations, too. Men who report that they have forced women to have intercourse against their will or who report that they would be willing to do so are much more likely than other men to have friends who have engaged in sexual violence.[95]

Certainly most men are not rapists, nor do most men condone rape. Although estimates of the number of rapes vary widely,[96] almost all women from an early age are aware of the possibility of rape and fear it.[97] As we noted earlier, one of the few ways middle-class parents treat males and females differently is greater chaperonage for girls. The fear of rape becomes an important mechanism by which the total system of male dominance is reinforced. In coping with this fear women often restrict their activities or depend on a male protector. The courts themselves in trying rape cases reinforce the idea that women should restrict their own freedom (including their sexual freedom) in order to avoid rape. This assumption is rarely made in the case of a person who is the victim of a nonsexual assault or robbery. Thus, to an extent, both men and women accept the idea that although men rape, women cause it. The victim is blamed for rape, and the threat of rape becomes a way of restricting women's freedom.[98]

The laws on rape and their enforcement are changing. Most especially, the traditional definition of rape not as a violation of a woman's integrity but as a violation of her chastity is being questioned. For many years courts questioned a rape victim's prior sexual behavior and expected her to prove her chastity by struggling against the rapist. The view behind this practice is also related to the opinion that a husband cannot rape his wife, because in effect he already owns her chastity. Until recently, the law reflected the general Victorian view that women are either good or bad, pure or impure, chaste or fair game. This view, although appearing to help good women, in fact defines all women in terms of their sexuality and its patterning, rather than as human beings who, just as men, need freedom to live in the world without fear.

An important exception to the pervasiveness of rape cross-culturally and historically is the absence of rape among the peace-loving, nonviolent Arapesh described by Margaret Mead.[99] As we have seen earlier, this is a society where there is a strong tradition of male nurturance. Certainly, rape and the motive to rape should be minimized in situations where violence, male bonding, and the sex objectification of women are minimized.

Growing Up Female

Although the significant biological event initiating adolescence for boys is ejaculation, the significant biological event for girls is menstruation. Unlike ejaculation, menstruation is not directly connected with genital sexuality, but is rather an event testifying to the possibility of motherhood. Apparently girls in adolescence do not generally see themselves as sexual beings, and very few girls report feeling sexually deprived during adolescence. Nevertheless, both boys and girls are sexual beings. In contrast to boys, whose budding sexuality is often painfully obvious, girls' sexuality may be less conscious and insistent. For instance, the avid interest many young girls show in horses and bike riding may stem at least partially from the sexual stimulation these activities provide. Moreover, many ways of sitting adopted by young girls can be stimulating.

For many years young women were far less likely than young men to be sexually active. Before the mid-1960s the sexual double standard was a fact of teenage life, enforced by adolescent peer groups. As Lillian Rubin described it, "A girl's 'rep' rested on being a virtuous maiden, a boy's was tied to being a macho stud."[100] Although girls needed to be sexually attractive to be popular, if they became sexually active they could greatly limit the range of possible marriage partners. Today both male and female adolescents are much more likely to be sexually active. Although middle-class girls of earlier generations often felt pressured to lose their virginity by the time they were in college, today's young women often face such pressure in high school.

Even though girls' sexual activity is now more similar to boys, sexuality still does not appear to be as central to young women's sense of self and status as it is for young men, nor is it as free. Boys who delay sexual activity are often degraded and taunted by their peers. In contrast, although for girls the disgrace attached to adolescent sexuality is no longer present, virginity is not stigmatized either.[101] Whereas men recall their first sexual experience as a critical time in defining their manhood, none of a large sample of women interviewed by Rubin saw her first sexual experience as defining of womanhood.[102]

Most indicative of how the double standard has not disappeared is the continuing controls on girls' sexuality. A norm of serial monogamy is strong among teenagers, but boys who violate this norm face few sanctions, whereas girls are uniformly disparaged.[103] Richard Udry and his associates have examined the influence of both hormonal changes and social controls on adolescents' sexual behavior. Their studies indicate that, at least for whites, social controls such as the influences of peers and parents, especially fathers, are much more important for girls than for boys in influencing restraint in sexual activity.[104]

Men as objects Men's sex objectification of women may have a parallel among women. Constantina Safilios-Rothschild has suggested that women make men into objects too, not objects of sexual conquest but objects to support them.[105] Men are then objectified by women as money-making machines. Certainly men have taken this view—witness the turn-of-the-century jokes about women as golddiggers. Women as sex objects to men was taken for granted, and then men complained that women used their sexuality to get what they wanted. Although women sometimes do calculate with regard to men and thus use them in that sense, the parallelism between men's objectification of women and women's objectification of men should not be allowed to obscure the basic asymmetry of the situation. Because men do, in fact, control most of the resources in the wider society, women are constrained to use their sexuality as a way of gaining access to the money, prestige, and power men control.

That women do calculate with regard to men is evidenced by the differences in men's and women's attitudes toward marrying for love. College men and women were once asked the following question: "If a boy (girl) had all the other qualities you desired, would you marry this person if you were not in love with him (her)?" Of the males 65% answered that they would not marry if they were not in love, but only 24% of the women were equally sure that they would not. The great majority of the women (72%) answered that they were undecided on this question. One young woman remarked that it was hard to give a clear-cut answer to this question because, she said, "If a boy had all the other qualities I desired, and I was not in love with him—well, I think I could talk myself into falling in love!"[106] This young woman was prepared to do what Arlie Hochschild calls emotion work.[107] She would try to make herself feel what her calculation tells her she needs to feel.

As Willard Waller pointed out years ago, when a man marries, he chooses a companion and a helpmate, but a women chooses a companion and also a standard of living. Therefore, "it is necessary for a woman to be mercenary."[108] Shulamith Firestone agrees and argues that women unlike men are in no position to love freely.[109] Women are not so financially dependent on men as they were 50 or 100 years ago yet they still earn far less than men do. One can still make sense of all the findings reported on differences between men's and women's love patterns in terms of two principles: First, marriage is more important to women than to men; second, courtship is less under women's direct control, and women are not expected to initiate relationships.

Contrary to stereotype, men fall in love more easily than women and are more devastated if a relationship ends.[110] Men, as it were, can afford to be more emotional and less calculating than women. Women, whose life chances depend a great deal on whom they marry, yet who cannot initiate courtship, are thus constrained to work on their emotions more than men. They learn how to manipulate their own emotions to make them fit with their choice of a man. A woman also learns how to manipulate the emotions of the man she wants in order to cause him to fall in love with her. As the old cliché goes, "It is just as easy to fall in love with a rich man as a poor man."

From young person to sex object The necessity of attracting men in order to gain a measure of power over them makes women's experiences in growing up very different from men's. Simone de Beauvoir in her now dated but insightful chapter on "The Young Girl" in *The Second Sex* described the conflicts girls experience as they learn to transform themselves from active child to false object. In order to attract men, the girl must lie. "But, above all, the lie to which the adolescent girl is condemned is that she must pretend to be an object, and a fascinating one, when she senses herself as an uncertain, dissociated being, well aware of her blemishes. Make up, false hair, girdles, and 'reinforced' brassieres are all lies. The very face itself becomes a mask: spontaneous expressions are artfully induced."[111]

Although the nature of the artifices changes through time, the woman and her body remain on display. The conception of women as display objects to be evaluated has been continuously reinforced by the practice of selling all kinds of products from bathtubs to cars with the image of the sexy, attractive, partially undressed woman.[112] Good-looking women are also used to enhance sports events. Cheerleaders are now a prominent part of not only scholastic but also professional football games. Beauty contests, of course, are another example of women as display objects.

Because they are display objects, women learn to look at themselves as such. They learn to look at their faces and figures objectively and then deliberately work at making the best of them, disguising them or transforming them to fit the current image. The psychological effect of viewing oneself as an object in this way can be alienating and makes it difficult for women to gain a sense of themselves as real people. The pathological starving (anorexia) or gorging (bulimia) pattern found almost exclusively among adolescent girls may be understood as an obsession with self-defeating attempts to change their bodies to fit an ideal image.[113]

The further irony of women transforming themselves into sex objects is that the very qualities of attractiveness to men are often also the qualities men use as the reason for refusing women legitimate power. Thus, a man may say, "How can I take you seriously when you are so beautiful?" or "You're so cute when you're mad." Fortunately, most men's and women's consciousnesses have been raised with regard to the most blatant forms of this tendency to objectify and then patronize women. Yet it remains true that physical appearance is more important for women than for men.

Female bonding In past times and in some contemporary situations involving relationships with extended kin, women have formed strong solidary bonds with one another. Carroll Smith-Rosenberg studied the correspondence and diaries of men and women in the late 18th and 19th centuries and found that friendship and love between women was of great importance in the lives of both groups. Married and unmarried women visited each other, wrote to each other, and helped each other in crises. The close emotional attachments women had with each other partially competed with their attachment to their husbands in empathy and depth of commitment.[114] At present in areas where extended kin live close to each other, mothers and their adult daughters may interact frequently in their daily lives and are closer to each other than they are to their husbands.[115] Even today, in a situation where extended kin are less important, deep friendships and loyalties between individual women continue to exist.[116]

These female friendships, however, differ from male friendships in important ways. Male bonding is more impersonal and is related to reinforcing masculinity, whereas female bonding is more personal, empathetic, and familistic. Men use their interest in women as a basis for bonding together as men in pursuit of women. With women, matters are very different. Although occasionally (and increasingly) women may talk together about men as sex objects ("What a hunk!"), generally women do not bond together on the basis of their common physical interest in men except as a kind of protest. More important, women cannot bond together on the basis of their interest in men as money, power, and prestige machines, because the initiative lies with men. They must be chosen by a man. Thus, women become separated from one another in the pursuit of men. Alix Shulman recounted how her sorority sisters turned on her because they thought she was beautiful and thus had an advantage over them in the competition for men: "*Surely I must be beautiful if she hates me for it!* Well let her hate me then, what do I care? Obviously this hatchery is not the world."[117] Generally, the informal rule among women is that all is fair in love and war. It is considered impolite to congratulate a bride precisely because it points up the truth that women compete for men. In a male-dominated society, heterosexuality, then, has tended to break up the bonds between women, whereas to some extent it has been used to solidify the bonds between men. To the extent that our society makes it necessary for a women to become attached to a man in order to survive socially and economically and to the extent that men define the nature of women, the bonds that women might have with women necessarily become tenuous.

SUMMARY

In this chapter we have used a role-oriented version of psychoanalytic theory and data from academic psychology and sociology to describe how gender roles and male dominance are reproduced within the family and within male peer groups. The central elements in this process are that both males' and females' first interaction tends to be with a maternal figure, and within this interaction infants of both sexes are hooked into social roles and become responsive to social sanctions. The meaning of the Oedipal phase in part is that children cease to interact in merely dyadic relations and instead internalize the rules and roles in the family system as a whole. This involves learning gender-differentiated roles, including heterosexuality and male dominance.

Gender roles may be differentiated into maternal and heterosexual aspects. The maternal aspect is learned in nurturant interactions in the early years of life. Because females are responsible for early child care in all cultures, this first reciprocal role interaction is ordinarily with a female, a maternal figure who holds great power over the child. Because we live in a male-dominant society, this early stage of female dominance cannot be the prototype for adult heterosexual relations. Specifically, gender typing becomes important at the Oedipal stage, when the father enters the child's world. Fathers are more concerned with gender typing of their children than mothers are. Males are also more concerned with maintaining the sexual double standard than females are. This is because ending the double standard would directly challenge patterns of male dominance.

At the Oedipal period, as boys develop their identity as males, they repress their earlier identification with the mother and tend to reject the nurturant and maternal aspect of their personalities. To reinforce their sense of masculinity males strongly stress segregation of gender roles, devalue women, and make women sex objects. The husband–father role, then, as the adult male role within the family, is the role that introduces the gender-differentiating principle into the family. The woman's status as a sex object is first played out in relation to her father, and the boy learns to be dominant from his father and other males.

On the other hand, daughters of fathers do not become total sex objects, because of the incest taboo. Fathers are more likely to break the taboo than mothers, but within the family wives and daughters have more equal status and are less likely to be merely sex objects to husbands and fathers than they are outside the family. It is within the male peer group that males are most likely to define women as objects of conquest and to devalue them. These groups tend to have a dominance hierarchy and function to reinforce a system of male dominance in the wider society. They are more prominent among adolescents than among older men in the United States, and some of the grosser aspects of males' devaluation of females may be mitigated by marriage.

SUGGESTED READINGS

Brownmiller, Susan. 1975. *Against Our Will: Men, Women, and Rape.* New York: Simon & Schuster. The classic case for the relevance of rape to understanding women's situation.

Fine, Gary Alan. 1987. *With the Boys: Little League Baseball and Preadolescent Culture.* Chicago: University of Chicago Press. A look at the peer group life of young boys as it appears in organized sports activities.

Johnson, Miriam M. 1988. *Strong Mothers, Weak Wives: The Search for Gender Equality.* Berkeley: University of California Press. An extended discussion of many of the theoretical points presented in this chapter.

Raphael, Ray. 1988. *The Men from the Boys: Rites of Passage in Male America.* Lincoln: University of Nebraska Press. Describes the many ways men try to affirm their masculine identity.

Rubin, Lillian B. 1990. *Erotic Wars: What Happened to the Sexual Revolution?* New York: Farrar, Straus, & Giroux. Discusses the changes in sexual attitudes and behaviors from the 1950s to the present.

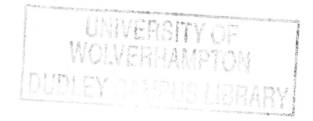

chapter 11

Gender throughout the Life Cycle

Any given individual ordinarily has a number of statuses, each with a corresponding set of role expectations. These statuses tend to be hierarchically ranked; some are more important and controlling than others.[1] For example, as we have seen, even when a woman in our society works at a very demanding job outside the home, the role obligations attached to her family statuses are expected to take priority: She is to be wife and mother first and jobholder second. For the man, on the other hand, the status of worker is considerably more salient in people's minds than his status as father and husband. These different *status sets*[2] of men and women are anticipated in adolescence, become most important during young adulthood, and ordinarily decline in importance during the later years of life.

Life-cycle changes may be classified differently in different cultures. For instance, Chippewa Indians divide a woman's life into four categories: birth to walking, walking to puberty, puberty to birth of first granddaughter, and first granddaughter to first great-granddaughter. People in our culture generally distinguish childhood and adolescence, young adulthood, middle age, and finally old age. Whatever the specific classification used, however, life stages generally reflect not only physical changes but, also and more importantly, changes in the social statuses an individual holds.

There are no strict age norms for entering a given stage; instead, there is a span of years in which a given behavior is considered appropriate. People in our society generally expect adults to marry or establish a close, intimate relationship with someone of the other sex by the age of 30 and for men to have made firm occupational decisions by the age of 40.[3] Yet there is a wide range of times at which people may actually enter one stage or another. Both the historical era in which one lives and demographic variables such as one's social class and racial and ethnic background can influence the age at which one enters a given life stage.[4] For instance, women are capable of bearing children from their teens into their 40s. In general, middle-class people tend to enter various life stages at an older age than working-class people. Middle-class women and men marry, have children, and also have grandchildren at older ages than do working-class men and women.[5] We also tend to expect that life events will occur in a given order—for example, finishing school, starting work, and then marrying—and some evidence exists that the order in which we experience these events can affect later life experiences.[6]

Each life stage has its own rewards and its own problems as individuals face different role expectations and demands. Sociologists tend to focus on the role strains that people experience, usually because of the different emphasis given to the various statuses that they hold. Psychoanalytic theorists also discuss developmental crises, ranging from the Oedipal crisis in early childhood through the identity crisis in adolescence to concerns about generativity and continuance of life in older years. In the following sections we discuss each of the life stages after childhood, looking at the different experiences of males and females. Because of the available data, much of our discussion will focus on middle-class whites in the United States. Also, much of our discussion will necessarily focus on typical experiences of individuals in each life stage rather than the broad range of exceptional behaviors that are possible.

ADOLESCENCE

Adult role expectations begin to exert a strong influence on the sex groups at adolescence, the time between childhood and adulthood. The length of the adolescent period varies from one culture to another, and in some cultures it is not socially recognized at all. In the United States its length also varies among subgroups and tends to be longer for middle-class children than for working-class children.

By the end of adolescence, gender segregation that foresees adult roles is widely apparent. Both males and females are beginning to move out of their family of orientation and to form their identities—boys centering on their status as workers, and girls centering on their status of spouse and parent, even though most also plan to be workers. Boys' and girls' different academic interests begin to parallel the occupations available to males and females. The young women and men perceive the roles that will be available to them in the years to come and adjust their interests and plans largely to fit these possibilities.

Social Roles in Adolescence

During adolescence young people begin to disengage themselves from their parents and siblings and to develop greater individual autonomy. Probably because of fears for their daughters' safety, parents allow adolescent sons to date earlier, to be left alone earlier, and to go places without parental permission more than daughters.[7] Although many adolescents hold paid jobs outside the home, boys work somewhat longer hours than girls.[8] As might be expected given this greater freedom, boys tend to have more conflicts with their parents regarding acceptable behaviors.[9]

As adolescents move away from their orientation to their family and their status as children, their friendships with their peers become more and more important. Although friends are very important to both adolescent boys and girls, girls more than boys want their friendships to contain elements of intimacy, support, and understanding. As we would expect from our discussion of gender differences in personality development, boys do not seem as interested in these affective qualities and emotional ties as they are in congenial companions with whom they can engage in activities,[10] and boys are less likely than girls to report that their friendships involve mutual intimacy and emotional closeness.[11] Neither boys nor girls, however, necessarily reject their parents' values or advice. They continue to recognize their parents' authority and, although relying on friends or other adults for advice in some areas, usually consult their parents when making decisions about their future educational and career plans.[12] Mothers, more than fathers, tend to maintain more regular contact and interest in their children's activities throughout adolescence.[13]

Adolescent males and females tend to pursue different leisure and extracurricular activities. In school girls tend to be cheerleaders, whereas boys are more likely to participate in most sports, even though the availability of sports activities for girls has increased greatly. Girls are more likely than boys to participate in extracurricular activities such as forensics, drama, glee club, and student publications and government.[14]

As we noted in Chapter 10, in recent years sexual activity among adolescents has generally increased. Yet although young women are apparently more knowledgeable about birth control than they were a few years ago, they do not use it consistently, probably because they feel guilty about their sexual activity.[15] Premarital sexual activity has occurred for many years. But only since the 1970s has sexual activity often involved young people who do not plan to marry each other. Thus, although pregnant teenagers in earlier years were likely to marry the father of their child, the majority today, especially in the African-American community, keep the child but do not marry the father. White teenagers are somewhat more likely than African-Americans to choose to have an abortion.[16] This situation illustrates the intense problems that can come with the too-rapid acquisition of new statuses at adolescence. A teenage mother, especially if she is from a poor family and is African-American, is more likely to live an economically marginal life, to not have a stable marriage, and to have children with behavioral and academic problems.[17] She is also more likely to live with her parents.[18] This can place a heavy burden on the young woman's mother who, as we will see below, is generally ready to put child rearing behind her and concentrate on other areas of life.

Although the acquisition of the status of parent in adolescence is rather rare, all adolescents appear to anticipate their future roles as worker and as spouse. For many years scholars thought that adolescent girls, in anticipating the wife role, began to hold down their academic achievement so that they did not appear "too brilliant," avoiding direct competition with potential future mates.[19] More extensive analyses have now demonstrated that girls do not exhibit more academic underachievement than boys. They receive higher grades than boys in all kinds of classes through high school, college, and graduate school.[20] In addition, they are more devoted to their studies, spend more of their free time on homework, and value achievement in general more highly than boys do. Generally both male and female peer groups, at least in the middle class, value academic achievement. Students with higher peer status are also those with better grades.[21] Moreover, gender differences in levels of educational aspiration are extremely small or indicate that girls actually have higher aspirations.[22] Clearly, adolescent girls do not sacrifice academic excellence to attract boys.

Teenage boys and girls do, however, have different high-school course preferences, college majors, and occupational aspirations, all of which parallel gender typing in the adult occupational world.[23] In recent years these gender differences appear to be even stronger among working-class, non-college-bound students than among those in the middle class, where girls are now more likely to aspire to male-typed professions.[24] Adolescent girls of all social classes are also less than fully committed to the work role, with many planning to interrupt their work careers to accommodate family plans.[25] These different orientations toward work show how adolescent girls anticipate the adult world of gender segregation, their being wives, and the greater valuation of males and their activities. They often choose occupations and course areas that do not compete with the boys and anticipate that they will subordinate the demands of their work role to those of the role of spouse and parent.

Developmental Crises in Adolescence

The anticipation of adult statuses and roles produces strains and conflicts for adolescents. Psychoanalysts describe the difficulties adolescents face in developing their identity and intimate relations with others as they anticipate these new roles. Erik Erikson popularized the idea of an identity crisis in adolescence.[26] Although a person's identity has of course been present since childhood, adolescents become crucially aware of the possibilities open to them and may become obsessed with the issue of who they are.

Because males and females face different role expectations in adult life, the nature of the identities they develop at adolescence differs. A number of years ago the psychologists Elizabeth Douvan and Joseph Adelson noted that for an adolescent boy

> identity revolves around the questions, "Who am I? What do I do?" The nature of his occupation plays a crucial defining role in a man's identity. The girl, on the other hand, depends on marriage for her critical defining element; she will take her self-definition, by and large, from the man she marries and the children she raises.[27]

Although adolescent girls today are more likely than in earlier years to anticipate having an occupational identity, their fantasies and life goals indicate that the differences observed a few years ago are still present. We recently asked high-school students to write essays describing their lives as they hoped them to be 10 years in the future. Boys' descriptions focused on their jobs and leisure activities; girls' focused on their husbands, children, and homes. Another study asked a large sample of high-school students how much they valued a wide range of life goals. Although boys and girls were equally likely to value finding an occupation that they wanted to be in, girls valued religion, making a contribution to society, and marriage and family more than boys, whereas boys valued showing others they could "make good" and obtain money and a secure, successful life more than girls.[28]

Boys face a more concrete task than girls of actively deciding what route they will pursue after finishing their schooling, for their future identification largely centers on their occupational role. The process of identity formation for girls is more ambiguous because most women still see their major adult statuses as wife and mother. What these statuses will actually entail largely depends on whom they marry.

Perhaps because so much of their future still depends on whom they marry, adolescent girls are much more likely than adolescent boys to be concerned about and less satisfied with their appearance, to have a less favorable attitude toward their own sex group, and, with at least some measures, to have lower self-esteem.[29] Although there are no gender differences among children in the incidence of clinical depression, adolescent girls and adult women suffer from this crippling psychological malady significantly more often than adolescent boys and men. Adolescent girls are also much more likely than boys to suffer from anorexia and bulimia nervosa, psychological ailments that involve extreme weight loss stemming from the girls' deluded belief that they are too fat and that weight loss will make them more attractive. Betty Allgood-Merten and her associates have shown that teenage girls' greater levels of depression are associated with a heightened concern with their body image.[30] In addition, although among children high self-esteem is associated, for both boys and girls, with the possession of both stereotypical masculine (self-efficacy) and stereotypical feminine (relationality) traits, among adolescents only stereotypical masculine traits are generally associated with self-esteem, the pattern commonly found with adults. This lack of association between femininity and self-esteem is particularly striking among adolescent girls. As Betty Allgood-Merten and Jean Stockard suggested, the coming of age for adolescent girls "brings with it a double bind—a marked devaluation of that which is female, yet being female—which makes it very difficult to feel good about oneself."[31] Both male and female adolescents seem well aware of the greater value accorded males in the adult world.

YOUNG ADULTHOOD

Both women and men usually hold at some time in young adulthood the statuses of worker, parent, and spouse. Yet the balance they have between these roles differs more markedly at this stage than perhaps at any other. Women are more involved in roles associated with wife and mother; men are more involved in work roles. These different balances contribute to the strains found in their young adult lives and the nature of their search for individual meaning in life.

Family responsibilities during young adulthood have undergone dramatic alterations over the years, partly because the childbearing period has been greatly compressed and adult women's life expectancy has greatly increased. Between 1800 and 1900 the total fertility rate among whites was cut in half as the average number of children born to a white woman surviving menopause fell from 7.04 to 3.56.[32] The birthrate in this century rose somewhat in the 1950s and 1960s from a low in the depression of the 1930s, but it now has dropped considerably. Furthermore, fewer children are spaced closer and closer together, allowing women much more time to devote to other tasks than child care. Finally, marriage itself is becoming less common, and young adults more often live outside family settings, alone, or with friends. This nonfamily living appears to promote, especially among young women, more nontraditional orientations, including less interest in marriage, more interest in a career, and expectations for fewer children.[33] Nevertheless, most men and women do eventually marry and most do have children.

The Status Sets of Men and Women

When viewed from a life-span perspective, the role of "only a housewife" for women seems to be largely disappearing. In the past women have been least likely to be in the labor force when they have young children in the home and most likely to reenter the labor force when their children are grown. In recent years the number of women in the labor force has increased, and the largest growth has been in the category of women with young children. In fact, the labor-force participation rate for married women without children under 18 is lower than that for mothers of children under 18,[34] primarily because so many women whose children are now grown are not in the labor force.

Do these statistics indicate a change in the work patterns of women throughout the life cycle? Undoubtedly this pattern is being modified from its earlier form, but the statistics confound differences between generations with differences in life-cycle stages in women's labor-force participation. Many women still lessen their labor-force participation when their children are young. However, many fewer women follow this pattern now than a few years ago. More young women either are not stopping work or are returning while their children are still infants and preschoolers. We suspect that as women who are now young reach the stage where their children are old enough to leave home, they will be more likely to reenter the labor force than were women who are now middle aged or nearing retirement. At that time the proportion of women without children under 18 who are in the labor force should be much higher than it is now. Numerous studies have documented that today's young women are more committed than their mothers' generation to careers and participation in the paid labor force.[35]

In general, young women probably have much more varied lifestyles than women did only a few years ago. They are much more likely than older generations were to combine work with parenting and marriage and to enter each of these statuses at a wide range of ages.[36] Middle-class men and women more often delay marriage and childbearing than working-class men and women, primarily because of the different educational demands and rewards of their anticipated occupations. Middle-class occupations usually require more education and have lower earnings early in the career than later, whereas working-class occupations typically have fewer educational requirements and smaller future earnings potential. Thus, in order to maximize family earnings at times when they are most needed (typically when setting up a household for childbearing and later with adolescent children in the home), it makes economic sense for middle-class couples to postpone marriage and childbearing, but no economic sense for working-class couples to do so.[37]

Even though there are a number of ways in which women balance the demands of home and work, their stage in the family life cycle largely influences the type of balance they make. In the newlywed stage, after marriage but before children are born, most young women work outside the home. Although newlywed women do not yet have families, they often anticipate motherhood, both in their temporary attitude toward work and also in their active lifestyle. Some observers suggest that women in the preparental stage tend to stress activity and to be involved in a wide variety of activities because they foresee the role constriction that will come with motherhood.[38]

Whether or not women with preschool children are in the paid labor force, they are likely to bear the primary responsibility for child care. Some statistics suggest that with no children in the family, about 1,000 hours of housework a year are needed to keep a household running. With no children under 6 about 1,500 hours a year are required. With children under 6, about 2,000 hours a year are needed, twice the amount of work required when there were no children in the home.[39] Husbands rarely give substantial help with this work, so a working mother essentially may have two full-time jobs.[40] Thus, as a result of sheer necessity, most mothers of young children concentrate more of their physical and emotional energy on the roles associated with their families than on those associated with work, even though many remain psychologically committed to their careers and plan to return to work in the future.[41]

As a woman's children grow older, she enters what Helena Lopata has called the full-house plateau, a time when there is an "increasing diversity of life styles."[42] Housework becomes less of a burden, and, as the children's interactions outside the family increase, so does child care. More women return to work as their children enter school, although some may return only sporadically. An increasing number of women enter the labor force at this stage out of financial necessity. As children get older, economic strains on the family increase, and many women must work to help out with the family's finances.[43] Because they may have been out of the labor market for a number of years, however, they often face even greater discrimination than women with continuous work histories. Their wages may be quite poor and their jobs unfulfilling.

Whereas women are likely to be involved in both family and work roles, men are more likely to be committed to work roles than to family roles. Most men do want to marry, and value the companionship, security, and emotional support of family life.[44] Evidence also suggests that men are more psychologically involved with their marriages and families than with their work.[45] Still, fathers are far less involved with their children and their care than mothers are, even when both parents are employed.[46] In addition, both men and women perceive that women must trade off time and energy invested in work and family roles, although they perceive that these roles operate independently for men. Men's involvement with work need not vary in response to family responsibilities.[47]

Strains at Young Adulthood

The different foci of men and women at young adulthood result in strain for both sexes. First, our society expects that a mother should be solely devoted to her child, and the isolated nuclear family increases the probability that a woman will be the only person involved in infant care. Second, the father is often heavily involved in his own work activities and other pursuits. He may be launching a career when the children are born, and he may have little time to spend with his family. Jessie Bernard has pointed out that our society is unusual in the isolation and stress placed on young mothers.[48] Fathers generally provide only a minimal amount of help with infant care, and there are rarely others such as relatives or servants who can help. Young mothers experience considerable stress from the increased responsibility as well as from their isolation from the adult world. When mothers of young children work outside the home, they are not as isolated as housewives are, but they still experience extreme psychological and physical stress from the demands of their families.

Although many women follow the pattern of marriage and motherhood, an increasing number of young women devote themselves exclusively to their careers in young adulthood. This pattern is more common among women in the professions than among women in other areas. Even though they avoid the parent and sometimes the spouse status, these young women do not escape role strains. Instead, it appears that as they get older, many of them reevaluate the course of their lives as they realize they have only a few years left in which they are able to bear a child. This appears to be a developmental crisis in the psychoanalytic sense as the women balance and evaluate the ways to find fulfillment for themselves and to contribute to the development of the next generation. Some of these women decide to have families and to assume the status of parent; others decide to remain devoted to their work-related roles.[49] Because a man is expected to focus his energies on work, his life tends to become divided not between work and family but between work and leisure, and he tends to specialize in a narrow range of interests that limit the possibilities of true communication with others. The man's focus on the often instrumental world of work deprives him of the more human and expressive qualities found in nurturant roles within the family.[50]

This lack of positive expressiveness in the male role can create intrapsychic strains for men to the extent that it involves a tendency to avoid self-disclosure and a desire not to expose areas of weakness or vulnerability.[51] Men's reluctance to disclose themselves may also function as a way of maintaining dominance. The lack of self-disclosure that characterizes the male role in this society is not just an unfortunate cultural trait, but may be a device that men use to maintain and exert power. If a man lets people know how he really feels—that he is hurt, that he is afraid—he may lose power.[52]

MIDDLE AGE

Middle age appears to occur when the person perceives that middle age has begun. Although there are wide class and subcultural variations, for both women and men, middle age involves physical changes, developmental crises, and role strains.

Physical Changes

Bernice Neugarten suggested that men look for signs of aging in the health of either themselves or their friends. In contrast, women do not "body-monitor" or look for illness in themselves so much as they look for such signs in their husbands, perhaps in preparation for widowhood that they will probably face in the future.[53] Yet both women and men show physical signs of middle age and aging. Their appearance changes as their bodies begin to age.

Unlike other primates and unlike men, women live past the period when they can reproduce, entering menopause.[54] From about 45 to 60 years of age the ovaries decrease their functioning and ovulation stops. Gradually a woman is no longer able to bear children. Although there are probably no accurate assessments of how many menopausal women experience physical symptoms, from 10% to 30% are so inconvenienced that they seek medical attention.[55] The possible symptoms include the hot flush or hot flashes—a "brief episode of feelings of warmth and flushing, accompanied by perspiration"—as well as dizziness, insomnia, headaches, tingling sensations, and anxiety.[56]

Yet a study of attitudes toward menopause found that a majority of older women saw postmenopausal women as "feeling better, more confident, calmer, [and] freer than before [menopause]," whereas the majority of younger women disagreed with this view. Middle-aged women seemed to be more likely than younger women to see menopause as creating no major discontinuities in a woman's life and to feel that a woman has some degree of control over her symptoms.[57] Women who are more privileged economically are also less likely to experience difficulties at menopause.[58]

Men do not experience a counterpart to women's menopause. Whereas women are born with their lifetime supply of ova, men continually produce sperm and can father children virtually until their death. Yet men do age, and some writers have noted what they call the male climacteric. All men experience a decline in testosterone levels as they age, and some popular writers suggest that about 15% of all men experience a sharp and sudden drop in these levels. The symptoms reported for males parallel to some extent the symptoms cited for females, including depression, nervousness, irritability, hot flashes, and dizziness.[59] Because men and their significant others do not ordinarily expect such changes to occur, these writers suggest that the climacteric may be more disconcerting for men who experience it than for women.[60]

Status and Role Changes

Along with physical changes, there are also role changes at middle age. In fact, as we noted above, women tend to define the departure of children from the home as the start of middle age. This can bring about basic changes in the lives of American women. As Lopata noted, when a woman's children reach preadulthood, the "basic tasks of womanhood, as defined by American society, those of bearing and rearing children, are completed."[61] If women do not find other ways to fill their lives, their self-definitions as a mother or a housewife can have "very narrow boundaries with empty lives."[62] Lopata suggested that the loss of children when they are launched into adulthood involves an "automatic drop of status for women," a situation similar to that of retired men. She found that this situation could be most disturbing to working-class or less well educated women who do not have the opportunity or resources to broaden their activities.

Most women today focus their energies on roles other than motherhood as their children grow older, maintaining a variety of commitments and responsibilities to others.[63] The vast majority spend some time working outside the home,[64] and many return to school for further education and job training.[65] Virtually all married middle-aged women assume the primary responsibility for household chores. Many also assume responsibilities for their own and/or their husband's aging parents. Given the growing life span of people in the United States, this responsibility can continue for many years, until the daughters or daughters-in-law are well into retirement years themselves.[66]

It should be noted that most of the studies of middle-aged women have involved the mothers of the "baby-boom" generation, women with an unusually high birthrate who often spent a number of years as housewives. Younger generations of women have generally had more continuous work experiences, less traditional attitudes toward women's roles, fewer children, and delayed childbearing. As they reach middle age, greater continuity of work roles from younger years to midlife may appear.[67]

In contrast to women, men do not experience sharp role changes at middle age, nor do they have the extensive multiple role commitments of women. They do not associate middle age with their children's leaving home but rather with the growing approach of old age. The middle-aged men in one large study tended to be actively involved in life, focusing on their work. The men were both more committed to their work and saw it as more central to their lives than did their working wives. It is not surprising that these men were happier than their wives.[68]

Role Strains and Developmental Crises in Middle Age

Erik Erikson has suggested that the last developmental crisis concerns integrity and despair, the point at which individuals try to come to grips with what they have done in their lives, accept their surroundings, and feel connected with the rest of humanity. From the empirical studies of Roger Gould it appears that this crisis may be a continuous process.[69] People in their early 30s often begin to question their life course. These questions continue with subjects in their late 30s and early 40s, who also begin to sense the finiteness of time and their lives. The subjects in their mid- and late-40s appear to have begun to live with these questions and to have developed more autonomous relations with their own children. Finally, in their 50s they show more self-acceptance and come to rely more on their spouses. (Unfortunately, Gould's studies were cross-sectional rather than longitudinal, and it is impossible to tell to what extent generational changes in experiences or situations can affect these stages.)

Although the popular literature tends to emphasize the "crises" associated with these developmental changes, it is important to realize that they usually do not reach crisis proportions. Many of the changes people experience at this time are not seen as losses but are seen as gains.[70] Midlife changes appear to be most stressful when they do not occur as expected, as for instance when adult children remain in the home or when a spouse dies at an early age.[71] The different roles of men and women influence the nature of their developmental changes. Although women must adjust to new combinations of demanding roles and their declining culturally defined physical attractiveness, men usually try to come to terms with what they have accomplished in their work role. They begin to realize that they are mortal, and they compare their achievements with the dreams of their youth.[72]

Strains for Women It was once thought that middle-aged women, when faced with the diminution of their maternal roles, were prone to experience depression.[73] We now know that this "empty-nest syndrome" was characteristic only of the generation of mothers born around the turn of the century who did not anticipate having a life span that extended long after their last child left home. Later generations have anticipated these postparental years and typically react to the empty nest with a sense of relief and enjoyment of their increased freedom.[74]

As in young adulthood, middle-aged women can face strains from the multiple roles they must fill. They may face extensive demands from older children, jobs, spouses, and, increasingly, elderly parents. In general, women in all social-class and racial-ethnic groups are much more likely than men to be responsive to and responsible for contact with and care for extended kin.[75] Studies indicate that women who are involved in several roles are generally healthier and have a stronger sense of well-being than those with fewer role demands. If, however, they are dissatisfied with these multiple roles, have little support from others, and/or face extreme time constraints, role strain and health problems may result.[76]

Besides experiencing these different role demands, middle-aged women begin to look older. Although many women are not disturbed by these changes, their aging appearance proves problematic for others.[77] In our society a middle-aged woman is often seen as losing her looks or going downhill, but a middle-aged man is perceived as sexually attractive and available. In fact, younger women often think an experienced older man is a good catch. Because men show signs of aging as much as or sometimes more than women do and because their sexual capacity declines to some extent whereas women's does not, it is probably not men's physical attractiveness or sexual prowess that allows them to continue to appeal to women but, at least within the middle class, their successful careers. The "trophy wife" has become a popular term in the media for the all too common phenomenon of the rich and powerful man who divorces his middle-aged wife to marry a sexy (and even accomplished) younger woman as a "trophy" for his success.

Strains for men Although women try to balance a variety of roles, such as work and elder care, men at middle age appear to take stock of their lives, to judge how well they have met earlier goals. Because men's lives center much more on work than on family, this stocktaking generally focuses on their status as worker. This illustrates a major strain in male gender roles in our society, for a man is not allowed to feel he is really a man unless he achieves in one sense or another. Thus, all through their lives most men are engaged in proving themselves. This activity in the middle class mainly centers on the world of work, but, because it is connected with maintaining masculine identity and male dominance, performance anxiety can spill over into all areas of life from sexuality to child rearing. Although men are subject to performance anxiety, performance also keeps many men going. When they can no longer perform, they become vulnerable. Thus, most men perceive old age as a threat because it endangers their performance capacities.[78]

OLD AGE

Attempts to find meaning from life continue into old age. However, as the possibility of death comes closer and as the roles of men and women change, the concerns of men and women may become somewhat more similar. Although gender roles in middle age and young adulthood involve a fair amount of divergence, in old age the roles men and women play appear to converge through changes both in the work patterns and in the family lives of men and women. The economic inequities women face in earlier life stages, however, continue to affect their later years.

Role Changes

Women are more likely to work when the children leave home, and when both men and women reach retirement age they leave the work force and tend to concentrate their energies in other areas. When there are no longer children at home, the energies of the mother need not be directed so much toward her children, and the father's role as breadwinner for his family becomes less important. When grandchildren are born, both grandmother and grandfather may take a nurturant or a playful role toward the grandchild. Some grandmothers may take over maternal functions, but rarely will the grandfather have to play either an authoritative or a breadwinner role.[79] In other words, the roles of grandfather and grandmother are much less differentiated than the roles of mother and father, even though some gender differences remain.[80]

Men and women also appear to come closer together on personality variables in old age. The noted gerontologist Bernice Neugarten has concluded that as they age "men seem to become more receptive to affiliative and nurturant promptings; women, more responsive toward and less guilty about aggressive and egocentric impulses."[81]

Jeanne McGee and Kathleen Wells caution that we must not exaggerate the extent of convergence of gender roles in old age.[82] Because aging inevitably involves the loss of a number of highly gender-differentiated roles acquired earlier in adulthood, some kind of convergence in roles of the sex groups is inevitable. Their observations of group behavior of older men and women document the persistence of male dominance in conversations and in decision-making patterns.[83] Women usually do not give up the role of housewife as they age, and the traditional division of household labor remains largely intact.[84] In addition, older women, much more than older men, retain responsibility for maintaining ties with family members and extended kin.[85]

Both men and women, as long as they are healthy, appear to maintain a wide variety of possible role patterns in old age. A number of studies indicate that older men and women who are more satisfied with life tend to participate in more social roles and have more interactions with other people.[86] For many older people the major source of social support and interaction, other than a spouse, is their children.[87] Daughters are much more likely than sons to provide this support.[88] Women's greater concern with relationality and connections with others continues throughout the life cycle, as older women tend to have larger social support networks than older men, regardless of their marital status.[89]

Still, retired women are less satisfied with life than retired men, and this appears to be related to their lower retirement incomes and, to some extent, their greater probability of being alone.[90] Both men and women tend to be more satisfied with retired life when they have better health, more varied leisure activities, and higher incomes and previous occupational status.[91] Yet retired women tend to have less financial security and lower incomes than retired men. Retirement pensions in the United States, both the federal Social Security system and private funds, are based on workers' earnings. Women are more likely than men to work intermittently and to have lower-paying jobs and thus have lower pensions.[92] Women also generally live longer than men, often resulting in the loss of a spouse's income and pension benefits and greater vulnerability to the detrimental effects of inflation on fixed incomes.[93]

The Death of a Spouse

The final stage of life for men and women often involves the death of a spouse. Although women have always lived longer than men, women are living even longer than men because of the increasing life span. By the time a woman is 65 years old there are only 68 men for every 100 women. This means that widowhood may well be part of a married woman's life. Married men are much less likely to be widowed than married women are. In the late 1980s, 77% of all women aged 45–54 were married, but only 24% of those 75 or older were married. Of all women, 6% were widowed at ages 45–54; 67% were widowed at age 75 or older. Because of the higher death rates for African-American men, the percentage of widows among African-American women is higher at each age group.[94]

Widowers are much more likely to remarry than are widows. Similarly, divorced men are much more likely to remarry than divorced women. Only part of this difference may be accounted for by the greater availability of marriageable women than men.[95]

An increasingly common situation is that of divorced older women. Divorced older women are often left without adequate financial resources, and if they have spent most of their lives as housewives, they often have inadequate job skills. They face many of the same financial hardships and problems of loneliness that widows do. In addition, older divorced women are not entitled to some of the financial benefits that widows can aquire. For instance, they often cannot collect Social Security payments earned by their ex-husbands. Older women who have never married tend to be well educated, with relatively continuous job histories and, at least for whites and Hispanics, have higher retirement incomes than men who have never married.[96]

Although widowhood may be a tragedy for an individual person, Helena Lopata has suggested that it is so common that it should be seen as the final stage in the typical career of a wife. Large differences are found between widows of different social classes and different social settings. Women who have the educational and social resources to participate in the larger community, maintaining social networks, are the most likely to adjust well to new social relations and the least likely to become isolated.[97]

TRENDS AND CONTINUITIES IN GENDER DURING THE LIFE CYCLE

Part of our discussion of gender throughout the life cycle has been based on studies of people at various life stages. Other evidence comes from cross-sectional studies of people at different stages of life, and a small amount of evidence is available from longitudinal studies of people over a number of years. In this final section, we briefly review information on general trends in self-concepts of men and women over the life cycle and then discuss evidence on continuities—that is, how behaviors and capabilities at one point in time influence later gender role behaviors.

Self-Concept over the Life Cycle

The changes in social roles and physiology over the life cycle are often accompanied by changes in self-conception and personality orientation. Marjorie Lowenthal and associates summarized the changes in the self-concepts of men in their sample at different life stages:

> In essence, there is reflected through the successive stages a change from an insecure and discontented self-image [in high school] through a buoyant and sometimes uncontrolled [newlywed] phase to the stage of control and industry [in middle age], to a later point of decreased demands on the self and greater acceptance of others and one's environment [at preretirement].[98]

As the authors noted, these changes parallel Erikson's overview of developmental stages throughout life.

Lowenthal and her associates found that women's self-concepts do not change as much as men's from one life stage to another. Generally, they found that high-school and newlywed women are similar to men of that age in being unsure of themselves and feeling powerless over the future. The newlywed women also tend to have less energy than their husbands and to exhibit greater warmth. The middle-aged women are least happy and see themselves as absent-minded. By preretirement, however, this pattern appears to dissipate, with the preretirement women feeling more effective and self-controlled than ever before. The Lowenthal group suggested that this comes from women's greater freedom at this stage as their children are on their own. They suggested that life stage may be more important in explaining psychological differences than chronological age.[99] Stage of life is more influential than age because life stages denote different kinds of interactions in different social situations.

Jack Block's follow-up study of young people involved in the University of California, Berkeley, Growth Study in the late 1920s supports at least part of the Lowenthal group's findings. Block's subjects were in their late 30s when they were contacted. The men were found at that time to have become more self-confident and certain; the women saw themselves as less sure of themselves.[100] When these subjects are contacted again in middle age we would expect that the women, whose responsibilities will have shifted so that they may focus more attention on themselves, will have regained some of their self-confidence.

Longitudinal Studies

Longitudinal studies, such as the Berkeley Growth Study, provide a unique opportunity to see continuities in gender roles as people grow older. Although longitudinal studies are very expensive and time consuming, they are often preferable to cross-sectional studies because we can control for different cultural and historical experiences of the subjects. For instance, a cross-sectional study may compare people who were 40 years old with some who were 70 years old in 1990. Yet these two groups of people had strikingly different experiences when they were in their 20s because of historical circumstances. For example, the 40-year-olds were young during the Vietnam War, while the 70-year-olds experienced World War II. Because, however, longitudinal studies deal only with a single generation, their results may not totally apply to other generations.

The results of three longitudinal studies can enhance our knowledge of continuities in gender roles over life: the Fels Institute study of children begun in 1929,[101] the Berkeley Growth Study of children and their parents that began about 60 years ago,[102] and Lewis Terman's studies of highly gifted children begun in the 1920s.[103] Although these studies were conducted a number of years ago, they are still important for showing how as children grow older they tend to mold their behaviors more in accordance with the societal definitions of gender-appropriate behavior. Also, because men do have more power and prestige in the society, it is somewhat more difficult to predict women's futures than men's futures from their early years. Women may traditionally have had less objective control over their fate.

Jerome Kagan and Howard Moss's follow-up study of the Fels Institute children illustrates how gender expectations in the society influence the development of personality characteristics and related behaviors. Stereotypically feminine traits that appeared in childhood were related to similar traits in adulthood in women, but not in men. Stereotypically masculine traits were related to adult behaviors for men, but not for women. Kagan and Moss found these results even in families "that did not consciously attempt to mold the child in strict concordance with traditional sex-role standards." They suggested that children in these families "responded to the pressures of the extrafamilial environment. The aggressive girls learned to inhibit direct expression of overt agressive and sexual behavior; the dependent boys gradually placed inhibition on urges toward dependent overtures to others."[104]

The children did not actually discard their childhood traits. Instead, when a child had behavior patterns that were not concordant with gender-role expectations, the adult behavior tended to be related to those behavior patterns, but was more in accord with traditional gender expectations. For instance:

> Passivity among boys predicted noncompetitiveness, sexual anxiety, and social apprehension in adult men, but not direct dependent overtures to parents or love

> objects. A tendency toward rage reactions in young girls predicted intellectual competitiveness, masculine interests, and dependency conflict in adult women, but not direct expression of aggression. It appears that when a childhood behavior is congruent with traditional sex-role characteristics, it is likely to be predictive of phenotypically similar behaviors in adulthood. When it conflicts with sex-role standards, the relevant motive is more likely to find expression in theoretically consistent substitute behaviors that are socially more acceptable than the original response. In sum, the individual's desire to mold his overt behavior in concordance with the culture's definition of sex-appropriate responses is a major determinant of the patterns of continuity and discontinuity in his development.[105]

Kagan and Moss did find that some characteristics show no continuity from childhood to adulthood. These traits included compulsivity, irrational fears, task persistence, and excessive irritability during the first 3 years of life. Yet when traits were consistent or stable over time, they tended to be congruent with acceptable gender roles.

Evidence that women are more affected than men by the opportunities they encounter comes both from studies that began with children and studies starting in adulthood. The parents in Henry Maas and Joseph Kuypers' study were first interviewed in the early 1930s when they were generally in their early 30s, and they were contacted again in 1968–69 when they were in their late 60s and early 70s.[106] In general the fathers in this study showed more continuity in lifestyle from their 30s to old age than the mothers did. Maas and Kuypers noted that "the continuities in [the] fathers' life styles are associated with few changes in context, aside from retirement, over their adult years."[107] In contrast, many mothers had extensive lifestyle changes from their early years of mothering. Changes in the women's situation and especially their age and health, economic conditions, and marital status all influenced whether their old age was more pleasant than their earlier lives. Mass and Kuypers suggested that because the women had to adapt to more changing conditions than the fathers over their lives, they showed less continuity.

Although Maas and Kuypers' study of parents shows how women more often experience changes in their lifestyles in adulthood than men do, Terman's study of gifted young people shows how the future occupational status of young women is much less likely than the status of young men to be related to their actual potential. Terman and his associates identified a large number of highly intelligent students in the 1920s and continued to follow them through their adult lives. Both boys and girls usually did very well in school, and the girls performed somewhat better than the boys in high school. Many of the men had very successful careers and were in the professions eight times as often as would be expected by chance.[108] Only about half of the women were employed in adulthood. Almost 35% of these employed women were in "business occupations, chiefly secretarial and clerical,"[109] 10% were college teachers in 4-year schools, and 22% taught in lower levels.[110] Although both the men and women generally did quite well in college, over half of the men but only 29% of the women graduating from college went on to get graduate degrees. In general, although highly gifted men may be expected to show occupational success, highly gifted women may be more hidden, and "there are highly gifted women working as secretaries, filing clerks, elementary teachers, and telephone operators."[111] Even though Terman's data were gathered a number of years ago, we suspect that the situation has changed only a little. Women and men are still equally represented among the gifted population, yet men overwhelmingly dominate the most prestigious and well-paid occupational areas.

SUMMARY

Men and women grow from childhood—where they have remarkably similar body shapes and abilities—through adolescence—where males become larger and stronger and both sex groups reach sexual maturity—and young adulthood—where women can bear and nurse children—to middle age—where women lose their reproductive capability and both sex groups begin to show signs of aging—and old age—where men tend to weaken and die earlier than women. At the same time, males and females enter different social roles and relationships. Young children gradually expand their relationships to involve their peers more, until by adolescence they tend to focus more on peers than on their families. By young adulthood most young people begin to form their own families through marriage and having children. Women tend to assume the primary responsibility for childcare, although they also usually remain in or soon return to the roles associated with the status of worker. Men's roles tend to center on their work, and they tend to see their main function in the family as that of provider or breadwinner. By the time parents reach middle age, children have usually left home, but many women find themselves caring for aging parents. By old age men's and women's roles become more similar as both leave the labor force and as they become grandparents, roles that in our culture emphasize nurturance. Children who display atypical gender-typed behaviors in childhood generally modify these to more gender-typical forms by adulthood. More continuities over the life span may be found in the lives of adult men than adult women, probably because men have traditionally had greater economic independence and control over their lives.

We have also seen how the achievement of males and females begins to diverge in anticipation of gender-differentiated adult roles. Even though the majority of women combine work with marriage, evidence indicates that their family roles are expected to take precedence over their outside work. Thus, men are much more likely to reach their intellectual potential in the occupational world than are women.

SUGGESTED READINGS

Baruch, Grace K., and Jeanne Brooks-Gunn. (Eds.). 1984. *Women in Midlife*. New York: Plenum. An extensive collection of articles related to middle-aged women.

Clausen, John A. 1986. *The Life Course: A Sociological Perspective*. Englewood Cliffs,

N.J.: Prentice Hall. An overview of sociological knowledge regarding the life cycle.

LOPATA, HELENA ZNANIECKA. 1987. *Widows: Vol. 2. North America.* Durham, N.C.: Duke University Press. An extensive collection of articles regarding the experience of widowhood in the United States and Canada.

LUEPTOW, LLOYD B. 1984. *Adolescent Sex Roles and Social Change.* New York: Columbia University Press.

SIMMONS, ROBERTA G., and DALE A. BLYTH. 1987. *Moving into Adolescence: The Impact of Pubertal Change and School Context.* New York: Aldine de Gruyter. Reports of extensive studies of adolescents in different time periods and locales.

chapter 12

The Future

The previous chapters have shown that male dominance exists in our cultural symbol system, in informal everyday interactions, and in social institutions and roles. Even in the same organizations, the activities of males and females tend to be separate, and what males do is more highly valued that what females do. In general, domestic roles for women and public roles for men are emphasized in all societies. This gender stratification is reproduced in each generation, in social institutions, and in the personalities of individuals as men's motive to deprecate women develops along with their early notions of their gender identity.

Although some sex differences, such as males' tendency to aggress more than females, may have some biological basis, psychological studies show few gender differences in basic capacities. Gender differences that do appear as people grow older can generally be better explained by the different social roles that males and females are expected to play. Children first develop their understandings of these different social roles, and boys first develop the motive underlying male dominance in their interactions in the family. As children grow older and interact more with their peers, their notions of appropriate gender roles are elaborated. The male peer group is especially important in reinforcing the deprecation of women. Throughout life, men and women generally face different role expectations, although the extent of gender differentiation and how this affects individuals' self-concepts may vary from one life stage to another.

We believe that the world would be a better place for all of its inhabitants—women and men, girls and boys—if male dominance and gender inequality could disappear. Both women and men could have more opportunities to enter new fields of work and to enjoy a greater variety of types of relationships with others. Girls and boys could grow up with stronger self-concepts, free of the poverty so many now experience, and able to explore a wide variety of interests. What would this world be like? How could our world be changed to approximate it? Could these changes really occur? In this chapter we explore each of these issues, linking our analysis to the three perspectives of feminist theory outlined in Chapter 1.

A WORLD WITHOUT MALE DOMINANCE

People, and perhaps especially liberal feminists, have often approached the question of gender inequality by asking, Why can't women be more like men? Our analysis is closer to that of some radical feminists, and suggests that a world without male dominance would not be one in which women become more like men, but one in which men become more like women in the sense that a female paradigm or world view would be substituted for the now-dominant male paradigm. This means that cultural symbols would be altered to show an equal valuation of females and males, and cultural values would express complementarity and interdependence rather than priority and social hierarchy.[1] It would be recognized that nurturance, expressiveness, and concern for other people are more important than the maintenance of hierarchies and dominance over others.[2] Aggression would be viewed as a threat to social integration and to human survival itself. Like many socialist feminists we suggest that in this world, all forms of domination would be seen as undesirable, and stratification by race, class, and gender would lessen.

Such changes in cultural values and symbols imply changes in social institutions and in the personalities of individuals. In a society without male dominance, there would be no unfair legal restrictions on women's activities, women and men would have equal access to educational opportunities, and gender segregation and wage disparities in the labor force would no longer exist. Women and men would have equal access to all roles in the society.

Because a society without male dominance would attach greater value to nurturant and expressive roles, work patterns and regulations would support family roles and the involvement of both women and men in the care of children. Most people would probably continue to marry, and marriage itself could temper tendencies toward male aggression and male bonding. Marriages would, however, be more egalitarian than they are now, with men and women sharing household tasks and important family decisions. Men would increase their involvement with kin beyond the nuclear family and, like women, would want to help maintain intergenerational ties. Children would be guaranteed access to quality-care programs, and both mothers and fathers would want to devote much time to their children's care.

Because men would be more involved with the early care of children, gender identities would be retained but would probably be stronger and less problematic than they are now because masculinity would seem less formidable. Gender itself would be less salient, and men would not feel a need to deprecate women to shore up their masculinity. Some gender differences in personalities and even social roles would probably remain, but there would be no different value attached to those of women and those of men.

Today these changes may seem unrealistic or at least very difficult to promote. The preponderance of evidence amassed in this book shows that male dominance persists in social institutions as well as day-to-day interactions.

Throughout the world, women still do the bulk of the housework, even when they also work many hours outside the home. Gender stratification permeates the economy. From country to country, women hold different jobs from men, and even when they have similar qualifications and do similar work, women are paid less than men are. In our own country, men and women have the same average amount of education; yet full-time, year-round women workers earn on the average about two-thirds what full-time men workers earn. Any attempts to alter male dominance must recognize the multiple areas in which it appears.

NEEDED INSTITUTIONAL CHANGES

Changes that would lead to a less male dominant society must attempt to deal with inequalities that are perpetuated in social institutions, within individual personalities, in everyday interactions, and in cultural symbols. Like many socialist and radical feminists, we believe that the most fruitful way to approach change is to focus not directly on individual motivation but on how the structure of social institutions and the patterns of interactions within them reinforce gender inequalities on the institutional, individual, and cultural levels. Because individuals live and mature within social institutions, one way to alter their motivations, self-definitions, and interaction patterns is to change these institutions. Because cultural symbols ultimately reflect existing social reality, they may eventually alter to reflect institutional changes. It must also be recognized that societies may more easily legislate changes in institutions than in individual attitudes, thus making institutions the easiest area in which to intervene.

Our analysis of gender inequality in social institutions has focused on the economy, the family, education, and the polity. As liberal feminists have stressed, providing women with education appears to be a basic necessity in starting the trend toward greater equality. In advanced industrial countries, with increased education, the birthrate tends to decline, more women become involved in occupations outside the home, and women themselves may begin to demand greater legal equality.[3] The extent of inequality in education, and to some extent in the polity, tends to vary from one society to another. For instance, although in many countries women have much less education than men and are much more likely to be illiterate, in this country and in some others, especially in Europe, women and men have virtually the same amount of education. Although no country has an equal representation of the sex groups in its governing bodies, many countries guarantee equal rights for women and men in the political sphere and have legislation that calls for equal treatment in the economy. This is especially true of industrialized countries. These legal guarantees, along with increased education, are necessary steps to guarantee the end of gender inequality and can help promote changes in other institutions. Yet laws requiring that women be treated like men ignore the fact that women are intimately and directly connected to the care of children much more than men are.[4] As socialist feminists have stressed, changes in the polity and education are probably not sufficient to guarantee the end of male dominance.

Despite legal guarantees and relatively equal educational opportunities, extensive inequalities persist in both the economy and the family. Cross-culturally, women remain the main providers of early child care, both in the home and in other care settings. Women's labor-force participation has increased in all developed Western nations, and the wage gap between men and women has generally declined, although less in the United States than in other countries. Yet in all societies women continue to do different work from men and receive less money and less prestige for their work than men. Changes in both the economy and the family will be necessary to lessen inequality in social institutions and to decrease men's motive to devalue women. These changes should be accompanied by, and reflected in, alterations in our cultural beliefs and values, as well as our day-to-day social interactions.

Dealing with Gender Stratification through the Economy

Laws requiring that men and women be paid the same amount for the same work and regulations such as affirmative action programs that call for an end to gender segregation of occupations provide the basis for the equal participation of women and men in the economy with equal rewards. Some laws also require the end of discrimination in admission to educational programs leading to certain kinds of jobs. By law in this country, women cannot be denied admission to vocational training programs in the traditionally male craft areas or to traditionally male professional areas in medicine or law solely on the basis of their sex. The various equal employment opportunity laws also give women who have experienced discrimination an opportunity to claim jobs. Proponents of these laws and regulations hope that as more women are trained in male-dominated areas, the sex ratio in the applicant pool for these jobs will change, and eventually employers will be forced to hire either unqualified men or the trained and qualified women. This assumes, of course, that the demand for these workers does not decline and that the services of all trained people will be needed.

If these economic changes occurred, they could help promote greater gender equality in the family. When women work outside the home *and* contribute a large proportion of the family income, they may have more input into family decisions. Moreover, at least when a family has young children, the father may contribute more time to child care if his wife works outside the home.

Even though the legal basis for ending gender segregation of occupations as well as gender disparities in income has been in place in the United States for a number of years, there has been relatively little progress toward this end. More women are employed than at any time in U.S. history. Middle-class young women are more likely than their older sisters and, especially, their mothers to train for and enter traditionally male-typed occupational areas. The gender gap in wages has narrowed slightly in the past 20 years, especially among young workers. Yet women workers still earn much less than men, and occupational segregation appears to be very tenacious. As more women are trained for an occupational area, they may begin to enter the field, but the field then appears to develop greater internal gender segregation, and the areas within the field where men are employed provide higher pay. Women in racial-ethnic minorities are even more likely than white women to hold low-paying jobs.

Some states have passed "comparable worth" or "pay equity" legislation designed to reward typically female jobs equally to typically male jobs requiring similar skills and training.[5] Implementation of these schemes within organizations has produced some lessening of the gender wage gap[6] but has fallen far short of the hoped-for success, primarily because the political process used in determining the equity plans were still controlled by a male-dominated establishment.[7]

Women are most conspicuously absent from the highest levels of the occupational and political world. Women generally have only token representation at the top government policymaking levels and at the highest levels of the corporate world. A *Fortune* magazine study of directors and highest executives at 799 major companies found almost 4,000 men, but only 19 women.[8] If gender stratification is to lessen significantly, it is critical that women be equally represented in these highest levels.[9]

Women's ties with children and the failure of employers and policymakers to deal consistently with this issue exacerbate the difficulties women face in the economy. Women continue to have the primary responsibility for housework and child care, even when they have extremely demanding jobs. Few employers in the United States provide help with child care, flexible work hours to accommodate children's needs, or paid maternity leaves. Women in blue-collar work as well as clerical jobs face rigid time schedules, low pay, and virtually no recognition or help from employers for their family responsibilities.[10] Professional women, although better paid, also face these problems. Career paths that lead to top-echelon positions generally require long work hours and uninterrupted work histories. Mothers cannot fulfill these requirements, unless they have partners who choose to forgo careers and take care of family responsibilities or unless they hire others (almost always women, at low pay) to care for their children and households. A number of studies of high-level executives have found that virtually all of the men have children, whereas one-half to one-third of the women are childless.[11] The vast majority of women want to have children at some time in their lives. Our present economic arrangements require them to compromise their career and family goals.

Working mothers, and a substantial number of their partners, at all levels of the occupational structure report experiencing a great deal of strain in their day-to-day lives because of the demands of work and family.[12] A recent survey of parents in the Los Angeles area found that 80% of mothers and nearly 40% of fathers would quit their jobs, if they could, to spend more time with their children.[13]

It appears, then, that economic changes, at least as they have been structured in this society, may be helpful but are not sufficient to produce lasting change in gender inequality. The laws related to job discrimination, although not strictly enforced, may not be sufficient to end inequities, and the motives underlying male dominance, role segregation, and the perpetuation of inequities appear unchanged. Most importantly, the balance of attention women and men give to their activities connected with work and family has not altered. Women have been expected to enter the job world as men have done while also maintaining their work in the family, generally without any additional help. Simply focusing on women's work for pay does not appear to directly change their greater responsibility than men for work in the family, nor does it assure that the various laws will be followed. To deal with these problems, we turn to additional changes that focus on the family.

Dealing with Gender Stratification through the Family

One step that might alter the distribution of family responsibilities as well as minimize the psychological motives underlying male dominance is for men to become more involved in the nurturing of young children. Based on our earlier analysis, we would hypothesize that as men become more involved in nurturing young children, gender identity will not disappear but will become less problematic and less salient. Studies of matrifocal societies where considerable worth is given by both men and women to the maternal role and of societies where males are more exposed to young children indicate that male dominance is less in these than in other societies.[14] Studies of adults in our own culture suggest that those who have grown up in loving households where both mothers and fathers participate in non-gender-typed tasks are less gender-typed themselves[15] and that couples who share parenting are more likely to be satisfied with themselves and their relationship.[16]

Because father–daughter incest is already all too common, it might be argued that if men were encouraged to nurture it would increase their tendency to sexualize their relationship with children even more. This could increase incest and the sex objectification of women even further. Yet, if fathers were actively involved in child care and felt genuinely responsible for their children's well-being, they might be less inclined toward a sexual and seductive relationship with them. In this case, incest might actually decline.

If male children were exposed to warmly supportive fathers in early childhood, their lessened need to dominate and to sex objectify women might also lessen the incidence of rape. As males no longer need to repress their positive expressiveness in denying "femininity," their overall agressiveness might lessen, especially because nurturing itself requires a repression of aggression. Finally, some evidence indicates that hererosexuality (whatever one may think of its desirability) would be promoted in both sexes by fathers interacting in a warm and caring, but not a seductive, manner with their children.*

---

*In speaking of fathers, mothers, and families, we do not mean to imply that the only desirable family situation is that of the isolated nuclear family with both parents present.

We have suggested that women's secondary status is much more linked to the wife role than to the mother role. Studies of families where mothers and fathers share parenting indicate that the mothers retain the primary authority for nurturing and, to a large extent, direct the father's participation.[17] To the extent that men's greater participation in child care involves an enhancement of their empathy, nurturance, and positive expressiveness in ways that accord with women's wishes, it could point toward a more caring, egalitarian marriage relationship where both partners provide emotional support for the other, rather than the wife primarily serving and deferring to the husband.[18] At the same time, a greater cultural emphasis on individuals' own identity and self-realization[19] may foster egalitarian relations and validate the assumption that all people, both men and women, deserve individual fulfillment.

In recent years the divorce rate has risen considerably, both women and men are less likely to marry than they have been in earlier years, and single mothers are much more common. Even though joint custody of children has become more common after divorce, fathers are much less likely to remain in contact with their children than are mothers, and over one-fifth of all families with children in the United States do not include a male adult. Within the African-American community, over half of the children under 18 live with only their mother. To some extent, for a variety of reasons discussed in Chapter 3, the definition of women as wives is weaker within our society than it was a few years ago. Fewer women are married. Women are becoming less dependent on men and may bond more with other women, both kin and friends.[20] Especially in single-parent families, women's more powerful mother role has become much more salient than the wife role.

Although these changes in the family may enhance the attention given to women's autonomy and ties with other kin, there may be other less salubrious results. As families increasingly live apart from fathers, they are much more likely to be poor. Women rarely earn enough money to support their families by themselves, fathers often do not pay required child support, these support payments are often inadequate, and the usual outcome of divorce is impoverishment.[21] Over half of all children living in families headed by women live in poverty, compared to only 10% of children in families with both a mother and father present. The link between marriage and economic security for women remains firm but has altered so that incomes of both husband and wife are needed to avoid poverty. Unlike only a few years ago, the majority of men in the United States, even though they earn far more than women, now do not make enough money to support a family by themselves. Two incomes are often necessary to support a family, and even single mothers holding professional jobs find it hard to make ends meet. Ironically, then, although the growing prevalence of nontraditional family styles has led to a deemphasis on the wife role, it has also led to women's impoverishment.

Another unintended consequence of changing family patterns may be a growing tendency for adult men to associate more with their peers, reinforcing tendencies to devalue and objectify women. Men have always bonded in "homosocial" fellowship, but, at least in the middle class, marriage has helped to weaken these peer ties.[22] As men increasingly choose to forgo intimate, long-term relationships with women and children, they may become even more likely to objectify and devalue women and girls. In fact, rates of rape and homicide tend to be higher in areas where more men live alone or only with other men.[23]

In addition, men's likelihood of involvement with caring, nurturant, intergenerational relationships lessens. Alice Rossi has suggested that this growing lack of intergenerational connectedness may have long-term consequences not just for the status of women, but for all people who live in deprived circumstances. She suggested that as fewer people are directly linked with the care and rearing of children, political incentives for altruistic policies that provide for the welfare of children and other vulnerable populations, both in this country and abroad, may diminish.[24] Other authors suggest that the growing focus in recent decades of adults on their own self-fulfillment, rather than the welfare of children, can be linked to the increasing incidence of alcohol and drug abuse, criminal behavior, and suicide among adolescents.[25]

Finally, although a growing number of men may participate in early child care and nurture both their young sons and daughters,[26] to the extent that men increasingly absent themselves from the home and contact with their offspring, many children will not experience such nurturant paternal relationships. Although women and men kin and friends may help fill this gap,[27] many mothers may find the heavy demands of child care even more difficult, and young children will be more likely to miss the possibility of nurturant, paternal interactions. These are precisely the interactions that can help foster stronger and more secure gender identities and ultimately less devaluation of women. As the feminist writer Barbara Ehrenreich noted, as long as women have sons, as well as daughters, consistent nurturant interactions for children with both adult men and women will be important ingredients of a healthy future adulthood and a society that has greater gender equality.[28]

THE POSSIBILITY OF CHANGE

Experiences with attempts to alter gender stratification since the beginning of the current wave of the feminist movement indicate that change can occur. Yet it will undoubtedly come slowly, and unanticipated consequences may provide setbacks along the way. In the past century, most countries throughout the world have recognized women as citizens, and many governments have enacted laws and established commissions to implement greater equality between women and men.[29] A major impetus for these changes has been the increased education of women and, in many places, their increased involvement in the public spheres of the economy and the polity. Within the United States, there is extensive evidence that attitudes toward women's roles have changed. Polls taken over a period of the past 50 years in this country show a consistent trend toward greater acceptance of equality for men and women by members of both sexes.[30]

As we noted in Chapter 1, changes can also be seen in cultural symbols.

Women who are attending seminaries or who are now ordained are challenging and altering the patriarchal symbolism characterizing their religions. Language usage has clearly changed. The names of jobs have been extensively revised, thanks in good part to the policies of the federal government. We now have flight attendants, mail carriers, and postal workers instead of stewardesses, mailmen, and postmen. Signs on construction sites now proclaim "crew working" instead of "men working." Publishing companies require their authors, whenever possible, to avoid sexist language. Images in the media also demonstrate changes. Women newscasters are much more common than just a few years ago. Although many prime-time shows maintain the traditional patterns of male dominance, other shows portray women professionals and deal with stories involving males caring for their children and the problems of balancing work and home life.

Some suggest that there has been a general cultural trend toward a greater emphasis and value on expressiveness, nurturance, and caring as opposed to competitive striving since the 1960s. Media are much more likely to depict men in nurturant, vulnerable roles.[31] Fathers are becoming more involved in the birth process and caring for young children on a day-to-day basis. Other cultural trends, however, suggest a very different picture. The "yuppie" concern with success at any cost, the popularity of warrior and combat movies, as well as popular music that vividly degrades and sexualizes women all indicate that many aspects of our society have not embraced cultural values that support a greater concern with expressiveness.[32] Nor do these aspects of our culture suggest a lessening of gender inequality.

Similarly, changes in the economy have led to greater employment of women, but few changes in the wage gap, occupational segregation, or the division of labor in the family. More women and children live in poverty today than 20 years ago, and women's probabilities relative to men of living in poverty have continually worsened since 1950.[33] Women's increased labor-force participation and legal guarantees to equal treatment do not appear to have necessarily improved their situation in the economy or the family.

We believe that further changes cannot be successful unless policy initiatives broaden to place a high priority on nurturance and care of children. If many segments of our society explicitly supported the importance of caring, nurturance, and positive expressiveness rather than exploitation and cut-throat competition, policies that provide support for mothers and children would logically result. Such policies would implicitly and explicitly deal with the problem of poverty, one that disproportionately affects children and their mothers, especially those who are members of racial and ethnic minorities. Income would be more evenly distributed between not only women and men, but also between childless families and those with children.[34] Both government bodies and the corporate world would expand their support of child-care services, provision of medical and welfare services to children, and support for working parents through paid leaves and other services. Provisions would be made for parents to work shorter hours without penalty so that they could provide more attention to children of all ages. Unions, feminist organizations, and other groups would actively lobby for a higher priority on children's welfare.[35]

If broad-based support could be developed for greater attention to the needs of children, cultural definitions of masculinity would alter. If the policies suggested above that stress nurturance, equality, and caring were implemented, we might hear that "real men love and help support their children" and "real men aren't threatened by successful women."

The nuclear family composed of a husband, wife and their children may well remain the type of family idealized within our culture for a number of years. Yet the much more diverse kin structures described in Chapter 3 that might be called the postmodern family are probably much more typical of family types that will be common in at least the foreseeable future. The conventional modern family heavily emphasizes women's role as wife. The postmodern family may deemphasize this role but often involves women carrying a double burden of responsibilities in the economy and family. Thus, neither form appears to promote greater gender equality. In calling for a change in the cultural definition of masculinity, we are not necessarily advocating either of these family forms but, instead, an alteration of values and norms to emphasize the importance of responsibility for the young among all adult members of the society as well as the equality of mothers and fathers.

To be truly effective, we believe that changes must proceed simultaneously within the family and the economy. Gender relations in both of these institutions must alter. Women must break through the "glass ceiling" and gain equity in top-level administrative positions in business and government. The "clockwork" of these typically male careers must change to accommodate women. Some of the most ardent supporters of family policy on the national political scene have been women, and we believe that extensive changes will require the intervention of women at high levels of authority in both the corporate and political world. Thus, to obtain the policy changes we suggest, it will be important to have much greater equity at all levels of the economic world; to have greater equity within the economy it will be important to develop more supportive family policies throughout our society.

Many mothers may be reluctant to relinquish their concern for child care and the organization and management of their families because these activities bring them status within the family as well as intrinsic pleasure. Yet the welfare of mothers and children would be enhanced if mothers received greater support both from the society and from male kin. This can only happen if our cultural definitions of masculinity broaden to include notions of caring, positive expressiveness, and nurturance.

The United States is unique among industrialized countries in its virtual lack of attention to families, child welfare, and support for mothers. In fact, Urie Bronfenbrenner has declared that simply because we ignore the situation, the family policy in this country is an antifamily policy.[36] Paternity leaves are almost unknown, paid maternity leaves are rarely available, quality child care is expensive and often extremely difficult to find, and an alarming number of mothers and children live in poverty. Parents must often work so many hours that they can give their children only cursory attention, and those who choose to cut back on their work hours or to leave work for periods of time to care for their children are often severely penalized in terms of career advancement or job security.[37]

In contrast, most other industrialized societies now provide paid parental leaves for working mothers (and often fathers), regulate and subsidize child care, allow parents to take paid leave when a child is sick, provide free medical care, and even provide monetary allowances to parents to help support children. These countries realize that their future well-being as a society rests on the health and welfare of their children. Indeed, these societies generally have lower infant mortality rates, lower crime and imprisonment rates, as well as a smaller wage gap between the sex groups. Experiences in these countries indicate that supporting women's mothering does as much, if not more, to enhance their status as do laws that require they be treated as men are. This occurs because child-care policies explicitly help to lessen women's double burdens at home and at work.[38]

In general, advances in our society that may be attributed to the feminist movement have benefited middle-class women, who are disproportionately white, more than working-class or poor women who are also more likely to belong to racial-ethnic minorities.[39] College-educated women, but not their blue-collar sisters, are more likely to aspire to and enter traditionally male jobs and have been most likely to enjoy the economic advantages that come from these successes. To the extent that they can hire help for housework and child care (usually other women at low wages) and the extent that their husbands are freer to embrace the cultural ideals of expressiveness and nurturance while not threatening their economic standing, these middle-class women may face somewhat less demanding double burdens of work and family roles.[40] Policies that would focus more directly on the welfare of children and families should help to redress more directly the concerns of working-class and poor women, who are also more likely to belong to racial or ethnic minorities.

Women's greater participation in the labor force, the passing of legislation that requires equality in the economy, and the increasing acceptance of egalitarian roles for men and women are certainly important steps toward a more egalitarian society. As feminists work toward additional changes that focus not just on increasing women's representation at all levels of the occupational world, but also on support for families and children and the specific concerns of working-class and poor women we may be able to move closer to a society in which greater equity exists for women and men in all areas of society.[41] Male dominance will no doubt be hard to change, but we believe that the results will be worth the effort.

SUGGESTED READINGS

CHAFETZ, JANET SALTZMAN. 1990. *Gender Equity: An Integrated Theory of Stability and Change*. Newbury Park, Calif.: Sage. A systematic development of propositions regarding variables that can help produce greater gender equality within industrialized societies.

EHRENREICH, BARBARA. 1983. *The Hearts of Men: American Dreams and the Flight from Commitment*. New York: Anchor Books. A feminist analysis of the changes in men's orientations toward women and children since the 1950s.

HAYES, CHERYL D., JOHN L. PALMER, and MARTHA J. ZASLOW. (Eds.). 1990. *Who Cares for America's Children? Child Care Policy for the 1990's*. Washington, D.C.: National Academy Press. Report of a national panel on child-care policy that examines the needs for child care in the United States and presents policy recommendations.

HEWLITT, SYLVIA ANN. 1986. *A Lesser Life: The Myth of Women's Liberation in America*. New York: Morrow. An impassioned plea for greater support for working mothers in the United States. Includes comparisons to other countries.

JOHNSON, MIRIAM M. Forthcoming. "Liberalism and Gender Equality: Problems of Social Integration." In Paul Colomy (Ed.). *Neofunctionalism: Dynamic Systems and the Problem of Social Integration*. Newbury Park: Sage. Discusses how current changes in the family can help improve the status of women.

SEDNEY, MARY ANNE. 1987. "Development of Androgyny: Parental Influences." *Psychology of Women Quarterly*. 11:311–326. Reviews a variety of studies that describe the long-term effects of parents' non-gender-typed behavior on their children's gender-typed behavior in adulthood.

Endnotes

CHAPTER 1

1. Jaggar, 1983, pp. 102–103; Rubin, 1975.
2. Key, 1975, p. 89.
3. Baron, 1986, p. 112.
4. Baron, 1986, pp. 171–172.
5. Schulz, 1975; see also Penelope, 1990.
6. Pagels, 1979.
7. Weitz, 1977.
8. Ruether, 1977, pp. 13–15.
9. Ruether, 1985, pp. 42–43.
10. Neal, 1979.
11. Ruether, 1985, p. 33.
12. Weitz, 1977, pp. 185–187.
13. Tuchman, 1978.
14. Cantor, 1987, pp. 202–203.
15. Lemon, 1978.
16. Waters and Huck, 1989, p. 48.
17. Barthel, 1987, p. 170.
18. Ferguson, 1983, p. 189.
19. Cantor, 1987, pp. 196–199, 211.
20. Courtney and Whipple, 1983.
21. Barthel, 1987.
22. Rak and McMullen, 1987.
23. Courtney and Whipple, 1983.
24. Brown and Campbell, 1986, pp. 98–104.
25. Saario et al., 1973; Huston, 1983, pp. 421–422; Grauerholz and Pescosolido, 1989; Williams et al., 1987; Ferree and Hall, 1990.
26. Tuchman, 1978.
27. West and Zimmerman, 1987; see also Gerson and Peiss, 1985, and Deaux and Major, 1987.
28. Stacey and Thorne, 1985.
29. McPherson and Smith-Lovin, 1986.
30. See Clawson, 1989, for a historical discussion of fraternal organizations.
31. Heuser, 1977; see also Cahill, 1986 a and b.
32. See Davis, 1988, for a historical discussion of gender and fashion, and Cahill, 1989, for a discussion of appearance management and the reproduction of gender.
33. See also Fine, 1987.
34. Stouffer et al., 1976, p. 180.
35. Eisenhart, 1975; see also Raphael, 1988.

36. Fry, 1972, p. 139.
37. Quinn and Lees, 1984; Gruber, 1990; Enarson, 1984; Farley, 1978; Korda, 1973; Swerdlow, 1989; Hearn and Parkin, 1987; Hearn, et al., 1989.
38. Aries, 1987, p. 157.
39. Fishman, 1983.
40. Kollock, et al., 1985; Smith-Lovin and Brody, 1989.
41. Wiley and Woolley, 1988.
42. West and Zimmerman, 1983, p. 109; West, 1982.
43. Henley, 1977.
44. Porter and Geis, 1981.
45. Hall, 1984, 1987.
46. Daniels, 1988.
47. Komarovsky, 1953, p. 78; 1974, p. 525; 1985, pp. 243–245; Dean et al., 1975.
48. Zimmer, 1986, 1987; see also Williams 1989; DeFleur, 1985.
49. Epstein, 1970, p. 979.
50. Kanter, 1975; Tavris and Offir, 1977, p. 211.
51. Kanter, 1975.
52. P. Johnson 1976; see also Kramarae, 1981, pp. 142–154.
53. Cott, 1987, p. 3.
54. Chafe, 1977; Chafetz and Dworkin, 1986; Rossi, 1982, pp. 9–13; Taylor, 1989.
55. Jaggar, 1983; Nielsen, 1990; Lindsey, 1990; Donovan, 1985; Deckard, 1983.
56. e.g. Friedan, 1963.
57. e.g. Sayers, 1982; Gimenez, 1978; Delphy, 1984; Hartmann, 1981; Benston, 1969.
58. e.g. Daly, 1978; Lerner, 1986; Moen, 1979; O'Brien, 1981; Rich, 1976, 1980.
59. Stacey, 1987; Rosenfelt and Stacey, 1987.
60. Epstein, 1988.
61. Wuthnow, 1988.
62. Briggs, 1987; Charlton, 1987; Ruether, 1985; Kaufman, 1989.
63. McLaughlin et al., 1988, p. 174.

CHAPTER 2

1. Frieze et al., 1978, pp. 342–344; Gallup, 1988, p. 11; see also Deitch, 1988; Miller, 1988; Goodman, 1990b.
2. See Mueller, 1988, for extensive discussion of these elections.
3. Gurin, 1985; Poole and Zeigler, 1985; Bennett, 1986; Wirls, 1986; Sears and Huddy, 1990.
4. Klatch, 1987, 1988.
5. Rossi, 1982.
6. Luker, 1984.
7. Tinker, 1983.
8. Travis, 1986; Bookman and Morgen, 1988; Milkman, 1990; Jones, 1990; Fernandez-Kelly and Garcia, 1990.
9. Lynn, 1979, pp. 410–411; Beckwith, 1986; pp. 147–152.
10. Cf. Mandel, 1988, pp. 85–88.
11. Mandel, 1988, pp. 90–92.
12. National Directory of Women Elected Officials, 1991.
13. National Directory of Women Elected Officials, 1987, pp. 6–10.
14. Diamond, 1977.
15. Goodman, 1990a.
16. Kincaid, 1978.
17. Poole and Zeigler, 1985, p. 156; Mandel, 1988, p. 94.
18. Goodman, 1988.
19. Mandel, 1988.
20. Sigelman and Sigelman, 1982; Sigelman and Welch, 1984; Zipp and Plutzer, 1985.
21. Bullock and Johnson, 1985.
22. Wilhite and Thielmann, 1986; Uhlaner and Schlozman, 1986; Burrell, 1985.
23. Miller, L., 1986, p. 89.
24. Carroll, 1985.

25. Carroll 1985; Darcy et al., 1985.
26. Ackelsberg and Diamond, 1987, p. 507.
27. Darcy and Hadley, 1988.
28. Foreman, 1977.
29. Epstein, 1988, pp. 188–190.
30. Gates, 1976, p. 62; Hoff-Wilson, 1987, pp. 9–10.
31. Mansbridge, 1986, p. 8; Freeman, 1986, p. 47.
32. Mansbridge, 1986, pp. 12–14.
33. Freeman, 1986, 1990.
34. Ingersoll, 1983.
35. Hoff-Wilson, 1987, p. 32.
36. Hoff-Wilson, 1987; Freeman, 1986.
37. Baron, 1987.
38. Freeman, 1990.
39. Mansbridge, 1986; Gelb and Palley, 1987.
40. Sisley, Becky, personal communication, 1991, University of Oregon.
41. Weitzman, 1985.
42. Hoff-Wilson, 1987, pp. 26–28.
43. Hoff-Wilson, 1987, p. 28.
44. Baron, 1987, p. 490.
45. MacKinnon, 1987; Scales, 1986; Rhode, 1987; Freeman, 1990.
46. Kreps and Clark, 1975.
47. U.S. Bureau of the Census, 1987, pp. 366, 373–374.
48. Oppenheimer, 1970.
49. Bergmann, 1986, pp. 24–27; Smith and Ward, 1985.
50. McLaughlin et al., 1988, pp. 179–183.
51. U.S. Bureau of the Census, 1987, p. 366; see also Almquist and Wehrle-Einhorn, 1978, pp. 66–67.
52. Blau and Ferber, 1986, pp. 107–108; Jones, 1986.
53. U.S. Bureau of the Census, 1987, p. 373; U.S. Bureau of the Census, 1990, p. 384.
54. Blau and Ferber, 1986, pp. 107–109; Wilson, 1987, pp. 81–82.
55. U.S. Bureau of the Census, 1990, p. 55.
56. Darien, 1976; McLaughlin et al., 1988, pp. 117–119, 170–179; San Francisco Chronicle, 1990.
57. Jacobs, 1989a.
58. Blau and Ferber, 1986, p. 161.
59. Rytina and Bianchi, 1984; Reskin and Hartmann, 1986, p. 20.
60. Taeuber, 1991, p.134.
61. Bielby and Baron, 1984, 1986, 1987; see also Strang and Baron, 1990.
62. Bianchi and Spain, 1986, p. 164; Jacobs, 1989 a and b.
63. Lillydahl, 1986; Russell and Rush, 1987; Reskin and Hartmann, 1986, pp. 25–26; Blau and Ferber, 1986, p. 168.
64. Waite and Berryman, 1985.
65. Reskin and Roos, 1990.
66. Kalleberg et al., 1986.
67. Higginbotham, 1987; Sokoloff, 1988.
68. U.S. Department of Commerce, 1976, p. 47.
69. U.S. Bureau of the Census, 1989, pp. 137–144.
70. Bergmann, 1986, pp. 119–123.
71. Kemp and Beck, 1986.
72. U.S. Bureau of the Census, 1990, p. 453.
73. Blau and Ferber, 1986, p. 178.
74. Blau and Ferber, 1986, pp. 280–302.
75. Pearce, 1985, 1987.
76. Allen, 1987, p. 1.
77. U.S. Bureau of the Census, 1987, p. 48.
78. U.S. Bureau of the Census, 1987, p. 434; Sidel, 1986.
79. Wilson, 1987, pp. 82–83; *Employment and Earnings*, 1991, p. 212.
80. U.S. Bureau of the Census, 1987, p. 48.
81. Simms, 1985–86. U.S. Bureau of the Census, 1990, p. 460.

82. Almquist and Wehrle-Einhorn, 1978; Smith and Tienda, 1988.
83. Becker, 1971.
84. Blau and Ferber, 1986; Marini, 1989; England and McCreary, 1987a.
85. Becker, 1975, 1985; Blau and Ferber, 1986, pp. 184–185; Fuchs, 1988; Mincer and Polachek, 1974; O'Neill, 1985.
86. Corcoran and Duncan, 1979; England and McCreary, 1987 a and b; Ferber et al., 1986; Felmlee, 1988; Gwartney-Gibbs and Taylor, 1986; Madden, 1985.
87. Bielby and Bielby, 1988.
88. Filer, 1985a; Killingsworth, 1985.
89. Jencks et al., 1988; see also England et al., 1988.
90. Blau and Ferber, 1986, pp. 251–252; Madden, 1985, pp. 96–97; Phelps, 1972.
91. E.g., Bielby and Baron, 1984, 1986, 1987.
92. Blau and Ferber, 1986, pp. 252–253.
93. Aigner and Cain, 1977.
94. Arrow, 1973; Blau and Ferber, 1986, pp. 252–254; Madden, 1985, pp. 97–101; Waite and Berryman, 1985; Bergmann, 1986, pp. 113–114.
95. Bergmann, 1971, 1973, 1986; Blau and Ferber, 1986, pp. 255–258.
96. Madden, 1975, p. 155.
97. Madden, 1973, 1975, 1985.
98. Blau and Ferber, 1986, p. 247.
99. Coverdill, 1988; Coverman, 1986; Edwards, 1979; Kalleberg and Berg, 1987; Lorence, 1987; Piore, 1975; Connor and Kemp, 1987; Perman and Stevens, 1989; Bulow and Summers, 1986.
100. Coverdill, 1988; Coverman, 1986; Hardesty et al., 1988; Taylor et al, 1986; Dickens and Lang, 1985, 1987.
101. Coverman, 1986; Lorence, 1987; Piore, 1975, p. 134.
102. Blau and Jusenius, 1976; Madden, 1975, pp. 107–108.
103. DiPrete and Soule, 1988; Mueller and Parcel, 1986; Rosenbaum, 1984; Rosenfeld, 1980.
104. Villemez and Bridges, 1988.
105. Fulbright, 1986; Mueller and Parcel, 1986; Rosenfeld, 1980.
106. DiPrete and Soule, 1986; DiPrete, 1987.
107. Quadragno, 1976; Lorber, 1984.
108. Patterson and Engelberg, 1978; Epstein, 1981; Schafran, 1987; Roach, 1990; Hagan, 1990.
109. Astin and Bayer, 1973; Bognanno, 1987; Fox, 1981; Harkess, 1985, pp. 501–504; Patterson, 1973; Weis, 1987; Kulis et al., 1986; Miller et al., 1988; Pfeffer and Ross, 1990.
110. Grimm, 1978; Stockard, 1984.
111. Carrick, 1986; Ray and Rubin, 1987; Stockard, 1980c.
112. Johnson, W., 1988; see also O'Farrell, 1988.
113. Cassell et al., 1975; Ferree, 1987.
114. Foner, 1987.
115. Falk, 1975; Needleman and Tanner, 1987.
116. Needleman and Tanner, 1987.
117. Fiorito and Greer, 1986; Moore, 1986.
118. Baron and Newman, 1990; Fletcher and Gill, forthcoming.
119. Kanter, 1977.
120. Zimmer, 1988, p. 66; Miller, J., 1986, p. 11.
121. Mainiero, 1986.
122. Deaux and Ullman, 1983; Gruber and Bjorn, 1982; both cited in Zimmer, 1988, p. 69.
123. Miller, J., 1986.
124. Zimmer, 1988, pp. 69–73; see also Blum and Smith, 1988; Williams, 1989.
125. Reich et al., 1975, p. 71.
126. Deckard and Sherman, 1974.
127. Cf. Bridges and Nelson, 1989; DiPrete and Grusky, 1990.
128. Reskin, 1988.

CHAPTER 3

1. Hareven, 1976b, p. 198.
2. Parsons, 1966.

3. Zaretsky, 1976, pp. 50–51; Zaretsky, 1982.
4. Aries, 1962.
5. Hareven, 1976a, p. 99.
6. LeVine and White, 1987.
7. Jeffrey, 1972.
8. Ehrenreich and English, 1976, p. 11.
9. Lerner, 1969.
10. Hareven, 1976a.
11. Zaretsky, 1976, p. 52; Cancian, 1987.
12. Hareven, 1976a, pp. 101–103; see also Bose, 1987.
13. Hareven, 1976a, p. 106.
14. McLaughlin et al., 1988, pp. 18–19.
15. Jones, 1987.
16. Parsons, 1954a.
17. Parsons, 1954a.
18. Chafe, 1972; Blau and Ferber, 1986; pp. 102–103.
19. Friedan, 1963.
20. Rubin, 1976, p. 115.
21. Stacey, 1990.
22. Bianchi and Spain, 1986, p. 12; U.S. Bureau of the Census, 1989, pp. 3–5.
23. Bianchi and Spain, 1986, pp. 21–22; U.S. Bureau of the Census, 1990, p. 86.
24. Bianchi and Spain, 1986, pp. 47–68.
25. Bianchi and Spain, 1986, pp. 12, 25, 47–68.
26. U.S. Bureau of the Census, 1990, p. 66.
27. Bianchi and Spain, 1986, pp. 74–79; Hogan and Kitagawa, 1985.
28. Staples, 1989; Cherlin, 1981; Walker, 1988; Bennett, et al., 1989, Lichter, et al., 1991.
29. Bianchi and Spain, 1986, pp. 84–101; Gwartney-Gibbs, 1986.
30. Bianchi and Spain, 1986; McLaughlin et al. 1988; Sorenson and McLanahan, 1987.
31. England and Farkas, 1986, pp. 17–18; McLaughlin et al., 1988, p. 201.
32. Bergmann, 1986, pp. 200–201; Blau and Ferber, 1986, pp. 51–52; Brown, 1982; DeVault, 1987; England and Farkas, 1986.
33. Becker, 1981; Blau and Ferber, 1986.
34. Oppenheimer, 1982, p. 265.
35. Blau and Ferber, 1986, p. 49.
36. Benston, 1969; Dalla Costa, 1973; Beechy, 1978.
37. England and Farkas, 1986, pp. 53–55.
38. E.g., Bergmann, 1986, p. 269; Blumstein and Schwartz, 1983, p. 139; McDonald, 1980.
39. England and Farkas, 1986, pp. 51–59.
40. Berk, 1985, pp. 70–77; Hochschild, 1989.
41. Spitze, 1986; Hochschild, 1989.
42. Blumstein and Schwartz, 1983, p. 561.
43. Blumstein and Schwartz, 1983, pp. 153–154.
44. England and Farkas, 1986, p. 99; Pleck, 1985, p. 50; Coverman, 1985; Barnett and Baruch, 1987; Ybarra, 1982.
45. Pleck, 1985; Huber and Spitze, 1983; Barnett and Baruch, 1987; Baruch and Barnett, 1986.
46. deTurck and Miller, 1986.
47. Blumstein and Schwartz, 1983, p. 146.
48. Baruch and Barnett, 1986.
49. Mason and Lu, 1988.
50. Weiss, 1987, p. 120.
51. Berk, 1985; see also Haavind and Andenes, 1990.
52. Dobash and Dobash, 1979; Okun, 1986; Shupe et al., 1987.
53. Pagelow, 1984, p. 45.
54. Okun, 1986, p. 43.
55. Gelles and Cornell, 1985, pp. 79–80; Berk et al., 1983; Dutton, 1988, pp. 19–20; Okun, 1986, pp. 39–42.
56. Stets, 1988.
57. Fagan et al., 1983; Gelles and Cornell, 1985, pp. 71–79; Okun, 1986; Zinn and Eitzen, 1987, pp. 314–315.

58. Ross and Sawhill, 1975; Simms, 1986; Bianchi and Spain, 1986; Wojtkiewicz et al., 1990.
59. Wilson, 1987; Staples, 1989.
60. Arendell, 1986; Weitzman, 1985, 1988; Peterson, 1989.
61. Bianchi and Spain, 1986; Duncan, 1984; Garfinkel and McLanahan, 1986.
62. Garfinkel and McLanahan, 1986; Morrissey, 1987; Simms, 1986.
63. Garfinkel and McLanahan, 1986; McLanahan and Booth, 1989.
64. McAdoo, 1986.
65. Fassinger, 1989.
66. Cancian, 1987.
67. Lasch, 1977, 1978; Bellah et al., 1985.
68. Cancian, 1987.
69. Kinsey et al., 1953, p. 158.
70. Kinsey et al., 1953, p. 584.
71. Kinsey et al., 1953, p. 375.
72. Masters and Johnson, 1966.
73. E.g., Koedt, 1973.
74. Blumstein and Schwartz, 1983.
75. Gallup, 1986.
76. Blumstein and Schwartz, 1989.
77. Peterson and Peterson, 1973.
78. Kinsey et al., 1953.
79. Maslow, 1942.
80. Morgan, 1977.
81. Blumstein and Schwartz, 1983, pp. 222–225.
82. Rossi, 1977.
83. Rossi, 1977, p. 16.
84. Rossi, 1977, p. 21; also see Rossi 1987; Rossi and Rossi, 1990.
85. Young and Willmott, 1975.
86. Lamb, 1987, p. 6.
87. Ehrensaft, 1987.
88. Gilbert, 1985; Berardo et al., 1987; Hertz, 1986.
89. Fowlkes, 1987; Hunt and Hunt, 1982.
90. Hertz, 1986; also see Rothman, 1989.
91. Ehrensaft, 1987; Smith and Reid, 1986; Coltrane, 1989; Hertz and Charlton, 1989.
92. Caldwell, 1973; Kamerman, 1985.
93. Lasch, 1977.
94. Madden, 1978.
95. Peng and Takai, 1983; Rumberger, 1983, 1987.
96. Stockard, 1980a, p. 27.
97. Campbell, 1973.
98. Stockard, 1980a, pp. 27–30; see also Walters, 1986.
99. Chamberlain, 1988, pp. 68–69.
100. See Chamberlain, 1988, pp. 193–253; Jacobs, 1985, 1986.
101. Snyder, 1988, pp. 194–201.
102. Snyder, 1989, pp. 238–239.
103. Suter and Miller, 1973.
104. Michelson, 1972.
105. Snyder, 1988, p. 175.
106. Hirschman and Wong, 1986.
107. Sewell and Shah, 1967; Alexander and Eckland, 1974; Treiman and Terrell, 1975.
108. Roby, 1976; Farmer and Sidney, 1985; Campbell, 1986; Thompson 1987; Burbridge, 1986.
109. Snyder, 1988, pp. 113, 194–201.
110. Wilson and Shin, 1983.
111. Fiorentine, 1987.
112. Lang, 1987 a, b, c; Kulis, 1988.
113. Chamberlain, 1988, pp. 17–18.
114. Cole, 1986.
115. Kulis and Miller, 1989; Kulis, 1988.
116. Snyder, 1988, p. 254.

117. Stockard, 1980a, 1985.
118. Crouse and Trusheim, 1988, p. 144.
119. Rosser, 1987.
120. Sandler, 1987.
121. Wong and Sanders, 1983.
122. Roby, 1973.
123. Freeman, 1975, p. 204.
124. Stockard and McGee, 1990; Wilson and Boldizar, 1990.
125. Stockard and McGee, 1990.
126. Cf. Stockard and McGee, 1990; Gaskell, 1985; Jacobs, 1989b.
127. Stockard, 1980b, 1985.
128. E.g., Mason et al., 1976; Mason and Bumpass, 1975.

CHAPTER 4

1. See Guttentag and Secord, 1983; Chafetz, 1984; and Ward and Pampel, 1985, for discussions of the relation of the sex-ratio of a population to women's participation in the labor force.
2. Galenson, 1973, pp. 14–19; Rijk, 1984.
3. Rijk, 1984, pp. 85–87; Lockwood and Knowles, 1984.
4. Kronick and Lieberthal, 1976.
5. Rijk, 1984; Galenson, 1973.
6. Bystydzienski, 1989.
7. Hijab, 1988.
8. Tiano, 1987; Joekes 1987; Deere and Leon, 1987; Hijab, 1988.
9. Tiano, 1987; Afshar, 1985; Deere and Leon, 1987; Joekes, 1987; Lele, 1986; Beneria, 1982; Hijab, 1988; Boserup, 1986; Ward, 1984.
10. Galenson, 1973.
11. Tiano, 1987; Ward, 1984, 1988; Acosta-Belén and Bose, 1990.
12. Youssef, 1974.
13. Haavio-Mannila, 1971; Kauppinen-Toropainen et al., 1984.
14. Joekes, 1987; Deere and Leon, 1987; Afshar, 1985.
15. Galenson, 1973, p. 24.
16. Galenson, 1973, p. 25.
17. Roos, 1985, pp. 53–56.
18. Davidson and Cooper, 1986.
19. Galenson, 1973, pp. 26–27; Scriven, 1984, p. 171; Schmuck, 1987.
20. Scriven, 1984, p. 170.
21. Kauppinen-Toropainen et al., 1984.
22. Cook 1984, p. 5, citing OECD, 1980, p. 46.
23. Lapidus, 1985, p. 16.
24. Lapidus, 1985; Moses, 1986; McAuley, 1981.
25. Lapidus, 1976b, pp. 125–126; Attwood and McAndrew, 1984, p. 294.
26. Lapidus, 1976, p. 129; see also Lapidus, 1978; McAuley, 1981, pp. 86–91; and Attwood and McAndrew, 1984, pp. 294–296.
27. Birdsell and McGreevey, 1983; Tiano, 1987; Rios, 1990, Ward, 1990.
28. Treiman and Roos, 1983; Rosenfeld and Kalleberg, 1990.
29. Galenson, 1973, p. 30; see also Pettman, 1975; Janjic, 1985, pp. 5–6; Davidson and Cooper, 1984.
30. Scott, 1982, p. 24.
31. Swafford, 1978; Lapidus, 1985; McAuley, 1981.
32. Seagert and Olson, 1986, pp. 93–99.
33. Tiano, 1987, pp. 223–224; Birdsell and McGreevey, 1983, pp. 10–11; Bowman and Anderson, 1982; Stromquist, 1989.
34. OECD, 1986, pp. 17–18.
35. Norderval, 1986, p. 69; Merkl, 1986, p. 32; Moses, 1986, p. 398; OECD, 1986, pp. 11–23.
36. Davis, 1987, Merkl, 1986, p. 33; Moses, 1986, p. 398.
37. Boulding et al., 1976, pp. 157–164; OECD, 1986, pp. 22–23.
38. Juillard, 1976, p. 118.

39. Porter and Venning, 1976, pp. 94–95.
40. Husen, 1967.
41. Van Allen, 1976, p. 35.
42. Bielli, 1976, p. 108.
43. Porter and Venning, 1986; see also Safa, 1990, regarding a similar linkage between education and women's activism in Latin America.
44. Koyama et al., 1967, pp. 297–298; Sugisaki, 1986, pp. 117–121.
45. Youssef, 1976; Hijab, 1988.
46. Rijk, 1984, p. 87.
47. Lockwood and Knowles, 1984; Kauppinen-Toropainen et al., 1984; Bystydzienski, 1989.
48. Weitz, 1977, p. 210; Bystydzienski, 1989, pp. 674–675.
49. Kalleberg and Rosenfeld, 1990.
50. Niemi et al., 1981; Ericsson, 1985.
51. Coser, 1974; Lapidus, 1985, 1988.
52. Wolf, 1985; Johnson, 1983; Stacey, 1983.
53. Niemi et al., 1981, pp. 26, 85.
54. Stiehm, 1976; Hijab, 1988; Fernea, 1985.
55. Van Allen, 1976, p. 36.
56. Jaquette, 1976, p. 67; Beuchler, 1986, pp. 178–180.
57. Roby, 1973.
58. Hayashi, 1985, p. 66.
59. Holter and Henriksen, 1979; Scriven, 1984, pp. 161–162; Juillard, 1986, p. 18.
60. Buric, 1985, p. 52.
61. Wolf, 1985, p. 40; Johnson, 1986, pp. 451–452.
62. Scott, 1979.
63. Schopp-Schilling, 1985, pp. 134–135.
64. Boulding et al., 1976, pp. 250–251.
65. Christy, 1987; Randall, 1987; Lovenduski, 1986; Skard and Haavio-Mannila, 1984; Epstein and Coser, 1981; Jaquette, 1986; Schmidt, 1986.
66. Blondel, 1985, p. 30.
67. Blondel, 1985, p. 32; Randall, 1987, pp. 96–102.
68. Skard and Haavio-Mannila, 1984, 1985; Blondel, 1985, pp. 30–32; Lovenduski, 1986, pp. 152–154; Moses, 1986.
69. Skard and Haavio-Mannila, 1985, p. 54; Rule, 1981; Kohn, 1980, pp. 236–237; Scriven, 1984.
70. Darcy and Song, 1986; Skard and Haavio-Mannila, 1985, pp. 64–76; Porter and Venning, 1986, p. 92.
71. Callaway and Schildkrout, 1986; Sanasarian, 1986.
72. Porter and Venning, 1986.
73. El Guindi, 1986.
74. Narain, 1967.
75. Holly and Bransfield, 1976.
76. Baude, 1979; Holter and Henriksen, 1979; Ericsson, 1985, p. 139; Skard and Haavio-Mannila, 1984, p. 154.
77. See Youssef and Hartley, 1979; Mascia-Lees, 1984.
78. Boulding et al., 1976, pp. 248–249.
79. Cf. Brinton, 1988; Papanek, 1985; Neuhauser, 1989; Chafetz, 1984; Holter, 1984; Ruggie, 1984; Mascia-Lees, 1984.

CHAPTER 5

1. Strathern, 1987, 1988.
2. Ortner and Whitehead, 1981.
3. Cf. Schneider, 1984; Collier et al., 1982.
4. Whyte, 1978, pp. 50–52.
5. Paige and Paige, 1981.
6. Friedl, 1975.
7. Durkheim, 1933.
8. D'Andrade, 1966.

9. Mukhopadhyay and Higgins, 1988, pp. 468–481.
10. Weiner, 1976.
11. Rosaldo, 1974.
12. Weiner, 1976; Dube, 1986.
13. Quinn, 1977, p. 183; Whyte, 1978.
14. See also Ross, 1986.
15. Cf. Coontz and Henderson, 1986a; Mukhopadhyay and Higgins, 1988, p. 468; Quinn, 1977, p. 183.
16. Rosaldo, 1974.
17. Mukhopadhyay and Higgins, 1988, pp. 480–481; Sharistanian, 1987.
18. Collier and Rosaldo, 1981; Ortner, 1981; Ortner and Whitehead, 1981.
19. Gailey, 1987; Sacks, 1979; Yanagisako and Collier, 1987.
20. Harris, 1977.
21. Whyte, 1978, pp. 132–133.
22. Cf. Chowning, 1987.
23. White and Burton, 1988.
24. Lamphere, 1977, p. 622.
25. Lloyd, 1965.
26. O'Brien, 1977.
27. Tanner, 1974.
28. Quoted by Tanner, 1974, p. 156.
29. Tanner, 1974, p. 155; see also Bolles and Samuels, 1989.
30. Lewis, 1975, p. 222.
31. Lewis, 1975, p. 230.
32. E.g., DeVore, 1965.
33. E.g., Wilson, 1975, 1978.
34. Sarich and Wilson, 1967; Wilson and Sarich, 1969; both cited by Zihlman, 1987, p. 12.
35. Wilson, 1978, p. 25.
36. Wilson, 1975, pp. 547–548.
37. Henley et al., 1989, Fedigan, 1982; Smuts et al., 1986.
38. Lancaster, 1984, pp. 6–7.
39. Wright, 1984; Hrdy, 1981; Robinson et al., 1986; Richard, 1986.
40. See DeVore and Washburn, 1963; Washburn and Devore, 1961.
41. Fedigan, 1982; Henley et al., 1989; Fedigan, 1986; p. 40, citing Goodall, 1976, and McGrew, 1981; Fedigan and Fedigan, 1989.
42. Fedigan, 1986, pp. 40–41.
43. DeWaal, 1982.
44. Fedigan, 1986, p. 41.
45. Fedigan, 1986, pp. 41–42.
46. Goodall, 1968; Teleki, 1973; both cited by Fedigan, 1986, p. 42.
47. Fedigan, 1986, pp. 42–43.
48. Smuts, 1985.
49. Smuts, 1985, pp. 258–259.
50. Johanson and Edey, 1981; Johanson, 1989.
51. E.g., Lovejoy, 1981.
52. Shipman, 1985.
53. Fedigan, 1986, citing McGrew 1981; Reynolds, 1966; Zihlman, 1978.
54. Linton, 1971; Tanner and Zihlman, 1976; Zihlman, 1978; Tanner, 1981.
55. Fedigan, 1986, p. 44.
56. Gough, 1971.
57. Myers, 1988; Fedigan, 1986, pp. 43–45.
58. Martin and Voorhies, 1975.
59. Friedl, 1975.
60. See also Brown, 1970.
61. Goodman et al., 1985, pp. 1203–1204.
62. Martin and Voorhies, 1975; Friedl, 1975.
63. Friedl, 1975, p. 20.
64. See also Coontz and Henderson, 1986b.
65. Friedl, 1975, p. 26.

66. Martin and Voorhies, 1975.
67. Coontz and Henderson, 1986b.
68. Martin and Voorhies, 1975, p. 229.
69. Engels, 1972.
70. Brown, 1975.
71. Friedl, 1975.
72. Friedl, 1975, p. 135; Sanday, 1973; Quinn, 1977, p. 203.
73. Blumberg, 1978, 1984, p. 29.
74. Burton and White, 1984; Ember, 1983.
75. Martin and Voorhies, 1975.
76. Whyte, 1978, p. 156.
77. Nelson and Oleson, 1977.
78. See Coontz and Henderson, 1986b; Gailey, 1987; Leacock, 1986; Lerner, 1986; Mukhopadhyay and Higgins, 1988, pp. 477–479; Quinn, 1977; Robertson and Berger, 1986; Sacks, 1979; Silverblatt, 1987.
79. Blumberg and Winch, 1974.

CHAPTER 6

1. E.g., Goldberg, 1974; Morris, 1970; and Tiger, 1969.
2. Rossi, 1977, pp. 16–17.
3. Mackie, 1977.
4. Rossi, 1977, p. 4.
5. See also Kenrick, 1987; Filsinger, 1988; Lee, 1988, pp. 161–163; Birke, 1986; Draper, 1985; Bleier, 1984; Marini, 1990.
6. Money and Tucker, 1975, pp. 41–42.
7. Otten, 1985, p. 171.
8. Money and Tucker, 1975, p. 44; Otten, 1985, pp. 155–163.
9. Money and Tucker, 1975, pp. 44–46.
10. Money and Tucker, 1975, pp. 46–47.
11. Fausto-Sterling, 1985, p. 81; Otten, 1985, p. 160.
12. Money and Tucker, 1975, pp. 48–49; Money and Ehrhardt, 1972, pp. 43–45.
13. Money and Tucker, 1976, p. 48.
14. Money and Tucker, 1976, p. 66; Barfield, 1976, pp. 63–65.
15. Money and Tucker, 1976, p. 78; Gladue, 1988, pp. 68–78; Otten, 1985, pp. 163–171.
16. For a full account see Money and Ehrhardt, 1972; Otten, 1985, pp. 173–184.
17. Money and Tucker, 1975, p. 50.
18. Money and Tucker, 1975, pp. 52–55.
19. Money and Tucker, 1975, pp. 55–57.
20. Money and Tucker, 1975, pp. 57–59.
21. Money and Tucker, 1975, p. 71; Money and Ehrhardt, 1972, p. 46.
22. See Hoenig, 1985b; Fausto-Sterling, 1985, pp. 85–88, for informative summaries.
23. Money et al., 1957; Money and Ehrhardt, 1972.
24. Money and Ehrhardt, 1972.
25. Money and Ehrhardt, 1972, p. 155.
26. Money and Ehrhardt, 1972.
27. Imperato-McGinley et al., 1979.
28. See Hoenig, 1985b; Diamond, 1965, 1976, 1982; Stoller, 1985, pp. 65–76.
29. See Ehrhardt, 1985.
30. Hoenig, 1985a, p. 33.
31. See Green, 1974; p. 327; Person and Ovesey, 1974; Steiner, 1985; Stoller, 1985; Docter, 1988; Kessler and McKenna, 1978.
32. Quoted in Money and Tucker, 1975, p. 31.
33. *People*, 1976, p. 18.
34. Steiner et al., 1985, p. 2.
35. Money and Tucker, 1975, pp. 32–33, Pauly and Edgerton, 1986; but see also Lindemalm et al., 1986.
36. Meyer and Reter, 1979.

37. Stoller, 1968, 1974, 1985; Person and Ovesey, 1974.
38. See Hoenig, 1985a, for a summary.
39. Bradley, 1985.
40. Zucker, 1985.
41. See Green, 1987; Stoller, 1985; Zucker, 1985.
42. Raymond, 1977, p. 12.
43. Raymond, 1977, p. 15.
44. Raymond, 1977, p. 22.
45. Barfield, 1976, p. 66.
46. Barfield, 1976, p. 67.
47. Barfield, 1976, pp. 69–70
48. Dyer, 1985, 1986.
49. Barfield, 1976, p. 67; Stillion, 1985.
50. Barfield, 1976, p. 67; Travis, 1988a, pp. 14–17.
51. Barfield, 1976, pp. 67–68.
52. E.g., Mumpower, 1970.
53. Otten, 1985, pp. 204–206.
54. Verbrugge, 1989, p. 345.
55. Gove, 1987; Johnson, 1987; Travis, 1988a and b.
56. Travis, 1988a.
57. Travis, 1988a, pp. 17–22; Otten, 1985, pp. 206–208; Stillion, 1985, pp. 22–26.
58. Barfield, 1976, pp. 68–69.
59. Verbrugge, 1976; Hibbard and Pope, 1983, 1986.
60. Barfield, 1976, p. 69, citing Potts, 1970, and Madigan, 1957.
61. Harrison, 1978.
62. Maccoby and Jacklin, 1974, pp. 19–35; Barfield, 1976, p. 70; McGuinness, 1985a.
63. Maccoby and Jacklin, 1974, pp. 91–94.
64. Halpern, 1986, pp. 75–102, 150–152.
65. E.g., Connor et al, 1978; Fausto-Sterling, 1985, pp. 34–36.
66. Sherman, 1967.
67. Money and Ehrhardt, 1972, p. 195.
68. Money and Ehrhardt, 1972, pp. 196–197.
69. Katchadourian and Lunde, 1975, p. 95.
70. Frisch and Revelle, 1969, 1970, 1971a, 1971b, all cited by Travis, 1988a.
71. Tanner, 1970; Bullough, 1981, both cited by Stark, 1989b.
72. Maccoby and Jacklin, 1974, pp. 214–215.
73. Maccoby and Jacklin, 1974, p. 215.
74. Jay, 1963, and DeVore, 1963, reported in Ehrhardt, 1973, p. 103; also Fedigan, 1982, pp. 188–189.
75. Whiting and Whiting, 1975; Whiting and Edwards, 1988; see also Chapter 7.
76. Chamove et al., 1967, cited by Maccoby and Jacklin, 1974, p. 218.
77. Draper, 1985; Ehrhardt, 1985, p. 41.
78. Ehrhardt, 1973, 1985; Ehrhardt and Baker, 1974; see also Ehrhardt and Meyer-Bahlburg, 1981.
79. Ehrhardt, 1985, pp. 50–53; Sandberg et al., 1987.
80. Rosenblatt, 1969, cited by Maccoby and Jacklin, 1974, p. 215; also see Moltz et al., 1970; Otten, 1985, p. 168.
81. Rosenblatt, 1969, cited by Maccoby and Jacklin, 1974, pp. 215–216; see also Trause et al., 1976.
82. Leifer et al., 1972; Leifer, 1970; Fabes and Filsinger, 1988; Klaus and Kennel, 1976; Maccoby and Martin, 1983, pp. 26–27.
83. Klaus and Kennel, 1976; Lamb et al., 1987; see also Risman, 1987, 1989. LaRossa and LaRossa, 1989.
84. Ehrhardt and Baker, 1974, p. 38.
85. Maccoby and Jacklin, 1974, pp. 242–423; Hyde, 1984; Parke and Slaby, 1983.
86. Edwards, 1969; Tieger, 1980, cited by Parke and Slaby, 1983.
87. Ehrhardt, 1973; Ehrhardt and Baker, 1974; Ehrhardt, 1985.
88. E.g., Fasto-Sterling, 1985, pp. 136–138, Bleier, 1984, pp. 99–100.
89. Reinisch, 1981.
90. Ehrhardt and Baker, 1974.
91. Maccoby and Jacklin, 1974, p. 245.

92. Moyer 1974, 1987a; Parke and Slaby, 1983, pp. 560–561.
93. See Parke and Slaby 1983, pp. 561–562; Moyer, 1987a, pp. 23–25.
94. Moyer, 1987a, b.
95. E.g., Mazur, 1985.
96. Moyer, 1974, 1976; Svare, 1983.
97. Moyer, 1976, citing DeVore, 1963, and Hamburg, 1971; Fedigan, 1982; Smuts, 1985.
98. Moyer, 1976, p. 182; also see Davis and Gandelman, 1972.
99. Parlee, 1984.
100. Ramey, 1976, p. 139; Ericksen, 1984, p. 178.
101. Parlee, 1976, p. 125, citing Luce, 1970; Travis, 1988a, pp. 58–59.
102. Bardwick, 1974, p. 29; Money and Ehrhardt, 1972, p. 222; Barfield, 1976, pp. 70–71.
103. Money and Ehrhardt, 1972, p. 222.
104. Hoyenga and Hoyenga, 1979, pp. 145–153.
105. Carter, 1984; Travis, 1988a; Fausto-Sterling, 1985; Olesen and Woods, 1986; Koeske, 1987.
106. Rossi and Rossi, 1977, cited by Fausto-Sterling, 1985, pp. 108–109; Ramey, 1976; Hersey, 1931, cited by Travis, 1988a, p. 60; Englander-Golden et al., 1986.
107. Doering et al., 1975, cited by Travis, 1988a, p. 60; see also Ramey, 1976, p. 139.
108. See Fausto-Sterling, 1985, and Parlee, 1973, for extended critiques of this work.
109. Friedl, 1975.
110. Cf. Rossi, 1977; Leakey and Lewin, 1977; Lee, 1988.
111. Cf. Ladewig et al., 1988; Filsinger, 1988; Birke, 1986; Kenrick; 1987, Marini, 1990.

CHAPTER 7

1. Broverman et al., 1972.
2. Archer and Lloyd, 1985, pp. 38–47; Deaux, 1985, pp. 66–67; Williams and Best, 1982; Martin, 1987.
3. Hansen and O'Leary, 1985; O'Leary and Hansen, 1985.
4. Eagly and Steffen, 1986b.
5. See Deaux, 1985, pp. 66–69; O'Leary and Hansen, 1985; Hansen and O'Leary, 1985; Swim, et al., 1989.
6. Garai and Scheinfeld, 1968.
7. Parlee, 1975, p. 128.
8. See McHugh et al., 1986; Walston and Grady, 1985.
9. Mead, 1963.
10. Mead, 1963, p. 279.
11. Mead, 1963, p. 289.
12. Barry et al., 1957.
13. Whiting and Whiting, 1975; Whiting and Edwards, 1988; see also Ember, 1981.
14. Whiting and Edwards, 1988.
15. E.g., Whiting and Edwards, 1988, pp. 239, 271.
16. Whiting and Whiting, 1975, pp. 183–184; Whiting and Edwards, 1988, p. 159.
17. Barry et al., 1957; see also Quinn, 1977, pp. 195–198.
18. Maccoby and Jacklin, 1974.
19. See Halpern, 1986, pp. 35–38; Hyde, 1986b; Hedges and Becker, 1986.
20. Goldberg and Lewis, 1969.
21. Maccoby and Jacklin, 1974, pp. 181–182.
22. Deaux, 1985, pp. 62–63; Halpern, 1986, pp. 31–34.
23. Eaton and Enns, 1986.
24. Deutsch, 1944–45.
25. Maccoby and Jacklin, 1974.
26. See Shields, 1987, for a discussion of the complexities involved in studying gender differences in emotion.
27. Maccoby and Jacklin, 1974; Archer and Lloyd, 1985, pp. 160–166.
28. Maccoby and Jacklin, 1974.
29. Maccoby and Jacklin, 1974.
30. Whiting and Edwards, 1988.
31. Maccoby and Jacklin, 1974; Whiting and Edwards, 1988.

32. Maccoby and Jacklin, 1974; Block 1976; Lennon and Eisenberg, 1987.
33. Maccoby and Jacklin, 1974, p. 214.
34. Maccoby, 1990a; Maccoby and Jacklin, 1987; Maccoby, 1988; Lockheed, 1986; Thorne and Luria, 1986.
35. Whiting and Edwards, 1988.
36. Maccoby, 1988.
37. Serbin et al., 1984.
38. Maccoby, 1990a.
39. Whiting and Edwards, 1988.
40. Eagly, 1987; Eagly and Crowley, 1986.
41. Maccoby and Jacklin, 1974, p. 373.
42. Escalona, 1949, p. 34.
43. Maccoby and Jacklin, 1974, p. 227; White 1983, p. 3; Macaulay 1985, pp. 196–198.
44. Omark et al., 1973.
45. Hyde, 1984, 1986a; see also Maccoby and Jacklin, 1974.
46. Hyde, 1986a, p. 57; Eagly and Steffen, 1986a.
47. Feshback, 1969.
48. Maccoby and Jacklin, 1974.
49. Peirce and Edwards, 1988; Keltikangas-Javinen and Kangas, 1988; Hyde, 1986a; Maccoby and Jacklin, 1974.
50. Eagly and Steffen, 1986a; Eagly, 1987; Hyde, 1984, 1986.
51. Hyde, 1984, 1986a.
52. Eagly, 1987.
53. Frodi et al., 1977; Eagly and Steffen, 1986a.
54. Goldberg, 1974, p. 263.
55. Maccoby and Jacklin, 1974.
56. See Brock-Utne, 1989, for an extensive discussion of biases in much of the research on gender differences in competitiveness.
57. Maltz and Borker, 1982; Sachs, 1987; Miller et al., 1986; all cited by Maccoby, 1990a.
58. Whiting and Edwards, 1988.
59. Maccoby, 1990a.
60. Becker, 1986; Eagly, 1987; Eagly and Wood, 1985.
61. Sheldon, 1989, cited by Maccoby, 1990a.
62. Maccoby, 1990a.
63. McGuinness, 1985b, 1985a, p. 95.
64. Maccoby and Jacklin, 1974, p. 350.
65. Linn and Petersen, 1986.
66. Halpern, 1986, pp. 54–55.
67. Maccoby and Jacklin, 1974.
68. Block, 1976.
69. Gardner, 1983; McGuinness, 1985a, pp. 95–96.
70. McGuinness, 1985a, p. 96.
71. Guilford, 1967, cited by McGuinness, 1985a, p. 96.
72. Stockard, 1990.
73. Maccoby and Jacklin, 1974; Halpern, 1986, pp. 47–48.
74. Corballis and Beale, 1983; Witelson, 1976; both cited by Halpern, 1986, p. 48.
75. Gates, 1961; Scott et al., 1985; Lummis and Stevenson, 1990.
76. Balow, 1963.
77. McGuinness, 1985a, p. 103.
78. Bock and Moore, 1984, cited in Tittle, 1986; see also Lummis and Stevenson, 1990.
79. Halpern, 1986, p. 47.
80. Maccoby and Jacklin, 1974, p. 84.
81. Goldman and Hewitt, 1976, p. 53.
82. Hyde and Linn, 1988; Linn and Hyde, 1989.
83. Maccoby and Jacklin, 1974.
84. Linn and Hyde, 1989, p. 119; Lummis and Stevenson, 1990.
85. Linn and Hyde, 1989; Hyde et al., 1990, Bellisari, 1989; see also Brandon et al., 1987; Friedman, 1989.
86. Benbow and Stanley, 1980, 1983.

87. Pallas and Alexander, 1983; Chipman and Thomas, 1985, pp. 13–14; VanFossen, 1987.
88. McGuinness, 1985a, p. 108, citing Stallings, 1979, see also Halpern, 1986, pp. 59–60, Connor and Serbin, 1985.
89. Linn and Petersen, 1985, Linn and Hyde, 1989.
90. Linn and Hyde, 1989.
91. Hackett, 1985; Selkow, 1985; Tittle, 1986; Wise, 1985; Boswell 1985; Eccles, 1983.
92. Stockard, 1985.
93. McClelland et al., 1953.
94. Horner, 1968, 1970, 1972.
95. Horner, 1972, p. 159.
96. Maccoby and Jacklin, 1974, p. 138.
97. Condry and Dyer, 1976; see also Tresemer, 1977.
98. Spence and Helmreich, 1983.
99. Veroff, 1983; Sutherland and Veroff, 1985, p. 113.
100. Sutherland and Veroff, 1985, p. 114.
101. Stein and Bailey, 1975, pp. 152–153.
102. Stein and Bailey, 1975, p. 153; Sutherland and Veroff, 1985; Kaufman and Richardson, 1982.
103. Cf. Stein and Bailey, 1975, pp. 153–155.
104. Gough, 1952.
105. Nichols, 1962.
106. Lewis, 1968, pp. 69–71.
107. Constantinople, 1973.
108. Pleck, 1975, p. 165.
109. Bem, 1974.
110. Spence et al., 1974, 1975; Spence and Helmreich, 1978.
111. Bem et al., 1976, Cook, 1985.
112. Bem, 1981, 1983, 1985.
113. Cook, 1985.
114. See Spence, 1985; Cook, 1985.
115. E.g., Bem, 1985.
116. Spence, 1985, pp. 76–77.
117. See Gill et al., 1987; M. Johnson, 1988.
118. Block, 1976.
119. Tyler, 1965, p. 264.
120. Carlson, 1971.
121. DeBeauvoir, 1953.
122. Gutmann, 1965.
123. Carlson, 1971, pp. 270–271.
124. Carlson, 1971, p. 271.
125. Bakan, 1966.
126. Bakan, 1966, p. 15.
127. Block, 1973.
128. Carlson, 1971.
129. Gilligan, 1978, 1982; Gilligan et al., 1988.
130. Gilligan, 1982, p. 69.
131. Walker, 1984; see also Greeno and Maccoby, 1986; Colby and Damon, 1983.
132. Lyons, 1983; Gilligan et al., 1988.
133. Belenky et al., 1986.
134. Cf. Spence, 1985; Mednick, 1989.
135. See Johnson et al., 1975; Gill et al., 1987; Johnson, 1988.
136. Balswick and Peek, 1971.
137. Johnson et al., 1975.
138. Bennett and Cohen, 1959, p. 125; Gill et al., 1987.
139. Carli, 1982, cited by Wood, 1987.
140. Maccoby, 1990a; Whiting and Edwards, 1988.
141. Gill et al., 1987.
142. Fagot, 1978; Goodwin, 1980; Whalen and Whalen, 1987.

CHAPTER 8

1. Maccoby and Jacklin, 1974, p. 284.
2. Joffe, 1971.
3. See Stagner, 1988, pp. 402–412.
4. Mischel, 1970; Bandura and Walters, 1963.
5. Huston, 1983; Fagot and Leinbach, 1987; Block, 1984.
6. Fagot and Hagan, 1985; Fagot et al., 1985.
7. Huston, 1983; M. Johnson, 1988; Siegal, 1987; Bradley and Gobbart, 1989.
8. Fagot, 1985a.
9. Serbin et al., 1977, 1978; Huston, 1983, pp. 441–442.
10. Maccoby and Jacklin, 1974, p. 326.
11. Maccoby and Martin, 1983, p. 8.
12. Maccoby and Martin, 1983, p. 8.
13. Hetherington, 1965; Maccoby and Jacklin, 1974; Smith and Daglish, 1977, cited by Maccoby and Martin, 1983, p. 8.
14. Mussen and Rutherford, 1963, p. 601.
15. Angrilli, 1960; Heller, 1959.
16. M. Johnson, 1988.
17. Lynn, 1969, 1976.
18. Johnson, 1963, 1975, 1988; Parsons and Bales, 1955; Chodorow, 1974; Stoller, 1974.
19. Huston, 1983, p. 422.
20. Johnston et al., 1980, cited by Huston, 1983, p. 426.
21. Quattelbaum, 1977.
22. Scott, 1971.
23. Scott, 1971, p. 149.
24. Perry and Bussey, 1979.
25. See also Maccoby and Martin, 1983, pp. 8–9; Huston, 1983; Perry, et al., 1984.
26. Kohlberg 1966, p. 89, our arrangement.
27. Kohlberg 1966, p. 104.
28. Kohlberg 1966, p. 101.
29. Kohlberg 1966, p. 101.
30. Kohlberg 1966, p. 123.
31. Intons-Peterson, 1988.
32. Leinbach and Fagot, 1986; Archer and Lloyd, 1985, pp. 266–267; Maccoby, 1990b.
33. Kohlberg 1966, p. 161.
34. Kohlberg 1966, p. 136, italics Kohlberg's.
35. Kohlberg, 1966, p. 137.
36. Ullian, 1976.
37. Ullian, 1976, p. 38.
38. Ullian, 1976, p. 39.
39. Ullian, 1976.
40. Kohlberg, 1966.
41. See Maccoby, 1990b; Huston, 1985, pp. 10–11; Serbin and Sprafkin, 1986.
42. Block, 1973.
43. Rebecca et al., 1976.
44. Bem, 1981; Martin and Halvorson, 1981; Markus et al., 1982.
45. Martin and Halvorson, 1981, p. 1121.
46. Martin and Halvorson, 1981, 1987.
47. Bem, 1981, 1983, 1985, 1987.
48. Fagot and Leinbach, 1985.
49. Maccoby and Jacklin, 1974; Leinbach and Fagot, 1986, p. 665.
50. Huston, 1985, p. 11.
51. Fagot and Leinbach, 1985; Maccoby and Martin, 1983, p. 8.
52. Fagot et al., 1986; Fagot and Leinbach, 1989; Leinbach and Fagot, 1986.
53. Fagot and Leinbach, 1989.
54. Cf. Perry and Bussey, 1979.
55. Maccoby and Martin, 1983, p. 9.
56. Maccoby and Jacklin, 1987; Carter, 1987.

57. Maccoby and Jacklin, 1987; Maccoby, 1990a, 1986, 1988.
58. Carter, 1987, p. 113.
59. Fagot, 1985a, pp. 1101–1102.
60. Fagot, 1981.
61. Fagot, 1985a, Maccoby, 1988.
62. Maccoby, 1988, p. 756; Fagot and Leinbach, 1985: Fagot 1985b.

CHAPTER 9

1. Cf. Dyrud, 1976, p. 23.
2. Lindzey, 1967.
3. Freud, 1963b, p. 66.
4. M. Johnson, 1988, p. 12.
5. For a summary of the object relations school, see Chodorow, 1978; also Eichenbaum and Orbach, 1983.
6. See "Task Force on Sex Bias," 1975.
7. Galenson and Roiphe, 1974; Galenson, 1986.
8. Freud, 1933, 1963a, 1963b.
9. Deutsch, 1944–45, vol. 1, p. 231.
10. Erikson, 1968, pp. 268–271.
11. Erikson, 1968, p. 275.
12. Freud, 1969, p. 62.
13. Freud, 1963c, p. 193.
14. See especially Freud, 1933; also Lerman, 1986.
15. Mitchell, 1974, p. 366.
16. Firestone, 1971.
17. Mitchell, 1974.
18. Chodorow, 1978.
19. Levi-Strauss, 1969.
20. Levi-Strauss, 1969, p. 115.
21. Rubin, 1975, p. 175, italics ours.
22. Rubin, 1975, p. 172.
23. Cited in Rubin, 1975, p. 178.
24. Rubin, 1975, p. 180.
25. Martin and Voorhies, 1975; see also Williams, 1986.
26. Rubin 1975, p. 199.
27. Deutsch 1944–45, vol. 1.
28. Fairbairn, 1952.
29. Fliess, 1961, p. 121.
30. Horner, 1985, Stern, 1985; also see Benjamin, 1988.
31. Deutsch, 1944–45, vol. 1, pp. 287–288; Klein, 1960.
32. Deutsch, 1944–45, p. 205.
33. E.g., Klein, 1960; Jones, 1935; Westkott, 1986; Fast, 1984; Chessick, 1984.
34. Horney, 1967b, p. 64.
35. Guntrip, 1961, p. 357; Fairbairn, 1952.
36. Deutsch, 1944–45.
37. Chodorow, 1978.
38. Deutsch, 1944–45, Chodorow, 1978; see also Fast, 1984; Kanefield, 1985.
39. Chodorow, 1978.
40. Chasseguet-Smirgel, 1970, p. 118; Honey and Broughton, 1985.
41. See Jones, 1933; Klein, 1960.
42. Chodorow, 1974.
43. Chodorow, 1978.
44. See Stoller, 1968, 1974; Person and Ovesey, 1983.
45. Chehrazi, 1986; Fliegel 1986, pp. 19–22; Alpert and Spencer, 1986; Fast, 1984; Mendell, 1982.
46. Freud, 1963d, pp. 76–79.
47. Jones, 1933.
48. Horney, 1967a, pp. 137–138.

49. Horney, 1967a, pp. 145–146.
50. Lederer, 1968, p. 37.
51. Hays, 1972.
52. Mead, 1974.
53. Bettleheim, 1954.
54. Mead, 1974, p. 97.
55. Lidz and Lidz, 1977; see also Salamone, 1986.
56. Horney, 1967b, p. 61.
57. Mead, 1949.
58. Mead, 1949, p. 166.
59. Dinnerstein, 1976, p. 189.
60. Dinnerstein, 1976, p. 191; see also Stannard, 1977.
61. Burton and Whiting, 1961; Murphy, 1959; Munroe et al., 1981.
62. Mead, 1949, pp. 168–169.
63. Keller, 1985; Benjamin 1988.
64. Chodorow, 1974, p. 50; see also Chodorow, 1989.
65. Rubin, 1975.
66. M. Johnson, 1988, pp. 85–86.

CHAPTER 10

1. Lasch, 1977, p. 93.
2. Parsons, 1955, 1970.
3. Parsons, 1970, p. 41.
4. Parsons, 1970, pp. 41–42.
5. M. Johnson, 1963, 1988.
6. M. Johnson, 1975, 1988.
7. Stayton et al., 1971, p. 1067.
8. Yarrow et al., 1968, p. 103.
9. M. Johnson 1976, 1988.
10. Chodorow, 1978.
11. M. Johnson, 1975, 1977, 1988; Stockard and Johnson, 1979.
12. M. Johnson, 1963, 1975.
13. Moscovici, 1972.
14. Maccoby and Jacklin, 1974, p. 306, first italics authors', second ours.
15. Goldsmith, 1970, p. 143.
16. Deaux, 1985.
17. M. Johnson, 1988; Maccoby, 1990a; Siegal, 1987.
18. M. Johnson, 1988, pp. 131–138.
19. Radin, 1981.
20. Gilbert et al., 1982; Fagot, 1978.
21. Hoffman, 1977.
22. Hetherington, 1979.
23. Margolin and Patterson, 1975; Bronfenbrenner, 1961; Bursik et al., 1985.
24. Parke and Tinsley, 1981; Pederson, 1980; Parke, 1981; Ricks, 1985; Lamb and Lamb, 1976; Hoffman et al., 1984.
25. Also see Rubin et al., 1976; Fagot, 1978; Langlois and Downs, 1980; Snow et al., 1983.
26. Block, 1984; Radin, 1981; Goodenough, 1957.
27. Droppleman and Schaefer, 1963; Bronstein, 1984; see also Lamb, 1987; Mackey, 1985.
28. Roberts et al., 1978; Kaats and Davis, 1970.
29. Johnson, 1977.
30. Parsons, 1967.
31. M. Johnson, 1988, pp. 140–143.
32. Jourard and Robin, 1968; Barber and Thomas, 1986.
33. Finkelhor, 1980.
34. Parke and Sawin, 1979.
35. Ehrensaft, 1985.
36. M. Johnson, 1988, pp. 139–144.

37. M. Johnson, 1988, pp. 144–152; Johnson et al., 1981.
38. Gladue, 1988; Bell et al., 1981, pp. 212–220; Whitan and Mathy, 1986; but see also Troiden, 1988, pp. 101–122; Risman and Schwartz, 1988.
39. M. Johnson, 1988; Siegelman, 1987, pp. 51–53; Bell et al., 1981; Green, 1987, pp. 376–377.
40. Reiss, 1986, pp. 159–161.
41. Bieber et al., 1962.
42. Kaye et al., 1967; see also Saghir and Robins, 1973.
43. Wolff, 1971.
44. M. Johnson, 1988, pp. 150–152; Wolff, 1981; Bene, 1965; Loney, 1973; Thompson et al., 1973; Johnson et al., 1981.
45. Leonard, 1966.
46. Chafetz et al., 1976; Jaggar, 1983.
47. Kaye et al., 1967, p. 629.
48. Kaye et al., 1967, p. 634.
49. Johnson et al., 1981.
50. Bell et al., 1981.
51. Herman and Hirschman, 1977, p. 741; see also Herman, 1981.
52. Herman and Hirschman, 1977, p. 740.
53. Herman, 1981.
54. Armstrong, 1978; Meiselman, 1978.
55. Quoted by Armstrong, 1978, p. 56.
56. Herman and Hirschman, 1977, p. 748.
57. See also Gelinas, 1983.
58. Meiselman, 1978.
59. Gordon and O'Keefe, 1984.
60. M. Johnson, 1988, p. 173.
61. Parsons, 1954b.
62. Parsons, 1954b, pp. 305–307.
63. Johnson et al., 1975.
64. Fiedler, 1968.
65. Parsons, 1954b, p. 306.
66. Whiting et al., 1958; Whiting, 1960.
67. Raphael, 1988.
68. Kagan, 1964; Stockard, 1980a, 1985.
69. Hartley, 1976; Fine, 1987.
70. Hartley, 1976.
71. Kohlberg, 1966, p. 121.
72. Thorne and Luria, 1986; Eisenhart and Holland, 1983.
73. Whiting and Edwards, 1988.
74. Maccoby and Jacklin, 1987; Maccoby, 1990a.
75. Udry, 1974, p. 73.
76. Kinsey et al., 1948, p. 168.
77. Grass, 1964.
78. Rubin, 1990, pp. 43–44.
79. Cosby, 1975.
80. Fine, 1987, p. 114.
81. See also Phillips, 1986, p. 323; Rubin, 1990, pp. 134–136; Franklin, 1984, pp. 165–168; Pleck, 1980, p. 424.
82. Pleck, 1980, p. 424.
83. Udry, 1974, p. 71; Rubin, 1990.
84. Franklin, 1984, pp. 163–165.
85. Stoltenberg, 1990, p. 131.
86. Hymowitz and Weissman, 1978, p. 348.
87. Blumstein and Schwartz, 1976, p. 19.
88. Giallombardo, 1966.
89. Udry, 1974, pp. 72–73.
90. See also Rubin, 1990.
91. Safilios-Rothschild, 1977, p. 61.
92. See Phillips, 1986; Franklin, 1984.

93. See Brownmiller, 1975; Griffin, 1975.
94. Kanin and Parcell, 1977; Russell, 1984; Finkelhor and Yllo, 1985.
95. Gwartney-Gibbs et al., 1987; Kanin, 1985; Alder, 1985; DeKeseredy, 1990.
96. Check and Malamuth, 1985.
97. Brownmiller, 1975, p. 175.
98. Schwendinger and Schwendinger, 1983, pp. 23–25.
99. Griffin, 1975; Brownmiller, 1975.
100. Rubin, 1990, p. 26.
101. Rubin, 1990, p. 10.
102. Rubin, 1990, p. 57.
103. Rubin, 1990, pp. 70–72.
104. Udry, 1988; Udry and Billy, 1987.
105. Safilios-Rothschild, 1977.
106. Kephart, 1967, p. 473.
107. Hochschild, 1983.
108. Waller, 1951, quoted in Rubin, 1977.
109. Firestone, 1971, p. 140.
110. Rubin, 1977.
111. deBeauvoir, 1953, pp. 357–358.
112. Israel and Eliasson, 1971.
113. Allgood-Merten, et al., 1990.
114. Smith-Rosenberg, 1975.
115. Young and Willmott, 1973.
116. Rubin, 1985.
117. Shulman, 1973, p. 58.

CHAPTER 11

1. McCall and Simmons, 1978.
2. Epstein, 1974, p. 370.
3. Clausen, 1986, p. 3.
4. Modell, 1989.
5. Neugarten and Moore, 1968, p. 7; Clausen, 1986, p. 3; Marini, 1985.
6. Rindfuss et al., 1987; Marini, 1984.
7. Simmons and Blyth, 1987, pp. 72–96; also see Bursik et al., 1985.
8. Greenberger, 1988; Greenberger and Steinberg, 1986.
9. Papini et al., 1989.
10. Douvan and Adelson, 1966.
11. Youniss and Smollar, 1985.
12. Sebald, 1989; Youniss and Smollar, 1985; Offer, 1969, pp. 60–61.
13. Youniss and Smollar, 1985, pp. 87–91.
14. Lueptow, 1984, pp. 252–255.
15. Rubin, 1990, pp. 76–77.
16. Furstenberg et al., 1987, pp. 1–4; Furstenberg and Brooks-Gunn, 1989; Taeuber, 1991, pp. 45–46.
17. Furstenberg et al., 1987; Farber, 1990; Upchurch and McCarthy, 1990; Furstenberg and Brooks-Gunn, 1989.
18. Goldscheider and DaVanzo, 1985.
19. E.g., Coleman, 1961.
20. Stockard and Wood, 1984; Stockard et al., 1985; Stockard, 1985; Lueptow, 1984; Simmons and Blyth, 1987.
21. Lueptow, 1984.
22. Simmons and Blyth, 1987, p. 97; Lueptow, 1984, pp. 128–131.
23. Stockard and McGee, 1990; Lueptow, 1984; Ireson and Gill, 1988.
24. Lueptow, 1984; Sundberg et al., 1984.
25. Simmons and Blyth, 1987, pp. 79–89.
26. Erikson, 1959, 1968.
27. Douvan and Adelson, 1966, p. 24; see also Lowenthal et al., 1975.

28. Lueptow, 1984, pp. 100–102.
29. Simmons and Blyth, 1987; see also Eder and Sanford, 1986.
30. Allgood-Merten et al., 1990.
31. Allgood-Merten and Stockard, 1991.
32. Hareven, 1976a, b.
33. Goldscheider and Waite, 1986a; Waite et al., 1986a; Mott 1982; McLaughlin et al., 1988; Oppenheimer, 1988.
34. U.S. Bureau of the Census, 1989, p. 386.
35. Mott, 1982; McLaughlin et al., 1988; Faver, 1984.
36. Lopata et al., 1985.
37. Oppenheimer, 1982.
38. Lowenthal et al., 1975, p. 17.
39. Bernard, 1975a, p. 116.
40. LaRossa and LaRossa, 1981; Hochschild, 1989.
41. Cf. Waite et al., 1986b; Mott and Shapiro, 1982.
42. Lopata, 1971.
43. Oppenheimer, 1974, 1982.
44. Nordstrom, 1986.
45. Pleck and Lange, 1978; cited by R. Lewis, 1986, p. 14.
46. C. Lewis, 1986; Hochschild, 1989; Bielby and Bielby, 1989.
47. DiBenedetto and Tittle, 1990.
48. Bernard, 1975b.
49. Gould, 1972; Sheehy, 1976; Walter, 1986; Gerson, 1985.
50. Parsons, 1954a.
51. See Rubin, 1983; Balswick, 1988; Grossman, 1987.
52. Sattel, 1976.
53. Neugarten, 1968b.
54. Williams, 1983, p. 398.
55. DeLovey 1984, p. 287; Williams 1983, p. 400; Katchadourian and Lunde, 1975, p. 102.
56. Williams, 1983, p. 111.
57. Neugarten et al., 1968, pp. 198–199.
58. Severne, 1982.
59. Sheehy, 1976, pp. 458–459, citing Ruebsaat and Hull, 1975; see also Flint, 1982, pp. 264–266.
60. Sheehy, 1976.
61. Lopata, 1971, p. 41.
62. Lopata, 1971, p. 41.
63. Lopata and Barnewolt, 1983; Long and Porter, 1984; Faver, 1984.
64. Shaw, 1983.
65. Schlossberg, 1984; Shaw and O'Brien, 1983.
66. Abel, 1987, 1989; Steuve and O'Donnell, 1984; Rossi and Rossi, 1990.
67. McLaughlin et al., 1988; Lopata and Barnewolt 1984; Moen et al., 1990.
68. Lowenthal et al., 1975, pp. 18–20.
69. Gould, 1972.
70. Baruch, 1984.
71. Neugarten, 1976; Brim, 1976.
72. Levinson et al., 1976; also see Vaillant, 1977; Wrightsman, 1988.
73. Bart, 1975.
74. Bernard, 1975a, b; Rubin, 1979; Neugarten, 1968b, p. 96; Faver, 1984, pp. 114–115; Cooper and Gutmann, 1987; White and Edwards, 1990.
75. Rossi and Rossi, 1990.
76. Long and Porter, 1984; Baruch, 1984; Waldron and Herold, 1986; Hibbard and Pope, 1985, 1991; Muller, 1986; Verbrugge, 1986; Lopata and Barnewolt, 1984; Thoits, 1983.
77. Berkun, 1983.
78. See also Rossi and Rossi, 1990, pp. 64–65.
79. Neugarten and Weinstein, 1968.
80. Cherlin and Furstenberg, 1986, pp. 122–127; Bengtson, 1985, p. 16; C.L. Johnson, 1988.
81. Neugarten, 1968a, p. 140; also see Taylor, 1987.
82. McGee and Wells, 1982.
83. See also Rossi and Rossi, 1990, pp. 56–61.

84. Brubaker and Hennon, 1982; Brubaker, 1985.
85. Rossi and Rossi, 1990.
86. Clausen 1986, p. 183; Riddick, 1982; Szinovacz, 1983, pp. 108–109.
87. Morgan et al., 1985, pp. 142–143.
88. Rubinstein, 1986; Fischer, 1986; Wilkinson, 1988; Sussman, 1976; Rossi and Rossi, 1990.
89. Depner and Ingersoll, 1982; see also Rossi and Rossi, 1990.
90. Seccombe and Lee, 1986.
91. Seccombe and Lee, 1986; Clausen, 1986, p. 181; Parnes and Lees, 1985; Crowley, 1985.
92. O'Rand and Henretta, 1982; Hess, 1985; Rogers, 1985; Meyer, 1990.
93. Haug and Folmar, 1986; Holden, 1989.
94. U.S. Bureau of the Census, 1989.
95. Bell, 1975, p. 147.
96. Braito and Anderson, 1983.
97. Lopata, 1973, 1987.
98. Lowenthal et al., 1975, pp. 67–68.
99. Lowenthal et al., 1975, pp. 72–76.
100. Block and Haan, 1971, pp. 66–76.
101. Kagan and Moss, 1962.
102. E.g., Block and Haan, 1971; Maas and Kuypers, 1974.
103. Terman and Oden, 1947; Burks et al., 1930.
104. Kagan and Moss, 1962, p. 268.
105. Kagan and Moss, 1962, pp. 268–269.
106. Maas and Kuypers, 1974.
107. Mass and Kuypers, 1974, pp. 130–131.
108. Terman and Oden, 1947, p. 193.
109. Terman and Oden, 1947, p. 194.
110. Terman and Oden, 1947, p. 181.
111. Terman and Oden, 1947, p. 311.

CHAPTER 12

1. Giele, 1978, p. x.
2. Cf. Neal, 1979.
3. Cf. Youssef and Hartley, 1979; Mason, 1984; Mascia-Lees, 1984.
4. Baron, 1987; MacKinnon, 1987; Scales, 1986; Rhode, 1987; Kessler-Harris, 1985.
5. See England and Dunn, 1988; Steinberg, 1987.
6. Orazem and Mattila, 1989; see also Gregory et al., 1989; Freeman, 1984.
7. Bridges and Nelson, 1989; Acker, 1989; see Paul, 1989; Blum, 1987; Brenner, 1987; and Reskin, 1988, for theoretical and philosophical critiques of comparable worth as a strategy for change.
8. Kilborn, 1990; see also Morrison and VonGlinow, 1990.
9. See Chafetz, 1990; Saltzstein, 1986; Martin et al., 1988.
10. Ferree, 1987.
11. Hewlett, 1986, pp. 397–398.
12. E.g., Emmons et al., 1990; Freyd, 1990.
13. Smith and Sipchen, 1990; see also Lamb, 1987.
14. Johnson, 1977, 1988; Coltrane, 1988; Tanner, 1974.
15. Sedney, 1987.
16. Cowan and Cowan, 1987, p. 170.
17. E.g., Ehrensaft, 1987; Hochschild, 1989.
18. See M. Johnson, 1988.
19. Bellah et al., 1985; Swidler, 1980.
20. Stacey, 1990; Rossi and Rossi, 1990; M. Johnson, forthcoming.
21. Weitzman, 1985, 1988; Krantz, 1988; Arendell, 1986.
22. Maccoby, 1990a.
23. Stark, 1989a, pp. 157–162.
24. Rossi, 1987, pp. 44–45.
25. Uhlenberg and Eggebeen, 1986.

26. Risman, 1987, 1989.
27. See especially Stacey, 1990.
28. Ehrenreich, 1983, pp. 181–182.
29. Boulding et al., 1976, pp. 248–254.
30. E.g., Mason et al., 1976; Chafetz, 1990, pp. 182–185.
31. Grief, 1985, p. 5.
32. Cf. Jeffords, 1989.
33. McLanahan, et al., 1989.
34. Ozawa, 1989, p. 206.
35. Cf. Skold, 1988; Hewlett, 1986; Hewlett et al., 1986; Lande et al., 1989; Hayes et al., 1990; Kahn and Kamerman, 1987; Kamerman and Kahn, 1981; Fernandez, 1986; Rosenfelt and Stacey, 1987.
36. Associated Press, 1977.
37. Hewlett, 1986; Auerbach, 1988, pp. 13–61; Hewlett et al., 1986; Goldberg and Kremen, 1987.
38. Hewlett, 1986; Hewlett et al., 1986; Kamerman and Kahn, 1981; Freeman, 1984.
39. Stockard, 1988.
40. Crosby and Herek, 1986.
41. Hunt and Hunt, 1987; Stanley et al., 1986.

References

Abel, Emily K. 1987. *Love Is Not Enough: Family Care of the Frail Elderly*. Washington, D.C.: American Public Health Association.

Abel, Emily K. 1989. "The Ambiguities of Social Support: Adult Daughters Caring for Frail Elderly Parents." *Journal of Aging Studies*. 3:211–230.

Ackelsberg, Martha, and Irene Diamond. 1987. "Gender and Political Life: New Directions in Political Science." Pp. 504–525 in Beth B. Hess and Myra Marx Ferree (Eds.). *Analyzing Gender: A Handbook of Social Science Research*. Newbury Park, Calif.: Sage.

Acker, Joan R. 1989. *Doing Comparable Worth: Gender, Class and Pay Equity*. Philadelphia: Temple University Press.

Acosta-Belen, Edna, and Christine E. Bose. 1990. "From Structural Subordination to Empowerment: Women and Development in Third World Contexts." *Gender and Society*. 4:299–320.

Afshar, Haleh. (Ed.). 1985. *Women, Work, and Ideology in the Third World*. London and New York: Tavistock.

Aigner, Dennis J., and Glen C. Cain. 1977. "Statistical Theories of Discrimination in Labor Markets." *Industrial and Labor Relations Review*. 30:175–187.

Alder, Christine. 1985. "An Exploration of Self-Reported Sexually Aggressive Behavior." *Crime and Delinquency*. 31:306–331.

Alexander, Karl L., and Bruce K. Eckland. 1974. "Sex Differences in the Educational Attainment Process." *American Sociological Review*. 39:668–682.

Allen, Michael Patrick. 1987. *The Founding Fathers: A New Anatomy of the Super-Rich Families in America*. New York: Dutton.

Allgood-Merten, Betty, Peter Lewinsohn, and Hyman Hops. 1990. "Sex Differences and Adolescent Depression." *Journal of Abnormal Psychology*. 1:55–63.

Allgood-Merten, Betty, and Jean Stockard. 1991. "Sex Role Identity and Self-Esteem: A Comparison of Children and Adolescents." *Sex Roles*, forthcoming.

Almquist, Elizabeth M., and Juanita Wehrle-Einhorn. 1978. "The Doubly Disadvantaged: Minority Women in the Labor Force." Pp. 63–88 in Ann Stromberg and Shirley Harkess (Eds.). *Women Working*. Palo Alto, Calif.: Mayfield.

Alpert, Judith L., and Jody Boghossian Spencer. 1986. "Morality, Gender, and Analysis." Pp. 83–111 in Judith L. Alpert (Ed.). *Psychoanalysis and Women: Contemporary Reappraisals*. New York: Analytic Press.

Angrilli, A. F. 1960. "The Psychosexual Identification of Pre-school Boys." *Journal of Genetic Psychology*. 97:329–340.

Archer, John, and Barbara Lloyd. 1985. *Sex and Gender*. New York: Cambridge University Press.

Arendell, Terry. 1986. *Mothers and Divorce: Legal, Economic and Social Dilemmas*. Berkeley: University of California Press.

Aries, Elizabeth. 1987. "Gender and Communication." Pp. 149–176 in Phillip Shaver and Clyde Hendrick (Eds.). *Sex and Gender: Vol. 7. Review of Personality and Social Psychology*. Newbury Park, Calif.: Sage.

Aries, Philippe. 1962. *Centuries of Childhood: A Social History of Family Life* (Robert Baldick, trans.). New York: Knopf.

Armstrong, Louise. 1978. *Kiss Daddy Goodnight: A Speak-Out on Incest*. New York: Hawthorn.

Arrow, Kenneth. 1973. "The Theory of Discrimination." Pp. 3–33 in Orley Ashenfelter and Albert Rees (Eds.). *Discrimination in Labor Markets*. Princeton. N.J.: Princeton University Press.

Associated Press. 1977. "Family Serves Prime Function." *Eugene Register Guard*. August 31, p. 12F.

Astin, Helen A., and Alan E. Bayer. 1973. "Sex Discrimination in Academe." Pp. 333–356 in Alice Rossi and Ann Calderwood (Eds.). *Academic Women on the Move*. New York: Russell Sage Foundation.

Attwood, Lynne, and Maggie McAndrew. 1984. "Women at Work in the USSR." Pp. 269–304 in Marilyn J. Davidson and Cary L. Cooper (Eds.). *Working Women: An International Survey*. Chicester, Eng., and New York: Wiley.

Auerbach, Judith D. 1988. *In the Business of Child Care: Employer Initiatives and Working Women*. New York: Praeger.

Bakan, David. 1966. *The Duality of Human Existence*. Chicago: Rand McNally.

Balow, Irving H. 1963. "Sex Differences in First Grade Reading." *Elementary English*. 40:303–320.

Balswick, Jack. 1988. *The Inexpressive Male*. Lexington, Mass.: Heath.

Balswick, Jack, and Charles Peek. 1971. "The Inexpressive Male: A Tragedy of American Society." *Family Coordinator*. 20:363–368.

Bandura, Albert, and R. H. Walters. 1963. *Social Learning and Personality Development*. New York: Holt, Rinehart, & Winston.

Barber, Brian K., and Darwin L. Thomas. 1986. "Dimensions of Fathers' and Mothers' Supportive Behavior: The Case for Physical Affection." *Journal of Marriage and the Family*. 48:783–794.

Bardwick, Judith M. 1974. "The Sex Hormones, the Central Nervous System and Affect Variability in Humans." Pp. 27–50 in Violet Franks and Vsanti Burtle (Eds.). *Women in Therapy: New Psychotherapies for a Changing Society*. New York: Brunner/Mazel.

Barfield, Ashton. 1976. "Biological Influences on Sex Differences in Behavior." Pp. 62–121 in Michael Teitelbaum (Ed.). *Sex Differences: Social and Biological Perspectives*. Garden City, N.Y.: Anchor Books.

Barnett, Rosalind C., and Grace K. Baruch. 1987. "Determinants of Fathers' Participation in Family Work." *Journal of Marriage and the Family*. 49:29–40.

Baron, Ava. 1987. "Feminism Legal Strategies: The Powers of Difference." Pp. 474–503 in Beth B. Hess and Myra Marx Ferree (Eds.). *Analyzing Gender: A Handbook of Social Science Research*. Newbury Park, Calif.: Sage.

Baron, Dennis. 1986. *Grammar and Gender*. New Haven, Conn., and London: Yale University Press.

Baron, James N., and Andrew E. Newman. 1990. "For What It's Worth: Organizations, Occupations, and the Value of Work Done by Women and Nonwhites." *American Sociological Review*. 55:155–175.

Barry, Herbert, Margaret K. Bacon, and Irvin L. Child. 1957. "A Cross-Cultural Survey of Some Sex Differences in Socialization." *Journal of Abnormal and Social Psychology*. 55:327–332.

Bart, Pauline. 1975. "The Loneliness of the Long-Distance Mother." Pp. 156–170 in Jo Freeman (Ed.). *Women: A Feminist Perspective*. Palo Alto, Calif.: Mayfield.

Barthel, Diane. 1987. *Putting on Appearances: Gender and Advertising*. Philadelphia: Temple University Press.

Baruch, Grace K. 1984. "The Psychological Well-Being of Women in the Middle Years." Pp. 161–180 in Grace Baruch and Jeanne Brooks-Gunn (Eds.). *Women in Midlife*. New York: Plenum.

Baruch, Grace K., and Rosalind C. Barnett. 1986. "Consequences of Fathers' Participation in Family Work: Parents' Role Strain and Well-Being." *Journal of Personality and Social Psychology*. 51:981–992.

Baude, Annika. 1979. "Public Policy and Changing Family Patterns in Sweden: 1930–1977." Pp. 145–176 in Jean Lipman-Blumen and Jessie Bernard (Eds.). *Sex Roles and Social Policy: A Complex Social Science Equation*. Beverly Hills, Calif.: Sage.

Beauvoir, Simone de. 1953. *The Second Sex* (H. M. Parshley, trans.). New York: Knopf.

Becker, Betsy Jane. 1986. "Influence Again: An Examination of Reviews and Studies of Gender Differences in Social Influence." Pp. 178–209 in Janet Shibley Hyde and Marcia C. Linn (Eds.). *The Psychology of Gender: Advances Through Meta-Analysis*. Baltimore: Johns Hopkins University Press.

Becker, Gary S. 1971. *The Economics of Discrimination* (2nd ed.). Chicago: University of Chicago Press.

Becker, Gary S. 1975. *Human Capital: A Theoretical and Empirical Analysis, with Special Reference to Education* (2nd ed.). Chicago: University of Chicago Press.

Becker, Gary S. 1981. *A Treatise on the Family*. Cambridge, Mass.: Harvard University Press.

Becker, Gary S. 1985. "Human Capital, Effort and the Sexual Division of Labor." *Journal of Labor Economics*. 3:S33–S58.

Beckwith, Karen. 1986. *American Women and Political Participation: The Impact of Work, Generation, and Feminism*. New York: Greenwood Press.

Beechy, Veronica. 1978. "Women and Production: A Critical Analysis of Some Sociological Theories of Women's Work." Pp. 155–197 in Annette Kuhn and AnnMarie Wolpe (Eds.). *Feminism and Materialism: Women and Modes of Production*. London: Routledge and Kegan Paul.

Belenky, Mary Field, Blythe McVicker Clinchy, Nancy Rule Goldberger, and Jill Mattuck Tarule. 1986. *Women's Ways of Knowing: The Development of Self, Voice and Mind*. New York: Basic Books.

Bell, Alan P., Martin S. Weinberg, and Sue Kiefer Hammersmith. 1981. *Sexual Preference: Its Development in Men and Women*. Bloomington: Indiana University Press.

Bell, Inge Powell. 1975. "The Double-Standard: Age." Pp. 145–155 in Jo Freeman (Ed.). *Women: A Feminist Perspective*. Palo Alto, Calif.: Mayfield.

Bellah, Robert, Richard Madsen, William Sullivan, Ann Swidler, and Steven Tipton. 1985. *Habits of the Heart*. Berkeley: University of California Press.

Bellisari, Anna. 1989. "Male Superiority in Mathematical Aptitude: An Artifact." *Human Organization*. 48:273–279.

Bem, Sandra Lipsitz. 1974. "The Measurement of Psychological Androgyny." *Journal of Consulting and Clinical Psychology*. 42:155–162.

Bem, Sandra Lipsitz. 1981. "Gender Schema Theory: A Cognitive Account of Sex Typing." *Psychological Review*. 88:354–364.

Bem, Sandra Lipsitz. 1983. "Gender Schema Theory and Its Implications for Child Development: Raising Gender-Aschematic Children in a Gender-Schematic Society." *Signs: Journal of Women in Culture and Society*. 8:598–616.

Bem, Sandra Lipsitz. 1985. "Androgyny and Gender Schema Theory: A Conceptual and Empirical Integration." Pp. 179–226 in Theo B. Sonderegger (Ed.). *Psychology and Gender: Nebraska Symposium on Motivation, 1984*. Lincoln: University of Nebraska Press.

Bem, Sandra Lipsitz. 1987. "Gender Schema Theory and the Romantic Tradition." In Phillip Shaver and Clyde Hendrick (Eds.). *Sex and Gender*. Newbury Park, Calif.: Sage.

Bem, Sandra Lipsitz, W. Martyna, and C. Watson. 1976. "Sex-Typing and Androgyny: Further Explorations of the Expressive Domain." *Journal of Personality and Social Psychology*. 34:1016–1023.

Benbow, Camilla Person, and Julian C. Stanley. 1980. "Sex Differences in Mathematical Ability: Fact or Artifact?" *Science*. 210:1262–1264.

Benbow, Camilla Person, and Julian C. Stanley. 1983. "Differential Course-Taking Hypothesis Revisited." *American Educational Research Journal*. 20:469–573.

Bene, Eva. 1965. "On the Genesis of Female Homosexuality." *British Journal of Psychiatry*. 111:815–821.

Beneria, Lourdes (Ed.). 1982. *Women and Development: The Sexual Division of Labor in Rural Societies*. New York: Praeger.

Bengston, Vern L. 1985. "Diversity and Symbolism in Grandparental Roles." Pp. 11–25 in Vern L. Bengtson and Joan F. Robertson (Eds.). *Grandparenthood*. Beverly Hills, Calif.: Sage.

Benjamin, Jessica. 1988. *The Bonds of Love: Psychoanalysis, Feminism, and the Problem of Domination*. New York: Pantheon Books.

Bennett, Edward M., and Larry R. Cohen. 1959. "Men and Women: Personality Patterns and Contrast." *Genetic Psychology Monographs*. 59:101–155.

Bennett, Linda L. M. 1986. "The Gender Gap: When an Opinion Gap Is Not a Voting Bloc." *Social Science Quarterly*. 67:613–625.

Bennett, Neil G., David E. Bloom, and Patricia H. Craig. 1989. "The Divergence of Black and White Marriage Patterns." *American Journal of Sociology*. 95:692–722.

Benston, Margaret. 1969. "The Political Economy of Women's Liberation." *Monthly Review*. 21:13–27.

Berardo, Donna Hodgkins, Constance L. Shehan, and Gerald R. Leslie. 1987. "A Residue of Tradition: Jobs, Careers, and Spouses' Time in Housework." *Journal of Marriage and the Family*. 49:381–390.

Bergmann, Barbara R. 1971. "The Effect on White Incomes of Discrimination in Employment." *Journal of Political Economy*. 79:294–313.

Bergmann, Barbara R. 1973. "The Economics of Women's Liberation." *Challenge*. 16:11–17.

Bergmann, Barbara R. 1986. *The Economic Emergence of Women*. New York: Basic Books.

Berk, Richard A., Sarah Fenstermaker Berk, Donileen R. Loseke, and David Rauma. 1983. "Mutual Combat and Other Family Violence Myths." Pp. 197–212 in David Finkelhor, Richard J. Gelles, Gerald T. Hotaling, and Murray A. Straus (Eds.). *The Dark Side of Families: Current Family Violence Research*. Beverly Hills, Calif.: Sage.

Berk, Sarah Fenstermaker. 1985. *The Gender Factory: The Apportionment of Work in American Households*. New York: Plenum.

Berkun, Cleo S. 1983. "Changing Appearance for Women in the Middle Years of Life: Trauma?" Pp. 11–35 in Elizabeth W. Markson (Ed.). *Older Women: Issues and Prospects*. Lexington, Mass.: Lexington Books.

Bernard, Jessie. 1975a. *The Future of Motherhood*. New York: Penguin.

Bernard, Jessie. 1975b. *Women, Wives, Mothers: Values and Options*. Chicago: Aldine.

Bettleheim, Bruno. 1954. *Symbolic Wounds: Puberty Rites and the Envious Male*. London: Thames & Hudson.

Beuchler, Judith-Maria. 1986. "Women in Petty Commodity Production in La Paz, Bolivia." Pp. 165–188 in June Nash and Helen I. Safa (Eds.). *Women and Change in Latin America*. South Hadley, Mass.: Bergin & Garvey.

Bianchi, Suzanne M., and Daphne Spain. 1986. *American Women in Transition*. New York: Russell Sage Foundation.

Bieber, Irving, J. J. Dain, P. R. Dince, M. G. Drellich, H. G. Grand, R. H. Gundlach, M. W. Kremer, A. H. Rifkin, C. B. Wilber, and Toby Bieber. 1962. *Homosexuality: A Psychoanalytic Study*. New York: Basic Books.

Bielby, Denise D., and William T. Bielby. 1988. "She Works Hard for the Money: Household Responsibilities and the Allocation of Work Effort." *American Journal of Sociology*. 93:1031–1059.

Bielby, William T., and James N. Baron. 1984. "A Woman's Place Is with Other Women: Sex Segregation Within Organizations." Pp. 27–55 in Barbara F. Reskin (Ed.). *Sex Segregation in the Workplace: Trends, Explanations, Remedies*. Washington, D.C.: National Academy Press.

Bielby, William T., and James N. Baron. 1986. "Men and Women at Work: Sex Segregation and Statistical Discrimination." *American Journal of Sociology*. 91:759–799.

Bielby, William T., and James N. Baron. 1987. "Undoing Discrimination: Job Integration and Comparable Worth." Pp. 211–229 in Christine Bose and Glenna Spitze (Eds.). *Ingredients for Women's Employment Policy.* Albany, N.Y.: SUNY Press.

Bielby, William T., and Denise D. Bielby. 1989. "Family Ties: Balancing Commitment to Work and Family in Dual Earner Households." *American Sociological Review.* 54:776–789.

Bielli, Carla. 1976. "Some Aspects of the Condition of Women in Italy." Pp. 105–114 in Lynne B. Iglitzin and Ruth Ross (Eds.). *Women in the World: A Comparative Study* (Beverly Springer, trans.). Santa Barbara, Calif.: Clio Books.

Birdsell, Nancy, and William Paul McGreevey. 1983. "Women, Poverty, and Development." Pp. 3–13 in Mayra Buvinic, Margaret A. Lycette, and William Paul McGreevey (Eds.). *Women and Poverty in the Third World.* Baltimore: Johns Hopkins University Press.

Birke, Lynda. 1986. *Women, Feminism, and Biology: The Feminist Challenge.* New York: Methuen.

Blau, Francine D., and Marianne A. Ferber. 1986. *The Economics of Women, Men, and Work.* Englewood Cliffs, N.J.: Prentice Hall.

Blau, Francine O. and Carol L. Jusenius. 1976. "Economists' Approaches to Sex Segregation in the Labor Market: An Appraisal." *Signs: Journal of Women in Culture and Society.* 1:181–200.

Bleier, Ruth. 1984. *Science and Gender: A Critique of Biology and Its Theories on Women.* New York: Pergamon Press.

Block, Jack and Norma Haan. 1971. *Lives Through Time.* Berkeley: Bancroft.

Block, Jeanne H. 1973. "Conceptions of Sex Role: Some Cross-Cultural and Longitudinal Perspectives." *American Psychologist.* 28:512–526.

Block, Jeanne H. 1976. "Issues, Problems, and Pitfalls in Assessing Sex Differences." *Merrill-Palmer Quarterly.* 22:283–308.

Block, Jeanne H. 1984. *Sex Role Identity and Ego Development.* San Francisco: Jossey-Bass.

Blondel, Jean. 1985. *Government Ministers in the Contemporary World.* Beverly Hills, Calif.: Sage.

Blum, Linda M. 1987. "Possibilities and Limits of the Comparable Worth Movement." *Gender and Society.* 1:380–399.

Blum, Linda, and Vicki Smith. 1988. "Women's Mobility in the Corporation: A Critique of the Politics of Optimism." *Signs: Journal of Women in Culture and Society.* 13:528–545.

Blumberg, Rae Lesser. 1978. *Stratification: Socioeconomic and Sexual Inequality.* Dubuque, Iowa: Wm. C. Brown.

Blumberg, Rae Lesser and Robert F. Winch. 1974. "Societal Complexity and Familial Complexity." Pp. 94–113 in Robert F. Winch and Graham B. Spanier (Eds.). *Selected Studies in Marriage and the Family.* (4th edition). New York: Holt, Rinehart, & Winston.

Blumberg, Rae Lesser. 1984. "A General Theory of Gender Stratification." Pp. 23–101 in Randall Collins (Ed.). *Sociological Theory 1984.* San Francisco: Jossey-Bass.

Blumstein, Philip W. and Pepper Schwartz. 1976. "Bisexuality: Some Social Psychological Issues." Available from P. W. Blumstein, Department of Sociology, University of Washington, Seattle, Washington.

Blumstein, Philip, and Pepper Schwartz. 1983. *American Couples: Money, Work, Sex.* New York: Morrow.

Blumstein, Philip, and Pepper Schwartz. 1989. "Intimate Relations and the Creation of Sexuality." Pp. 120–129 in Barbara J. Risman and Pepper Schwartz (Eds.). *Gender in Intimate Relations: A Microstructural Approach.* Belmont, Calif.: Wadsworth.

Bock, R. D., and E. G. J. Moore. 1984. *Profile of American Youth: Demographic Influences on ASVAB Test Performance.* Washington, D.C.: Office of the Assistant Secretary of Defense.

Bognanno, Mario F. 1987. "Women in Professions: Academic Women." Pp. 245–264 in Karen Shallcross Koziara, Michael H. Moskow, and Lucretia Dewey Tanner (Eds.). *Working Women: Past, Present, Future.* Washington, D.C.: Bureau of National Affairs.

Bolles, A. Lynn and Deborah D'Amico Samuels. 1989. "Anthropological Scholarship on Gender in the English-speaking Carribean." Pp. 171–188 in Sandra Morgen (Ed.). *Gender and Anthropology: Critical Reviews for Research and Teaching.* Washington, D.C.: American Anthropological Association.

Bookman, Ann, and Sandra Morgen. (Eds.). 1988. *Women and the Politics of Empowerment.* Philadelphia: Temple University Press.

Bose, Christine E. 1987. "Dual Spheres." Pp. 267–288 in Beth B. Hess and Myra Marx Ferree (Eds.). *Analyzing Gender: A Handbook of Social Science Research.* Newbury Park, Calif.: Sage.

Boserup, Ester. 1986. *Woman's Role in Economic Development.* Aldershot, Eng.: Gower. (Originally published 1970.)

Boswell, Sally Y. 1985. "The Influence of Sex-Role Stereotyping on Women's Attitudes and Achievement in Mathematics." Pp. 175–197 in Susan F. Chipman, Lorelei R. Brush, and Donna M. Wilson (Eds.). *Women and Mathematics: Balancing the Equation.* Hillsdale, N.J.: Erlbaum.

Boulding, Elise, Shirley A. Nuss, Dorothy Lee Carson, and Michael A. Greenstein. 1976. *Handbook of International Data on Women.* New York: Halsted Press.

Bowman, Mary Jean, and C. Arnold Anderson. 1982. "The Participation of Women in Education in the Third World." Pp. 11–30 in Gail P. Kelly and Carolyn M. Elliott (Eds.). *Women's Education in the Third World: Comparative Perspectives.* Albany, N.Y.: SUNY Press.

Bradley, Ben S. and Susan K. Gobbart. 1989. "Determinants of Gender-Typed Play in Toddlers." *Journal of Genetic Psychology.* 150:453–455.

Bradley, Susan J. 1985. "Gender Disorders in Childhood: A Formulation." Pp. 175–188 in Betty W. Steiner (Ed.). *Gender Dysphoria: Development, Research, Management.* New York: Plenum.

Braito, Rita, and Donna Anderson. 1983. "The Ever-Single Elderly Woman." Pp. 195–225 in Elizabeth W. Markson (Ed.). *Older Women: Issues and Prospects.* Lexington, Mass.: Lexington Books.

Brandon, Paul R., Barbara J. Newton, and Ormond W. Hammond. 1987. "Children's Mathematics Achievement in Hawaii: Sex Differences Favoring Girls." *American Educational Research Journal.* 24:437–461.

Brenner, Johanna. 1987. "Feminist Political Discourses: Radical Versus Liberal Approaches to the Feminization of Poverty and Comparable Worth." *Gender and Society.* 1:447–465.

Bridges, William P., and Robert L. Nelson. 1989. "Markets in Hierarchies: Organizational and Market Influences on Gender Inequality in a State Pay System." *American Journal of Sociology.* 95:616–658.

Briggs, Sheila. 1987. "Women and Religion." Pp. 408–441 in Beth B. Hess and Myra Marx Ferree (Eds.). *Analyzing Gender: A Handbook of Social Science Research.* Newbury Park, Calif.: Sage.

Brim, Orville. 1976. "Theories of the Male Mid-Life Crisis." *Counseling Psychologist.*" 6:2–9.

Brinton, Mary C. 1988. "The Social-Institutional Bases of Gender Stratification: Japan as an Illustrative Case." *American Journal of Sociology.* 94:300–334.

Brock-Utne, Birgit. 1989. "Gender and Cooperation in the Laboratory." *Journal of Peace Research.* 26:47–56.

Bronfenbrenner, Urie. 1961. "Some Familial Antecedents of Responsibility and Leadership in Adolescents." Pp. 239–271 in L. Petrullo and B. M. Bass (Eds.). *Leadership and Interpersonal Behavior.* New York: Holt, Rinehart, & Winston.

Bronstein, Phyllis. 1984. "Differences in Mothers' and Fathers' Behaviors Toward Children: A Cross-Cultural Comparison." *Developmental Psychology.* 20:995–1003.

Broverman, Inge K., Susan R. Vogel, Donald M. Broverman, Frank E. Clarkson, and Paul S. Rosenkrantz. 1972. "Sex-Role Stereotypes: A Current Appraisal." *Journal of Social Issues.* 28:59–78.

Brown, Clair (Vickery). 1982. "Home Production for Use in a Market Economy." Pp. 151–167 in Barrie Thorne with Marilyn Yalom (Eds.). *Rethinking the Family: Some Feminist Questions.* New York: Longman.

Brown, Jane D., and Kenneth Campbell. 1986. "Race and Gender in Music Videos: The Same Beat but a Different Drummer." *Journal of Communication.* 36:94–106.

Brown, Judith K. 1970. "A Note on the Division of Labor by Sex." *American Anthropologist.* 72:1073–1078.

Brown, Judith K. 1975. "Iroquois Women: An Ethnohistoric Note." Pp. 235–251 in Rayna R. Reiter (Ed.). *Toward an Anthropology of Women.* New York: Monthly Review Press.

Brownmiller, Susan. 1975. *Against Our Will: Men, Women and Rape.* New York: Simon & Schuster.

Brubaker, Timothy H. 1985. "Responsibility for Household Tasks: A Look at Golden Anniversary Couples Aged 75 Years and Older." Pp. 27–36 in Warren A. Peterson and Jill Quadagno (Eds.). *Social Bonds in Later Life: Aging and Interdependence.* Beverly Hills, Calif.: Sage.

Brubaker, Timothy H., and Charles B. Hennon. 1982. "Responsibility for Household Tasks: Comparing Dual-Earner and Dual-Retired Marriages." Pp. 205–219 in Maximiliane Szinovacz (Ed.). *Women's Retirement: Policy Implications of Recent Research.* Beverly Hills, Calif.: Sage.

Bullock, Charles S., and Loch K. Johnson. 1985. "Sex and the Second Primary." *Social Science Quarterly.* 66:933–944.

Bullough, Vern L. 1981. "Age at Menarche: A Misunderstanding." *Science.* 213:365–366.

Bulow, Jeremy I. and Lawrence H. Summers. 1986. "A Theory of Dual Labor Markets with Application to Industrial Policy, Discrimination, and Keynesian Unemployment." *Journal of Labor Economics.* 4:376–414.

Burbridge, Lynn C. 1986. "Black Women in Employment and Training Programs." Pp. 115–129 in Margaret C. Simms and Julianne Malveaux (Eds.). *Slipping Through the Cracks: The Status of Black Women.* New Brunswick, N.J.: Transaction Books.

Buric, Olivera. 1985. "Yugoslavia." Pp. 49–56 in Jennie Farley (Ed.). *Women Workers in Fifteen Countries: Essays in Honor of Alice Hanson Cook.* Ithaca, N.Y.: ILR Press.

Burks, Barbara Stoddard, Dortha Williams Jensen, and Lewis H. Terman. 1930. *The Promise of Youth.* Stanford, Calif.: Stanford University Press.

Burrell, Barbara C. 1985. "Women's and Men's Campaigns for the U.S. House of Representatives, 1972–1982: A Finance Gap?" *American Politics Quarterly.* 13:251–272.

Bursik, Robert J., Jr., Don Merten, and Gary Schwartz. 1985. "Appropriate Age-Related Behavior for Male and Female Adolescents: Adult Perceptions." *Youth and Society.* 17:115–130.

Burton, Michael L., and Douglas R. White. 1984. "Sexual Division of Labor in Agriculture." *American Anthropologist.* 86:568–583.

Burton, Roger V., and John W. M. Whiting. 1961. "The Absent Father and Cross-Sex Identity." *Merrill-Palmer Quarterly.* 7:85–95.

Bystydzienski, Jill M. 1989. "Women and Socialism: A Comparative Study of Women in Poland and the USSR." *Signs: Journal of Women in Culture and Society.* 14:668–684.

Cahill, Spencer E. 1986a. "Childhood Socialization as a Recruitment Process: Some Lessons from the Study of Gender Development." Pp. 163–186 in P. Adler and P. Adler (Eds.). *Sociological Studies of Child Development.* Greenwich, Conn.: JAI Press.

Cahill, Spencer E. 1986b. "Language Practices and Self-Definition: The Case of Gender Identity Acquisition." *Sociological Quarterly.* 27:295–311.

Cahill, Spencer E. 1989. "Fashioning Males and Females: Appearance Management and the Social Reproduction of Gender." *Symbolic Interaction.* 12:281–298.

Caldwell, Bettye M. 1973. "Infant Day Care—The Outcast Gains Respectability." Pp. 20–36 in Pamela Roby (Ed.). *Child Care: Who Cares?* New York: Basic Books.

Callaway, Barbara J., and Enid Schildkrout. 1986. "Law Education, and Social Change: Implications for Hausa Muslim Women in Nigeria." Pp. 181–206 in Lynne B. Itlitzin and Ruth Ross (Eds.). *Women in the World: 1975–1985 The Women's Decade* (2nd rev. ed.). Santa Barbara, Calif.: ABC–Clio.

Campbell, Jean W. 1973. "Women Drop Back In: Educational Innovation in the Sixties." Pp. 93–124 in Alice S. Rossi and Ann Calderwood (Eds.). *Academic Women on the Move.* New York: Russell Sage.

Campbell, Paul B. 1986. "Vocational Education: Access, Equity, and Consequence." *Educational Horizons.* 65(1):10–15.

Cancian, Francesca M. 1987. *Love in America: Gender and Self-Development.* New York: Cambridge University Press.

Cantor, Muriel G. 1987. "Popular Culture and the Portrayal of Women: Content and Control." Pp. 190–214 in Beth B. Hess and Myra Marx Feree (Eds.). *Analyzing Gender: A Handbook of Social Science Research.* Newbury Park, Calif.: Sage.

Carli, L. 1982. "Are Women More Social and Men More Task-Oriented? A Meta-Analytic Review of Sex Differences in Group Interaction, Reward Allocation, Coalition Formation, and Cooperation in the Prisoner's Dilemma Game." Unpublished manuscript, University of Massachusetts–Amherst.

Carlson, Rae. 1971. "Sex Differences in Ego Functioning: Exploratory Studies of Agency and Communion." *Journal of Consulting and Clinical Psychology.* 37:267–277.

Carrick, Kathleen. 1986. "Silk v. Corduroy: The Status of Men and Women in Law Librarianship." *Law Library Journal.* 78:425–441.

Carroll, Susan J. 1985. *Women as Candidates in American Politics.* Bloomington: Indiana University Press.

Carter, Bonnie Frank. 1984. "Premenstrual Syndrome: Studies in Interdisciplinary Problem Solving." Pp. 3–14 in Benson E. Ginsburg and Bonnie Frank Carter (Eds.). *Premenstrual Syndrome: Ethical and Legal Implications in a Biomedical Perspective.* New York: Plenum.

Carter, D. B. 1987. "The Roles of Peers in Sex Role Socialization." Pp. 101–121 in D. Bruce Carter (Ed.). *Current Conceptions of Sex Roles and Sex Typing: Theory and Research.* New York: Praeger.

Cassell, Frank H., Steven M. Director, and Samuel I. Doctors. 1975. "Discrimination Within Internal Labor Markets." *Industrial Relations.* 14:337–344.

Chafe, William H. 1972. *The American Woman: Her Changing Social, Economic, and Political Role.* New York: Oxford University Press.

Chafe, William. 1977. *Women and Equality.* New York: Oxford University Press.

Chafetz, Janet Saltzman, Paula Beck, Patricia Sampson, Joyce West, and Bonnye Jones. 1976. *Who's Queer? A Study of Homo- and Heterosexual Women.* Sarasota, Fla.: Omni Press.

Chafetz, Janet Saltzman. 1984. *Sex and Advantage: A Comparative, Macro-Structural Theory of Sex Stratification.* Totowa, N.J.: Rowman & Allanheld.

Chafetz, Janet Saltzman. 1990. *Gender Equity: An Integrated Theory of Stability and Change.* Newbury Park, Calif.: Sage.

Chafetz, Janet Saltzman, and Anthony Gary Dworkin. 1986. *Female Revolt: Women's Movements in World and Historical Perspective.* Totowa, N.J.: Rowman & Allanheld.

Chamberlain, Mariam K. (Ed.). 1988. *Women in Academe: Progress and Prospects.* New York: Russell Sage Foundation.

Chamove, A., H. Harlow, and G. D. Mitchell. 1967. "Sex Differences in the Infant-Directed Behavior of Preadolescent Rhesus Monkeys." *Child Development.* 38:329–335.

Charlton, Joy. 1987. "Women in Seminary: A Review of Current Social Science Research." *Review of Religious Research.* 28:305–318.

Chasseguet-Smirgel, Janine. 1970. "Feminine Guilt and the Oedipus Complex." Pp. 94–134 in Janine Chasseguet-Smirgel (Ed.). *Female Sexuality.* Ann Arbor: University of Michigan Press.

Check, James V., and Neil Malamuth. 1985. "An Empirical Assessment of Some Feminist Hypotheses About Rape." *International Journal of Women's Studies.* 8:414–423.

Chehrazi, Shahla. 1986. "Female Psychology: A Review." *Journal of the American Psychoanalytic Association.* 34:111–162.

Cherlin, Andrew J., and Frank F. Furstenberg, Jr. 1986. *The New American Grandparent: A Place in the Family, a Life Apart.* New York: Basic Books.

Cherlin, Andrew J. 1981. *Marriage, Divorce, Remarriage.* Cambridge, Mass.: Harvard University Press.

Chessick, Richard D. 1984. "Was Freud Wrong About Feminine Psychology?" *American Journal of Psychoanalysis.* 44:355–367.

Chipman, Susan F., and Veronica G. Thomas. 1985. "Women's Participation in Mathematics: Outlining the Problem." Pp. 1–24 in Susan F. Chipman, Lorelei R. Brush, and Donna M. Wilson (Eds.). *Women and Mathematics: Balancing the Equation.* Hillsdale, N.J.: Erlbaum.

Chodorow, Nancy J. 1974. "Family Structure and Feminine Personality." Pp. 43–66 in Michelle Zimbalist Rosaldo and Louise Lamphere (Eds.). *Women, Culture, and Society.* Stanford, Calif.: Stanford University Press.

Chodorow, Nancy J. 1978. *The Reproduction of Mothering.* Berkeley: University of California Press.

Chodorow, Nancy J. 1989. *Feminism and Psychoanalytic Theory.* New Haven: Yale University Press.

Chowning, Ann. 1987. "'Women Are Our Business': Women, Exchange and Prestige in Kove." Pp. 130–149 in Marilyn Strathern (Ed.). *Dealing with Inequality: Analysing Gender Relations in Melanesia and Beyond.* New York: Cambridge University Press.

Christy, Carol A. 1987. *Sex Differences in Political Participation: Processes of Change in Fourteen Nations.* New York: Praeger.

Clausen, John A. 1986. *The Life Course: A Sociological Perspective.* Englewood Cliffs, N.J.: Prentice Hall.

Clawson, Mary Ann. 1989. *Constructing Brotherhood: Class, Gender and Fraternalism.* Princeton, N.J.: Princeton University Press.

Colby, Anne, and William Damon. 1983. "Listening to a Different Voice: A Review of Gilligan's *In a Different Voice.*" *Merrill-Palmer Quarterly.* 29:473–481.

Cole, Stephen. 1986. "Sex Discrimination and Admission to Medical School, 1929–1984." *American Journal of Sociology.* 92:549–567.

Coleman, James. 1961. *The Adolescent Society.* New York: Free Press.

Collier, Jane F., and Michelle Z. Rosaldo. 1981. "Politics and Gender in Simple Societies." Pp. 275–329 in *Sexual Meanings: The Cultural Construction of Gender and Sexuality.* New York: Cambridge University Press.

Collier, Jane, Michelle Z. Rosaldo, and Sylvia Yanagisako. 1982. "Is There a Family? New Anthropological Views." Pp. 25–39 in Barrie Thorne with Marilyn Yalom (Eds.). *Rethinking the Family: Some Feminist Questions.* New York: Longman.

Coltrane, Scott. 1988. "The Father–Child Relationship and the Status of Women." *American Journal of Sociology.* 93:1060–1095.

Coltrane, Scott. 1989. "Household Labor and the Routine Production of Gender." *Social Problems.* 36:473–490.

Condry, John, and Sharon Dyer. 1976. "Fear of Success: Attribution of Cause to the Victim." *Journal of Social Issues.* 32:63–84.

Connor, Jane Marantz, Maxine Schackman, and Lisa A. Serbin. 1978. "Sex-Related Differences in Response to Practice on a Visual–Spatial Test and Generalization to a Related Test." *Child Development.* 49:24–29.

Connor, Jane M., and Lisa A. Serbin. 1985. "Visual–Spatial Skill: Is It Important for Mathematics? Can It Be Taught?" Pp. 151–174 in Susan F. Chipman, Lorelei R. Brush, and Donna M. Wilson (Eds.). *Women and Mathematics: Balancing the Equation.* Hillsdale, N.J.: Erlbaum.

Connor, Patricia Joan, and Alice Abel Kemp. 1987. "Gender Differences in Labor Market Wages: A Comparison of Industrial Sector Effects and a Decomposition Within Four Occupations." *Social Science Journal.* 24:429–442.

Constaninople, Anne. 1973. "Masculinity–Femininity: An Exception to a Famous Dictum." *Psychological Bulletin.* 80:389–407.

Cook, Alice H. 1984. "Introduction." Pp. 3–36 in Alice H. Cook, Val. R. Lorwin, and Arlene Kaplan Daniels (Eds.). *Women and Trade Unions in Eleven Industrialized Countries.* Philadelphia: Temple University Press.

Cook, Ellen Piel. 1985. *Psychological Androgyny.* New York: Pergamon Press.

Coontz, Stephanie, and Peta Henderson. 1986a. "Introduction: 'Explanations of Male Dominance.'" Pp. 1–42 in Stephanie Coontz and Peta Henderson (Eds.). *Women's Work, Men's Property: The Origins of Gender and Class.* London: Verso.

Coontz, Stephanie, and Peta Henderson. 1986b. "Property Forms, Political Power, and Female Labour in the Origins of Class and State Societies." Pp. 108–155 in Stephanie Coontz and Peta Henderson (Eds.). *Women's Work, Men's Property: The Origins of Gender and Class.* London: Verso.

Cooper, Kathryn L., and David L. Gutmann. 1987. "Gender Identity and Ego Mastery Style in Middle Aged, Pre– and Post–Empty Nest Women." *Gerontologist.* 27:347–352.

Corballis, M. C., and I. L. Beale. 1983. *The Ambivalent Mind: The Neuropsychology of Left and Right.* Chicago: Nelson-Hall.

Corcoran, Mary, and Greg J. Duncan. 1979. "Work History, Labor Force Attachment and Earnings Differences Between Races and Sexes." *Journal of Human Resources.* 14:3–20.

Cosby, Bill. 1975. "The Regular Way." Pp. 58–62 in John W. Petras (Ed.). *Sex Male Gender Masculine: Selected Readings in Male Sexuality.* Port Washington, N.Y.: Alfred Publishing.

Coser, Lewis A. 1974. "Some Aspects of Soviet Family Policy." Pp. 412–429 in Rose Laub Coser (Ed.). *The Family: Its Structures and Functions* (2nd ed.). New York: St. Martin's Press.

Cott, Nancy. 1987. *The Grounding of Modern Feminism.* New Haven, Conn.: Yale University Press.

Courtney, Alice E., and Thomas W. Whipple. 1983. *Sex Stereotyping in Advertising.* Lexington, Mass.: Lexington Books.

Coverdill, James E. 1988. "The Dual Economy and Sex Differences in Earnings." *Social Forces.* 66:970–993.

Coverman, Shelley. 1985. "Explaining Husbands' Participation in Domestic Labor." *Sociological Quarterly.* 26:81–97.

Coverman, Shelley. 1986. "Occupational Segmentation and Sex Differences in Earnings." Pp. 139–172 in Robert V. Robinson (Ed.). *Research in Social Stratification and Mobility: A Research Annual.* Greenwich, Conn.: JAI Press.

Cowan, Carolyn Pope, and Philip A. Cowan. 1987. "Men's Involvement in Parenthood: Identifying the Antecedents and Understanding the Barriers." Pp. 145–174 in Phyllis W. Berman and Frank A. Pedersen (Eds.). *Men's Transitions to Parenthood: Longitudinal Studies of Early Family Experience.* Hillsdale, N.J.: Erlbaum.

Crosby, Faye, and Gregory M. Herek. 1986. "Male Sympathy with the Situation of Women: Does Personal Experience Make a Difference?" *Journal of Social Issues.* 42:55–66.

Crouse, James, and Dale Trusheim. 1988. *The Case Against the SAT.* Chicago: University of Chicago Press.

Crowley, Joan E. 1985. "Longitudinal Effects of Retirement on Men: Psychological and Physical Well-Being." Pp. 147–173 in Herbert S. Parnes, Joan E. Crowley, R. Jean Haurin, Lawrence J. Less, William R. Morgan, Frank L. Mott, and Gilbert Nestel. *Retirement Among American Men.* Lexington, Mass.: Lexington Books.

Dalla Costa, Mariarosa. 1972. "Women and the Subversion of Community." *Radical America.* 6:67–102.

Daly, Mary. 1978. *Gyn/ecology: The Metaethics of Radical Feminism.* Boston: Beacon Press.

D'Andrade, Roy G. 1966. "Sex Differences and Cultural Institutions." Pp. 173–203 in Eleanor E. Maccoby (Ed.). *The Development of Sex Differences.* Stanford, Calif.: Stanford University Press.

Daniels, Arlene Kaplan. 1988. *Invisible Careers: Women Civic Leaders from the Volunteer World.* Chicago: University of Chicago Press.

Darcy, R., and Charles D. Hadley. 1988. "Black Women in Politics: The Puzzle of Success." *Social Science Quarterly.* 69:629–645.

Darcy, R., and Sunhee Song. 1986. "Men and Women in the South Korean National Assembly: Social Barriers to Representational Roles." *Asian Survey.* 26:670–687.

Darcy, R., Susan Welch, and Janet Clark. 1985. "Women Candidates in Single- and Multi-Member Districts: American State Legislative Races." *Social Science Quarterly.* 66:945–953.

Darien, Jean C. 1976. "Factors Influencing the Rising Labor Force Participation Rates of Married Women with Pre-School Children." *Social Science Quarterly.* 56:614–630.

Davidson, Marilyn J., and Cary L. Cooper. (Eds.). 1984. *Working Women: An Interational Survey.* Chicester, Eng., and New York: Wiley.

Davidson, Marilyn J., and Cary L. Cooper. 1986. "Executive Women Under Pressure." *International Review of Applied Psychology*. 35:301–326.

Davis, Denis J. 1987. "Do You Want Your Daughter or Son in Your Trade? A Study of the Attitudes of Job Incumbents to Females Entering Male-Dominated Trades." *Comparative Education*. 23:279–285.

Davis, Fred. 1988. "Clothing, Fashion, and the Dialectic of Identity." Pp. 23–38 in David R. Maines and Carl J. Couch (Eds.). *Communication and Social Structure*. Springfield, Ill.: Chas C. Thomas.

Davis, P. G., and R. D. Gandelman. 1972. "Pup-Killing Produced by the Administration of Testosterone Propionate to Adult Female Mice." *Hormones and Behavior*. 3:169–173.

Dean, Dwight G., Rita Braito, Edward A. Powers, and Brent Bruton. 1975. "Cultural Contradictions and Sex Roles Revisited: A Replication and a Reassessment." *Sociological Quarterly*. 16:207–215.

Deaux, Kay. 1985. "Sex and Gender." *Annual Review of Psychology*. 36:49–81.

Deaux, Kay, and Brenda Major. 1987. "Putting Gender into Context: An Interactive Model of Gender-Related Behavior." *Psychological Review*. 94:369–389.

Deaux, Kay, and Joseph Ullman. 1983. *Women of Steel*. New York: Praeger.

Deckard, Barbara Sinclair. 1983. *The Women's Movement: Political, Socioeconomic and Psychological Issues*. New York: Harper and Row.

Deckard, Barbara, and Howard Sherman. 1974. "Monopoly Power and Sex Discrimination." *Politics and Society*. 4:475–482.

Deere, Carmen Diana, and Magdalena Leon. (Eds.). 1987. *Rural Women and State Policy: Feminist Perspectives on Latin American Agricultural Development*. Boulder, Colo.: Westview Press.

DeFleur, Lois B. 1985. "Organizational and Ideological Barriers to Sex Integration in Military Groups." *Work and Occupations*. 12:206–228.

Deitch, Cynthia. 1988. "Sex Differences in Support for Government Spending." Pp. 192–216 in Carol M. Mueller (Ed.). *The Politics of the Gender Gap: The Social Construction of Political Influence*. Newbury Park, Calif.: Sage.

Delphy, Christine. 1984. *Close to Home: A Materialist Analysis of Women's Oppression*. (Diana Leonard, Trans. and Ed.) Amherst: University of Massachusetts Press.

DeKeseredy, Walter S. 1990. "Woman Abuse in Dating Relationships: The Contribution of Male Peer Support." *Sociological Inquiry*. 60:236–243.

DeLorey, Catherine. 1984. "Health Care and Midlife Women." Pp. 277–301 in Grace Baruch and Jeanne Brooks-Gunn (Eds.). *Women in Midlife*. New York: Plenum.

Depner, Charlene, and Berit Ingersoll. 1982. "Employment Status and Social Support: The Experience of the Mature Woman." Pp. 61–76 in Maximiliane Szinovacz (Ed.). *Women's Retirement: Policy Implications of Recent Research*. Beverly Hills, Calif.: Sage.

deTurck, Mark A., and Gerald R. Miller. 1986. "The Effects of Husbands' and Wives' Social Cognition on Their Marital Adjustment, Conjugal Power, and Self-Esteem." *Journal of Marriage and the Family*. 48:715–724.

Deutsch, Helene. 1944–45. *The Psychology of Women: A Psychoanalytic Interpretation: Vol. 1. Girlhood, Vol. 2. Motherhood*. New York: Bantam.

DeVault, Marjorie L. 1987. "Doing Housework: Feeding and Family Life." Pp. 178–191 in Naomi Gerstel and Harriet Engle Gross (Eds.). *Families and Work*. Philadelphia: Temple University Press.

DeVore, Irven. 1963. "Mother–Infant Relations in Free Ranging Baboons." Pp. 305–335 in H. L. Rheingold (Ed.). *Maternal Behavior in Mammals*. New York: Wiley.

DeVore, Irven. 1965. *Primate Behavior: Field Studies of Monkeys and Apes*. New York: Holt, Rinehart, & Winston.

DeVore, L., and Washburn, S. L. 1963. "Baboon Ecology and Human Evolution." Pp. 335–367 in F. C. Howell and F. Bourliere (Eds.). *African Ecology and Human Evolution*. Chicago: Aldine.

DeWaal, Frans. 1982. *Chimpanzee Politics: Power and Sex Among Apes*. New York: Harper & Row.

Diamond, Irene. 1977. *Sex Roles in the State House*. New Haven, Conn.: Yale University Press.

Diamond, Milton. 1965. "A Critical Evaluation of the Ontogeny of Human Sexual Behavior." *Quarterly Review of Biology*. 40:147–175.

Diamond, Milton. 1976. "Human Sexual Development: Biological Foundations for Sexual Development." Pp. 22–61 in F. Beach (Ed.). *Human Sexuality in Four Perspectives*. Baltimore: Johns Hopkins University Press.

Diamond, Milton. 1982. "Sexual Identity, Monozygotic Twins Reared in Discordant Sex Roles and a BBC Follow-Up." *Archives of Sexual Behavior*. 11:181–186.

DiBenedetto, Barbara, and Carol Kehr Tittle. 1990. "Gender and Adult Roles: Role Commitment of Women and Men in a Job-Family Trade-Off Context." *Journal of Counseling Psychology*. 37:41–48.

Dickens, William T. and Kevin Lang. 1985. "A Test of Dual Labor Market Theory." *American Economic Review*. 75:792–805.

Dickens, William T. and Kevin Lang. 1986. "Where Have All the Good Jobs Gone? Deindustrialization and Labor Market Segmentation." Pp. 90–102 in Kevin Lang and Jonathan S. Leonard (Eds.). *Unemployment and the Structure of Labor Markets*. New York: Basil Blackwell.

Dinnerstein, Dorothy. 1976. *The Mermaid and the Minotaur: Sexual Arrangements and Human Malaise*. New York: Harper & Row.

DiPrete, Thomas A. 1987. "The Professionalization of Administration and Equal Employment Opportunity in the U.S. Federal Government." *American Journal of Sociology*. 93:119–140.

DiPrete, Thomas A., and David B. Grusky. 1990. "Structure and Trend in the Process of Stratification for American Men and Women." *American Journal of Sociology*. 96:107–143.

DiPrete, Thomas A., and Whitman Soule. 1986. "The Organization of Career Lines: Equal Employment Opportunity and Status Advancement in a Federal Bureaucracy." *American Sociological Review*. 51:295–309.

DiPrete, Thomas A., and Whitman Soule. 1988. "Gender and Promotion in Segmented Job Ladder Systems." *American Sociological Review*. 53:26–40.

Dobash, R. Emerson, and Russell Dobash. 1979. *Violence Against Wives*. New York: Free Press.

Docter, Richard F. 1988. *Transvestites and Transsexuals: Toward a Theory of Cross-Gender Behavior*. New York: Plenum.

Doering, C. H., H. Kraemer, H. Brodie, and D. Hamburg. 1975. "A Cycle of Plasma Testosterone in the Human Male." *Journal of Clinical Endocrinology*. 40:492–500.

Donovan, Josephine. 1985. *Feminist Theory: The Intellectual Traditions of American Feminism*. New York: Frederick Ungar.

Douvan, Elizabeth, and Joseph Adelson. 1966. *The Adolescent Experience*. New York: Wiley.

Draper, Patricia. 1985. "Two Views of Sex Differences in Socialization." Pp. 5–25 in Roberta L. Hall, with Patricia Draper, Margaret E. Hamilton, Diane McGuinness, Charlotte M. Otten, and Eric A. Roth. *Male–Female Differences: A Bio-Cultural Perspective*. New York: Praeger.

Droppleman, L. F., and E. S. Schaefer. 1963. "Boys' and Girls' Reports of Maternal and Paternal Behavior." *Journal of Abnormal and Social Psychology*. 67:648–654.

Dube, Leela. 1986. "Introduction." Pp. xiv–xliv in Leela Dube, Eleanor Leacock, and Shirley Ardener (Eds.). *Visibility and Power: Essays on Women in Society and Development*. Delhi: Oxford University Press.

Duncan, Greg J. 1984. *Years of Poverty, Years of Plenty*. Ann Arbor, Mich.: Institute for Social Research.

Durkheim, Emile. 1933. *Emile Durkheim on the Division of Labor in Society* (trans. by W. O. Halls). New York: MacMillan (originally published in 1892).

Dutton, Donald G. 1988. *The Domestic Assault of Women: Psychological and Criminal Justice Perspectives*. Boston: Allyn & Bacon.

Dyer, K. F. 1985. "Making Up the Difference: Some Explanations for Recent Improvements in Women's Athletic Performances." *Search*. 16:264–269.

Dyer, K. F. 1986. "The Trend of the Male–Female Differential in Various Speed Sports 1936–1984." *Journal of Biosocial Science*. 18:169–177.

Dyrud, Jarl. 1976. "Toward a Science of the Passions." *Saturday Review*. February 21, pp. 22–27.

Eagly, Alice H. 1987. *Sex Differences in Social Behavior: A Social-Role Interpretation*. Hillsdale, N.J.: Erlbaum.

Eagly, Alice H., and Maureen Crowley. 1986. "Gender and Helping Behavior: A Meta-Analytic Review of the Social Psychological Literature." *Psychological Bulletin*. 100:283–308.

Eagly, Alice H., and Valerie J. Steffen. 1986a. "Gender and Aggressive Behavior: A Meta-Analytic Review of the Social Psychological Literature." *Psychological Bulletin*. 100:309–330.

Eagly, Alice H., and Valerie J. Steffen. 1986b. "Gender Stereotypes, Occupational Roles, and Beliefs About Part-Time Employees." *Psychology of Women Quarterly*. 10:252–262.

Eagly, Alice H., and Wendy Wood. 1985. "Gender and Influenceability: Stereotype Versus Behavior." Pp. 225–256 in Virginia E. O'Leary, Rhoda Kesler Unger, and Barbara Strudler Wallston (Eds.). *Women, Gender, and Social Psychology*. Hillsdale, N.J.: Erlbaum.

Eaton, Warren O., and Lesley Reid Enns. 1986. "Sex Differences in Human Motor Activity Level." *Psychological Bulletin*. 100:19–28.

Eccles (Parsons), Jacquelynne. 1983. "Expectancies, Values, and Academic Behaviors." Pp. 75–146 in Janet T. Spence (Ed.). *Achievement and Achievement Motives: Psychological and Sociological Approaches*. San Francisco: Freeman.

Eder, Donna, and Stephanie Sanford. 1986. "The Development and Maintenance of Interactional Norms Among Early Adolescents." *Sociological Studies of Child Development*. 1:283–300.

Edwards, D. A. 1969. "Early Androgen Stimulation and Aggressive Behavior in Male and Female Mice." *Physiology and Behavior*. 4:333–338.

Edwards, Richard. 1979. *Contested Terrain: The Transformation of the Workplace in the Twentieth Century*. New York: Basic Books.

Ehrenreich, Barbara. 1983. *The Hearts of Men: American Dreams and the Flight from Commitment*. New York: Anchor Books.

Ehrenreich, Barbara, and Deirdre English. 1976. "The Manufacture of Housework." Pp. 7–42 in Mina Davis Caulfield et al. (Eds.). *Capitalism and the Family*. San Francisco: Agenda.

Ehrensaft, Diane. 1985. "Dual Parenting and the Duel of Intimacy." Pp. 323–337 in Gerald Handel (Ed.). *The Psychosocial Interior of the Family* (3rd ed.). New York: Aldine.

Ehrensaft, Diane. 1987. *Parenting Together: Men and Women Sharing the Care of Their Children*. New York: Free Press.

Ehrhardt, Anke A. 1973. "Maternalism in Fetal Hormonal and Related Syndromes." Pp. 99–116 in Joseph Zubin and John Money (Eds.). *Contemporary Sexual Behavior: Critical Issues in the 1970's*. Baltimore: Johns Hopkins University Press.

Ehrhardt, Anke A. 1985. "Gender Differences: A Biosocial Perspective." Pp. 37–57 in Theo B. Sonderegger (Ed.). *Nebraska Symposium on Motivation, 1984: Psychology and Gender*. Lincoln: University of Nebraska Press.

Ehrhardt, Anke A., and Susan W. Baker. 1974. "Fetal Androgens, Human Central Nervous System, Differentiation, and Behavior Sex Differences." Pp. 33–52 in R. C. Friedman et al. (Eds.). *Sex Differences in Behavior*. New York: Wiley.

Ehrhardt, Anke A., and H. F. L. Meyer-Bahlburg. 1981. "The Effects of Prenatal Hormones on Gender Identity, Sex-Dimorphic Behavior, Sexual Orientation, and Cognition." *Science*. 211:1312–1318.

Eichenbaum, Luise, and Susie Orbach. 1983. *Understanding Women: A Feminist Psychoanalytic Approach*. New York: Basic Books.

Eisenhart, Margaret A., and Dorothy C. Holland. 1983. "Learning Gender from Peers: The Role of Peer Groups in the Cultural Transmission of Gender." *Human Organization*. 42:321–332.

Eisenhart, R. Wayne. 1975. "You Can't Hack It, Little Girl: A Discussion of the Covert Psychological Agenda of Modern Combat Training." *Journal of Social Issues*. 31:13–23.

El Guindi, Fadwa. 1986. "The Egyptian Woman: Trends Today, Alternatives Tomorrow." Pp. 225–242 in Lynne B. Itlitzin and Ruth Ross (Eds.). *Women in the World: 1975–1985 The Women's Decade* (2nd rev. ed.). Santa Barbara, Calif.: ABC–Clio.

Ember, Carol R. 1981. "A Cross-Cultural Perspective on Sex Differences." Pp. 531–583 in Ruth H. Munroe, Robert L. Munroe, and Beatrice B. Whiting (Eds.). *Handbook of Cross-Cultural Human Development*. New York: Garland.

Ember, Carol R. 1983. "The Relative Decline in Women's Contribution to Agriculture with Intensification." *American Anthropologist.* 85:285–304.

Emmons, Carol-Ann, Monica Biernat, Linda Beth Tiedje, Eric L. Lang, and Camille B. Wortman. 1990. "Stress, Support, and Coping Among Women Professionals with Preschool Children." Pp. 61–93 in John Eckenrode and Susan Gore (Eds.). *Stress Between Work and Family.* New York: Plenum Press.

Employment and Earnings. 1991. Volume 38.

Enarson, Elaine. 1984. *Woodsworking Women: Sexual Integration in the U.S. Forest Service.* Birmingham: University of Alabama Press.

Engels, Frederick. 1972. *The Origin of the Family, Private Property, and the State* (Eleanor Leacock, ed.). New York: International Publishers. (Originally published 1884.)

England, Paula, and Dana Dunn. 1988. "Evaluating Work and Comparable Worth." *Annual Review of Sociology.* 14:227–248.

England, Paula, and George Farkas. 1986. *Households, Employment, and Gender.* New York: Aldine.

England, Paula, George Farkas, Barbara Stanek Kilbourne, and Thomas Dou. 1988. "Explaining Occupational Sex Segregation and Wages: Findings from a Model with Fixed Effects." *American Sociological Review.* 53:544–558.

England, Paula, and Lori McCreary. 1987a. "Gender Inequality in Paid Employment." Pp. 286–320 in Beth B. Hess and Myra Marx Ferree (Eds.). *Analyzing Gender: A Handbook of Social Science Research.* Newbury Park, Calif.: Sage.

England, Paula, and Lori McCreary. 1987b. "Integrating Sociology and Economics to Study Gender and Work." Pp. 143–172 in Ann H. Stromberg, Laurie Larwood, and Barbara Gutek (Eds.). *Women and Work: An Annual Review* (Vol. 2). Newbury Park, Calif.: Sage.

Englander-Golden, Paula, Frank J. Sonleitner, Mary R. Whitmore, and Gail J. M. Corbley. 1986. "Social and Menstrual Cycles: Methodological and Substantive Findings." Pp. 77–96 in Virginia L. Olesen and Nancy Fugate Woods (Eds.). *Culture, Society, and Menstruation.* Washington, D.C.: Hemisphere.

Epstein, Cynthia Fuchs. 1970. "Encountering the Male Establishment: Sex Status Limits on Women's Careers in the Professions." *American Journal of Sociology.* 75:965–982.

Epstein, Cynthia Fuchs. 1981. *Women in Law.* New York: Basic Books.

Epstein, Cynthia Fuchs. 1974. "Reconciliation of Women's Roles." Pp. 473–489 in Rose L. Coser (Ed.). *The Family: Its Structures and Functions* (2nd ed.). New York: St. Martin's Press.

Epstein, Cynthia Fuchs. 1988. *Deceptive Distinctions: Sex, Gender, and the Social Order.* New Haven: Yale University Press.

Epstein, Cynthia Fuchs, and Rose Laub Coser. (Eds.). 1981. *Access to Power: Cross-National Studies of Women and Elites.* London: Allen & Unwin.

Ericsson, Ylva. 1985. "Sweden." Pp. 138–146 in Jennie Farley (Ed.). *Women Workers in Fifteen Countries: Essays in Honor of Alice Hanson Cook.* Ithaca, N.Y.: ILR Press.

Ericksen, Karen Paige. 1984. "Menstrual Symptoms and Menstrual Beliefs: National and Cross-National Patterns." Pp. 175–187 in Benson E. Ginsburg and Bonnie Frank Carter (Eds.). *Premenstrual Syndrome: Ethical and Legal Implications in a Biomedical Perspective.* New York: Plenum.

Erikson, Erik H. 1959. "Identity and the Life Cycle." *Psychological Issues.* 1:18–171.

Erikson, Erik H. 1968. *Identity: Youth and Crisis.* New York: Norton.

Escalona, Sibylle. 1949. "The Psychological Situation of Mother and Child Upon Return from the Hospital." In Milton J. E. Senn (Ed.). *Problems of Infancy and Childhood: Transactions of the Third Conference.* New York: Josiah Macy, Jr., Foundation.

Fabes, Richard A., and Erik E. Filsinger. 1988. "Odor Communication and Parent–Child Interaction." Pp. 93–118 in Erik E. Filsinger (Ed.). *Biosocial Perspectives on the Family.* Newbury Park, Calif.: Sage.

Fagan, Jeffrey A., Douglas K. Stewart, and Karen V. Hansen. 1983. "Violent Men or Violent

Husbands? Background Factors and Situational Correlates." Pp. 49–67 in David Finkelhor, Richard J. Gelles, Gerald T. Hotaling, and Murray A. Straus (Eds.). *The Dark Side of Families: Current Family Violence Research.* Beverly Hills, Calif.: Sage.

Fagot, Beverly I. 1978. "The Influence of Sex of Child on Parental Reactions to Toddler Children." *Child Development.* 49:459–465.

Fagot, Beverly I. 1981. "Continuity and Changes in Play Styles as a Function of Sex of the Child." *International Journal of Behavioral Development.* 4:37–43.

Fagot, Beverly I. 1985a. "Beyond the Reinforcement Principle: Another Step Toward Understanding Sex Role Development." *Developmental Psychology.* 21:1097–1104.

Fagot, Beverly I. 1985b. "Changes in Thinking About Early Sex Role Development." *Developmental Review.* 5:83–98.

Fagot, Beverly I., and Richard Hagan. 1985. "Aggression in Toddlers: Responses to the Assertive Acts of Boys and Girls." *Aggression.* 12:341–351.

Fagot, Beverly I., Richard Hagan, Mary Driver Leinbach, and Sandra Kronsberg. 1985. "Differential Reactions to Assertive and Communicative Acts of Toddler Boys and Girls." *Child Development.* 56:1499–1505.

Fagot, Beverly I., and Mary Driver Leinbach. 1985. "Gender Identity: Some Thoughts on an Old Concept." *Journal of the American Academy of Child Psychiatry.* 24:684–688.

Fagot, Beverly I., and Mary Driver Leinbach. 1987. "Socialization of Sex Roles within the Family." Pp. 89–100 in D. B. Carter (Ed.). *Current Conceptions of Sex Roles and Sex Typing: Theory and Research.* New York: Praeger.

Fagot, Beverly I., and Mary Driver Leinbach. 1989. "The Young Child's Gender Schema: Environmental Input, Internal Organization." *Child Development.* 60:663–672.

Fagot, Beverly I., Mary Driver Leinbach, and Richard Hagan. 1986. "Gender Labeling and the Adoption of Sex-Typed Behaviors." *Developmental Psychology.* 22:655–666.

Fairbairn, Ronald. 1952. *An Object-Relations Theory of the Personality.* New York: Basic Books.

Falk, Gail. 1975. "Sex Discrimination in the Trade Unions: Legal Resources for Change." Pp. 254–276 in Jo Freeman (Ed.). *Women: A Feminist Perspective.* Palo Alto, Calif.: Mayfield.

Farber, Naomi. 1990. "The Significance of Race and Class in Marital Decisions Among Unmarried Adolescent Mothers." *Social Problems.* 37:51–63.

Farley, Lin. 1978. *Sexual Shakedown: The Sexual Harrassment of Women on the Job.* New York: McGraw-Hill.

Farmer, Helen S., and Joan Seliger Sidney. 1985. "Sex Equity in Career and Vocational Education." Pp. 338–359 in Susan S. Klein (Ed.). *Handbook for Achieving Sex Equity Through Education.* Baltimore: Johns Hopkins University Press.

Fassinger, Polly A. 1989. "The Impact of Gender and Past Marital Experiences on Heading a Household Alone. Pp. 165–180 in Barbara J. Risman and Pepper Schwartz (Eds.). *Gender in Intimate Relationships: A Microstructural Approach.* Belmont, Calif.: Wadsworth.

Fast, Irene. 1984. *Gender Identity: A Differentiation Model.* Hillsdale, N.J.: Erlbaum.

Fausto-Sterling, Anne. 1985. *Myths of Gender: Biological Theories About Women and Men.* New York: Basic Books.

Faver, Catherine A. 1984. *Women in Transition: Career, Family, and Life Satisfaction in Three Cohorts.* New York: Praeger.

Fedigan, Linda Marie. 1982. *Primate Paradigms: Sex Roles and Social Bonds.* Montreal: Eden Press.

Fedigan, Linda Marie. 1986. "The Changing Role of Women in Models of Human Evolution." *Annual Review of Anthropology.* 15:25–66.

Fedigan, Linda Marie and Laurence Fedigan. 1989. "Gender and the Study of Primates." Pp. 41–64 in Sandra Morgen (Ed.). *Gender and Anthropology: Critical Reviews of Research and Teaching.* Washington, D.C.: American Anthropological Asssociation.

Felmlee, Diane H. 1988. "Returning to School and Women's Occupational Attainment." *Sociology of Education.* 61:29–41.

Ferber, Marianne A., Carole A. Green, and Joe L. Spaeth. 1986. "Work Power and Earnings of Women and Men." *AEA Papers and Proceedings.* 76:53–56.

Ferguson, Marjorie. 1983. *Forever Feminine: Women's Magazines and the Cult of Femininity.* London and Exeter, N.H.: Heinemann.

Fernandez, John P. 1986. *Child Care and Corporate Productivity: Resolving Family/Work Conflicts.* Lexington, Mass.: Lexington Books.

Fernandez-Kelly, M. Patricia and Anna M. Garcia. 1990. "Power Surrendered, Power Restored: The Politics of Work and Family Among Hispanic Garment Workers in California and Florida." Pp. 130–149 in Louise A. Tilly and Patricia Gurin (Eds.). *Women, Politics, and Change.* New York: Russell Sage Foundation.

Fernea, Elizabeth Warnock. (Ed.). 1985. *Women and the Family in the Middle East: New Voices of Change.* Austin: University of Texas Press.

Ferree, Myra Marx. 1987. "She Works Hard for a Living: Gender and Class on the Job." Pp. 322–347 in Beth B. Hess and Myra Marx Ferree (Eds.). *Analyzing Gender: A Handbook of Social Science Research.* Newbury Park, Calif.: Sage.

Ferree, Myra Marx and Elaine J. Hall. 1990. "Visual Images of American Society: Gender and Race in Introductory Sociology Textbooks." *Gender and Society.* 4:500–533.

Feshback, N. D. 1969. "Sex Differences in Children's Modes of Aggressive Responses Towards Outsiders." *Merrill-Palmer Quarterly.* 15:249–258.

Fielder, Leslie A. 1968. *The Return of the Vanishing American.* New York: Stein & Day.

Filer, Randall. 1985. "Male-Female Wage Differences: The Importance of Compensating Differentials." *Industrial and Labor Relations Review.* 38:426–437.

Filsinger, Erik E. 1988. "Biology Reexamined: The Quest for Answers." Pp. 9–38 in Erik E. Filsinger (Ed.). *Biosocial Perspectives on the Family.* Newbury Park, Calif.: Sage.

Fine, Gary Alan. 1987. *With the Boys: Little League Baseball and Preadolescent Culture.* Chicago: University of Chicago Press.

Finkelhor, David. 1980. "The Sexual Climate in Families." Mimeograph, Family Violence Research Laboratory, University of New Hampshire, Durham.

Finkelhor, David, and Kersti Yllo. 1985. *License to Rape: Sexual Abuse of Wives.* New York: Holt, Rinehart, & Winston.

Fiorentine, Robert. 1987. "Men, Women and the Premed Persistence Gap: A Normative Alternatives Approach." *American Journal of Sociology.* 92:1118–1139.

Fiorito, Jack, and Charles R. Greer. 1986. "Gender Differences in Union Membership, Preferences, and Beliefs." *Journal of Labor Research.* 7:145–164.

Firestone, Shulamith. 1971. *The Dialectic of Sex.* New York: Bantam.

Fischer, Lucy Rose. 1986. *Linked Lives: Adult Daughters and Their Mothers.* New York: Harper & Row.

Fishman, Pamela M. 1983. "Interaction: The Work Women Do." Pp. 89–101 in Barrie Thorne, Cheris Kramarae, and Nancy Henley (Eds.). *Language, Gender and Society.* Rowley, Mass.: Newbury House.

Fletcher, Jean, and Sandra K. Gill. Forthcoming. "Union Density and Women's Relative Wage Gains: An International Comparison." Barbara Bergmann and Nancy Folber (Eds.). *Women in the World Economy.* London: Macmillan.

Fliegel, Zenia Odes. 1986. "Women's Development in Analytic Theory: Six Decades of Controversy." Pp. 3–31 in Judith L. Alpert (Ed.). *Psychoanalysis and Women: Contemporary Reappraisals.* New York: Analytic Press.

Fliess, Robert. 1961. *Ego and Body Ego: Contributions to Their Psychoanalytic Psychology.* New York: Schulte.

Flint, Marcha. 1982. "Male and Female Menopause: A Cultural Put-On." Pp. 363–375 in Ann M. Voda, Myra Dinnerstein, and Sheryl R. O'Donnell (Eds.). *Changing Perspectives on Menopause.* Austin: University of Texas Press.

Foner, Philip S. 1987. "Women and the American Labor Movement: A Historical Perspective." Pp. 154–186 in Karen Shallcross Koziara, Michael H. Moskow, and Lucretia Dewey Tanner (Eds.). *Working Women: Past, Present, Future.* Washington, D.C.: Buerau of National Affairs.

Foreman, Laura. 1977. "Congress Facing Proposals to Improve Its Standards as an Employer." *New York Times.* August 13, p. I.7.

Fowlkes, Martha R. 1987. "The Myth of Merit and Male Professional Careers: The Roles of Wives." Pp. 347–360 in Naomi Gerstel and Harriet Engel Gross (Eds.). *Families and Work.* Philadelphia: Temple University Press.

Fox, Mary Frank. 1981. "Sex, Salary, and Achievement: Reward-Dualism in Academia." *Sociology of Education.* 54:71–84.

Franklin, Clyde W. II. 1984. *The Changing Definition of Masculinity.* New York: Plenum.

Freeman, J. 1975. "How to Discriminate Against Women Without Really Trying." Pp. 194–208 in Jo Freeman (Ed.). *Women: A Feminist Perspective.* Palo Alto, Calif.: Mayfield.

Freeman, Jo. 1986. "The Quest for Equality: The ERA vs. Other Means." Pp. 46–78 in Winston A. Van Horne (Ed.). *Ethnicity and Women.* Milwaukee: University of Wisconsin System American Ethnic Studies Coordinating Committee.

Freeman, Jo. 1990. "From Protection to Equal Opportunity: The Revolution in Women's Legal Status." Pp. 457–481 in Louise A. Tilly and Patricia Gurin (Eds.). *Women, Politics, and Change.* New York: Russell Sage Foundation.

Freeman, Richard B. 1984. "Affirmative Action: Good, Bad, or Irrelevant?" *New Perspectives.* 16:23–27.

Freud, Sigmund. 1933. "Femininity." Pp. 112–135 in *New Introductory Lectures in Psychoanalysis.* New York: Norton.

Freud, Sigmund. 1963a. "Female Sexuality." Pp. 194–211 in *Sexuality and the Psychology of Love* (Philip Reiff, ed.). New York: Collier. (Originally published 1931.)

Freud, Sigmund. 1963b. "The Most Prevalent Form of Degradation in Erotic Life." Pp. 58–70 in *Sexuality and the Psychology of Love* (Philip Reiff, ed.). New York: Collier. (Originally published 1912.)

Freud, Sigmund. 1963c. "Some Psychological Consequences of the Anatomical Distinction Between the Sexes." Pp. 183–193 in *Sexuality and the Psychology of Love* (Philip Reiff, ed.). New York: Collier. (Originally published 1925.)

Freud, Sigmund. 1963d. "The Taboo of Virginity." Pp. 70–86 in *Sexuality and the Psychology of Love* (Philip Reiff, ed.). New York: Collier. (Originally published 1918.)

Freud, Sigmund. 1969. *An Outline of Psychoanalysis.* New York: Norton. (Originally published 1940.)

Freyd, Jennifer. 1990. "Faculty Members with Young Children Need More Flexible Schedules." *Chronicle of Higher Education,* February 21, p. B2.

Friedan, Betty. 1963. *The Feminine Mystique.* New York: Dell.

Friedl, Ernestine. 1975. *Women and Men: An Anthropologist's View.* New York: Holt, Rinehart, & Winston.

Friedman, Lynn. 1989. "Mathematics and the Gender Gap: A Meta-Analysis of Recent Studies on Sex Differences in Mathematical Tasks." *Review of Educational Research.* 59:185–213.

Frieze, Irene H., Jacquelynne E. Parsons, Paula B. Johnson, Diane N. Ruble, and Gail L. Zellman. 1978. *Women and Sex Roles: A Social Psychological Perspective.* New York: Norton.

Frisch, R. E., and R. Revelle. 1969. "The Height and Weight of Adolescent Boys and Girls at the Time of Peak Velocity of Growth in Height and Weight: Longitudinal Data." *Human Biology.* 41:536–559.

Frisch, R. E., and R. Revelle. 1970. "Height and Weight at Menarche and a Hypothesis of Critical Body Weights and Adolescent Events." *Science.* 169:397–399.

Frisch, R. E., and R. Revelle. 1971a. "Height and Weight at Menarche and a Hypothesis of Menarche." *Archives of Disease in Childhood.* 46:695–701.

Frische, R. E., and R. Revelle. 1971b. "The Height and Weight of Girls and Boys at the Time of Initiation of the Adolescent Growth Spurt in Height and Weight and the Relationship to Menarche." *Human Biology.* 43:140–159.

Frodi, Ann, Jacqueline Macaulay, and Pauline Ropert-Thome. 1977. "Are Women Always Less

Aggressive than Men? A Reivew of the Experimental Literature." *Psychological Bulletin*. 84:634–660.

Fry, William. 1972. "Psycho-Dynamics of Sexual Humor: Women's View of Sex." *Medical Aspects of Human Sexuality*. 6:124–139.

Fuchs, Victor R. 1988. *Women's Quest for Economic Equality*. Cambridge, Mass.: Harvard University Press.

Fulbright, Karen. 1986. "The Myth of the Double-Advantage: Black Female Managers. Pp. 33–45 in Margaret C. Simms and Julianne Malveaux (Eds.). *Slipping Through the Cracks: The Status of Black Women*. New Brunswick, N.J.: Transaction Books.

Furstenberg, Frank F., Jr., and J. Brooks-Gunn. 1989. "Causes and Consequences of Teenage Pregnancy and Childbearing." Pp. 71–100 in Martha N. Ozawa (Ed.). *Women's Life Cycle and Economic Insecurity: Problems and Proposals*. New York: Greenwood Press.

Furstenberg, Frank F., Jr., J. Brooks-Gunn, and S. Philip Morgan. 1987. *Adolescent Mothers in Later Life*. Cambridge, Eng.: Cambridge University Press.

Gailey, Christine Ward. 1987. *Kinship to Kingship*. Austin: University of Texas Press.

Galenson, Eleanor. 1986. "Early Pathways to Female Sexuality in Advantaged and Disadvantaged Girls." Pp. 37–48 in Toni Bernay and Dorothy W. Cantor (Eds.). *The Psychology of Today's Woman: New Psychoanalytic Visions*. New York: Analytic Press.

Galenson, Eleanor, and Herman Roiphe. 1974. "The Emergence of Genital Awareness During the Second Year of Life." Pp. 223–232 in R. C. Friedman et al. (Eds.). *Sex Differences in Behavior*. New York: Wiley.

Galenson, Marjorie. 1973. *Women and Work: An International Comparison*. Ithaca: Publications Division, New York School of Industrial Labor Relations, Cornell University.

Gallup, George. 1988. "Campaign Issues." *The Gallup Report*, Report #273, July, pp. 4–17.

Gallup, Gordon G., Jr. 1986. "Unique Features of Human Sexuality in the Context of Evolution." Pp. 13–42 in Donn Byrne and Kathryn Kelley (Eds.). *Alternative Approaches to the Study of Sexual Behavior*. Hillsdale, N.J.: Erlbaum.

Garai, J. E., and Aram Scheinfeld. 1968. "Sex Differences in Mental and Behavior Traits." *Genetic Psychology Monographs*. 77:169–299.

Gardner, Howard. 1983. *Frames of Mind*. New York: Basic Books.

Garfinkel, Irwin, and Sara S. McLanahan. 1986. *Single Mothers and Their Children: A New American Dilemma*. Washington, D.C.: Urban Institute.

Gaskell, Jane. 1985. "Course Enrollment in the High School: The Perspective of Working-Class Females." *Sociology of Education*. 58:48–59.

Gates, Arthur I. 1961. "Sex Differences in Reading Ability." *Elementary School Journal*. 61:431–434.

Gates, Margaret J. 1976. "Occupational Segregation and the Law." *Signs: Journal of Women in Culture and Society*. 1:61–74.

Gelb, Joyce, and Marian Lief Palley. 1987. *Women and Public Policies*. Princeton, N.J.: Princeton University Press.

Gelinas, Denise J. 1983. "The Persisting Negative Effects of Incest." *Psychiatry*. 46:312–333.

Gelles, Richard J., and Claire Pedrick Cornell. 1985. *Intimate Violence in Families*. Beverly Hills, Calif.: Sage.

Gerson, Kathleen. 1985. *Hard Choices: How Women Decide About Work, Career, and Motherhood*. Berkeley: University of California Press.

Gerson, Judith M., and Kathy Peiss. 1985. "Boundaries, Negotiation, Consciousness: Reconceptualizing Gender Relations." *Social Problems*. 32:317–331.

Giallombardo, Rose. 1966. *Society of Women: A Study of a Women's Prison*. New York: Wiley.

Giele, Janet Z. 1978. *Women and the Future: Changing Sex Roles in Modern America*. New York: Free Press.

Gilbert, Lucia Albino. 1985. *Men in Dual-Career Families: Current Realities and Future Prospects*. Hillsdale, N.J.: Erlbaum.

Gilbert, Lucia A., Gary R. Hanson, and Beverly Davis. 1982. "Perceptions of Parental Role Responsibilities: Differences Between Mothers and Fathers." *Family Relations*. 31:261–269.

Gill, Sandra, Jean Stockard, Miriam Johnson, and Suzanne Williams. 1987. "Measuring Gender Differences: The Expressive Dimension and the Critique of Androgyny Scales." *Sex Roles*. 17:375–400.

Gilligan, Carol. 1978. "In a Different Voice: Women's Conceptions of Self and Morality." *Harvard Educational Review*. 47:481–517.

Gilligan, Carol. 1982. *In a Different Voice: Psychological Theory and Women's Development*. Cambridge, Mass.: Harvard University Press.

Gilligan, Carol, Jane Victoria Ward, and Jill McLean Taylor, with Betty Bardige (Eds.). 1988. *Mapping the Moral Domain: A Contribution of Women's Thinking to Psychological Theory and Education*. Cambridge, Mass.: Harvard University Press.

Gimenez, Martha. 1978. "Structuralist Marxism on 'the Woman Question'." *Science and Society*. 42:301–323.

Gladue, Brian Anthony. 1988. "Biological Influences upon the Development of Sexual Orientation." Pp. 61–91 in Erik E. Filsinger (Ed.). *Biosocial Perspectives on the Family*. Newbury Park, Calif.: Sage.

Goldberg, Gertrude, and Eleanor Kremen. 1987. "The Feminization of Poverty: Only in America?" *Social Policy*. 17:3–14.

Goldberg, Steven. 1974. *The Inevitability of Patriarchy*. New York: Morrow.

Goldberg, Susan, and Michael Lewis. 1969. "Play Behavior in the Year-Old Infant: Early Sex Differences." *Child Development*. 40:21–31.

Goldman, Roy D., and Barbara Newlin Hewitt. 1976. "The Scholastic Aptitude Test Explains Why College Men Major in Science More Often than College Women." *Journal of Counseling Psychology*. 23:50–54.

Goldscheider, Frances Kobrin, and Julie DaVanzo. 1985. "Living Arrangements and the Transition to Adulthood." *Demography*. 22:545–563.

Goldscheider, Frances Kobrin, and Linda J. Waite. 1986. "Sex Differences in the Entry into Marriage." *American Journal of Sociology*. 92:91–109.

Goldsmith, Barbara. 1970. "Grass, Women and Sex: An Interview with Mike Nichols." *Harper's Bazaar*. November, p. 142.

Goodall, Jane. 1968. "The Behavior of Free-Living Chimpanzees of the Gombe Stream Reserve." *Animal Behavior Monographs*. 1:161–311.

Goodall, Jane. 1976. "Continuities Between Chimpanzee and Human Behavior." Pp. 81–95 in G. Isaac and E. R. McCown (Eds.). *Human Origins: Louis Leakey and the East African Evidence*. Menlo Park, Calif.: Benjamin.

Goodenough, Evelyn W. 1957. "Interest in Persons as an Aspect of Sex Difference in the Early Years." *Genetic Psychology Monographs*. 55:287–323.

Goodman, Ellen. 1988. "Women Have 345 Years to Wait." *Durham Morning Herald*. November 15, p. 5a.

Goodman, Ellen. 1990a. "In Politics, Glass Ceiling Got Cracked." *Eugene Register Guard*. November 11, p. 3C.

Goodman, Ellen. 1990b. "'The Ladies' Speak Against War." *The Register Guard*. Eugene, Oregon, December 4, p. 11a.

Goodman, Madeleine, J., P. Bion Griffin, Agnes A. Estioko-Griffin, and John S. Grove. 1985. "The Compatibility of Hunting and Mothering Among the Agta Hunter-Gatherers of the Philippines." *Sex Roles*. 12:1199–1209.

Goodwin, Marjorie H. 1980. "Directive-Response Speech Sequences in Girls' and Boys' Task Activities." In Sally McConnell-Ginet, Ruth A. Borker, and Nell Furman (Eds.). *Women and Language in Literature and Society*. New York: Praeger.

Gordon, Linda, and Paul O'Keefe. 1984. "Incest as a Form of Family Violence: Evidence from Historical Case Records." *Journal of Marriage and the Family*. 46:27–34.

Gough, Harrison G. 1952. "Identifying Psychological Femininity." *Educational and Psychological Measurement*. 12:427–439.

Gough, Kathleen. 1971. "The Origin of the Family." *Journal of Marriage and the Family.* 33:760–770.

Gould, Roger L. 1972. "The Phases of Adult Life: A Study in Developmental Psychology." *American Journal of Psychiatry.* 129:521–531.

Gove, Walter R. 1987. "Mental Illness and Psychiatric Treatment Among Women." Pp. 102–118 in Mary Roth Walsh (Ed.). *The Psychology of Women: Ongoing Debates.* New Haven, Conn.: Yale University Press. (Originally published 1980.)

Grass, Günter. 1964. *Cat and Mouse* (Ralph Manheim, trans.) New York: New American Library.

Grauerholz, Elizabeth, and Bernice A. Pescosolido. 1989. "Gender Representation in Children's Literature: 1900–1984." *Gender and Society.* 3:113–125.

Green, Richard. 1974. *Sexual Identity Conflict in Children and Adults.* New York: Basic Books.

Green, Richard. 1987. *The "Sissy Boy Syndrome" and the Development of Homosexuality.* New Haven, Conn.: Yale University Press.

Greenberger, Ellen. 1988. "Working in Teenage America." Pp. 21–50 in Jeylan T. Mortimer and Kathryn M. Borman (Eds.). *Work Experience and Psychological Development Through the Life Span.* Boulder, Colo.: Westview Press.

Greenberger, Ellen, and Laurence Steinberg. 1986. *When Teenagers Work: The Psychological and Social Costs of Adolescent Employment.* New York: Basic Books.

Greeno, C. G., and Eleanor E. Maccoby. 1986. "How Different Is the 'Different Voice'?" *Signs: Journal of Women in Culture and Society.* 11:310–316.

Gregory, Robert F., Roslyn Anstie, Anne Daly, and Vivian Ho. 1989. "Women's Pay in Australia, Great Britain, and the United States: The Role of Laws, Regulations, and Human Capital." Pp. 222–242 in Robert T. Michael, Heidi I. Hartmann, and Brigid O'Farrell (Eds.). *Pay Equity: Empirical Inquiries.* Washington, D.C.: National Academy Press.

Grief, Geoffrey L. 1985. *Single Fathers.* Lexington, Mass.: Lexington Books.

Griffin, Susan. 1975. "Rape: The All-American Crime." Pp. 24–39 in Jo Freeman (Ed.). *Women: A Feminist Perspective.* Palo Alto, Calif.: Mayfield.

Grimm, James W. 1978. "Women in Female-Dominated Professions." Pp. 293–315 in Ann Stromberg and Shirley Harkess (Eds.). *Women Working.* Palo Alto, Calif.: Mayfield.

Grossman, Frances Kaplan. 1987. "Separate and Together: Men's Autonomy and Affiliation in the Transition to Parenthood." Pp. 89–112 in Phyllis W. Berman and Frank A. Pedersen (Eds.). *Men's Transition to Parenthood: Longitudinal Studies of Early Family Experience.* Hillsdale, N.J.: Erlbaum.

Gruber, James E. 1990. "Methodological Problems and Policy Implications in Sexual Harassment Research." *Population Research and Policy Review.* 9:235–254.

Gruber, James, and Lars Bjorn. 1982. "Blue-Collar Blues: The Sexual Harassment of Women Autoworkers." *Work and Occupations.* 9:271–298.

Guilford, J.P. 1967. *The Nature of Human Intelligence.* New York: McGraw-Hill.

Guntrip, Harry. 1961. *Personality Structure and Human Interaction: The Developing Synthesis of Psychodynamic Theory.* New York: International University Press.

Gurin, Patricia. 1985. "Women's Gender Consciousness." *Public Opinion Quarterly.* 49:143–163.

Guttentag, Marcia, and Paul Secord. 1983. *Two Many Women: The Sex Ratio Question.* Beverly Hills, Calif.: Sage.

Gutmann, David. 1965. "Women and the Conception of Ego Strength." *Merrill-Palmer Quarterly.* 11:229–240.

Gwartney-Gibbls, Patricia A. 1986. "The Institutionalization of Premarital Cohabitation: Estimates from Marriage License Applications, 1970 and 1980." *Journal of Marriage and the Family.* 48:423–434.

Gwartney-Gibbs, Patricia A., Jean Stockard, and Susanne Bohmer. 1987. "Learning Courtship Aggression: The Influence of Parents, Peers, and Personal Experiences." *Family Relations.* 36:276–282.

Gwartney-Gibbs, Patricia A., and Patricia A. Taylor. 1986. "Black Women Workers' Earnings Progress in Three Industrial Sectors." *Sage.* 3:20–25.

Haavind, Hanne, and Agnes Andenes. 1990. "Care and the Responsibility for Children: Creating the Life of Women Creating Themselves." Paper presented at the Fourth International Interdisciplinary Congress on Women, New York, June.

Haavio-Mannila, Elina. 1971. "Convergences Between East and West: Tradition and Modernity in Sex Roles in Sweden, Finland, and the Soviet Union." *Acta Sociologica.* 14:114–125.

Hackett, Gail. 1985. "Role of Mathematics Self-Efficacy in the Choice of Math-Related Majors of College Women and Men: A Path Analysis." *Journal of Counseling Psychology.* 32:47–56.

Hagan, John. 1990. "The Gender Stratification of Income Inequality Among Lawyers." *Social Forces.* 68:835–855.

Hall, Judith A. 1984. *Nonverbal Sex Differences: Communication Accuracy and Expressive Style.* Baltimore: Johns Hopkins University Press.

Hall, Judith A. 1987. "On Explaining Gender Differences: The Case of Nonverbal Communication." Pp. 177–200 in Phillip Shaver and Clyde Hendrick (Eds.). *Sex and Gender: Vol. 7. Review of Personality and Social Psychology.* Newbury Park, Calif.: Sage.

Halpern, Diane F. 1986. *Sex Differences in Cognitive Abilities.* Hillsdale, N.J.: Erlbaum.

Hamburg, O. A. 1971. "Aggressive Behavior of Chimpanzees and Baboons in Natural Habitats." *Journal of Psychiatric Research.* 8:385–398.

Hansen, Ranald D., and Virginia E. O'Leary. 1985. "Sex-Determined Attributions." Pp. 67–99 in Virginia E. O'Leary, Rhoda Kesler Unger, and Barbara Strudler Wallston (Eds.). *Women, Gender, and Social Psychology.* Hillsdale, N.J.: Erlbaum.

Hardesty, Scarlett G., Malcolm D. Holmes, and James D. Williams. 1988. "Economic Segmentation and Worker Earnings in a U.S.-Mexico Border Enclave." *Sociological Perspectives.* 31:466–489.

Hareven, Tamara K. 1976a. "The Family and Gender Roles in Historical Perspective." Pp. 93–118 in Libby A. Carter, Anne Firor Scott, and Wendy Martyna (Eds.). *Women and Men: Changing Roles, Relationships, and Perceptions.* New York: Aspen Institute for Humanistic Studies.

Hareven, Tamara K. 1976b. "Modernization and Family History: Perspectives on Social Change." *Signs: Journal of Women in Culture and Society.* 2:190–206.

Harkess, Shirley. 1985. "Women's Occupational Experiences in the 1970's: Sociology and Economics." *Signs: Journal of Women in Culture and Society.* 10:495–516.

Harris, Marvin. 1977. "Why Men Dominate Women." *New York Times Magazine.* November 13, p. 46.

Harrison, James. 1978. "Warning: The Male Sex Role May Be Dangerous to Your Health." *Journal of Social Issues.* 34:65–86.

Hartley, Ruth E. 1976. "Sex-Role Pressures and the Socialization of the Male Child." Pp. 235–252 in Deborah S. David and Robert Brannon (Eds.). *The Forty-Nine Percent Majority: The Male Sex Role.* Reading, Mass.: Addison Wesley. (Originally published 1959.)

Hartmann, Heidi I. 1981. "The Family as the Locus of Gender, Class and Political Struggle: The Example of Housework." *Signs: Journal of Women in Culture and Society.* 6:366–394.

Haug, Marie R., and Steven J. Folmar. 1986. "Longevity, Gender, and Life Quality." *Journal of Health and Social Behavior.* 27:332–345.

Hayashi, Hiroko. 1985. "Japan." Pp. 57–67 in Jennie Farley (Ed.). *Women Workers in Fifteen Countries: Essays in Honor of Alice Hanson Cook.* Ithaca, N.Y.: ILR Press.

Hayes, Cheryl D., John L. Palmer, and Martha J. Zaslow (Eds.). 1990. *Who Cares for America's Children? Child Care Policy for the 1990's.* Washington, D.C.: National Academy Press.

Hays, H. R. 1972. *The Dangerous Sex.* New York: Pocket Books.

Hearn, Jeff and Wendy Parkin. 1987. *'Sex at Work': The Power and Paradox of Organization Sexuality.* New York: St. Martin's Press.

Hearn, Jeff, Deborah L. Sheppard, Peta Tancred-Sheriff, and Gibson Burrell. (Eds.). 1989. *The Sexuality of Organization.* London and Newbury Park: Sage.

Hedges, Larry V., and Betsy Jane Becker. 1986. "Statistical Methods in the Meta-Analysis of Research on Gender Differences." Pp. 14–50 in Janet Shibley Hyde and Marcia C. Linn (Eds.). *The Psychology of Gender: Advances Through Meta-Analysis.* Baltimore: Johns Hopkins University Press.

Heller, D. O. 1959. "The Relationship Between Sex-Appropriate Behavior in Young Children and the Clarity of the Sex-Role of the Like-Sexed Parent as Measured by Tests." *Dissertation Abstracts*. 19:3365–3366.

Henley, Nancy M. 1977. *Body Politics: Power, Sex, and Non-Verbal Communication*. Englewood Cliffs, N.J.: Prentice Hall.

Henley, Nancy M., Rose Laub Coser, Jane Flax, Naomi Quinn, and Kathryn Kish Sklar. 1989. "Gender Studies." Pp. 161–189 in R. Duncan Luce, Neil J. Smelser, and Dean R. Gurstein (Eds.). *Leading Edges in the Social and Behavioral Sciences*. New York: Russell Sage Foundation.

Herman, Judith. 1981. *Father–Daughter Incest*. Cambridge, Mass.: Harvard University Press.

Herman, Judith, and Lisa Hirschman. 1977. "Father–Daughter Incest." *Signs: Journal of Women in Culture and Society*. 2:735–756.

Hersey, P. 1931. "Emotional Cycles of Man." *Journal of Mental Science*. 77:151–169.

Hertz, Rosanna. 1986. *More Equal than Others: Women and Men in Dual-Career Marriages*. Berkeley: University of California Press.

Hertz, Rosanna, and Joy Charlton. 1989. "Making Family Under a Shiftwork Schedule: Air Force Security Guards and Their Wives." *Social Problems*. 36:491–507.

Hess, Beth B. 1985. "Aging Policies and Old Women: The Hidden Agenda." Pp. 319–331 in Alice S. Rossi (Ed.). *Gender and the Life Course*. New York: Aldine.

Hetherington, E. Mavis. 1965. "A Developmental Study of the Effects of Sex of the Dominant Parent on Sex-Role Preference, Identification, and Imitation in Children." *Journal of Personality and Social Psychology*. 2:188–194.

Hetherington, E. Mavis. 1979. "Divorce: A Child's Perspective." *American Psychologist*. 34:851–858.

Heuser, Linda. 1977. "Sex Typing in Daycare: A Preliminary View." Paper presented at the annual meeting of the Pacific Sociological Association, April; Sacramento, Cal.

Hewlett, Sylvia Ann. 1986. *A Lesser Life: The Myth of Women's Liberation in America*. New York: Morrow.

Hewlett, Sylvia Ann, Alice S. Ilchman, and John J. Sweeney. (Eds.). *Family and Work: Bridging the Gap*. Cambridge, Mass.: Ballinger.

Hibbard, Judith H., and Clyde R. Pope. 1983. "Gender Roles, Illness Orientation and Use of Medical Services." *Social Science and Medicine*. 17:129–137.

Hibbard, Judith H., and Clyde R. Pope. 1985. "Employment Status, Employment Characteristics, and Women's Health." *Women and Health*. 10:59–77.

Hibbard, Judith H., and Clyde R. Pope. 1986. "Another Look at Sex Differences in the Use of Medical Care: Illness Orientation and the Types of Morbidities for Which Services Are Used." *Women and Health*. 11:21–36.

Hibbard, Judith H., and Clyde R. Pope. 1991. "The Effect of Domestic and Occupational Roles on Morbidity and Mortality." *Social Science and Medicine*, forthcoming.

Higginbotham, Elizabeth. 1987. "Employment for Professional Black Women in the Twentieth Century." Pp. 73–91 in Christine Bose and Glenna Spitze (Eds.). *Ingredients for Women's Employment Policy*. Albany, N.Y.: SUNY Press.

Hijab, Nadia. 1988. *Womanpower: The Arab Debate on Women at Work*. New York: Cambridge University Press.

Hirschman, Charles, and Morrison G. Wong. 1986. "The Extraordinary Educational Attainment of Asian-Americans: A Search for Historical Evidence and Explanations." *Social Forces*. 65: 1–27.

Hochschild, Arlie. 1983. *The Managed Heart*. Berkeley: University of California Press.

Hochschild, Arlie (with Anne Machung). 1989. *The Second Shift*. New York: Avon.

Hoenig, John. 1985a. "Etiology of Transsexualism." Pp. 33–73 in Betty W. Steiner (Ed.). *Gender Dysphoria: Development, Research, Management*. New York: Plenum.

Hoenig, John. 1985b. "The Origin of Gender Identity." Pp. 11–32 in Betty W. Steiner (Ed.). *Gender Dysphoria: Development, Research, Management*. New York: Plenum.

Hoffman, Charles D., Sandra Eido Tsuneyoshi, Marilyn Ebina, and Heather Fite. 1984. "A Comparison of Adult Males' and Females' Interactions with Girls and Boys." *Sex Roles.* 11:799–811.

Hoffman, Lois Wladis. 1977. "Changes in Family Roles, Socialization, and Sex Differences." *American Psychologist.* 32:644–657.

Hoff-Wilson, Joan. 1987. "The Unfinished Revolution: Changing Legal Status of U.S. Women." *Signs: Journal of Women in Culture and Society.* 13:7–36.

Hogan, Dennis P., and Evelyn M. Kitagawa. 1985. "The Impact of Social Status, Family Structure, and Neighborhood on the Fertility of Black Adolescents." *American Journal of Sociology.* 90:825–855.

Holden, Karen C. 1989. "Women's Economic Status in Old Age and Widowhood." Pp. 143–169 in Martha N. Ozawa (Ed.). *Women's Life Cycle and Economic Insecurity: Problems and Prospects.* New York: Greenwood Press.

Holly, Aleen, and Christine Towne Bransfield. 1976. "The Marriage Law: Basis of Change for China's Women." Pp. 363–374 in Lynne B. Iglitzin and Ruth Ross (Eds.). *Women in the World: A Comparative Study.* Santa Barbara, Calif.: Clio Books.

Holter, Harriet. 1984. "Women's Research and Social Theory." Pp. 9–25 in Harriet Holter (Ed.). *Patriarchy in a Welfare State.* Oslo: Universitetsforlaget.

Holter, Harriet, and Hildur Ve Henriksen. 1979. "Social Policy and the Family in Norway." Pp. 199–224 in Jean Lipman-Blumen and Jessie Bernard (Eds.). *Sex Roles and Social Policy: A Complex Social Science Equation.* Beverly Hills, Calif.: Sage.

Honey, Margaret, and John Broughton. 1985. "Feminine Sexuality: An Interview with Janine Chasseguet-Smirgel." *Psychoanalytic Review.* 72:527–548.

Horner, Matina S. 1968. "Sex Differences in Achievement Motivation and Preference in Competitive and Non-Competitive Situations." Unpublished Ph.D. dissertation, University of Michigan.

Horner, Matina S. 1970. "Femininity and Successful Achievement: A Basic Inconsistency." In Judith M. Bardwick, Elizabeth Douvan, Matina S. Horner, and David Guttmann. *Feminine Personality and Conflict.* Monterey, Calif.: Brooks/Cole.

Horner, Matina S. 1972. "Toward an Understanding of Achievement-Related Conflicts in Women." *Journal of Social Issues.* 28:157–175.

Horner, Thomas M. 1985. "The Psychic Life of the Young Infant: Review and Critique of the Psychoanalytic Concepts of Symbiosis and Infantile Omnipotence." *American Journal of Orthopsychiatry.* 55:324–343.

Horney, Karen. 1967a. "The Dread of Woman: Observations on a Specific Difference in the Dread Felt by Men and by Women Respectively for the Opposite Sex." Pp. 133–146 in Harold Kelman (Ed.). *Feminine Psychology.* New York: Norton. (Originally published 1932.)

Horney, Karen. 1967b. "The Flight from Womanhood: The Masculinity Complex in Women as Viewed by Men and by Women." Pp. 54–70 in Harold Kelman (Ed.). *Feminine Psychology.* New York: Norton. (Originally published 1926.)

Hoyenga, Katherine Blick, and Kermit T. Hoyenga. 1979. *The Question of Sex Differences: Psychological, Cultural, and Biological Issues.* Boston: Little, Brown.

Hrdy, Sarah Blaffer. 1981. *The Woman that Never Evolved.* Cambridge, Mass.: Harvard University Press.

Huber, Joan, and Glenna Spitze. 1983. *Sex Stratification: Children, Housework, and Jobs.* New York: Academic Press.

Hunt, Janet G., and Larry L. Hunt. 1982. "Dual-Career Families: Vanguard of the Future or Residue of the Past?" Pp. 41–59 in Joan Aldous (Ed.). *Two Paychecks: Life in Dual-Earner Families.* Beverly Hills, Calif.: Sage.

Hunt, Janet G., and Larry L. Hunt. 1987. "Male Resistance to Role Symmetry in Dual-Earner Households: Three Alternative Explanations." Pp. 192–203 in Naomi Gerstel and Harriet Engel Gross (Eds.). *Families and Work.* Philadelphia: Temple University Press.

Husen, Torsten. 1967. *International Study of Achievement in Mathematics: A Comparison of Twelve Countries.* New York: Wiley.

Huston, Aletha C. 1983. "Sex-Typing." Pp. 387–467 in *Handbook of Child Psychology: Volume 4. Socialization, Personality, and Social Development* (4th ed.). Paul H. Mussen (series editor), E. Mavis Hetherington (volume editor). New York: Wiley.

Huston, Aletha C. 1985. "The Development of Sex Typing: Themes from Recent Research." *Developmental Review*. 5:1–17.

Hyde, Janet Shibley. 1984. "How Large Are Gender Differences in Aggression? A Meta-Analysis." Developmental Psychology. 20:722–736.

Hyde, Janet Shibley. 1986a. "Gender Differences in Aggression." Pp. 51–66 in Janet Shibley Hyde and Marcia C. Linn (Eds.). *The Psychology of Gender: Advances Through Meta-Analysis.* Baltimore: Johns Hopkins University Press.

Hyde, Janet Shibley. 1986b. "Introduction: Meta-Analysis and the Psychology of Gender." Pp. 1–13 in Janet Shibley Hyde and Marcia C. Linn (Eds.). *The Psychology of Gender: Advances Through Meta-Analysis.* Baltimore: Johns Hopkins University Press.

Hyde, Janet Shibley, and Marcia C. Linn. 1988. "Gender Differences in Verbal Ability: A Meta-Analysis." *Psychological Bulletin.* 104:53–69.

Hyde, Janet Shibley, E. Fennema, and S. J. Lamon. 1990. "Gender Differences in Mathematics Performance: A Meta-Analysis." *Psychological Bulletin.* 107:139–155.

Hymowitz, Carol and Michaele Weissman. 1978. *A History of Women in America.* New York: Bantam.

Imperato-McGinley, J., R. E. Peterson, T. Gautier, and E. Sturla. 1979. "Androgens and the Evolution of Male-Gender Identity Among Male Pseudohermaphrodites with 5(Reductase Deficiency." *New England Journal of Medicine.* 300:1233–1237.

Ingersoll, Fern S. 1983. "Former Congresswomen Look Back." Pp. 191–207 in Irene Tinker (Ed.). *Women in Washington: Advocates for Public Policy.* Beverly Hills, Calif.: Sage.

Intons-Peterson, Margaret Jean. 1988. *Children's Concepts of Gender.* Norwood, N.J.: Ablex.

Ireson, Carol, and Sandra K. Gill. 1988. "Girls' Socialization for Work." Pp. 132–166 in Ann Stromberg and Shirley Harkess (Eds.). *Women Working* (2nd ed.). Palo Alto, Calif.: Mayfield.

Israel, Joachim, and Rosmari Eliasson. 1971. "Consumption Society, Sex Roles, and Sexual Behavior." *Acta Sociologica.* 14:68–82.

Jacobs, Jerry A. 1985. "Sex Segregation in American Higher Education." Pp. 191–214 in Laurie Larwood, Ann H. Stromberg, and Barbara A. Gutek (Eds.). *Women and Work: An Annual Review* (Vol. 1). Beverly Hills, Calif.: Sage.

Jacobs, Jerry A. 1986. "The Sex-Segregation of Fields of Study: Trends During the College Years." *Journal of Higher Education.* 57:134–154.

Jacobs, Jerry A. 1989a. "Long-Term Trends in Occupational Segregation by Sex." *American Journal of Sociology.* 95:160–173.

Jacobs, Jerry A. 1989b. *Revolving Doors: Sex Segregation and Women's Careers.* Stanford, Calif.: Stanford University Press.

Jaggar, Alison M. 1983. *Feminist Politics and Human Nature.* Totowa, N.J.: Rowman and Allanheld.

Janjic, Marion. 1985. "Women's Work in Industrialized Countries: An Overview from the Perspective of the International Labour Organization." Pp. 1–12 in Jennie Farley. (Ed.). *Women Workers in Fifteen Countries: Essays in Honor of Alice Hanson Cook.* Ithaca, N.Y.: ILR Press.

Jaquette, Jane S. 1986. "Female Political Participation in Latin America: Raising Feminist Issues." Pp. 243–271 in Lynne B. Iglitzin and Ruth Ross (Eds.). *Women in the World: 1975–1985 The Women's Decade* (2nd rev. ed.). Santa Barbara, Calif.: ABC–Clio.

Jay, P. 1963. "Mother-Infant Relations in Langurs." in H. L. Rheingold (Ed.). *Maternal Behavior in Mammals.* New York: Wiley.

Jeffords, Susan. 1989. *The Remasculinization of America: Gender and the Vietnam War.* Bloomington: Indiana University Press.

Jeffrey, Kirk. 1972. "The Family as Utopian Retreat from the City: The Nineteenth Century Contribution," Pp. 21–41 in Sallie Teselle (Ed.). *The Family, Communes, and Utopian Communities.* New York: Harper & Row.

Jencks, Christopher, Lauri Perman, Lee Rainwater. 1988. "What Is a Good Job? A New Measure of Labor-Market Success." *American Journal of Sociology.* 93:1322–1357.

Joekes, Susan P. 1987. *Women in the World Economy: An INSTRAW Study.* New York: Oxford University Press.

Joffe, Carole. 1971. "Sex Role Socialization and the Nursery School, or as the Twig Is Bent." *Journal of Marriage and the Family.* 33:467–476.

Johanson, Donald C. 1989. *Lucy's Child: The Discovery of a Human Ancestor.* New York: Morrow.

Johanson, Donald C., and Maitland A. Edey. 1981. *Lucy: the Beginnings of Humankind.* New York: Simon & Schuster.

Johnson, Coleen Leahy. 1988. *Ex Familia: Grandparents, Parents, and Children Adjust to Divorce.* New Brunswick, N.J.: Rutgers University Press.

Johnson, Kay. 1986. "Women's Rights, Family Reform, and Population Control in the People's Republic of China." Pp. 439–462 in Lynne B. Itlitzin and Ruth Ross (Eds.). *Women in the World: 1975–1985 The Women's Decade* (2nd rev. ed.). Santa Barbara, Calif.: ABC–Clio.

Johnson, Kay Ann. 1983. *Women, the Family, and Peasant Revolution in China.* Chicago: University of Chicago Press.

Johnson, Marilyn. 1987. "Mental Illness and Psychiatric Treatment Among Women: A Response." Pp. 119–1226 in Mary Roth Walsh (Ed.). *The Psychology of Women: Ongoing Debates.* New Haven, Conn.: Yale University Press. (Originally published 1980.)

Johnson, Miriam M. 1963. "Sex Role Learning in the Nuclear Family." *Child Development.* 34: 319–333.

Johnson, Miriam M. 1975. "Fathers, Mothers and Sex Typing." *Sociological Inquiry.* 45:15–26.

Johnson, Miriam M. 1976. "Misogyny and the Superego: Chauvinism in the Moral Sphere." *Indian Journal of Social Research.* 16:372–383.

Johnson, Miriam M. 1977. "Androgyny and the Maternal Principle." *School Review.* 86:50–69.

Johnson, Miriam M. 1988. *Strong Mothers, Weak Wives: The Search for Gender Equality.* Berkeley: University of California Press.

Johnson, Miriam M. Forthcoming. "Liberalism and Gender Equality: Problems of Social Integration." In Paul Colomy (Ed.) Neofunctionalism: Dynamic Systems and the Problems of Social Integration. Newbury Park: Sage.

Johnson, Miriam M., Jean Stockard, Joan Acker, and Claudeen Naffziger. 1975. "Expressiveness Reevaluated." *School Review.* 83:617–644.

Johnson, Miriam M., Jean Stockard, Mary Rothbart, and Lisa Friedman. 1981. "Sexual Preference, Feminism, and Women's Perceptions of Their Parents." *Sex Roles.* 6:1–18.

Johnson, Paula. 1976. "Women and Power: Toward a Theory of Effectiveness." *Journal of Social Issues.* 32:99–110.

Johnson, Wendy. 1988. "Women in Road Construction." Pp. 247–251 in *The American Woman 1988–89.* (Edited by Sara E. Rix for the Women's Research and Education Institute.) New York: Norton.

Johnson, J., J. Ettema, and T. Davidson. 1980. *An Evaluation of Freestyle: A Television Series to Reduce Sex-Role Stereotypes.* Report from the Center for Research on Utilization of Scientific Knowledge. Ann Arbor: Institute for Social Research, University of Michigan.

Jones, Barbara A. P. 1986. "Black Women and Labor Force Participation: An Analysis of Sluggish Growth Rates." Pp. 11–31 in Margaret C. Simms and Julianne Malveaux (Eds.). *Slipping Through the Cracks: The Status of Black Women.* New Brunswick: Transaction Books.

Jones, Ernest. 1933. "The Phallic Phase." *International Journal of Psychoanalysis.* 14:1–33.

Jones, Ernest. 1935. "Early Female Sexuality." *International Journal of Psychoanalysis.* 16: 263–273.

Jones, Jacqueline. 1987. "Black Women, Work, and the Family Under Slavery." Pp. 84–110 in Naomi Gerstel and Harriet Engle Gross (Eds.). *Families and Work.* Philadelphia: Temple University Press.

Jones, Jacqueline. 1990. "The Political Implications of Black and White Women's Work in the South, 1890-1965." Pp. 108–129 in Louise A. Tilly and Patricia Gurin (Eds.). *Women, Politics, and Change.* New York: Russell Sage Foundation.

Jourard, Sidney M., and Jane E. Robin. 1968. "Self-Disclosure and Touching: A Study of Two Modes of Interpersonal Encounter and Their Interrelation." *Journal of Humanistic Psychology.* 8:39–48.

Juillard, Joelle Rutherford. 1976. "Women in France." Pp. 115–128 in Lynne B. Iglitzin and Ruth Ross (Eds.). *Women in the World: A Comparative Study.* Santa Barbara, Calif.: Clio Books.

Juillard, Joelle Rutherford. 1986. "Policy Impacts and Women's Roles in France." Pp. 7–26 in Lynne B. Itlitzin and Ruth Ross (Eds.). *Women in the World: 1975–1985 The Women's Decade* (2nd rev. ed.). Santa Barbara, Calif.: ABC–Clio.

Kaats, Gilbert R., and Keith E. Davis. 1970. "The Dynamics of Sexual Behavior of College Students." *Journal of Marriage and the Family.* 32:390–399.

Kagan, Jerome. 1964. "The Child's Sex Role Classification of School Objects." *Child Development.* 35:1051–1056.

Kagan, Jerome, and Howard A. Moss. 1962. *Birth to Maturity: A Study in Psychological Development.* New York: Wiley.

Kahn, Alfred J., and Sheila B. Kamerman. 1987. *Child Care: Facing the Hard Choices.* Dover, Mass.: Auburn House.

Kalleberg, Arne L., and Ivar Berg. 1987. *Work and Industry: Structures, Markets, and Processes.* New York: Plenum.

Kalleberg, Arne L., and Rachel A. Rosenfeld. 1990. "Work in the Family and in the Labor Market: A Cross-National, Reciprocal Analysis." *Journal of Marriage and the Family.* 52:331–346.

Kalleberg, Arne, Michael Wallace, Karyn A. Loscocco, Kevin T. Leicht, and Hans-Melnut Ehm, 1986. "The Eclipse of Craft: The Changing Face of Labor in the Newspaper Industry." Pp. 47–71 in Daniel B. Cornfield (Ed.). *Workers, Managers, and Technological Change: Emerging Patterns of Labor Relations.* New York: Plenum.

Kamerman, Sheila B. 1985. "Child Care Services: An Issue for Gender Equity and Women's Solidarity." *Child Welfare.* 64:259–271.

Kamerman, Sheila B., and Alfred J. Kahn. 1981. *Child Care, Family Benefits, and Working Parents: A Study in Comparative Policy.* New York: Columbia University Press.

Kanefield, Linda. 1985. "Psychoanalytic Constructions of Female Development and Women's Conflicts About Achievement—Part II." *Journal of the American Academy of Psychoanalysis.* 13:347–366.

Kanin, Eugene J. 1985. "Date Rapists: Differential Socialization and Relative Deprivation." *Archives of Sexual Behavior.* 14:219–231.

Kanin, Eugene J., and Stanley R. Parcell. 1977. "Sexual Aggression: A Second Look at the Offended Female." *Archives of Sexual Behavior.* 6:67–76.

Kanter, Rosabeth Moss. 1975. "Women and the Structure of Organizations: Explorations in Theory and Behavior." Pp. 34–74 in Marcia Millman and R. M. Kanter (Eds.). *Another Voice.* Garden City, N.Y.: Doubleday.

Kanter, Rosabeth Moss. 1977. *Men and Women of the Corporation.* New York: Basic Books.

Katchadourian, Herant A. and Donald T. Lunde. 1975. *Fundamentals of Human Sexuality* (2nd Ed.). New York: Holt, Rinehart, and Winston.

Kaufman, Debra Renee. 1989. "Patriarchal Women: A Case Study of Newly Orthodox Jewish Women." *Symbolic Interaction.* 12:299–314.

Kaufman, Debra R., and Barbara L. Richardson. 1982. *Achievement and Women: Challenging the Assumptions.* New York: Free Press.

Kauppinen-Toropainen, Kaisa, Elina Haavio-Mannila, and Irja Kandolin. 1984. "Women at Work in Finland." Pp. 183–208 in Marilyn J. Davidson and Cary L. Cooper (Eds.). *Working Women: An International Survey.* Chichester, Eng.: Wiley.

Kaye, Harvey E., Soll Berl, Jack Clare, Mary R. Eleston, Benjamin S. Gershwin, Patricia Gershwin, Leonard S. Kogan, Clara Torda, and Cornelia B. Wilbur. 1967. "Homosexuality in Women." *Archives of General Psychiatry.* 17:626–634.

Keller, Evelyn Fox. 1985. *Reflections on Gender and Science.* New Haven, Conn.: Yale University Press.

Keltikangas-Jarvinen, Liisa, and Paula Kangas. 1988. "Problem-Solving Strategies in Aggressive and Nonaggressive Children." *Aggressive Behavior*. 14:255–264.

Kemp, Alice Abel, and E. M. Beck. 1986. "Equal Work, Unequal Pay: Gender Discrimination Within Work-Similar Occupations." *Work and Occupations*. 13:324–347.

Kenrick, Douglas T. 1987. "Gender, Genes, and the Social Environment: A Biosocial Interactionist Perspective." Pp. 14–43 in Phillip Shaver and Clyde Hendrick (Eds.). *Sex and Gender*. Newbury Park, Calif.: Sage.

Kephart, William M. 1967. "Some Correlates of Romantic Love." *Journal of Marriage and the Family*. 229:470–474.

Kessler, Suzanne J. and Wendy McKenna. 1978. *Gender: An Ethnomethodological Approach*. New York: Wiley.

Kessler-Harris, Alice. 1985. "The Debate over Equality for Women in the Work Place: Recognizing Differences." Pp. 141–161 in Laurie Larwood, Ann H. Stromberg, and Barbara A. Gutek (Eds.). *Women and Work: An Annual Review* (Vol. 1). Beverly Hills, Calif.: Sage.

Key, Mary Ritchie. 1975. *Male/Female Language*. Metuchen, N.J.: Scarecrow Press.

Kilborn, Peter. 1990. "Executive Hiring: Is It for All?" *Eugene Register Guard*. July 30, pp. 1A, 4A.

Killingsworth, Mark. 1985. "The Economics of Comparable Worth: Analytical, Empirical, and Policy Questions." Pp. 86–115 in Heidi Hartmann (Ed.). *Comparable Worth: New Directions for Research*. Washington, D.C.: National Academy Press.

Kincaid, Diane D. 1978. "Over His Dead Body: A Positive Perspective on Widows in the U.S. Congress." *Western Political Quarterly*. 31:96–104.

Kinsey, Alfred C., Wardell B. Pomeroy, and Clyde E. Martin. 1948. *Sexual Behavior in the Human Male*. Philadelphia: Saunders.

Kinsey, Alfred C., Wardell B. Pomeroy, Clyde E. Martin, and Paul H. Gebhard. 1953. *Sexual Behavior in the Human Female*. Philadelphia: Saunders.

Klatch, Rebecca. 1987. *Women of the New Right*. Philadelphia: Temple University Press.

Klatch, Rebecca. 1988. "Coalition and Conflict Among Women of the New Right." *Signs: Journal of Women in Culture and Society*. 13:671–694.

Klaus, Marshall H., and John H. Kennel. 1976. *Maternal-Infant Bonding*. St. Louis, Mo.: Mosby.

Klein, Melanie. 1960. *The Psychoanalysis of Children*. New York: Grove Press. (Originally published 1932.)

Koedt, Anne. 1973. "The Myth of the Vaginal Orgasm." Pp. 198–207 in Anne Koedt, Ellen Levine, and Anita Rapone (Eds.). *Radical Feminism*. New York: Quadrangle/New York Times Book Co.

Koeske, Randi Daimon. 1987. "Premenstrual Emotionality: Is Biology Destiny?" Pp. 137–146 in Mary Roth Walsh (Ed.). *The Psychology of Women: Ongoing Debates*. New Haven, Conn.: Yale University Press.

Kohlberg, Lawrence. 1966. "A Cognitive-Developmental Analysis of Children's Sex Role Concepts and Attitudes." Pp. 82–172 in Eleanor Maccoby (Ed.). *The Development of Sex Differences*. Stanford, Calif.: Stanford University Press.

Kohn, Walter S. G. 1980. *Women in National Legislatures: A Comparative Study of Six Countries*. New York: Praeger.

Kollock, Peter, Philip Blumstein, and Pepper Schwartz. 1985. "Sex and Power in Interaction: Conversational Privileges and Duties." *American Sociological Review*. 50:34–46.

Komarovsky, Mirra. 1953. *Women in the Modern World*. Boston: Little, Brown.

Komarovsky, Mirra. 1974. "Thirty Years Later: The Masculine Case." Pp. 520–531 in Rose L. Coser (Ed.). *The Family: Its Structures and Functions* (2nd ed.). New York: St. Martin's Press.

Komarovsky, Mirra. 1985. *Women in College: Shaping New Feminine Identities*. New York: Basic Books.

Korda, Michael. 1973. *Male Chauvinism! How It Works*. New York: Random House.

Koyama, Takashi, Hachiro Nakamura, and Masako Hiramatsu. 1967. "Japan." Pp. 290–314 in Raphael Patai (Ed.). *Women in the Modern World*. New York: Free Press.

Kramarae, Cheris. 1981. *Women and Men Speaking*. Rowley, Mass.: Newbury House.

Krantz, Susan E. 1988. "Divorce and Children." Pp. 249–273 in Sanford M. Dornbusch and Myra H. Strober (Eds.). *Feminism, Children, and the New Families.* New York: Guilford Press.

Kreps, Juanita, and Robert Clark. 1975. *Sex, Age and Work: The Changing Composition of the Labor Force.* Baltimore: Johns Hopkins University Press.

Kronick, Jane C., and Jane Lieberthal. 1976. "Predictors of Cross-Cultural Variation in the Percentage of Women Employed in Europe." *International Journal of Comparative Sociology.* 27:92–96.

Kulis, Stephen. 1988. "The Representation of Women in Top Ranked Sociology Departments." *American Sociologist.* 19:203–217.

Kulis, Stephen, and Karen A. Miller. 1989. "Are Minority Women Sociologists in Double Jeopardy?" *American Sociologist.* 19:323–339.

Kulis, Stephen, Karen A. Miller, Morris Axelrod, and Leonard Gordon. 1986. "Minorities and Women in the Pacific Sociological Association Region: A Five-Year Progress Report." *Sociological Perspectives.* 29:147–170.

Ladewig, Becky Heath, Stephen J. Thoma, and John H. Scanzoni. 1988. "Sociobiology and the Family: A Focus on the Interplay Between Social Science and Biology." Pp. 173–187 in Erik E. Filsinger (Ed.). *Biosocial Perspectives on the Family.* Newbury Park, Calif.: Sage.

Lamb, Michael E. (Ed.). 1987. *The Father's Role: Cross-Cultural Perspectives.* Hillsdale, N.J.: Erlbaum.

Lamb, Michael E., and Jamie E. Lamb. 1976. "The Nature and Importance of the Father–Infant Relationship." *The Family Coordinator.* 25:379–387.

Lamb, Michael E., Joseph H. Pleck, Eric L. Charnov, and James A. Levine. 1987. "A Biosocial Perspective on Paternal Behavior and Involvement." Pp. 111–142 in Jane B. Lancaster, Jeanne Altmann, Alice S. Rossi, and Connie R. Sherrod (Eds.). *Parenting Across the Life Span: Biosocial Dimensions.* New York: Aldine de Gruyter.

Lamphere, Louise. 1977. "Review Essay: Anthropology." *Signs: Journal of Women in Culture and Society.* 2:612–627.

Lancaster, Jane B. 1984. "Introduction." Pp. 1–10 in Meredith F. Small (Ed.). *Female Primates: Studies by Women Primatologists.* New York: Liss.

Lande, Jeffrey S., Sandra Scarr, and Nina Gunzenhauser. (Eds.). 1989. *Caring for Children: Challenge to America.* Hillsdale, N.J.: Erlbaum.

Lang, Dwight. 1987a. "Equality, Prestige, and Controlled Mobility in the Academic Hierarchy." *American Journal of Education.* 95:441–467.

Lang, Dwight. 1987b. "Patterns of Status and Prestige Inequality in Professional Education: A Research Note." *Journal of Research and Development in Education.* 20:66–69.

Lang, Dwight. 1987c. "Stratification and Prestige Hierarchies in Graduate and Professional Education." *Sociological Inquiry.* 57:12–31.

Langlois, Judith, and A. Chris Downs. 1980. "Mothers, Fathers and Peers as Socialization Agents of Sex-Typed Play Behaviors in Young Children." *Child Development.* 51:1217–1247.

Lapidus, Gail W. 1976. "Occupational Segregation and Public Policy: A Comparative Analysis of American and Soviet Patterns." *Signs: Journal of Women in Culture and Society.* 1:119–136.

Lapidus, Gail Warshofsky. 1978. *Women in Soviet Society: Equality, Development and Social Change.* Berkeley: University of California Press.

Lapidus, Gail W. 1985. "The Soviet Union." Pp. 13–32 in Jennie Farley (Ed.). *Women Workers in Fifteen Countries: Essays in Honor of Alice Hanson Cook.* Ithaca, N.Y.: ILR Press.

Lapidus, Gail W. 1988. "The Interaction of Women's Work and Family Roles in the U.S.S.R." Pp. 87–121 in Barbara A. Gutek, Ann H. Stromberg, and Laurie Larwood (Eds.). *Women and Work: An Annual Review* (Vol. 3). Newbury Park, Calif.: Sage.

LaRossa, Ralph, and Maureen Mulligan LaRossa. 1981. *Transition to Parenthood: How Infants Change Families.* Beverly Hills, Calif.: Sage.

LaRossa, Ralph, and Maureen Mulligan LaRossa. 1989. "Baby Care: Fathers vs. Mothers." Pp. 138–154 in Barbara J. Risman and Pepper Schwartz (Eds.). *Gender in Intimate Relations: A Microstructural Approach.* Belmont, Calif.: Wadsworth.

Lasch, Christopher. 1977. *Haven in a Heartless World.* New York: Basic Books.

Lasch, Christopher. 1978. *The Culture of Narcissism: American Life in an Age of Diminishing Expectations*. New York: Norton.

Leacock, Eleanor. 1986. "Women, Power, and Authority." Pp. 107–135 in Leela Dube, Eleanor Leacock, and Shirley Ardener (Eds.). *Visibility and Power: Essays on Women in Society and Development*. Delhi: Oxford University Press.

Leakey, Richard E., and Roger Lewin. 1977. *Origins*. New York: Dutton.

Lederer, Wolfgang. 1968. *The Fear of Women*. New York: Grune & Stratton.

Lee, Gary R. 1988. "The Feasibility of an Integration." Pp. 159–172 in Erik E. Filsinger (Ed.). *Biosocial Perspectives on the Family*. Newbury Park, Calif.: Sage.

Leifer, A. D. 1970. "Effects of Early, Temporary Mother–Infant Separation on Later Maternal Behavior in Humans." Unpublished Ph.D. dissertation, Stanford University.

Leifer, A. D., P. H. Leiderman, C. R. Barnett, and J. A. Williams. 1972. "Effects of Mother–Infant Separation on Maternal Attachment Behavior." *Child Development*. 43:1203–1218.

Leinbach, Mary Driver, and Beverly I. Fagot. 1986. "Acquisition of Gender Labels: A Test for Toddlers." *Sex Roles*. 15:655–666.

Lele, Uma. 1986. "Women and Structural Transformation." *Economic Development and Cultural Change*. 34:195–221.

Lemon, Judith. 1978. "Dominant or Dominated? Women on Prime-Time Television." Pp. 51–68 in G. Tuchman, A. K. Daniels, and J. Benet (Eds.). *Hearth and Home: Images of Women in the Mass Media*. New York: Oxford University Press.

Lennon, Randy, and Nancy Eisenberg. 1987. "Gender and Age Differences in Empathy and Sympathy." Pp. 195–217 in Nancy Eisenberg and Janet Strayer (Eds.). *Empathy and Its Development*. New York: Cambridge University Press.

Leonard, Marjorie. 1966. "Fathers and Daughters: The Significance of Fathering in the Psychosexual Development of the Girl." *International Journal of Psychoanalysis*. 47:325–334.

Lerman, Hannah. 1986. *A Mote in Freud's Eye: From Psychoanalysis to the Psychology of Women*. New York: Springer.

Lerner, Gerda. 1969. "The Lady and the Mill Girl: Changes in the Status of Women in the Age of Jackson." *American Studies Journal*. 10:5–15.

Lerner, Gerda. 1986. *The Creation of Patriarchy*. New York: Oxford University Press.

LeVine, Robert A., and Merry White. 1987. "Parenthood in Social Transformation." Pp. 271–293 in Jane B. Lancaster, Jeanne Altmann, Alice S. Rossi, and Lonnie R. Sherrod (Eds.). *Parenting Across the Life Span: Biosocial Dimensions*. New York: Aldine de Gruyter.

Levinson, Daniel J., Charlotte M. Darrow, Edward B. Klein, Maria H. Levinson, and Braxton McKee. 1976. "Periods in the Adult Development of Men: Ages 18 to 45." *Counseling Psychologist*. 6:21–25.

Levi-Strauss, Claude. 1969. *The Elementary Structures of Kinship*. Boston: Beacon.

Lewis, Charlie. 1986. *Becoming a Father*. Milton Keynes, Eng.: Open University Press.

Lewis, Diane K. 1975. "The Black Family: Socialization and Sex Roles." *Phylon*. 36:221–237.

Lewis, Edwin C. 1968. *Developing Women's Potential*. Ames: Iowa State University Pres.

Lewis, Robert A. 1986. "Introduction: What Men Get Out of Marriage and Parenthood." Pp. 11–25 in Robert E. Lewis and Robert E. Salt (Eds.). *Men in Families*. Beverly Hills, Calif.: Sage.

Lichter, Daniel T., Felicia B. LeClerc, and Diane K. McLaughlin. 1991. "Local Marriage Markets and the Marital Behavior of Black and White Women." *American Journal of Sociology*. 96:843–867.

Lidz, Ruth W., and Theodore Lidz. 1977. "Male Menstruation: A Ritual Alternative to the Oedipal Transition." *International Journal of Psychoanalysis*. 58:17–31.

Lillydahl, Jane H. 1986. "Women and Traditionally Male Blue-Collar Jobs." *Work and Occupations*. 13:307–323.

Lindemalm, Gunnar, Dag Korlin, and Nils Uddenberg. 1986. "Long-Term Follow-Up of 'Sex Change' in 13 Male-to-Female Transsexuals." *Archives of Sexual Behavior*. 15:187–210.

Lindsey, Linda L. 1990. *Gender Roles: A Sociological Perspective*. Englewood Cliffs, N.J.: Prentice Hall.

Lindzey, Gardner. 1967. "Some Remarks Concerning Incest, the Incest Taboo, and Psychoanalytic Theory." *American Psychologist.* 22:1051–1059.

Linn, Marcia C., and Janet Shibley Hyde. 1989. "Gender, Mathematics, and Science." *Educational Researcher.* 18(8):17–27.

Linn, Marcia C., and Anne C. Petersen. 1985. "Emergence and Characterization of Sex Differences in Spatial Ability: A Meta-Analysis." *Child Development.* 56:1479–1498.

Linn, Marcia C., and Anne C. Petersen. 1986. "A Meta-Analysis of Gender Differences in Spatial Ability: Implications for Mathematics and Science Achievement." Pp. 67–101 in Janet Shibley Hyde and Marcia C. Linn (Eds.). *The Psychology of Gender: Advances Through Meta-Analysis.* Baltimore: Johns Hopkins University Press.

Linton, Sally. 1971. "Woman the Gatherer: Male Bias in Anthropology." Pp. 9–21 in S. E. Jacobs (Ed.). *Women in Perspective: A Guide for Cross-Cultural Studies.* Urbana: University of Illinois Press.

Lloyd, Peter C. 1965. "The Yoruba of Nigeria." Pp. 547–582 in James L. Gibbs (Ed.). *Peoples of Africa.* New York: Holt, Rinehart, & Winston.

Lockheed, Marlaine E. 1986. "Reshaping the Social Order: The Case of Gender Segregation." *Sex Roles.* 14:617–628.

Lockwood, Betty, and Wilf Knowles. 1984. "Women at Work in Great Britain." Pp. 3–38 in Marilyn J. Davidson and Cary L. Cooper (Eds.). *Working Women: An International Survey.* Chichester, Eng.: Wiley.

Loney, Jan. 1973. "Family Dynamics in Homosexual Women." Archives of Sexual Behavior. 2: 343–350.

Long, Judy, and Karen L. Porter. 1984. "Multiple Roles of Midlife Women: A Case for New Directions in Theory, Research, and Policy." Pp. 109–159 in Grace Baruch and Jeanne Brooks-Gunn (Eds.). *Women in Midlife.* New York: Plenum.

Lopata, Helena Znaniecka. 1971. *Occupation: Housewife.* New York: Oxford University Press.

Lopata, Helena Znaniecka. 1973. *Widowhood in an American City.* Cambridge, Mass.: Schenkman.

Lopata, Helena Znaniecka. 1987. *Widows: Vol. 2. North America.* Durham, N.C.: Duke University Press.

Lopata, Helena Z., and Debra Barnewolt. 1984. "The Middle Years: Change and Variation in Social-Role Commitments." Pp. 83–108 in Grace Baruch and Jeanne Brooks-Gunn (Eds.). *Women in Midlife.* New York: Plenum.

Lopata, Helena Z., D. Barnewolt, and C. A. Miller. 1985. *City Women: Work, Jobs, Occupations, Careers: Vol. 2. Chicago.* New York: Praeger.

Lorber, Judith. 1984. *Women Physicians: Careers, Status and Power.* New York: Tavistock.

Lorence, Jon. 1987. "Gender Differences in Occupational Labor Market Structure." *Work and Occupations.* 14:23–61.

Lovejoy, C. Owen. 1981. "The Origin of Man." *Science.* 23:341–350.

Lovenduski, Joni. 1986. *Women and European Politics: Contemporary Feminism and Public Policy.* Amherst: University of Massachusetts Press.

Lowenthal, Marjorie Fiske, Majda Thurnher, and David Chiriboga. 1975. *Four Stages of Life.* San Francisco: Jossey-Bass.

Luce, G. G. 1970. *Biological Rhythms in Psychiatry and Medicine.* USPHS Pub. No. 2088. Washington, D.C.: U.S. Department of Health, Education, and Welfare.

Lueptow, Lloyd B. 1984. *Adolescent Sex Roles and Social Change.* New York: Columbia University Press.

Luker, Kristin. 1984. *Abortion and the Politics of Motherhood.* Berkeley: University of California Press.

Lummis, Max, and Harold W. Stevenson. 1990. "Gender Differences in Beliefs and Achievement: A Cross-Cultural Study." *Developmental Psychology.* 26:254–263.

Lynn, David B. 1969. *Parental and Sex-Role Identification.* Berkeley, Calif.: McCutchan.

Lynn, David B. 1976. "Father and Sex-Role Development." *Family Coordinator.* 25:403–428.

Lynn, Naomi B. 1979. "American Women and the Political Process." Pp. 404–429 in Jo Freeman (Ed.). *Women: A Feminist Perspective* (2nd ed.). Palo Alto, Calif.: Mayfield.

Lyons, Nono Plessner. 1983. "Two Perspectives: On Self, Relationships, and Morality." *Harvard Educational Review*. 53:125–145.

McAdoo, Harriette Pipes. 1986. "Strategies Used by Black Single Mothers Against Stress." Pp. 153–166 in Margaret C. Simms and Julianne Malveaux (Eds.). *Slipping Through the Cracks: The Status of Black Women*. New Brunswick, N.J.: Transaction Books.

Macaulay, Jacqueline. 1985. "Adding Gender to Aggression Research: Incremental or Revolutionary Change?" Pp. 191–224 in Virginia E. O'Leary, Rhoda Kesler Unger, and Barbara Strudler Wallston (Eds.). *Women, Gender, and Social Psychology*. Hillsdale, N.J.: Erlbaum.

McAuley, Alastair. 1981. *Women's Work and Wages in the Soviet Union*. London: Allen & Unwin.

McCall, George J., and J. L. Simmons. 1978. *Identities and Interactions*. New York: Free Press.

McClelland, D. C., J. W. Atkinson, R. A. Clark, and E. L. Lowell. 1953. *The Achievement Motive*. New York: Appleton-Century-Crofts.

Maccoby, Eleanor E. 1986. "Social Groupings in Childhood: Their Relationship to Prosocial and Antisocial Behavior in Boys and Girls." Pp. 263–284 in Dan Olweus, Jack Block, and Marian Radke-Yarrow (Eds.). *Development of Antisocial and Prosocial Behavior: Research Theories and Issues*. Orlando: Academic Press.

Maccoby, Eleanor E. 1988. "Gender as a Social Category." *Developmental Psychology*. 24:755–765.

Maccoby, Eleanor E. 1990b. "The Role of Gender Identity and Gender Constancy in Sex-Differentiated Development." Pp. 5–20 in Dawn E. Schrader (Ed.). *The Legacy of Lawrence Kohlberg*. San Francisco: Jossey-Bass.

Maccoby, Eleanor E. 1990a. "Gender and Relationships: A Developmental Account." *American Psychologist*. 45:513–520.

Maccoby, Eleanor E., and Carol Nagy Jacklin. 1974. *The Psychology of Sex Differences*. Stanford, Calif.: Stanford University Press.

Maccoby, Eleanor E., and Carol Nagy Jacklin. 1987. "Gender Segregation in Childhood." *Advances in Child Development and Behavior*. 20:239–287.

Maccoby, Eleanor E., and John A. Martin. 1983. "Socialization in the Context of the Family: Parent–Child Interaction." Pp. 1–102 in *Handbook of Child Psychology: Volume 4. Socialization, Personality, and Social Development* (4th ed.). Paul H. Mussen (series editor), E. Mavis Hetherington (volume editor). New York: Wiley.

McDonald, Gerald W. 1980. "Family Power: The Assessment of a Decade of Theory and Research, 1970–1979." *Journal of Marriage and the Family*. 42:841–854.

McGee, Jeanne and Kathleen Wells. 1982. "Gender Typing and Androgyny in Later Life: New Directions for Theory and Research." *Human Development*. 25:116–139.

McGrew, W. C. 1981. "The Female Chimpanzee as a Human Evolutionary Prototype." Pp. 35–73 in F. Dahlberg (Ed.). *Woman the Gatherer*. New Haven, Conn.: Yale University Press.

McGuinness, Diane. 1985a. "Sensorimotor Biases in Cognitive Development." Pp. 57–126 in Roberta L. Hall, with Patricia Draper, Margaret E. Hamilton, Diane McGuinness, Charlotte M. Otten, and Eric A. Roth. *Male–Female Differences: A Bio-Cultural Perspective*. New York: Praeger.

McGuinness, Diane. 1985b. *When Children Don't Learn*. New York: Basic Books.

McHugh, Maureen C., Randi Daimon Koeske, and Irene Hanson Frieze. 1986. "Issues to Consider in Conducting Nonsexist Psychological Research: A Guide for Researchers." *American Psychologist*. 41:879–890.

Mackey, Wade C. 1985. *Fathering Behaviors: The Dynamics of the Man–Child Bond*. New York: Plenum.

MacKinnon, Catharine A. 1987. *Feminism Unmodified: Discourses on Life and Law*. Cambridge, Mass., and London: Harvard University Press.

McLanahan, Sara S., and Karen Booth. 1989. "Mother-Only Families: Problems, Prospects, and Politics." *Journal of Marriage and the Family*. 51:557–580.

McLanahan, Sara S., Annemette Sorenson, and Dorothy Watson. 1989. "Sex Differences in Poverty, 1950–1980." *Signs: Journal of Women in Culture and Society*. 15:102–122.

McLaughlin, Steven D., Barbara D. Melber, John O. G. Billy, Denise M. Zimmerle, Linda D. Winges, and Terry R. Johnson. 1988. *The Changing Lives of American Women*. Chapel Hill: University of North Carolina Press.

McPherson, J. Miller, and Lynn Smith-Lovin. 1986. "Sex Segregation in Voluntary Associations." *American Sociological Review*. 51:61–79.

Maas, Henry S. and Joseph A. Kuypers. 1974. *From Thirty to Seventy*. San Francisco: Jossey-Bass.

Mackie, Marlene. 1977. "On Congenial Truths: A Perspective on Women's Studies." *Canadian Review of Sociology and Anthropology*. 14:117–128.

Madden, Janice F. 1973. *The Economics of Sex Discrimination*. Lexington, Mass.: Lexington Books.

Madden, Janice F. 1975. "Discrimination—A Manifestation of Male Market Power?" Pp. 146–174 in Cynthia B. Lloyd (Ed.). *Sex Discrimination and the Division of Labor*. New York: Columbia University Press.

Madden, Janice F. 1978. "Economic Rationale for Sex Differences in Education." *Southern Economic Journal*. 44:778–797.

Madden, Janice F. 1985. "The Persistence of Pay Differentials: The Economics of Sex Discrimination." Pp. 115–140 in Laurie Larwood, Ann H. Stromberg, and Barbara A. Gutek (Eds.). *Women and Work: An Annual Review* (Vol. 1). Beverly Hills, Calif.: Sage.

Madigan, F. C. 1957. "Are Sex Mortality Differentials Biologically Caused?" *Milbank Memorial Fund Quarterly*. 32:202–223.

Mainiero, Lisa A. 1986."Coping with Powerlessness: The Relationship of Gender and Job Dependency to Empowerment-Strategy Usage." *Administrative Science Quarterly*. 31:633–653.

Maltz, D. N., and R. A. Borker. 1982. "A Cultural Approach to Male–Female Miscommunication." Pp. 195–216 in John A. Gumperz (Ed.). *Language and Social Identity*. New York: Cambridge University Press.

Mandel, Ruth B. 1988. "The Political Woman." Pp. 78–122 in *The American Woman 1988–89*. (Edited by Sara E. Rix for the Women's Research and Education Institute.) New York: Norton.

Mansbridge, Jane J. 1986. *Why We Lost the ERA*. Chicago and London: University of Chicago Press.

Margolin, Gayla, and Gerald R. Patterson. 1975. "Differential Consequences Provided by Mothers and Fathers for Their Sons and Daughters." *Developmental Psychology*. 11:537–38.

Marini, Margaret Mooney. 1984. "Women's Educational Attainment and the Timing of Entry into Parenthood." *American Sociological Review*. 49:491–511.

Marini, Margaret Mooney. 1985. "Determinants of the Timing of Adult Role Entry." *Social Science Research*. 14:309–350.

Marini, Margaret Mooney. 1989. "Sex Differences in Earnings in the United States." *Annual Review of Sociology*. 15:343–380.

Marini, Margaret Mooney. 1990. "Sex and Gender: What Do We Know?" *Sociological Forum*. 5: 95–120.

Markus, H., M. Crane, S. Bernstein, and M. Saladi. 1982. "Self-Schemas and Gender." *Journal of Personality and Social Psychology*. 42:38–50.

Martin, Carol Lynn. 1987. "A Ratio Measure of Sex Stereotyping." *Journal of Personality and Social Psychology*. 52:489–499.

Martin, Carol Lynn, and Charles F. Halvorson, Jr. 1981. "A Schematic Processing Model of Sex Typing and Stereotyping in Children." *Child Development*. 52:1119–1134.

Martin, Carol Lynn, and Charles F. Halvorson. 1987. "The Roles of Cognition in Sex Role Acquisition." Pp. 123–137 in D. B. Carter (Ed.). *Current Conceptions of Sex Roles and Sex Typing: Theory and Research*. New York: Praeger.

Martin, M. Kay, and Barbara Voorhies. 1975. *Female of the Species*. New York: Columbia University Press.

Martin, Patricia Yancey, Sandra Seymour, Myrna Courage, Karolyn Godbey, and Richard Tate. 1988. "Work-Family Policies: Corporate, Union, Feminist, and Pro-Family Leaders Views." *Gender and Society*. 3:385–400.

Mascia-Lees, Frances E. 1984. *Toward a Model of Women's Status*. New York: Lang.

Maslow, Abraham H. 1942. "Self-Esteem (Dominance-Feeling) and Sexuality in Women." *Journal of Social Psychology*. 16:259–294.

Mason, Karen Oppenheim. 1984. *The Status of Women: A Review of Its Relationships to Fertility and Mortality*. New York: Rockefeller Foundation.

Mason, Karen Oppenheim, and Larry L. Bumpass. 1975. "U.S. Women's Sex-Role Ideology, 1970." *American Journal of Sociology*. 80:1212–1219.

Mason, Karen Oppenheim, John L. Czajka, and Sara Arber. 1976. "Change in U.S. Women's Sex-Role Attitudes, 1964–1974." *American Sociological Review*. 41:573–596.

Mason, Karen Oppenheim, and Yu-Hsia Lu. 1988. "Attitudes Toward Women's Familial Roles: Changes in the United States, 1977–1985." *Gender and Society*. 2:39–57.

Masters, William H., and Virginia E. Johnson. 1966. *Human Sexual Response*. Boston: Little, Brown.

Mazur, Allan. 1985. "A Biosocial Model of Status in Face-to-Face Primate Groups." *Social Forces*. 64:377–402.

Mead, Margaret. 1949. *Male and Female: A Study of the Sexes in a Changing World*. New York: Dell.

Mead, Margaret. 1963. *Sex and Temperament in Three Primitive Societies*. New York: Morrow. (Originally published 1935.)

Mead, Margaret. 1974. "On Freud's View of Female Psychology." Pp. 95–106 in Jean Strouse (Ed.). *Women and Analysis*. New York: Grossman.

Mednick, Martha T. 1989. "On the Politics of Psychological Constructs: Stop the Bandwagon, I Want to Get Off." *American Psychologist*. 44:1118–1123.

Meiselman, Karen C. 1978. *Incest*. San Francisco: Jossey-Bass.

Mendell, Dale. (Ed.). 1982. *Early Female Development: Current Psychoanalytic Views*. New York: Spectrum Press Medical and Scientific Books.

Merkl, Peter H. 1986. "West German Women: A Long Way from *Kinder, Kuche, Kirche*." Pp. 27–52 in Lynne B. Iglitzin and Ruth Ross (Eds.). *Women in the World: 1975–1985 The Women's Decade* (2nd rev. ed.). Santa Barbara, Calif.: ABC–Clio.

Meyer, Jon K., and Donna J. Reter. 1979. "Sex Reassignment Follow-Up." *Archives of General Psychiatry*. 36:1010–1015.

Meyer, Madonna Harrington. 1990. "Family Status and Poverty among Older Women: The Gendered Distribution of Retirement Income in the United States." *Social Problems*. 37:551–563.

Michelson, Stephan. 1972. "Rational Income Decisions of Blacks and Everybody Else." Pp. 100–119 in Martin Carnoy (Ed.). *Schooling in a Corporate Society: The Political Economy of Education in America*. New York: McKay.

Milkman, Ruth. 1990. "Gender and Trade Unionism in Historical Perspective." Pp. 87–107 in Louise A. Tilly and Patricia Gurin (Eds.) *Women, Politics, and Change*. New York: Russell Sage Foundation.

Miller, Arthur. 1988. "Gender and the Vote: 1984." Pp. 258–282 in Carol M. Mueller (Ed.). *The Politics of the Gender Gap: The Social Construction of Political Influence*. Newbury Park, Calif.: Sage.

Miller, Karen A., Stephen Kulis, Leonard Gordon, and Morris Axelrod. 1988. "Representation of Women in U.S. Sociology Departments." *Footnotes*. Washington, D.C.: American Sociological Association, April, p. 3.

Miller Jon. 1986. *Pathways in the Workplace: The Effects of Gender and Race on Access to Organizational Resources*. New York: Cambridge University Press.

Miller, Lawrence W. 1986. "Political Recruitment and Electoral Success: A Look at Sex Differences in Municipal Elections." *Social Science Journal*. 23:75–90.

Miller, P., D. Danaher, and D. Forbes. 1986. "Sex-Related Strategies for Coping with Interpersonal Conflict in Children Aged Five and Seven." *Developmental Psychology*. 22:543–548.

Mincer, Jacob, and Solomon Polacheck. 1974. "Family Investments in Human Capital: Earnings of Women." *Journal of Political Economy*. 82:S76–S108.

Mischel, Walter. 1970. "Sex Typing and Socialization." Pp. 3–72 in Paul H. Mussen (Ed.). *Carmichael's Manual of Child Psychology* (Vol. 2, 3rd ed.). New York: Wiley.

Mitchell, Juliet. 1974. *Psychoanalysis and Feminism.* New York: Vintage.

Modell, John. 1989. *Into One's Own: From Youth to Adulthood in the United States 1920–1975.* Berkeley: University of California Press.

Moen, Elizabeth W. 1979. "What Does 'Control Over Our Bodies' Really Mean?" *International Journal of Women Studies.* 2:129–143.

Moen, Phyllis, Geraldine Downey, and Niall Bolger. 1990. "Labor-Force Reentry Among U.S. Homemakers in Midlife: A Life-Course Analysis." *Gender and Society.* 4:230–243.

Moltz, H., M. Lubin, M. Loon, and M. Numan. 1970. "Hormonal Indication of Maternal Behavior in the Ovarisectionized Rat." *Physiology and Behavior.* 5:1373–1377.

Money, John, and Anke A. Ehrhardt. 1972. *Man and Woman, Boy and Girl.* Baltimore: Johns Hopkins University Press.

Money, J., J. G. Hampson, and J. L. Hampson. 1957. "Imprinting and the Establishment of Gender Role." *Archives of Neurological Psychiatry.* 77:333–336.

Money, John, and Patricia Tucker. 1975. *Sexual Signatures: On Being a Man or a Woman.* Boston: Little, Brown.

Moore, Thomas S. 1986. "Are Women Workers 'Hard to Organize?'" *Work and Occupations.* 13: 97–111.

Morgan, Robin. 1977. "The Politics of Sado-Masochistic Fantasies." Pp. 227–240 in R. Morgan. *Going Too Far.* New York: Random House.

Morgan, William R., Herbert S. Parnes, and Lawrence J. Less. 1985. "Leisure Activities and Social Networks." Pp. 119–145 in Herbert S. Parnes, Joan E. Crowley, R. Jean Haurin, Lawrence J. Less, William R. Morgan, Frank L. Mott, and Gilbert Nestel. *Retirement Among American Men.* Lexington, Mass.: Lexington Books.

Morris, Desmond. 1970. *The Human Zoo.* New York: McGraw-Hill.

Morrison, Ann M. and Mary Ann Von Glinow. 1990. "Women and Minorities in Management." *American Psychologist.* 45:200–208.

Morrissey, Marietta. 1987. "Female-Headed Families: Poor Women and Choice." 302–314 in Naomi Gerstel and Harriet Engle Gross (Eds.). *Families and Work.* Philadelphia: Temple University Press.

Moscovici, Serge. 1972. *Society Against Nature.* (Sacha Rabinovitch, trans.) Atlantic Highlands, N.J.: Humanities Press.

Moses, Joel C. 1986. "The Soviet Union in the Women's Decade, 1975–1985." Pp. 385–413 in Lynne B. Iglitzin and Ruth Ross (Eds.). *Women in the World: 1975–1985 The Women's Decade* (2nd rev. ed.). Santa Barbara, Calif.: ABC–Clio.

Mott, Frank L. (Ed.). 1982. *The Employment Revolution: Young American Women in the 1970s.* Cambridge, Mass.: MIT Press.

Mott, Frank L., and David Shapiro. 1982. "Continuity of Work Attachment Among New Mothers." Pp. 80–101 in Frank L. Mott (Ed.). *The Employment Revolution: Young American Women in the 1970s.* Cambridge, Mass.: MIT Press.

Moyer, Kenneth E. 1974. "Sex Differences in Aggression." Pp. 335–372 in R. C. Friedman et al. (Eds.). *Sex Differences in Behavior.* New York: Wiley.

Moyer, Kenneth E. 1976. *The Psychobiology of Aggression.* New York: Harper & Row.

Moyer, Kenneth E. 1987a. "The Biological Basis of Dominance and Aggression." Pp. 1–34 in Diane McGuinness (Ed.). *Dominance, Aggression, and War.* New York: Paragon House.

Moyer, Kenneth E. 1987b. *Violence and Aggression: A Physiological Perspective.* New York: Paragon.

Mueller, Carol M. (Ed.). 1988. *The Politics of the Gender Gap: The Social Construction of Political Influence.* Newbury Park, Calif.: Sage.

Mueller, Charles W., and Toby L. Parcel. 1986. "Ascription, Dimensions of Authority and Earnings: The Case of Supervisors." Pp. 199–222 in Robert V. Robinson (Ed.). *Research in Social Stratification and Mobility: A Research Annual.* Greenwich, Conn.: JAI Press.

Mukhopadhyay, Carol C., and Patricia J. Higgins. 1988. "Anthropological Studies of Women's Status Revisited: 1977–1987." *Annual Review of Anthropology*. 17:461–495.

Muller, Charlotte. 1986. "Health and Health Care of Employed Women and Homemakers: Family Factors." *Women and Health*. 11:7–26.

Mumpower, D. L. 1970. "Sex Ratios Found in Various Types of Referred Exceptional Children." *Exceptional Children*. 36:621–624.

Munroe, Robert L., Ruth H. Munroe, and John W. M. Whiting. 1981. "Male Sex-Role Resolutions." Pp. 611–632 in Ruth H. Munroe, Robert L. Munroe, and Beatrice B. Whiting (Eds.). *Handbook of Cross-Cultural Human Development*. New York: Garland.

Murphy, Robert F. 1959. "Social Structure and Sex Antagonism." *Southwestern Journal of Anthropology*. 15:407–416.

Mussen, Paul, and E. Rutherford. 1963. "Parent–Child Relations and Parental Personality in Relation to Young Children's Sex-Role Preferences." *Child Development*. 34:589–607.

Myers, Fred R. 1988. "Critical Trends in the Study of Hunter-Gatherers." *Annual Review of Anthropology*. 17:261–282.

Narain, Vatsala. 1967. "India." Pp. 21–41 in Raphael Patai (Ed.). *Women in the Modern World*. New York: Free Press.

National Directory of Women Elected Officials. 1987. Washington, D.C.: National Women's Political Caucus.

National Directory of Women Elected Officials. 1991. Washington, D.C.: National Women's Political Caucus.

Neal, Marie Augusta. 1979. "Women in Religious Symbolism and Organization." *Sociological Inquiry*. 49:218–250.

Needleman, Ruth, and Lucretia Dewey Tanner. 1987. "Women in Unions: Current Issues." Pp. 187–224 in Karen Shallcross Koziara, Michael H. Moskow, and Lucretia Dewey Tanner (Eds.). *Working Women: Past, Present, Future*. Washington, D.C.: Bureau of National Affairs.

Nelson, Cynthia, and Virginia Oleson. 1977. "Veil of Illusion: A Critique of the Concept of Equality in Western Thought." *Catalyst*. 10–11:8–36.

Neugarten, Bernice L. 1968a. "Adult Personality: Toward a Psychology of the Life Cycle." Pp. 137–147 in Bernice L. Neugarten (Ed.). *Middle Age and Aging*. Chicago: University of Chicago Press.

Neugarten, Bernice L. 1968b. "The Awareness of Middle Age." Pp. 93–98 in Bernice L. Neugarten (Ed.). *Middle Age and Aging*. Chicago: University of Chicago Press.

Neugarten, Bernice L. 1976. "Adaptation and the Life Cycle." *Counseling Psychologist*. 6:16–20.

Neugarten, Bernice L., and Joan W. Moore. 1968. "The Changing Age-Status System." Pp. 5–21 in Bernice L. Neugarten (Ed.). *Middle Age and Aging*. Chicago: University of Chicago Press.

Neugarten, Bernice L., Joan W. Moore, and John C. Lowe. 1968. "Age Norms, Age Constraints, and Adult Associalization." Pp. 22–28 in Bernice L. Neugarten (Ed.). *Middle Age and Aging*. Chicago: University of Chicago Press.

Neugarten, Bernice L., and Karol K. Weinstein. 1968. "The Changing American Grandparent." Pp. 280–285 in Bernice L. Neugarten (Ed.). *Middle Age and Aging*. Chicago: University of Chicago Press.

Neuhauser, Kevin. 1989. "Sources of Women's Power and Status Among the Urban Poor in Contemporary Brazil." *Signs: Journal of Women in Culture and Society*. 14:685–702.

Nichols, R. C. 1962. "Subtle, Obvious, and Stereotype Measures of Masculinity–Femininity." *Educational and Psychological Measurement*. 22:449–461

Nielsen, Joyce McCarl. 1990. *Sex and Gender in Society: Perspectives on Stratification* (2nd Edition). Prospect Heights, Illinois: Waveland Press.

Niemi, Iiris, Salme Kiiski, and Mirja Liikkanen. 1981. *Use of Time in Finland*. Helsinki: Central Statistical Office of Finland.

Norderval, Ingunn. 1986. "Elusive Equality: The Limits of Public Policy." Pp. 53–83 in Lynne B. Iglitzin and Ruth Ross (Eds.). *Women in the World: 1975–1985 The Women's Decade* (2nd rev. ed.). Santa Barbara, Calif.: ABC–Clio.

Nordstrom, Bruce. 1986. "Why Men Get Married: More and Less Traditional Men Compared." Pp. 31–53 in Robert E. Lewis and Robert E. Salt (Eds.). *Men in Families*. Beverly Hills, Calif.: Sage.

O'Brien, Denise. 1977. "Female Husbands in Southern Bantu Societies." Pp. 109–126 in Alice Schlegel (Ed.). *Sexual Stratification: A Cross-Cultural View*. New York: Columbia University Press.

O'Brien, Mary. 1981. *The Politics of Reproduction*. Boston: Routledge and Kegan Paul.

O'Farrell, Brigid. 1988. "Women in Blue-Collar Occupations: Traditional and Nontraditional." Pp. 258–272 in Ann Helton Stromberg and Shirley Harkess (Eds.). *Women Working: Theories and Facts in Perspective* (2d Ed.). Mountain View, Calif.: Mayfield.

Offer, Daniel. 1969. *The Psychological World of the Teenager*. New York: Basic Books.

Okun, Lewis. 1986. *Woman Abuse: Facts Replacing Myths*. Albany: State University of New York Press.

O'Leary, Virginia E., and Ranald D. Hansen. 1985. "Sex as an Attributional Fact." Pp. 133–177 in Theo B. Sonderegger (Ed.). *Nebraska Symposium on Motivation 1984: Psychology and Gender*. Lincoln: University of Nebraska Press.

Olesen, Virginia L., and Nancy Fugate Woods. 1986. *Culture, Society, and Menstruation*. Washington, D.C.: Hemisphere.

Omark, D. R., M. Omark, and M. Edelman. 1973. "Dominance Hierarchies in Young Children." Paper presented at the International Congress of Anthropological and Ethnological Sciences, Chicago.

O'Neill, June. 1985. "Role Differentiation and the Gender Gap in Wage Rates." Pp. 50–75 in Laurie Larwood, Ann H. Stromberg, and Barbara A. Gutek (Eds.). *Women and Work: An Annual Review* (Vol. 1). Beverly Hills, Calif.: Sage.

Oppenheimer, Valerie Kincade. 1970. "The Female Labor Force in the United States: Demographic and Economic Factors Governing Its Growth and Changing Composition." Population Monograph, Series No. 5, University of California, Berkeley: Institute of International Studies.

Oppenheimer, Valerie Kincade. 1974. "The Life-Cycle Squeeze: The Interaction of Men's Occupational and Family Life Cycles." *Demography*. 11:227–245.

Oppenheimer, Valerie Kincade. 1982. *Work and the Family: A Study in Social Demography*. New York: Academic Press.

Oppenheimer, Valerie Kincade. 1988. "A Theory of Marriage Timing." *American Journal of Sociology*. 94:563–591.

O'Rand, Angela, and John C. Henretta. 1982. "Midlife Work History and Retirement Income." Pp. 25–44 in Maximiliane Szinovacz (Ed.). *Women's Retirement: Policy Implications of Recent Research*. Beverly Hills, Calif.: Sage.

Orazem, Peter F., and J. Peter Mattila. 1989. "Comparable Worth and the Structure of Earnings: The Iowa Case." Pp. 179–199 in Robert T. Michael, Heidi I. Hartmann, and Brigid O'Farrell (Eds.). *Pay Equity: Empirical Inquiries*. Washington, D.C.: National Academy Press.

Organization for Economic Cooperation and Development. 1980. *Women and Employment: Policies for Equal Opportunity*. Paris: OECD.

Organization for Economic Cooperation and Development. 1986. *Girls and Women in Education: A Cross-National Study of Sex Inequalities in Upbringing and in Schools and Colleges*. Paris: OECD.

Ortner, Sherry B. 1981. "Gender and Sexuality in Hierarchical Societies: The Case of Polynesia and Some Comparative Implications." Pp. 359–409 in Sherry Ortner and Harriet Whitehead (Eds.). *Sexual Meanings: The Cultural Construction of Gender and Sexuality*. New York: Cambridge University Press.

Ortner, Sherry B., and Harriet Whitehead. 1981. "Introduction: Accounting for Sexual Meanings." Pp. 1–27 in *Sexual Meanings: The Cultural Construction of Gender and Sexuality*. Cambridge, Eng.: Cambridge University Press.

Otten, Charlotte M. 1985. "Genetic Effects on Male and Female Development and on the Sex Ratio." Pp. 155–217 in Roberta L. Hall, with Patricia Draper, Margaret E. Hamilton, Diane

McGuinness, Charlotte M. Otten, and Eric A. Roth. *Male–Female Differences: A Bio-Cultural Perspective.* New York: Praeger.

Ozawa, Martha N. 1989. "Conclusions: Women and Society." Pp. 194–210 in Martha N. Ozawa (Ed.). *Women's Life Cycle and Economic Insecurity: Problems and Proposals.* New York: Greenwood Press.

Pagelow, Mildred Daley. 1984. *Family Violence.* New York: Praeger.

Pagels, Elaine. 1979. *The Gnostic Gospels.* New York: Random House.

Paige, Karen Ericksen, and Jeffery M. Paige. 1981. *The Politics of Reproductive Ritual.* Berkeley: University of California Press.

Pallas, Aaron M., and Karl L. Alexander. 1983. "Sex Differences in Quantitative SAT Performance: New Evidence on the Differential Coursework Hypothesis." *American Educational Research Journal.* 20:165–182.

Papanek, Hanna. 1985. "Class and Gender in Education-Employment Linkages." *Comparative Education Review.* 29:317–346.

Papini, Dennis R., Steven Clark, Jawanda K. Barnett, and Catherine L. Savage. 1989. "Grade, Pubertal Status, and Gender-Related Variations in Conflictual Issues Among Adolescents." *Adolescence.* 24:978–987.

Parke, Ross D. 1981. *Fathers.* Cambridge, Mass.: Harvard University Press.

Parke, Ross D., and D. B. Sawin. 1979. "Children's Privacy in the Home: Developmental, Ecological and Child-Rearing Determinants." *Environment and Behavior.* 11:87–104.

Parke, Ross D., and Ronald G. Slaby. 1983. "The Development of Aggression." Pp. 547–641 in *The Handbook of Child Psychology* (Vol. 4). New York: Wiley.

Parke, Ross D., and Barbara R. Tinsley. 1981. "The Father's Role in Infancy: Determinants of Involvement in Caregiving and Play." In Michael E. Lamb (Ed.). *The Role of the Father in Child Development* (2nd ed.). New York: Wiley.

Parlee, Mary Brown. 1973. "The Premenstrual Syndrome." *Psychological Bulletin.* 80:454–465.

Parlee, Mary Brown. 1975. "Review Essay: Psychology." *Signs: Journal of Women in Culture and Society.* 1:119–138.

Parlee, Mary Brown. 1984. "Media Treatment of Premenstrual Syndrome." Pp. 189–205 in Benson E. Ginsburg and Bonnie Frank Carter (Eds.). *Premenstrual Syndrome: Ethical and Legal Implications in a Biomedical Perspective.* New York: Plenum.

Parnes, Herbert S., and Lawrence Lees. 1985. "Variation in Selected Forms of Leisure Activity Among Elderly Males." *Current Perspectives on Aging and the Life Cycle.* 1:223–242.

Parsons, Anne. 1967. "Is the Oedipus Complex Universal?" In Robert McVicker Hunt (Ed.). *Personalities and Cultures.* Garden City, N.Y.: Natural History Press.

Parsons, Talcott. 1954a. "Age and Sex in the Social Structure of the United States." Pp. 89–103 in *Essays in Sociological Theory* (rev. ed.). Glencoe, Ill.: Free Press.

Parsons, Talcott. 1954b. "Certain Primary Sources and Patterns of Aggression in the Social Structure of the Western World." Pp. 298–335 in *Essays in Sociological Theory* (rev. ed.). Glencoe, Ill.: Free Press.

Parsons, Talcott. 1955. "Family Structure and the Socialization of the Child." Pp. 35–131 in T. Parsons and R. F. Bales. *Family Socialization and Interaction Process.* Glencoe, Ill.: Free Press.

Parsons, Talcott. 1966. *Societies: Evolutionary and Comparative Perspectives.* Englewood Cliffs, N.J.: Prentice Hall.

Parsons, Talcott. 1970. *Social Structure and Personality.* New York: Free Press.

Parsons, Talcott, and Robert F. Bales. 1955. *Family Socialization and Interaction Process.* Glencoe, Ill.: Free Press.

Patterson, Michelle. 1973. "Sex and Specialization in Academe and the Professions." Pp. 313–332 in Alice Rossi and Ann Calderwood (Eds.). *Academic Women on the Move.* New York: Russell Sage Foundation.

Patterson, Michelle, and Laurie Engelberg. 1978. "Women in Male-Dominated Professions." Pp. 266–292 in Ann Helton Stromberg and Shirley Harkess (Eds.). *Women Working.* Palo Alto, Calif.: Mayfield.

Paul, Ellen Frankel. 1989. *Equity and Gender: The Comparable Worth Debate*. New Brunswick, N.J.: Transaction Books.

Pauly, Ira B., and Milton T. Edgerton. 1986. "The Gender Identity Movement: A Growing Surgical–Psychiatric Liaison." *Archives of Sexual Behavior*. 15:315–329.

Pearce, Diana M. 1985. "Toil and Trouble: Women Workers and Unemployment Compensation." *Signs: Journal of Women in Culture and Society*. 10:439–459.

Pearce, Diana M. 1987. "On the Edge: Marginal Women Workers and Employment Policy." Pp. 197–210 in Christine Bose and Glenna Spitze (Eds.). *Ingredients for Women's Employment Policy*. Albany, N.Y.: SUNY Press.

Pederson, Frank A. (Ed.). 1980. *The Father–Infant Relationship: Observational Studies in the Family Setting*. New York: Praeger.

Peirce, Kate, and Emily D. Edwards. 1988. "Children's Construction of Fantasy Stories: Gender Differences in Conflict Resolution Strategies." *Sex Roles*. 18:393–404.

Penelope, Julia. 1990. *Speaking: Unlearning the Lies of the Fathers' Tongues*. New York: Pergamon.

Peng, Samuel S., and Ricky T. Takai. 1983. *High School Dropouts: Descriptive Information from High School and Beyond*, Bulletin, National Center for Education Statistics, Washington, D.C.

People. 1976. "Renee Richards." September 6, p. 18.

Perman, Lauri, and Beth Stevens. 1989. "Industrial Segregation and the Gender Distribution of Fringe Benefits." *Gender and Society*. 3:388–404.

Perry, David G., and Kay Bussey. 1979. "The Social Learning Theory of Sex Differences: Imitation Is Alive and Well." *Journal of Personality and Social Psychology*. 37:1699–1712.

Perry, David G., A. V. White, and L. C. Perry. 1984. "Is Early Sex-Typing Due to Children's Attempts to Match Their Behavior to Sex-Role Stereotypes?" *Child Development*. 55: 2114–2121.

Person, Ethel S., and Lionel Ovesey. 1974. "The Psychodynamics of Male Transsexualism." Pp. 315–326 in R. C. Friedman et al. (Eds.). *Sex Differences in Behavior*. New York: Wiley.

Person, Ethel S., and Lionel Ovesey. 1983. "Psychoanalytic Theories of Gender Identity." *Journal of the American Academy of Psychoanalysis*. 11:203–226.

Peterson, Gail Beaton, and Larry R. Peterson. 1973. "Sexism in the Treatment of Sexual Dysfunction." *Family Coordinator*. 22:397–404.

Peterson, Richard R. 1989. *Women, Work and Divorce*. Albany: SUNY Press.

Pettman, Barrie O. (Ed.). 1975. *Equal Pay for Women: Progress and Problems in Seven Countries*. Bradford, West Yorkshire, Eng.: McB Books.

Pfeffer, Jeffrey and Jerry Ross. 1990. "Gender-Based Wage Differences: The Effects of Organizational Context." *Work and Occupations*. 17:55–78.

Phelps, Edmund S. 1972. "The Statistical Theory of Racism and Sexism." *American Economic Review*. 62:659–661.

Phillips, Gerald M. 1986. "Men Talking to Men About Their Relationships." *American Behavioral Scientist*. 29:321–341.

Piore, M.J. 1975. "Notes for a Theory of Labor Market Stratification." Pp. 125–150 in R. C. Edwards, M. Reich, and D. M. Gordon (Eds.). *Labor Market Segmentation*. Lexington, Mass.: Heath.

Pleck, Joseph H. 1975. "Masculinity, Femininity: Current and Alternative Paradigms." *Sex Roles*. 1:161–178.

Pleck, Joseph H. 1980. "Men's Power with Women, Other Men, and Society." Pp. 417–433 in Elizabeth J. Pleck and Joseph Pleck (Eds.). *The American Man*. Englewood Cliffs, N.J.: Prentice Hall.

Pleck, Joseph H. 1985. *Working Wives/Working Husbands*. Beverly Hills, Calif.: Sage.

Pleck, Joseph H., and L. Lange, 1978. *Men's Family Role: Its Nature and Consequences* (Working Paper). Wellesley, Mass.: Wellesley College Center for Research on Women.

Poole, Keith T., and L. Harmon Zeigler. 1985. *Women, Public Opinion, and Politics: The Changing Political Attitudes of American Women*. New York: Longman.

Porter, Mary Cornelia, and Corey Venning. 1976. "Catholicism and Women's Role in Italy and Ireland." Pp. 81–104 in Lynn B. Iglitzin and Ruth Ross (Eds.). *Women in the World: A Comparative Study.* Santa Barbara, Calif.: Clio Books.

Porter, Mary Cornelia, and Corey Venning. 1986. "Italy and Ireland: Women, Church, and Politics in Two Catholic Countries." Pp. 85–108 in Lynne B. Iglitzin and Ruth Ross (Eds.). *Women in the World: 1975–1985 The Women's Decade* (2nd rev. ed.). Santa Barbara, Calif.: ABC–Clio.

Porter, Natalie, and Florence Geis. 1981. "Women and Nonverbal Leadership Cues: When Seeing Is Not Believing." Pp. 39–61 in Clara Mayo and Nancy M. Henley (Eds.). *Gender and Nonverbal Behavior.* New York: Springer-Verlag.

Potts, D. M. 1970. "Which Is the Weaker Sex?" *Journal of Biosociological Science Supplement.* 2:147–157.

Quadragno, Jill. 1976. "Occupational Sex-Typing and Internal Labor Market Distributions: An Assessment of Medical Specialties." *Social Problems.* 23:442–453.

Quattelbaum, Cynthia. 1977. "Perceived Television Model Attributes and Consequent Modeling Behavior as Described by the Viewer." Unpublished paper, Department of Speech, University of Oregon.

Quinn, Naomi. 1977. "Anthropological Studies on Women's Status." *Annual Review of Anthropology.* 6:181–225.

Quinn, Robert E., and Patricia L. Lees. 1984. "Attraction and Harassment: Dynamics of Sexual Politics in the Work Place." *Organizational Dynamics.* 13:35–46.

Radin, Norma. 1981. "Childrearing Fathers in Intact Families I: Some Antecedents and Consequences." *Merrill-Palmer Quarterly.* 27:489–514.

Rak, Diana S., and Linda M. McMullen. 1987. "Sex-Role Stereotyping in Television Commercials: A Verbal Response Mode and Content Analysis." *Canadian Journal of Behavioural Science.* 19:25–39.

Ramey, Estelle. 1976. "Men's Cycles (They Have Them, Too, You Know)." Pp. 138–142 in Alexandra G. Kaplan and Joan P. Bean (Eds.). *Beyond Sex-Role Stereotypes: Reading Toward a Psychology of Androgyny.* Boston: Little, Brown.

Randall, Vicky. 1987. *Women and Politics: An International Perspective* (2nd ed.). Houndmills, Eng.: MacMillan Education.

Raphael, Ray. 1988. *The Men from the Boys: Rites of Passage in Male America.* Lincoln: University of Nebraska Press.

Ray, Jean Meyer, and Angela Battaglia Rubin. 1987. "Pay Equity for Women in Academic Libraries: An Analysis of ARL Salary Surveys, 1976/77–1983/84." *College and Research Libraries.* 48:36–49.

Raymond, Janice. 1977. "Transsexualism: The Ultimate Homage to Sex-Role Power." *Chrysalis.* 3:11–23.

Rebecca, Meda, Robert Hefner, and Barbara Oleshansky. 1976. "A Model of Sex-Role Transcendence." Pp. 90–97 in Alexandra G. Kaplan and Joan P. Bean (Eds.). *Beyond Sex Role Stereotypes.* Boston: Little, Brown.

Reich, Michael, David M. Gordon, and Richard C. Edwards. 1975. "A Theory of Labor Market Segmentation." Pp. 69–97 in Martin Carnoy (Ed.). *Schooling in a Corporate Society.* New York: McKay.

Reinisch, J. M. 1981. "Prenatal Exposure to Synthetic Progestins Increases Potential for Aggression in Humans." *Science.* 222:1171–1173.

Reiss, Ira L. 1986. *Journey into Sexuality: An Exploratory Voyage.* Englewood Cliffs, N.J.: Prentice Hall.

Reskin, Barbara F. 1988. "Bringing the Men Back In: Sex Differentiation and the Devaluation of Women's Work." *Gender and Society.* 2:58–81.

Reskin, Barbara F., and Heidi I. Hartmann. (Eds.). 1986. *Women's Work, Men's Work: Sex Segregation on the Job.* Washington, D.C.: National Academy Press.

Reskin, Barbara F. and Patricia A. Roos. 1990. *Job Queues, Gender Queues: Explaining Women's Inroads into Male Occupations.* Philadelphia: Temple University Press.

Reynolds, V. 1966. "Open Groups Hominid Evolution." *Man.* 1:441–452.

Rhode, Deborah. 1987. "Justice, Gender, and the Justices." Pp. 13–34 in Laura L. Crites and Winifred L. Hepperle (Eds.). *Women, the Courts, and Equality*. Newbury Park, Calif.: Sage.

Rich, Adrienne. 1976. *Of Women Born: Motherhood as Experience and Institution*. New York: W. W. Norton.

Rich, Adrienne. 1980. "Compulsory Heterosexuality and Lesbian Existence." *Signs: Journal of Women in Culture and Society*. 5:631–660.

Richard, Alison F. 1986. "Malagasy Prosimians: Female Dominance." Pp. 25–33 in Barbara B. Smuts, Dorothy L. Cheney, Robert M. Seyfarth, Richard W. Wrangham, and Thomas T. Struhsaker (Eds.). *Primate Societies*. Chicago: University of Chicago Press.

Ricks, Shirley S. 1985. "Father–Infant Interactions: A Review of the Empirical Literature." *Family Relations*. 34:505–511.

Riddick Carol Cutler. 1982. "Life Satisfaction Among Aging Women: A Causal Model." Pp. 45–59 in Maximiliane Szinovacz (Ed.). *Women's Retirement: Policy Implications of Recent Research*. Beverly Hills, Calif.: Sage.

Rijk, Tineke de. 1984. "Women at Work in Holland." Pp. 83–102 in Marilyn J. Davidson and Cary L. Cooper (Eds.). *Working Women: An Interational Survey*. Chichester, Eng.: Wiley.

Rindfuss, Ronald R., C. Gray Swicegood, and Rachel A. Rosenfeld. 1987. "Disorder in the Life Course: How Common and Does It Matter?" *American Sociological Review*. 52:785–801.

Rios, Palmira N. 1990. "Export-Oriented Industrialization and the Demand for Female Labor: Puerto-Rican Women in the Manufacturing Sector, 1952–1980." *Gender and Society*. 4: 321–337.

Risman, Barbara J. 1987. "Intimate Relations from a Microstructural Perspective: Men Who Mother." *Gender and Society*. 1:6–32.

Risman, Barbara J. 1989. "Can Men 'Mother'? Life as a Single Father." Pp. 155–164 in Barbara J. Risman and Pepper Schwartz (Eds.). *Gender in Intimate Relations: A Microstructural Approach*. Belmont, Calif.: Wadsworth.

Risman, Barbara, and Pepper Schwartz. 1988. "Sociological Research on Male and Female Homosexuality." *Annual Review of Sociology*. 14:125–147.

Roach, Sharyn. 1990. "Men and Women Lawyers in In-House Legal Departments: Recruitment and Career Patterns." *Gender and Society*. 4:207–219.

Roberts, Elizabeth J., David Kline, and John Gagnon. 1978. *Family Life and Sexual Learning: Vol. 1. Summary Report*. Prepared by Project on Human Sexual Development. Cambridge, Mass. Population Education.

Robertson, Claire, and Iris Berger. (Eds.). 1986. *Women and Class in Africa*. New York: African Publishing Company.

Robinson, John G., Patricia C. Wright, and Warren G. Kinzey. 1986. "Monogamous Cebids and Their Relatives: Intergroup Calls and Spacing." Pp. 44–53 in Barbara B. Smuts, Dorothy L. Cheney, Robert M. Seyfarth, Richard W. Wrangham, and Thomas T. Struhsaker (Eds.). *Primate Societies*. Chicago: University of Chicago Press.

Roby, Pamela A. (Ed.). 1973. *Child Care—Who Cares? Foreign and Domestic Infant and Early Childhood Development Policies*. New York: Basic Books.

Roby, Pamela A. 1976. "Toward Full Equality: More Job Education for Women." *School Review*. 84:181–211.

Rogers, Gayle Thompson. 1985. "Nonmarried Women Approaching Retirement: Who Are They and When Do They Retire?" *Current Perspectives on Aging and the Life Cycle*. 1:169–191.

Roos, Patricia A. 1985. *Gender and Work: A Comparative Analysis of Industrial Societies*. Albany, N.Y.: SUNY Press.

Rosaldo, Michelle Z. 1974. "Woman, Culture, and Society: A Theoretical Overview." Pp. 17–42 in Michelle Z. Rosaldo and Louise Lamphere (Eds.). *Women, Culture, and Society*. Stanford, Calif.: Stanford University Press.

Rosenbaum, James E. 1984. *Career Mobility in a Corporate Hierarchy*. Orlando, Fla.: Academic Press.

Rosenblatt, J. S. 1969. "The Development of Maternal Responsiveness in the Rat." *American Journal of Orthopsychiatry*. 39:38–56.

Rosenfeld, Rachel A. 1980. "Race and Sex Differences in Career Dynamics." *American Sociological Review.* 45:583–609.

Rosenfeld, Rachel A., and Arne L. Kalleberg. 1990. "A Cross-National Comparison: The Gender Gap in Earnings." *American Journal of Sociology.* 96:69–106.

Rosenfelt, Deborah, and Judith Stacey. 1987. "Second Thoughts on the Second Wave." *Feminist Studies.* 13:341–361.

Ross, Heather L., and Isabel V. Sawhill. 1975. *Time of Transition: The Growth of Families Headed by Women.* Washington, D.C.: Urban Institute.

Ross, Marc Howard. 1986. "Female Political Participation: A Cross-Cultural Explanation." *American Anthropologist.* 88:843–858.

Rosser, Phyllis. 1987. *Sex Bias in College Admissions Tests: Why Women Lose Out* (2nd ed.). Cambridge, Mass.: National Center for Fair and Open Testing.

Rossi, Alice S. 1977. "A Biosocial Perspective on Parenting." *Daedulus.* 106:1–31.

Rossi, Alice S. 1982. *Feminists in Politics: A Panel Analysis of the First National Women's Conference.* New York: Academic Press.

Rossi, Alice S. 1987. "Parenthood in Transition: From Lineage to Child to Self-Orientation." Pp. 31–81 in Jane B. Lancaster, Jeanne Altmann, Alice S. Rossi, and Lonnie R. Sherrod (Eds.). *Parenting Across the Life Span: Biosocial Dimensions.* New York: Aldine de Gruyter.

Rossi, Alice, and Peter Rossi. 1977. "Body Time and Social Time: Mood Patterns by Menstrual Cycle Phase and Day of the Week." *Social Science Research.* 6:273–308.

Rossi, Alice S., and Peter H. Rossi. 1990. *Of Human Bonding: Parent–Child Relations Across the Life Course.* New York: Aldine de Gruyter.

Rothman, Barbara Katz. 1989. "Women as Fathers: Motherhood and Child Care Under a Modified Patriarchy." *Gender and Society.* 3:89–104.

Rubin, Gayle. 1975. "The Traffic in Women: Notes on the Political Economy of Sex." Pp. 157–210 in Rayna Reiter (Ed.). *Toward an Anthropology of Women.* New York: Monthly Review Press.

Rubin, Jeffrey Z., Frank J. Provenzano, and Zella Luria. 1976. "The Eye of the Beholder: Parents' Views on Sex of Newborns." Pp. 178–186 in Alexandra G. Kaplan and Joan P. Bean (Eds.). *Beyond Sex-Role Stereotypes: Readings Toward a Psychology of Androgyny.* Boston: Little, Brown.

Rubin, Lillian B. 1976. *Worlds of Pain: Life in the Working Class Family.* New York: Basic Books.

Rubin, Lillian B. 1979. *Women of a Certain Age: The Midlife Search for Self.* New York: Harper & Row.

Rubin, Lillian B. 1983. *Intimate Strangers.* New York: Harper & Row.

Rubin, Lillian B. 1985. *Just Friends: The Role of Friendship in Our Lives.* New York: Harper & Row.

Rubin, Lillian B. 1990. *Erotic Wars: What Happened to the Sexual Revolution?* New York: Farrar, Straus, & Giroux.

Rubin, Zick. 1977. "The Love Research." *Human Behavior.* 6:56–59.

Rubinstein, Robert L. 1986. *Singular Paths: Old Men Living Alone.* New York: Columbia University Press.

Ruebsaat, Helmut J., and Raymond Hull. 1975. *The Male Climacteric.* New York: Hawthorne.

Ruether, Rosemary Radford. 1977. *Mary—The Feminine Face of the Church.* Philadelphia: Westminster Press.

Ruether, Rosemary Radford. 1985. *Women–Church: Theology and Practice of Feminist Liturgical Communities.* San Francisco: Harper & Row.

Ruggie, Mary. 1984. *The State and Working Women.* Princeton, N.J.: Princeton University Press.

Rule, Wilma. 1981. "Why Women Don't Run: The Critical Contextual Factors in Women's Legislative Recruitment." *Western Political Quarterly.* 34:60–77.

Rumberger, Russell W. 1983. "Dropping Out of High School: The Influence of Race, Sex, and Family Background." *American Educational Research Journal.* 20:199–220.

Rumberger, Russell W. 1987. "High School Dropouts: A Review of Issues and Evidence." *Review of Educational Research.* 57:101–121.

Russell, Diana E. 1984. *Sex Exploitation: Rape, Sexual Abuse, and Workplace Harassment.* Beverly Hills, Calif.: Sage.

Russell, Joyce E. A., and Michael C. Rush. 1987. "A Comparative Study of Age-Related Variation in Women's Views of a Career in Management." *Journal of Vocational Behavior.* 30:280–294.

Rytina, Nancy F., and Suzanne M. Bianchi. 1984. "Occupational Reclassification and Changes in Distribution by Gender." *Monthly Labor Review.* 107:11–17.

Saario, Terry N., Carol Nagy Jacklin, and Carol Kehr Tittle. 1975. "Sex Role Stereotyping in the Public Schools." *Harvard Educational Review.* 43:386–416.

Sachs, J. 1987. "Preschool Boys' and Girls' Language Use in Pretend Play. Pp. 178–189 in S. U. Phillips, S. Steele, and C. Tanz (Eds.). *Language, Gender and Sex in Comparative Perspective.* New York: Cambridge University Press.

Sacks, Karen. 1979. *Sisters and Wives: The Past and Future of Sexual Equality.* Westport, Conn.: Greenwood Press.

Safa, Helen Icken. 1990. "Women's Social Movements in Latin America." *Gender and Society.* 4:354–369.

Safilios-Rothschild, Constantina. 1977. *Love, Sex, and Sex Roles.* Englewood Cliffs, N.J.: Prentice Hall.

Saghir, Marcel T., and Eli Robins. 1973. *Male and Female Homosexuality: A Comprehensive Investigation.* Baltimore: Williams & Wilkins.

Salamone, Frank A. 1986. "Religion and Repression: Enforcing Feminine Inequality in an 'Egalitarian' Society." *Anthropos.* 81:517–528.

Saltzstein, Grace Hall. 1986. "Female Mayors and Women in Municipal Jobs." *American Journal of Political Science.* 30:140–164.

Sanasarian, Eliz. 1986. "Political Activism and Islamic Identity in Iran." Pp. 207–224 in Lynne B. Iglitzin and Ruth Ross (Eds.). *Women in the World: 1975–1985 The Women's Decade* (2nd rev. ed.). Santa Barbara, Calif.: ABC–Clio.

Sanday, Peggy R. 1973. "Toward a Theory of the Status of Women." *American Anthropologist.* 75:1682–1700.

Sandberg, David E., Anke A. Ehrhardt, Claude A. Mellins, Susan E. Ince, and Heino F. L. Meyer-Bahlburg. 1987. "The Influence of Individual and Family Characteristics upon Career Aspirations of Girls During Childhood and Adolescence." *Sex Roles.* 16:649–668.

Sandler, Bernice Resnick. 1987. "The Classroom Climate: Still a Chilly One for Women." Pp. 113–123 in *Educating Men and Women Together: Coeducation in a Changing World.* Urbana and Chicago: University of Illinois Press.

San Francisco Chronicle. 1990. "Americans Wait Longer to Marry." *The Register-Guard.* Eugene, Oregon, July 12, p. 5a.

Sarich, V. M., and A. C. Wilson. 1967. "Immunological Time Scale for Hominid Evolution." *Science.* 158:1200–1203.

Sattel, Jack W. 1976. "The Inexpressive Male: Tragedy or Sexual Politics?" *Social Problems.* 23: 469–477.

Sayers, Janet. 1982. *Biological Politics: Feminist and Anti-Feminist Perspectives.* New York: Tavistock.

Scales, Ann. 1986. "The Emergence of Feminist Jurisprudence: An Essay." *Yale Law Journal.* 95:1373–1403.

Schafran, Lynn Hecht. 1987. "Practicing Law in a Sexist Society." Pp. 191–207 in Laura L. Crites and Winnifred L. Hepperle (Eds.). *Women, the Courts, and Equality.* Newbury Park, Calif.: Sage.

Schlossberg, Nancy K. 1984. "The Midlife Woman as Student." Pp. 315–339 in Grace Baruch and Jeanne Brooks-Gunn (Eds.). *Women in Midlife.* New York: Plenum.

Schmidt, Steffen W. 1986. "Women in Columbia." Pp. 273–304 in Lynne B. Iglitzin and Ruth Ross (Eds.). *Women in the World: 1975–1985 The Women's Decade* (2nd rev. ed.). Santa Barbara, Calif.: ABC–Clio.

Schmuck, Patricia A. (Ed.). 1987. *Women Educators: Employees of Schools in Western Countries.* Albany: State University of New York Press.

Schneider, David M. 1984. *A Critique of the Study of Kinship*. Ann Arbor: University of Michigan Press.

Schopp-Schilling, Hanna Beate. 1985. "Federal Republic of Germany." Pp. 124–137 in Jennie Farley (Ed.). *Women Workers in Fifteen Countries: Essays in Honor of Alice Hanson Cook*. Ithaca, N.Y.: ILR Press.

Schulz, Muriel R. 1975. "The Semantic Derogation of Women." Pp. 64–75 in Barrie Thorne and Nancy Henley (Eds.). *Language and Sex: Difference and Dominance*. Rowley, Mass.: Newbury House.

Schwendinger, Julia R., and Herman Schwendinger. 1983. *Rape and Inequality*. Beverly Hills, Calif.: Sage.

Scott, Hilda. 1979. "Women in Eastern Europe." Pp. 177–198 in Jean Lipman-Blumen and Jessie Bernard (Eds.). *Sex Roles and Social Policy: A Complex Social Science Equation*. Beverly Hills, Calif.: Sage.

Scott, Hilda. 1982. *Sweden's "Right to Be Human" Sex Role Equality: The Goal and the Reality*. Armonk, N.Y.: Sharpe.

Scott, John Finley. 1971. *Internalization of Norms: A Sociological Theory of Moral Commitment*. Englewood Cliffs, N.J.: Prentice Hall.

Scott, K. P., C. A. Dwyer, and B. Lieb-Brilhart. 1985. "Sex Equity in Reading and Communication Skills." Pp. 269–279 in *Handbook for Achieving Sex Equity Through Education*. Baltimore: Johns Hopkins University Press.

Scriven, Jeannie. 1984. "Women at Work in Sweden." Pp. 153–181 in Marilyn J. Davidson and Cary L. Cooper (Eds.). *Working Women: An International Survey*. Chichester, Eng.: Wiley.

Seagert, Joni, and Ann Olson. 1986. *Women in the World: An International Atlas*. New York: Simon & Schuster.

Sears, David O., and Leonie Huddy. 1990. "On the Origins of Political Disunity Among Women." Pp. 249–277 in Louise A. Tilly and Patricia Gurin (Eds.). *Women, Politics, and Change*. New York: Russell Sage Foundation.

Sebald, Hans. 1989. "Adolescents' Peer Orientation: Changes in the Support System During the Past Three Decades." *Adolescence*. 24:937–946.

Seccombe, Karen, and Gary R. Lee. 1986. "Gender Differences in Retirement Satisfaction and Its Antecedents." *Research on Aging*. 8:426–440.

Sedney, Mary Anne. 1987. "Development of Androgyny: Parental Influences." *Psychology of Women Quarterly*. 11:311–326.

Selkow, Paula. 1985. "Male/Female Differences in Mathematical Ability: A Function of Biological Sex or Perceived Gender Role?" *Psychological Reports*. 57:551–557.

Serbin, L. A., C. Sprafkin, M. Elman, and A. Doyle. 1984. "The Early Development of Sex Differentiated Patterns of Social Influence." *Canadian Journal of Social Science*. 14:350–363.

Serbin, Lisa A., J. M. Connor, and C. C. Citron. 1978. "Environmental Control of Independent and Dependent Behaviors in Preschool Girls and Boys: A Model for Early Independence Training." *Sex Roles*. 4:867–875.

Serbin, Lisa A., and Carol Sprafkin. 1986. "The Salience of Gender and the Process of Sex Typing in Three- to Seven-Year-Old Children." *Child Development*. 57:1188–1199.

Serbin, Lisa A., I. J. Tonick, and S. H. Sternglanz. 1977. "Shaping Cooperative Cross-Sex Play." *Child Development*. 48:924–929.

Severne, Liesbeth. 1982. "Psychosocial Aspects of the Menopause." Pp. 239–247 in Ann M. Voda, Myra Dinnerstein, and Sheryl R. O'Donnell (Eds.). *Changing Perspectives on Menopause*. Austin: University of Texas Press.

Sewell, William H., and Vimal P. Shah. 1967. "Socioeconomic Status, Intelligence, and the Attainment of Higher Education." *Sociology of Education*. 40:1–23.

Sharistanian, Janet. (Ed.). 1987. *Beyond the Public/Domestic Dichotomy: Contemporary Perspectives on Women's Public Lives*. New York: Greenwood Press.

Shaw, Lois Banfill, (Ed.). 1983. *Unplanned Careers: The Working Lives of Middle-Aged Women*. Lexington, Mass.: Lexington Books.

Shaw, Lois B., and Theresa O'Brien. 1983. "Introduction and Overview." Pp. 1–31 in Lois Banfill Shaw (Ed.). *Unplanned Careers: The Working Lives of Middle-Aged Women.* Lexington, Mass.: Lexington Books.

Sheehy, Gail. 1976. *Passages: Predictable Crises of Adult Life.* New York: Bantam.

Sheldon, A. 1989. "Conflict Talk: Sociolinguistic Challenges to Self-Assertion and How Young Girls Meet Them." Paper presented at the biennial meeting of the Society for Research in Child Development, Kansas City.

Sherman, Julia. 1967. *On the Psychology of Women.* Springfield, Ill.: Chas C Thomas.

Shields. Stephanie A. 1987. "Women, Men, and the Dilemma of Emotion." Pp. 229–250 in Phillip Shaver and Clyde Hendrick (Eds.). *Sex and Gender.* Newbury Park, Calif.: Sage.

Shipman, Pat. 1985. "The Ancestor That Wasn't." *The Sciences.* (March/April): 43–48.

Shulman, Alix Kates. 1973. *Memoirs of an Ex-Prom Queen.* New York: Bantam.

Shupe, Anson, William A. Stacey, and Lonnie R. Hazlewood. 1987. *Violent Men, Violent Couples: The Dynamics of Domestic Violence.* Lexington, Mass.: Lexington Books.

Sidel, Ruth. 1986. *Women and Children Last: The Plight of Poor Women in Affluent America.* New York: Viking.

Siegal, Michael. 1987. "Are Sons and Daughters Treated More Differently by Fathers than by Mothers?" *Developmental Review.* 7:183–209.

Siegelman, Marvin. 1987. "Kinsey and Others: Empirical Input." Pp. 33–79 in Louis Diamant (Ed.). *Male and Female Homosexuality: Psychological Approaches.* Washington, D.C.: Hemisphere.

Sigelman, Lee, and Carol K. Sigelman. 1982. "Sexism, Racism, and Ageism in Voting Behavior: An Experimental Analysis." *Social Psychology Quarterly.* 45:263–269.

Sigelman, Lee, and Susan Welch. 1984. "Race, Gender, and Opinion Toward Black and Female Presidential Candidates." *Public Opinion Quarterly.* 48:467–475.

Silverblatt, Irene. 1987. *Moon, Sun and Witches: Gender Ideologies and Class in Inca and Colonial Peru.* Princeton, N.J.: Princeton University Press.

Simmons, Roberta G., and Dale A. Blyth. 1987. *Moving into Adolescence: The Impact of Pubertal Change and School Context.* New York: Aldine de Gruyter.

Simms, Margaret C. 1985–86. "Black Women Who Head Families: An Economic Struggle." *Review of Black Political Economy.* 14:141–151.

Simms, Margaret C. 1986. "Black Women Who Head Families: An Economic Struggle." Pp. 141–151 in Margaret C. Simms and Julianne Malveaux (Eds.). *Slipping Through the Cracks: The Status of Black Women.* New Brunswick, N.J.: Transaction Books.

Skard, Torild, and Elina Haavio-Mannila. 1984. "Equality Between the Sexes—Myth or Reality in Norden?" *Daedulus* 113:141–167.

Skard, Torild, and Elina Haavio-Mannila. 1985. "Women in Parliament." Pp. 51–80 in Elina Haavio-Mannila and Associates (Eds.). *Unfinished Democracy: Women in Nordic Politics.* Oxford: Pergamon Press.

Skold, Karen. 1988. "The Interests of Feminists and Children in Child Care." Pp. 113–136 in Sanford M. Dornbusch and Myra H. Strober (Eds.). *Feminism, Children, and the New Families.* New York: Guilford Press.

Smith, Audrey D., and William J. Reid. 1986. *Role-Sharing Marriage.* New York: Columbia University Press.

Smith, James P., and Michael P. Ward. 1985. "Time-Series Growth in the Female Labor Force." *Journal of Labor Economics.* 3:s59–s90.

Smith, Lynn, and Bob Sipchen. 1990. "Parents Report Work Taking Toll on Family Life." *Eugene Register-Guard.* August 12, p. 4C.

Smith, P. K., and L. Daglish. 1977. "Sex Differences in Parent and Infant Behavior in the Home." *Child Development.* 48:1250–1254.

Smith, Shelly A. and Marta Tienda. 1988. "The Doubly Disadvantaged: Women of Color in the U.S. Labor Force." Pp. 61–80 in Ann Helton Stromberg and Shirley Harkess (Eds.). *Women Working: Theories and Facts in Perspective* (2nd ed.). Mountain View, Calif.: Mayfield.

Smith-Lovin, Lynn and Charles Brody. 1989. "Interruptions in Group Discussions: The Effects of Gender and Group Composition." *American Sociological Review*. 54:424–435.

Smith-Rosenberg, Carroll. 1975. "The Female World of Love and Ritual: Relations Between Women in Nineteenth Century America." *Signs: Journal of Women in Culture and Society*. 1:1–29.

Smuts, Barbara B. 1985. *Sex and Friendship in Baboons*. New York: Aldine.

Smuts, Barbara B., Dorothy L. Cheney, Robert M. Seyfarth, Richard W. Wrangham, and Thomas T. Struhsaker. (Eds.). 1986. *Primate Societies*. Chicago: University of Chicago Press.

Snow, M., Carol Jacklin, and Eleanor Maccoby. 1983. "Sex-of-Child Differences in Father–Child Interaction at One Year of Age." *Child Development*. 54:227–232.

Snyder, Thomas D. 1988. *Digest of Education Statistics, 1988*. Washington, D.C.: National Center for Education Statistics.

Snyder, Thomas D. 1989. *Digest of Education Statistics, 1989*. Washington, D.C.: National Center for Education Statistics.

Sokoloff, Natalie J. 1988. "Evaluating Gains and Losses by Black and White Men in the Professions, 1960–1980." *Social Problems*. 35:36–53.

Sorenson, Annemette, and Sara McLanahan. 1987. "Married Women's Economic Dependency, 1940–1980." *American Journal of Sociology*. 93:659–687.

Spence, Janet T. 1985. "Gender Identity and Its Implications for the Concepts of Masculinity and Femininity." Pp. 59–95 in Theo B. Sonderegger (Ed.). *Psychology and Gender: Nebraska Symposium on Motivation, 1984*. Lincoln: University of Nebraska Press.

Spence, Janet T., and Robert L. Helmreich. 1978. *Masculinity and Femininity: Their Psychological Dimensions, Correlates, and Antecedents*. Austin: University of Texas Press.

Spence, Janet T., and Robert L. Helmreich. 1983. "Achievement-Related Motives and Behaviors." Pp. 7–74 in Janet T. Spence (Ed.). *Achievement and Achievement Motives: Psychological and Sociological Approaches*. San Francisco: Freeman.

Spence, Janet T., Robert L. Helmreich, and J. Stapp. 1974. "The Personality Attributes Questionnaire: A Measure of Sex-Role Stereotypes and Masculinity–Femininity." *JSAS Catalog of Selected Documents in Psychology*. 4:43.

Spence, Janet T., Robert L. Helmreich, and J. Stapp. 1975. "Ratings of Self and Peers on Sex-Role Attributes and Their Relation to Self-Esteem and Conceptions of Masculinity and Femininity." *Journal of Personality and Social Psychology*. 32:29–39.

Spitze, Glenna. 1986. "The Division of Task Responsibility in U.S. Households: Longitudinal Adjustments to Change." *Social Forces*. 64:689–701.

Stacey, Judith. 1983. *Patriarchy and Socialist Revolution in China*. Berkeley: University of California Press.

Stacey, Judith. 1987. "Sexism by a Subtler Name? Postindustrial Conditions and Postfeminist Consciousness in the Silicon Valley." *Socialist Review*. 96:7–28.

Stacey, Judith. 1990. *Brave New Families: Sources of Domestic Upheaval in Late Twentieth Century America*. New York: Basic Books.

Stacey, Judith, and Barrie Thorne. 1985. "The Missing Feminist Revolution in Sociology." *Social Problems*. 32:301–316.

Stagner, Ross. 1988. *A History of Psychological Theories*. New York: Macmillan.

Stallings, J. A. 1979. "Comparisons of Men's and Women's Behaviors in High School Math Classes." Paper presented to the American Psychological Association, New York.

Stanley, Sandra C., Janet G. Hunt and Larry L. Hunt. 1986. "The Relative Deprivation of Husbands in Dual-Earner Households." *Journal of Family Issues*. 7:3–20.

Stannard, Una. 1977. *Mrs. Man*. San Francisco: Germain Books.

Staples, Robert. 1989. "Changes in Black Family Structure: The Conflict Between Family Ideology and Structural Conditions." Pp. 235–244 in Barbara J. Risman and Pepper Schwartz (Eds.). *Gender in Intimate Relationships: A Microstructural Approach*. Belmont, Calif.: Wadsworth.

Stark, Rodney. 1989a. *Instructor's Resource Book with Demonstrations and Activities to Accompany Sociology, Third Edition*. Belmont, Calif.: Wadsworth.

Stark, Rodney. 1989b. *Sociology* (3rd ed.). Belmont, Calif.: Wadsworth.

Stayton, Donelda J., Robert Hogan, and Mary D. S. Ainsworth. 1971. "Infant Obedience and Maternal Behavior: The Origins of Socialization Reconsidered." *Child Development.* 42:1057–1069.

Stein, Aletha H., and Margaret M. Bailey. 1975. "The Socialization of Achievement Motivation in Females." Pp. 151–157 in Martha Mednick et al. (Eds.). *Women and Achievement.* Washington, D.C.: Hemisphere.

Steinberg, Ronnie. 1987. "Radical Challenges in a Liberal World: The Mixed Success of Comparable Worth." *Gender and Society.* 1:466–475.

Steiner, Betty W. (Ed.). 1985. *Gender Dysphoria: Development, Research, Management.* New York: Plenum.

Steiner, Betty W., Ray Blanchard, and Kenneth J. Zuker. 1985. "Introduction." Pp. 1–10 in Betty W. Steiner (Ed.). *Gender Dysphoria: Development, Research, Management.* New York: Plenum.

Stern, Daniel N. 1985. *The Interpersonal World of the Infant.* New York: Basic Books.

Stets, Jan E. 1988. *Domestic Violence and Control.* New York: Springer-Verlag.

Steuve, Ann, and Lydia O'Donnell. 1984. "The Daughter of Aging Parents." Pp. 203–225 in Grace Baruch and Jeanne Brooks-Gunn (Eds.). *Women in Midlife.* New York: Plenum.

Stiehm, Judith. 1976. "Algerian Women: Honor, Survival, and Islamic Socialism." Pp. 229–242 in Lynne B. Iglitzin and Ruth Ross (Eds.). *Women in the World: A Comparative Study.* Santa Barbara, Calif.: Clio Books.

Stillion, Judith M. 1985. *Death and the Sexes: An Examination of Differential Longevity, Attitudes, Behaviors, and Coping Skills.* Washington, D.C.: Hemisphere.

Stockard, Jean. 1980a. "Sex Inequities in the Experiences of Students." Pp. 11–48 in Jean Stockard, Patricia A. Schmuck, Ken Kempner, Peg Williams, Sakre K. Edson, and Mary Ann Smith. *Sex Equity in Education.* New York: Academic Press.

Stockard, Jean. 1980b. "Why Sex Inequities Exist for Students." Pp. 49–77 in Jean Stockard, Patricia A. Schmuck, Ken Kempner, Peg Williams, Sakre K. Edson, and Mary Ann Smith. *Sex Equity in Education.* New York: Academic Press.

Stockard, Jean. 1980c. "Why Sex Inequities Exist in the Profession of Education." Pp. 99–115 in Jean Stockard, Patricia A. Schmuck, Ken Kempner, Peg Williams, Sakre K. Edson, and Mary Ann Smith. *Sex Equity in Education.* New York: Academic Press.

Stockard, Jean. 1984. "Career Patterns of High-Level Women School Administrators." *Journal of the National Association for Women Deans, Administrators, and Counselors.* 48:36–44.

Stockard, Jean. 1985. "Education and Gender Equality: A Critical View." Pp. 293–321 in Alan Kerckhoff (Ed.). *Research in Sociology of Education and Socialization Volume* 5. Greenwich, Conn.: JAI Press.

Stockard, Jean. 1988. "On Women's Aspirations and Equal Opportunity." Paper presented at a Plenary Session in honor of Martin Luther King, Jr., at the annual meeting of the Pacific Sociological Association, Las Vegas, Nevada.

Stockard, Jean. 1990. "Gender Differences in Attitudes Toward the Language Arts: Why Do They Persist?" Paper presented at the annual meeting of the Pacific Sociological Association, Spokane, Washington.

Stockard, Jean, and Miriam M. Johnson. 1979. "The Social Origins of Male Dominance." *Sex Roles.* 5:199–218.

Stockard, Jean, Dwight Lang, and J. Walter Wood. 1985. "Academic Merit, Status Variables, and Students' Grades." *Journal of Research and Development in Education.* 18:12–20.

Stockard, Jean, and Jeanne McGee. 1990. "Children's Occupational Preferences: The Influence of Sex and Perceptions of Occupational Characteristics." *Journal of Vocational Behavior.* 36:287–303.

Stockard, Jean, and J. Walter Wood. 1984. "The Myth of Female Underachievement: A Reexamination of Sex Differences in Academic Underachievement." *American Educational Research Journal.* 21:825–838.

Stoller, Robert J. 1968. *Sex and Gender: On the Development of Masculinity and Femininity.* New York: Science House.

Stoller, Robert J. 1974. "Facts and Fancies: An Examination of Freud's Concept of Bisexuality." Pp. 343–364 in Jean Strouse (Ed.). *Women and Analysis: Dialogues on Psychoanalytic Views of Femininity.* New York: Grossman.

Stoller, Robert J. 1985. *Presentations of Gender.* New Haven, Conn.: Yale University Press.

Stoltenberg, John. 1990. *Refusing to Be a Man: Essays on Sex and Justice.* New York: Penguin.

Stouffer, Samuel A., et al. 1976. "Masculinity and the Role of the Combat Soldier." Pp. 179–183 in Deborah David and Robert Brannon (Eds.). *The Forty-Nine Percent Majority: The Male Sex Role.* Reading, Mass.: Addison-Wesley. Excerpted from *The American Soldier: Combat and Its Aftermath.* Princeton, N.J.: Princeton University Press. 1949.

Strang, David, and James N. Baron. 1990. "Categorical Imperatives: The Structure of Job Titles in California State Agencies." *American Sociological Review.* 55:479–495.

Strathern, Marilyn. (Ed.). 1987. *Dealing with Inequality: Analysing Gender Relations in Melanesia and Beyond.* New York: Cambridge University Press.

Strathern, Marilyn. 1988. *The Gender of the Gift: Problems with Women and Problems with Society in Melanesia.* Berkeley: University of California Press.

Stromquist, Nelly P. 1989. "Determinants of Educational Participation and Achievement of Women in the Third World: A Review of the Evidence and a Theoretical Critique." *Review of Educational Research.* 59:143–183.

Sugisaki, Kazuko. 1986. "From the Moon to the Sun: Women's Liberation in Japan." Pp. 109–124 in Lynne B. Iglitzin and Ruth Ross (Eds.). *Women in the World: 1975–1985 The Women's Decade* (2nd rev. ed.). Santa Barbara, Calif.: ABC–Clio.

Sundberg, Norman D., Leona F. Tyler, and Millicent E. Poole. 1984. "Decade Differences in Rural Adolescents' Views of Life Possibilities." *Journal of Youth and Adolescence.* 12:45–56.

Sussman, Marvin. 1976. "The Family Life of Old People." Pp. 218–293 in R. Binstock and E. Shanas (Eds.). *Handbook of Aging and the Social Sciences.* New York: Van Nostrand Reinhold.

Suter, Larry E., and Herman P. Miller. 1973. "Income Differences Between Men and Career Women." *American Journal of Sociology.* 78:962–974.

Sutherland, Elyse, and Joseph Veroff. 1985. "Achievement Motivation and Sex Roles." Pp. 101–128 in Virginia E. O'Leary, Rhoda Kesler Unger, and Barbara Strudler Wallston (Eds.). *Women, Gender, and Social Psychology.* Hillsdale, N.J.: Erlbaum.

Svare, Bruce. 1983. "Psychobiological Determinants of Maternal Aggressive Behavior." Pp. 129–146 in Edward C. Simmel, Martin E. Hahn, and James K. Walters (Eds.). *Aggressive Behavior: Genetic and Neural Approaches.* Hillsdale, N.J.: Erlbaum.

Swafford, Michael. 1978. "Sex Differences in Soviet Earnings." *American Sociological Review.* 43:657–673.

Swerdlow, Marian. 1989. "Men's Accommodations to Women Entering a Nontraditional Occupation: A Case of Rapid Transit Operators." *Gender and Society.* 3:373–387.

Swidler, Ann. 1980. "Love and Adulthood in American Culture." Pp. 120–147 in Neil J. Smelser and Erik H. Erikson (Eds.). *Themes of Work and Love in Adulthood.* Cambridge, Mass.: Harvard University Press.

Swim, Janet, Eugene Borgida, Geoffrey Maruyama, and David G. Myers. 1989. "Joan McKay Versus John McKay: Do Gender Stereotypes Bias Evaluations?" *Psychological Bulletin.* 105: 409–429.

Szinovacz, Maximiliane. 1983. "Beyond the Hearth: Older Women and Retirement." Pp. 93–120 in Elizabeth W. Markson (Ed.). *Older Women: Issues and Prospects.* Lexington, Mass.: Lexington Books.

Taeuber, Cynthia. 1991. *Statistical Handbook on Women in America.* Phoenix, Ariz.: Oryx Press.

Tanner, James M. 1970. "Physical Growth." Pp. 77–155 in Paul Mussen (Ed.). *Carmichael's Manual of Child Psychology* (3rd ed.). New York: Wiley.

Tanner, Nancy. 1974. "Matrifocality in Indonesia and Among Black Americans." Pp. 129–156 in Michelle Z. Rosaldo and Louise Lamphere (Eds.). *Women, Culture and Society.* Stanford, Calif.: Stanford University Press.

Tanner, Nancy M. 1981. *On Becoming Human.* Cambridge, Eng.: Cambridge University Press.

Tanner, Nancy, and Adrienne Zihlman. 1976. "Women in Evolution: Part I. Innovation and Selection in Human Origins." *Signs: Journal of Women in Culture and Society.* 1:585–608.

Task Force on Sex Bias and Sex-Role Stereotyping in Psycho-Therapeutic Practice. 1975. "Report." *American Psychologist.* 30:1169–1175.

Tavris, Carol, and Carole Offer. 1977. *The Longest War: Sex Differences in Perspective.* New York: Harcourt Brace Jovanovich.

Taylor, Ann. 1987. "Sex Roles and Aging." Pp. 287–304 in David J. Hargreaves and Ann M. Colley (Eds.). *The Psychology of Sex Roles.* New York: Hemisphere.

Taylor, Patricia A., Patricia A. Gwartney-Gibbs, and Reynolds Farley. 1986. "Changes in the Structure of Earnings Inequality by Race, Sex, and Industrial Sector, 1960–1980." Pp. 105–138 in Robert V. Robinson (Ed.). *Research in Social Stratification and Mobility: A Research Annual.* Greenwich, Conn.: JAI Press.

Taylor, Verta. 1989. "Social Movement Continuity: The Women's Movement in Abeyance." *American Sociological Review.* 54:761–775.

Teleki, G. 1973. *The Predatory Behavior of Wild Chimpanzees.* Lewisburg, Pa.: Bucknell University Press.

Terman, Lewis M., and Melita H. Oden. 1947. *The Gifted Child Grows Up.* Stanford, Calif.: Stanford University Press.

Thoits, Peggy. 1983. "Multiple Identities and Psychological Well-Being: A Reformation and Test of the Social Isolation Hypothesis." *American Sociological Review.* 48:174–187.

Thompson, Hilda G. 1987. *Oregon Women: A Report on Their Education, Employment, and Economic Status.* Salem: Oregon Department of Education.

Thompson, Norman L., Jr., David M. Schwartz, Boyd R. McCandless, and David A. Edwards. 1973. "Parent–Child Relationships and Sexual Identity in Male and Female Homosexuals and Heterosexuals." *Journal of Consulting and Clinical Psychology.* 41:120–127.

Thorne, Barrie, and Zella Luria. 1986. "Sexuality and Gender in Children's Daily Worlds." *Social Problems.* 33:176–190.

Tiano, Susan. 1987. "Gender, Work and World Capitalism: Third World Women's Role in Development." Pp. 216–243 in Beth B. Hess and Myra Marx Ferree (Eds.). *Analyzing Gender: A Handbook of Social Science Research.* Newbury Park, Calif.: Sage.

Tieger, T. 1980. "On the Biological Basis of Sex Differences in Aggression." *Child Development.* 51:943–963.

Tiger, Lionel. 1969. *Men in Groups.* New York: Random House.

Tinker, Irene. (Ed.). 1983. *Women in Washington: Advocates for Public Policy.* Beverly Hills, Calif.: Sage.

Tittle, Carol Kehr. 1986. "Gender Research and Education." *American Psychologist.* 41:1161–1168.

Trause, Mary Anne, Marshall H. Klaus, and John H. Kennel. 1976. "Maternal Behavior in Mammals." Pp. 16–37 in M. H. Klaus and J. H. Kennel (Eds.). *Maternal-Infant Bonding.* St. Louis, Mo.: Mosby.

Travis, Cheryl Brown. 1988a. *Women and Health Psychology: Biomedical Issues.* Hillsdale, N.J.: Erlbaum.

Travis, Cheryl Brown. 1988b. *Women and Health Psychology: Mental Health Issues.* Hillsdale, N.J.: Erlbaum.

Travis, Toni-Michelle C. 1986. "Women as an Emerging Power Bloc: Ethnic and Racial Considerations." Pp. 79–112 in Winston A. Van Horne (Ed.). *Ethnicity and Women.* Milwaukee: University of Wisconsin System American Ethnic Studies Coordinating Committee.

Treiman, Donald J., and Patricia A. Roos. 1983. "Sex and Earnings in Industrial Society: A Nine-Nation Comparison." *American Journal of Sociology.* 89:612–650.

Treiman, Donald J., and Kermet Terrell. 1975. "Sex and the Process of Status Attainment: A Comparison of Working Women and Men." *American Sociological Review.* 40:174–200.

Tresemer, David W. 1977. *Fear of Success.* New York: Plenum.

Troiden, Richard R. 1988. *Gay and Lesbian Identity: A Sociological Analysis.* Dix Hills, N.Y.: General Hall.

Tuchman, Gaye. 1978. "Introduction: The Symbolic Annihilation of Women by the Mass Media." Pp. 3–38 in Gaye Tuchman, A. K. Daniels, and J. Benet (Eds.). *Hearth and Home: Images of Women in the Mass Media.* New York: Oxford University Press.

Tyler, Leona E. 1965. *The Psychology of Human Differences* (3rd ed.). New York: Appleton-Century-Crofts.

Udry, J. Richard. 1974. *The Social Context of Marriage* (3rd ed.). Philadelphia: Lippincott.

Udry, J. Richard. 1988. "Biological Predispositions and Social Control in Adolescent Sexual Behavior." *American Sociological Review.* 53:709–722.

Udry, J. Richard, and John O. G. Billy. 1987. "Initiation of Coitus in Early Adolescence." *American Sociological Review.* 52:841–855.

Uhlaner, Carole Jean, and Kay Lehman Schlozman. 1986. "Candidate Gender and Congressional Campaign Receipts." *Journal of Politics.* 48:30–50.

Uhlenberg, Peter, and David Eggebeen. 1986. "The Declining Well-Being of American Adolescents." *The Public Interest.* 82:25–38.

Ullian, Dorothy Z. 1976. "The Development of Conceptions of Masculinity and Femininity." Pp. 25–48 in Barbara Lloyd and John Archer (Eds.). *Exploring Sex Differences.* New York: Academic Press.

United States Bureau of the Census. 1987. *Statistical Abstract of the United States, 1988* (108th ed.). Washington, D.C.: U.S. Government Printing Office.

United States Bureau of the Census. 1989. *Money Income of Households, Families, and Persons in the United States: 1987.* Current Population Reports, Series P-60, No. 162. Washington, D.C.: U.S. Government Printing Office.

United States Bureau of the Census. 1990. *Statistical Abstract of the United States: 1990.* (110th Edition). Washington, D.C.: U.S. Government Printing Office.

United States Department of Commerce. 1976. *A Statistical Portrait of Women in the U.S.* Bureau of the Census, Current Population Reports, Special Studies Series P-23, No. 58.

Upchurch, Dawn M., and James McCarthy. 1990. "The Timing of First Birth and High School Completion." *American Sociological Review.* 55:224–234.

Vaillant, George E. 1977. *Adaptation to Life.* Boston: Little, Brown.

Van Allen, Judith. 1976. "African Women, 'Modernization,' and National Liberation." Pp. 25–54 in Lynne B. Iglitzin and Ruth Ross (Eds.). *Women in the World: A Comparative Study.* Santa Barbara, Calif.: Clio Books.

Vanfossen, Beth E. 1987. "Gender Differences in Mathematics Performance: Continuing Evidence." Presented at 1987 meeting of the American Sociological Association, Chicago.

Verbrugge, Lois M. 1976. "Sex Differentials in Morbidity and Mortality in the United States." *Social Biology.* 23:275–296.

Verbrugge, Lois M. 1986. "Role Burdens and Physical Health of Women and Men." *Women and Health.* 11:47–77.

Verbrugge, Lois M. 1989. "Recent, Present, and Future Health of American Adults." *Annual Review of Public Health.* 10:333–361.

Veroff, Joseph. 1983. "Assertive Motivation: Achievement Vs. Power." Pp. 99–132 in A. Stewart (Ed.). *Motivation and Society.* San Francisco: Jossey-Bass.

Villemez, Wayne J., and William P. Bridges. 1988. "When Bigger Is Better: Differences in Individual-Level Effect of Firm Size and Establishment Size." *American Sociological Review.* 53:237–255.

Waite, Linda J., and Sue E. Berryman. 1985. *Women in Nontraditional Occupations: Choice and Turnover.* Santa Monica, Calif.: Rand Corporation.

Waite, Linda J., Francis Kobrin Goldscheider, and Christina Witsberger. 1986a. "Nonfamily Living and the Erosion of Traditional Family Orientations Among Young Adults." *American Sociological Review.* 51:541–554.

Waite, Linda J., Gus Haggstrom, and David E. Kanouse. 1986b. "The Effects of Parenthood on the Career Orientation and Job Characteristics of Young Adults." *Social Forces.* 65:43–73.

Waldron, Ingrid, and Joan Herold. 1986. "Employment, Attitudes Toward Employment, and Women's Health." *Women and Health.* 11:79–98.

Walker, Henry A. 1988. "Black-White Differences in Marriage and Family Patterns." Pp. 87–112 in Sanford M. Dornbusch and Myra H. Strober (Eds.). New York: Guilford Press.

Walker, Lawrence J. 1984. "Sex Differences in the Development of Moral Reasoning: A Critical Review." *Child Development.* 55:677–691.

Waller, Willard. 1951. *The Family, a Dynamic Interpretation.* (Revised by Reuben Hill.) New York: Holt, Rinehart, & Winston.

Walston, Barbara Struder, and Kathleen E. Grady. 1985. "Integrating the Feminist Critique and the Crisis in Social Psychology: Another Look at Research Methods." Pp. 7–33 in Virginia E. O'Leary, Rhoda Kesler Unger, and Barbara Strudler Walston (Eds.). *Women, Gender, and Social Psychology.* Hillsdale, N.J.: Erlbaum.

Walter, Carolyn Ambler. 1986. *The Timing of Motherhood.* Lexington, Mass.: Heath.

Walters, Pamela Barnhouse. 1986. "Sex and Institutional Differences in Labor Market Effects on the Expansion of Higher Education, 1952–1980." *Sociology of Education.* 59:199–211.

Ward, Kathryn B. 1984. *Women in the World System: Its Impact on Status and Fertility.* New York: Praeger.

Ward, Kathryn B. 1988. "Women in the Global Economy." Pp. 17–48 in Barbara A. Gutek, Ann H. Stromberg, and Laurie Larwood (Eds.). *Women and Work: An Annual Review* (*Vol.* 3). Newbury Park, Calif.: Sage.

Ward, Kathryn B., and Fred C. Pampel. 1985. "Structural Determinants of Female Labor Force Participation in Developed Nations, 1955–1975." *Social Science Quarterly.* 66:654–667.

Ward, Kathryn (Ed.). 1990. *Women Workers and Global Restructuring.* Ithaca, N.Y.: Cornell University Press.

Washburn, S. L., and I. DeVore. 1961. "Social Behavior of Baboons and Early Man." Pp. 91–103 in S. L. Washburn (Ed.). *Social Life of Early Man.* Chicago: Aldine.

Waters, Harry F., and Janet Huck. 1989. "Networking Women." *Newsweek*, March 13, pp. 48–54.

Weiner, Annette B. 1976. *Women of Value Men of Renown: New Perspectives in Trobriand Exchange.* Austin: University of Texas Press.

Weis, Lois. 1987. "Academic Women in Science: 1977–1984." *Academe, #73.* (January-February): pp. 43–47.

Weiss, Robert S. 1987. "Men and Their Wives' Work." Pp. 109–121 in Faye J. Crosby (Ed.). *Spouse, Parent, Worker: On Gender and Multiple Roles.* New Haven, Conn.: Yale University Press.

Weitz, Shirley. 1977. *Sex Roles: Biological, Psychological, and Social Foundations.* New York: Oxford University Press.

Weitzman, Lenore. 1985. *The Divorce Revolution: The Unexpected Social and Economic Consequences for Women and Children in America.* New York: Free Press.

Weitzman, Lenore. 1988. "Women and Children Last: The Social and Economic Consequences of Divorce Law Reforms." Pp. 212–248 in Sanford M. Dornbusch and Myra H. Strober (Eds.). *Feminism, Children, and the New Families.* New York: Guilford Press.

West, Candace. 1982. "Why Can't a Woman be More Like a Man? An Interactional Note on Organizational Game-Playing for Managerial Women." *Work and Occupations.* 9:5–29.

West, Candace, and Don H. Zimmerman. 1983. "Small Insults: A Study of Interruptions in Cross-Sex Conversations Between Unacquainted Persons." Pp. 102–117 in Barrie Thorne, Cheris Kramarae, and Nancy Henley (Eds.). *Language, Gender and Society.* Rowley, Mass.: Newbury House.

West, Candace, and Don H. Zimmerman. 1987. "Doing Gender." *Gender and Society.* 1:125–151.

Westkott, Marcia. 1986. *The Feminist Legacy of Karen Horney.* New Haven, Conn.: Yale University Press.

Whalen, Jack, and Marilyn Whalen. 1987. "The Accomplishment of Sexual Status Through Children's Everyday Language Practices." Paper presented at the annual meeting of the American Sociological Association, Chicago, Ill.

Whitam, F. L., and R. M. Mathy. 1986. *Male Homosexuality in Four Societies: Brazil, Guatemala, Philippines, and the United States.* New York: Praeger.

White, Douglas R., and Michael L. Burton. 1988. "Causes of Polygyny: Ecology, Economy, Kinship, and Warfare." *American Anthropologist.* 90:871–887.

White, Jacquelyn Weygandt. 1983. "Sex and Gender Issues in Aggression Research." Pp. 1–26 in

Russell G. Geen and Edward I. Donnerstein (Eds.). *Aggression: Theoretical and Empirical Reviews: Vol. 2. Issues in Research.* New York: Academic Press.

White, Lynn, and John N. Edwards. 1990. "Emptying the Nest and Parental Well-Being: An Analysis of National Panel Data." *American Sociological Review.* 55:235–242.

Whiting, Beatrice Blyth, and Carolyn Pope Edwards. 1988. *Children of Different Worlds: The Formation of Social Behavior.* Cambridge, Mass.: Harvard University Press.

Whiting, Beatrice B., and John W. M. Whiting. 1975. *Children of Six Cultures: A Psychocultural Analysis.* Cambridge, Mass.: Harvard University Press.

Whiting, John W. M. 1960. "Resource Mediation and Learning by Identification." Pp. 112–126 in Ira Iscoe and Harold W. Stevenson (Eds.). *Personality Development in Children.* Austin: University of Texas Press.

Whiting, John W. M., Richard Kluckhorn, and Albert Anthony. 1958. "The Function of Male Initiation Ceremonies at Puberty." Pp. 359–370 in E. Maccoby, T. Newcomb, and E. Hartley (Eds.). *Readings in Social Psychology.* New York: Wiley.

Whyte, Martin King. 1978. *The Status of Women in Preindustrial Societies.* Princeton, N.J.: Princeton University Press.

Wiley, Mary Glenn, and Dale E. Woolley. 1988. "Interruptions Among Equals: Power Plays that Fail." *Gender and Society.* 2:90–102.

Wilhite, Allen, and John Theilmann. 1986. "Women, Blacks, and PAC Discrimination." *Social Science Quarterly.* 67:283–298.

Wilkinson, Doris Y. 1988. "Mother–Daughter Bonds in the Later Years: Transformation of the 'Help Pattern.'" Pp. 183–195 in Suzanne K. Steinmetz (Ed.). *Family and Support Systems Across the Life Span.* New York: Plenum.

Williams, Christine L. 1989. *Gender Differences at Work: Women and Men in Nontraditional Occupations.* Berkeley: University of California Press.

Williams, J. Allen, JoEtta A. Vernon, Martha C. Williams, and Karen Maleca. 1987. "Sex Role Socialization in Picture Books: An Update." *Social Science Quarterly.* 68:148–156.

Williams, John E., and Deborah L. Best. 1982. *Measuring Sex Stereotypes: A Thirty-Nation Study.* Beverly Hills, Calif.: Sage.

Williams, Juanita H. 1983. *Psychology of Women: Behavior in a Biosocial Context* (2nd ed.). New York: Norton.

Williams, Walter L. 1986. *The Spirit and the Flesh: Sexual Diversity in American Indian Culture.* Boston: Beacon Press.

Wilson, A. C., and V. M. Sarich. 1969. "A Molecular Time Scale for Human Evolution." *Proceedings of the National Academy of Sciences, USA.* 63:1088–1093.

Wilson, Edward O. 1975. *Sociobiology: The New Synthesis.* Cambridge, Mass.: Harvard University Press.

Wilson, Edward O. 1978. *On Human Nature.* Cambridge, Mass.: Harvard University Press.

Wilson, Kenneth L., and Janet P. Boldizar. 1990. "Gender Segregation in Higher Education: Effects of Aspirations, Mathematics Achievement, and Income." *Sociology of Education.* 63:62–74.

Wilson, Kenneth L., and Eui Hang Shin. 1983. "Reassessing the Discrimination Against Women in Higher Education." *American Educational Research Journal.* 20:529–551.

Wilson, William Julius. 1987. *The Truly Disadvantaged: The Inner City, the Underclass, and Public Policy.* Chicago: University of Chicago Press.

Wirls, Daniel. 1986. "Reinterpreting the Gender Gap." *Public Opinion Quarterly.* 50:316–330.

Wise, Lauress L. 1985. "Project TALENT: Mathematics Course Participation in the 1960s and Its Career Consequences." Pp. 25–58 in Susan F. Chipman, Lorelei R. Brush, and Donna M. Wilson (Eds.). *Women and Mathematics: Balancing the Equation.* Hillsdale, N.J.: Erlbaum.

Witelson, S. F. 1976. "Sex and the Single Hemisphere: Specialization of the Right Hemisphere for Spatial Processing." *Science.* 1973:425–427.

Wojtkiewicz, Roger A., Sara S. McLanahan, and Irwin Garinkel. 1990. "The Growth of Families Headed by Women: 1950–1980." *Demography.* 27:19–30.

Wolf, Margery. 1985. "The People's Republic of China." Pp. 33–48 in Jennie Farley (Ed.). *Women*

Workers in Fifteen Countries: Essays in Honor of Alice Hanson Cook. Ithaca, N.Y.: ILR Press.

Wolff, Charlotte. 1971. *Love Between Women*. London: Duckworth.

Wong, Herbert Y., and Jimy M. Sanders. 1983. "Gender Differences in the Attainment of Doctorates." *Sociological Perspectives*. 26:29–50.

Wood, Wendy. 1987. "Meta-Analytic Review of Sex Differences in Group Performance." *Psychological Bulletin*. 102:53–71.

Wright, Patricia C. 1984. "Biparental Care in *Aotus trivirgatus* and *Callicebus moloch*." Pp. 59–75 in Meredith F. Small (Ed.). *Female Primates: Studies by Women Primatologists*. New York: Liss.

Wrightsman, Lawrence S. 1988. *Personality Development in Adulthood*. Newbury Park, Calif.: Sage.

Wuthnow, Robert. 1988. *The Restructuring of American Religion: Society and Faith Since World War II*. Princeton, N.J.: Princeton University Press.

Yanagisako, Sylvia Junko, and Jane Fishburne Collier. 1987. "Toward a Unified Analysis of Gender and Kinship." Pp. 14–50 in J. F. Collier and S. J. Yanagisako (Eds.). *Gender and Kinship: Essays Toward a Unified Analysis*. Stanford, Calif.: Stanford University Press.

Yarrow, Marian R., John D. Campbell, and Roger V. Burton. 1968. *Child Rearing: An Inquiry into Research and Methods*. San Francisco: Jossey-Bass.

Ybarra, Lea. 1982. "When Wives Work: The Impact on the Chicano Family." *Journal of Marriage and the Family*. 15:169–178.

Young, Michael, and Peter Willmott. 1973. *The Symmetrical Family*. New York: Pantheon.

Youniss, James, and Jacqueline Smollar. 1985. *Adolescent Relations with Mothers, Fathers, and Friends*. Chicago: University of Chicago Press.

Youssef, Nadia Haggag. 1974. *Women and Work in Developing Societies*. Population Monograph, Series No. 15. Berkeley: Institute of International Studies, University of California.

Youssef, Nadia Haggag. 1976. "Women in the Muslim World." Pp. 203–218 in Lynne B. Iglitzin and Ruth Ross (Eds.). *Women in the World: A Comparative Study*. Santa Barbara, Calif.: Clio Books.

Youssef, Nadia H., and Shirley Foster Hartley. 1979. "Demographic Indicators of the Status of Women in Various Societies." Pp. 83–112 in Jean Lipman-Blumen and Jessie Bernard (Eds.). *Sex Roles and Social Policy: A Complex Social Science Equation*. Beverly Hills, Calif.: Sage.

Zaretsky, Eli. 1976. "Socialist Politics and the Family." Pp. 43–58 in Mina Davis Caulfield, Barbara Ehrenreich, Deirdre English, David Fernback, and Eli Zaretsky. *Capitalism and the Family*. San Francisco: Agenda.

Zaretsky, Eli. 1982. "The Place of the Family in the Origins of the Welfare State." Pp. 188–224 in Barrie Thorne with Marilyn Yalom (Eds.). *Rethinking the Family: Some Feminist Questions*. New York: Longman.

Zihlman, Adrienne L. 1978. "Women in Evolution: Part II. Subsistence and Social Organization Among Early Hominids." *Signs: Journal of Women and Culture in Society*. 4:4–20.

Zihlman, Adrienne L. 1987. "American Association of Physical Anthropologists Annual Luncheon Address, April, 1985: Sex, Sexes, and Sexism in Human Origins." *Yearbook of Physical Anthropology*. 30:11–19.

Zimmer, Lynn. 1986. *Women Guarding Men*. Chicago: University of Chicago Press.

Zimmer, Lynn. 1987. "How Women Reshape the Prison Guard Role." *Gender and Society*. 1: 415–431.

Zimmer, Lynn. 1988. "Tokenism and Women in the Workplace: The Limits of Gender-Neutral Theory." *Social Problems*. 35:64–77.

Zinn, Maxine Baca, and D. Stanley Eitzen. 1987. *Diversity in American Families*. New York: Harper & Row.

Zipp, John F., and Eric Plutzer. "Gender Differences in Voting for Female Candidates: Evidence from the 1982 Election." *Public Opinion Quarterly*. 49:179–197.

Zucker, Kenneth J. 1985. "Cross Gender-Identified Children." Pp. 75–174 in Betty W. Steiner (Ed.). *Gender Dysphoria: Development, Research, Management*. New York: Plenum.

Name Index

Subject Index